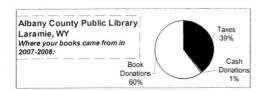

SPLENDID
SOLUTION

SPLENDID SOLUTION

Jonas Salk and the Conquest of Polio

❧

JEFFREY KLUGER

G. P. Putnam's Sons   New York

IIP

G. P. Putnam's Sons
Published by the Penguin Group
Penguin Group (USA) Inc., 375 Hudson Street, New York, NY 10014, USA • Penguin Group
(Canada), 10 Alcorn Avenue, Toronto, Ontario, Canada M4V 3B2 (a division of Pearson Penguin
Canada Inc.) • Penguin Books Ltd, 80 Strand, London WC2R 0RL, England • Penguin Ireland,
25 St Stephen's Green, Dublin 2, Ireland (a division of Penguin Books Ltd) • Penguin Group
(Australia), 250 Camberwell Road, Camberwell, Victoria 3124, Australia (a division of Pearson
Australia Group Pty Ltd) • Penguin Books India Pvt Ltd, 11 Community Centre,
Panchsheel Park, New Delhi–110 017, India • Penguin Group (NZ), Cnr Airborne and
Rosedale Roads, Albany, Auckland 1310, New Zealand (a division of Pearson New Zealand Ltd) •
Penguin Books (South Africa) (Pty) Ltd, 24 Sturdee Avenue, Rosebank,
Johannesburg 2196, South Africa

Penguin Books Ltd, Registered Offices: 80 Strand, London WC2R 0RL, England

Grateful acknowledgment is made to the March of Dimes Birth Defects Foundation
for permission to reproduce the photographs used throughout the text.

Library of Congress Cataloging-in-Publication Data
Kluger, Jeffrey.
Splendid solution : Jonas Salk and the conquest of polio / Jeffrey Kluger.
p.   cm.
Includes bibliographical references.
ISBN 0-399-15216-4
1. Salk, Jonas, 1914–1995.   2. Virologists—United States—Biography.
3. Poliomyelitis—United States—History.   4. Poliomyelitis—Vaccination—History.
5. Poliomyelitis vaccine—History.   I. Title.
QR31.S25K58   2004   2004050527
610'.92—dc22
[B]

Printed in the United States of America
1   3   5   7   9   10   8   6   4   2

This book is printed on acid-free paper. ∞

Book design by Meighan Cavanaugh

To Elisa Isabel and Paloma Arianne,
mis angelitas preciosas,

and to Alejandra,
mi amor

SPLENDID
SOLUTION

PROLOGUE

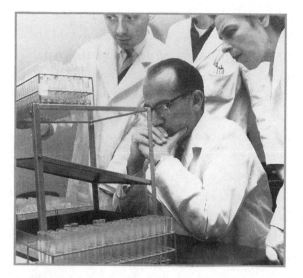

April 1951

All the talk about the little white coffins seemed to start out of
nowhere, but when it did, the word spread fast. Tens of thousands
of them were out there, it was said, stashed in depots around the
country. The location of the depots was never specified, and that was just as
well. If you knew where the caches of coffins were kept, you'd know where
the government expected the people to start dying. All of those people would
be children, of course. That's why the coffins were little—and white.

Jonas Salk, it was said, would be the person responsible for the deaths.
It was Salk who had cultured up the virus that would be injected into the
boys and girls. Salk himself was certain this version of the preparation

A list of captions for the photographs above, and all others, can be found on pages 360–61.

would not do anyone any harm. The virus he was using was dead, after all—he had killed it himself.

Months before, Salk and his colleagues had tried his formula out on monkeys, and the results had been good. Only then had he injected himself and his lab workers, not to mention his wife and his three young sons—the oldest of the boys barely ten, the youngest barely four. And only after inoculating all of them had he similarly treated the 7,500 children whose parents had willingly, indeed desperately, offered them up. In just a few more weeks, 400,000 other children around the country would be lining up to receive Salk's injections too. It was perhaps the greatest experiment of its kind ever attempted by medical science.

Salk tried not to be troubled by the coffin story as it got around, but it wasn't easy. It wasn't his injections that were dangerous, after all, it was a wild virus—a virus that had killed uncounted children for generations and had been attacking with a special savageness in the past few years.

In the summer of 1952 alone, more than 55,000 children in the United States had gone to bed with what their mothers believed was a cold and had woken up feverish, chilled, and rubber-limbed the next day. When the worried-looking doctor was led into the children's rooms, where they lay flat on their clammy backs beneath their wilted sheets, he'd ask them almost casually if they wouldn't mind lifting up their heads to look at their belly buttons. When they couldn't, it was as sure a sign as any that the cold was actually poliomyelitis and that the queerly rubbery limbs would soon grow much worse. The following summer, over 35,000 more children went to bed sick and failed the belly-button test and were hurried off to hospitals, where they waited to learn if the virus would quit when it had claimed their legs, or if it would go after their arms and their torsos and their very breath as well.

Now it was April 1954, and the fast-warming spring weather was as sure a reminder as any that the polio season was again approaching, following the heat from south to north, picking off children as it went like shot hitting skeet. It was against that onrushing danger that Salk had been racing—and it was against that same danger that all the whispering about the coffins got started. It was whispering that was begun, not surprisingly, by Walter Winchell.

During the Second World War, Winchell had been one of the glitteriest if most rough-cut stones in Hollywood's jewel box of celebrity reporters. In recent years, however, the appeal of his carnival-barker reporting had faded, and while plenty of newspapers still carried his column, his true soapbox was now radio, where he'd shout out his stories in a fifteen-minute slot every Sunday night. The show wasn't quite the backwater his critics liked to say it was, but it was clearly a banishment to the provinces compared with the vast stage he had once commanded.

For a man not often received in polite journalistic company, Winchell did do his homework. He made it a habit to keep his ear to the ground, listening not just for big stories but also for the emotional details that gave them their headline-making power. Winchell knew that Salk's vaccine, like any new vaccine, made a lot of people nervous, because a vaccine made sloppily or improperly could give you the very illness you were trying to avoid. This was why Winchell's words at the beginning of his April 4 broadcast carried such force.

"Good evening, Mr. and Mrs. America and all the ships at sea," he began, the familiar introduction by now grown tired. "Attention everyone. In a few moments I will report on a new polio vaccine—it may be a killer."

Fifteen seconds elapsed while Winchell's director played a commercial message, and then the newsman was back on the air.

"Attention all doctors and families," he announced. "The National Foundation for Infantile Paralysis plans to inoculate one million children this month. The U.S. Public Health Service tested ten batches of this new vaccine. They found, I am told, that seven of the ten contained live—not dead—virus. That it killed seven monkeys. The name of the vaccine is the Salk vaccine, named for Dr. Jonas Salk of the University of Pittsburgh. The Michigan State Medical Society has refused approval, the first state to do so. The polio foundation is trying to kill this story, but the U.S. Public Health Service will confirm it in about ten days. Why wait ten days?" The air crackled for a moment while the question hung and spun.

The performance was vintage Winchell. The brief, syntactically snapped sentences. The repetition of the sensationally obvious: the virus wasn't just "live," it was also "not dead." The slight feint toward an unnamed source. Winchell could sell the real thing and he could sell swill, and as always, he wasn't revealing on which one this was. But the pitch would continue the next morning in the 150 newspapers that still carried his column. And it would continue the following Sunday night, when he would boost the rumor's voltage by adding the ghastly detail about the coffins and the luckless children who would soon be occupying them, courtesy of Jonas Salk and his madman's vaccine.

Salk himself was unaware of what Winchell was up to the night of the first broadcast. The Salks owned a radio, but it wasn't much listened to. They owned a television too, but it wasn't much watched. Like all their neighbors, they subscribed to one of the three local newspapers. People who had the time to read in the morning took the early risers' *Pittsburgh Post-Gazette.* Afternoon readers chose the *Pittsburgh Sun-Telegraph.* Salk, who was generally in his lab before the sun came up, preferred the evening *Pittsburgh Press.* That Monday morning, Salk woke up as early as always, and was thus ignorant of Winchell's broadcast when he arrived at his lab. It was only when he saw the way the lab staff looked at him as he entered that he suspected something was up.

"You heard?" a technician asked him uncertainly, approaching with the morning paper.

"Heard what?" Salk asked.

With a shrug, the technician handed over the paper, folded open to the column. Salk took in the story in two or three bites, then read it again, a little more slowly. Then he did what he always did in such moments— which is to say he did almost nothing at all. He filled his cheeks up with air and let it out in a long puff—something the lab staff had seen him do a thousand times. He nodded his head slowly and deliberately—something they'd grown accustomed to also.

Salk, clearly, was furious. Stupidity always made him angry; malevolent stupidity made him angrier still. He wouldn't show it; he never did. You couldn't run the kind of lab he ran and conduct the kind of research he

conducted and allow yourself the luxury of pique. But it was more than the
need for a disciplined mind and a disciplined workplace that kept Salk's
anger in check. It was also mere bewilderment. For a man with such a deep
regard for scientific facts, he had a naïve belief that other people felt the
same way. When they would abuse those facts—wrench them out of
shape, turn them on their heads so that they said things they were never intended to say—he'd have a hard time believing they'd done it at all. Facts
were precious enough commodities when you needed them; why violate
them once you'd got them in hand?

"But this isn't true," he said to his technician at last, looking up from
Winchell's column in confusion.

Salk went through his workday saying little else about Winchell's ma-
lignant fiction. He had 400,000 children to inoculate before the hard
march of summer began and he could afford to think about little but that.
Salk knew his vaccine and he knew that it worked, and with a clear and
calm scientific certainty, he knew that it was safe.

What he didn't know was that in a small cage in a government lab, a
group of mice that had been receiving his shots would soon go lame,
falling to their sides and struggling for breath. If you didn't know better,
you'd almost think they had polio. If you didn't know better still, you'd
think they'd contracted it from the shot Salk, his sons, and so many thousands of others had already received.

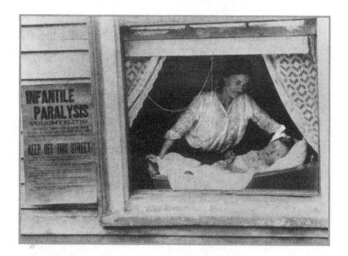

Summer 1916

There was a time when a black car with lacquered doors would not have attracted much attention on East 106th Street—but that was before the cars started coming to take the babies away. The mothers of New York learned to avoid a lot of things that summer: the nurses at the edges of the playgrounds; the policemen with their leaflets; the crowds in the streetcars and the food on the pushcarts and the water in the rivers with its odd, loamy smell. But most of all, they learned to avoid the black cars.

Like all the mothers on her small block, Dora Salk would have frozen when the car rounded the corner from Madison Avenue and began cruising slowly down 106th Street. Automobiles were an increasingly common sight even in the neighborhoods so far from midtown; 116,000 of them were now registered in the city, with up to 5,000 new owners signing up in a single month. But when the doors bore the seal of the City of New York and the car was slowing down and speeding up as it drifted past houses—a sure sign of a driver checking for an address—it meant trouble.

The city would claim, of course, that there was no reason at all to fear the black cars. They were sent only to find—and care for—the babies who had begun exhibiting the flushed look and wobbly limbs so characteristic of the unfolding plague. But caring for the babies in that limp and logy summer often as not meant sending them on a mandatory trip to Swineburne Island or one of the other facilities the city had set up to isolate the newly afflicted. There the babies might recover—or might not.

Certainly, measures as extreme as the cars and the island facility weren't necessary every year. Sure as crocuses, the paralysis would arrive whenever the warm weather did, twisting bodies and ruining families with a randomness that confounded even the best doctors. Some summers, the contagion would be mild, claiming a comparatively small crop of luckless children and then moving on. Other summers, the character of the disease would turn far blacker. Once alighted, it would range out everywhere, swallowing neighborhoods whole until the arrival of autumn and the sudden drop in temperature at last cooled its frenzy. It had happened that way back in 1907, and now, nine years later, it appeared to be happening again.

At first, most people thought less about the plague descending again this summer than about the developments on the other side of the Atlantic. There the nations of Europe were deep in the war that had been bleeding the continent for two years. Spill enough European blood and before long the call would start going out for Americans to come over and spill some of their own. That was what was on the minds of New Yorkers that season when the first indications of the paralysis started to appear. It was cardboard placards that initially brought the news of the growing epidemic, official signs that began appearing on houses around the city like ugly paper boils.

"INFANTILE PARALYSIS," the signs would announce in block letters, and then, parenthetically, the more bookish name: "Poliomyelitis." The warning that followed was always the same:

All persons not occupants of
these premises are advised of the
presence of Infantile Paralysis in
it and are advised not to enter.

The person having Infantile Paralysis
must not leave the apartment until
the removal of this notice by an
employee of the Department of Health.

By order of the BOARD OF HEALTH

When more than a few houses on a single street were infected, the whole block would be required to wear the warning mark: "Infantile paralysis is very prevalent in this part of the city. Keep off this street."

After the placards appeared, the nurses did too, and in their own way, they were even more fearsome. They were at first a welcome sight when they showed up in the playgrounds and parks, wandering up to mothers and children with friendly reminders of where the closest milk stations were—summer being a hard season in which to keep milk fresh and the babies needing plenty of it to stay strong. The few mothers who weren't attracted by the promise of milk might be drawn by the tickets for free ice, great blocks of the pricey stuff, enough to keep your food and milk chilled for days, if only you'd accompany the nurse to one of the city's designated pickup points. The ice and the milk would always be at the stations as promised, but while you were on your way, you could be sure the nurse would be eyeing your baby for signs of paralysis, signs that could be reported to the Board of Health and earn the baby another free ticket, this one off to Swineburne Island.

The mothers soon got wise to this, and the nurses disappeared, only to be replaced by the policemen, this time offering flyers filled with tips on how to keep babies safe from the illness. The flyers were tempting, but by now the mothers were wary and simply began avoiding the playgrounds altogether, walking with their babies only on the streets in front of their homes and darting inside at the first sign of trouble. Hiding would do you little good, however, the day the black car with the lacquered doors stopped at your house.

M ost nice days—at least until the start of that summer—Dora Salk made it a point to be outside early, promenading her twenty-month-old son, Jonas, before the day grew too warm. Dora was not the most popular mother on the block, perhaps because she was too good a mother—or at least that's how she saw it. Her house would be cleaned by early morning, and by nine A.M., she and Jonas would be taking their constitutional. As the other mothers emerged at ten or eleven or even later—their less fresh, less plump toddlers in tow—Dora would have nothing but cordial words for them, but it seemed a cordiality bred out of a belief that her day was being better, more profitably spent. Dora was always the first on the block to get her washing in, her shopping done, and her errands run, and when the other ladies' husbands would come home in the evenings and they would hurry off to finish preparing dinner, Dora would make a bit of a show of ambling home slowly.

"All the rushing for supper," she'd say. "Mine is finished and warming."

Such days spent on 106th Street were decidedly more relaxed before the black cars started showing up. When they did, things always played out the same way. Each mother would stiffen as the driver approached her address—and then go weak in relief as he passed. Finally, the car would slow in front of one door and the doctor would get out. If he got out alone, that was considered a good sign.

Mothers did not surrender their sick babies easily, often kicking and cursing the city physicians as soon as they arrived. Things typically went a bit smoother if a social worker came along, since the mothers seemed more inclined to turn a child over to a woman than to a man. The absence of a social worker usually meant that the doctor did not intend to take the sick child away, though lately that had become an unreliable sign, since as the epidemic progressed, the city's overworked Health Department simply had fewer of the ladies to spare. Alone or accompanied, the doctor would walk quickly up the steps to the house, casting a fast glance at the knot of mothers who stood avoiding his eyes.

The first thing the doctor would do when he entered a paralysis house was look around the parlor to determine whether the father had taken to sleeping there. If he had, that would count in the family's favor. The rules of the plague required that at the initial signs of illness, the child and the mother retreat to the family bedrooms and stay there until the infectious phase of the disease had passed. The father, who would have to continue working and otherwise moving through the community, was to isolate himself as well as he could. This meant that he was not to go up the stairs—beyond carrying up food and other essentials—and the mother and child were not to come down until there was no risk of either of them carrying the contagion further.

If a cot and clothes in the parlor convinced the doctor that the father was complying with the regulations, he would next go up to the bedrooms to examine the patient. The scene that greeted him there would almost always be a bleak one. By June, it was proving to be a punishing summer, with temperatures typically rising high into the 80s before noon and staying fixed there until well after sundown. The bedrooms of poliomyelitis patients would often be stifling, since the windows would be closed against the blueflies, stable flies, and houseflies that were widely suspected of carrying the virus. The Health Department permitted quarantined families to open their windows if they had metal screens in place, but screens were expensive and not always available.

In the room, the doctor would first ask the mother to describe how the child's illness had struck, though he knew what the answer would be—the same aches, the same chills, the same sudden loss of strength. Then he'd turn to the patient, feeling the child's head and neck to determine if there was any fever. He'd move the legs and arms to see if there was any pain; he'd bend the legs at the knees and ask the child to push back to determine if there was any lingering strength in the muscles. Then he'd lay the limbs back down.

If he concluded that the disease was still burning inside the child and that the parents had been sloppy about the quarantine rules, he'd interpose himself between the mother and the bed and gather the child up, prepared to fight the curses and kicks of the woman as he did. Carrying the child downstairs, he'd hope the father would restrain the mother—to say nothing of himself—so that he could take the patient to the car with a minimum of unpleasantness. If necessary, he would summon his driver, whom he'd have left behind the wheel, for assistance. If that didn't work, he'd summon the police.

If, on the other hand, the doctor found that the fever had passed and that the house was well sealed against leakage of the virus, he'd leave the home in peace. The disease, after all, would by now be through with the child, having entered and left, cutting a hot path through the spinal cord along the way. The wasted legs might never be of any use again, but the child would no longer be a danger to anyone else.

If the doctor did announce that the child could stay, the mother would cover her face with her hands in relief. When the doctor clumped back down the stairs with no child in his arms, the grateful father would often as not offer up an impulsive gift. The cigar man would insist that the doctor take a cigar; the boot man would offer him laces; the baker would offer a ring of cake. They'd press the unwanted tributes on the doctor, and he would mostly take them. Once in his car, he'd pass them on to his driver.

Dora Salk—or Dora Press, as folks once knew her—was surely not worrying about poliomyelitis or any other illness when she first arrived in New York City at the turn of the century. It was in Minsk, where she had been born, that you worried about paralysis and pox and other such plagues. In New York, you worried about getting rich.

There were a lot of things the twelve-year-old Dora didn't know how to do very well when she landed in New York, read and write English among them. But she knew how to speak it passably well—well enough that when she was careful, you didn't even always hear the Russian inflections welling up underneath. That kind of quick learning was more than enough to impress the men who did the hiring in the factories in the midtown garment district and to land her a steady job doing cut-and-stitch work. She performed so well in that position that by the time she was sixteen or so, the factory supervisor realized that the short, slight girl with the sharp voice and the crisp way might be even better suited to overseeing a team of other women doing the same kind of piecework she did, never mind that the women she'd be supervising would be two or even three times her age.

It was when she was working in her new job that the quick and driven Dora Press met the gentle and pleasant Daniel Salk, another garment worker, who designed lace scarves and collars and whose fine, filigreed work was matched only by his fine, filigreed temperament. A quiet man was perfectly all right with Dora—as long as that quiet man earned a re-spectable living, and Daniel did. The two young workers soon married, and Dora happily left her never well-loved job. She promptly turned her ferocious attention to making a sharp and spotless home out of the cou-ple's flat on the upper end of Manhattan, getting it ready for the children she intended to have before long—the first of whom, Jonas, arrived in 1914.

For a woman who conducted her affairs so tidily, it was an unsettlingly messy development when the summer of 1916 arrived and the city sud-denly began publishing reports of the spreading infantile paralysis prob-lem. The blaze had begun burning in Brooklyn and was now spreading toward Manhattan. Keeping up with the newspaper dispatches about the epidemic was not easy for Dora, still struggling to unknot printed English. An inability to read the local language was not something the proud Dora was inclined to admit, and she'd developed ways to conceal the problem when she was outside her home.

"Can you help me read that?" she'd ask a passerby, affecting a near-sighted squint at a street sign. "I don't know why they make those letters so small."

Behind closed doors, things were different. When word of the paralysis started getting around, she instructed Daniel to read her every report he found in the newspapers on how babies could be protected from the scourge. What she learned, she put straight to work in her home.

Young Jonas was kept impeccably clean; his nose and throat were regu-larly rinsed with a solution of one teaspoon of salt to one quart of warm water, a mixture that was said to prevent the polio virus from gaining purchase in the throat membranes. The foods in Dora's kitchen were always kept covered, and while everyone in the family ate well, none of them ate too much meat or sugar—such dense foods were believed to weigh too heavily on the gut and weaken the constitution. Most important of all, Dora would see to it that her clean, strong, well-nourished son was kept away from other children, with their questionable hygiene and diets and the germs they might be spreading to anyone who came near.

"Avoid the babies," Dora would warn Daniel each morning as he'd head off to his job.

"There are no babies at work," he'd answer.

"There are babies in the streets," she'd say. "There are babies in the carriages."

But as the summer ground on, it began to appear that merely avoiding the babies was not likely to make much difference for anyone in New York. The number of infected children in the city was growing beyond anything the health commissioner's office had ever considered possible. By the first of July, 350 children had contracted the paralysis and 75 of them had died. In one week alone, 52 new cases were reported—43 of them in Brooklyn and 9 in Manhattan.

New York was not alone in facing a contagion. Up and down the East Coast, Philadelphia, Boston, Baltimore, and other major cities were reporting outbreaks of their own. At least scattered cases appeared in thirty-three states. But so far, it was New York that was being hit the hardest, with one out of three cases in the entire country occuring within the boroughs that made up the city. Numbers that had already climbed so high in the relatively cool weeks of early summer would explode into the thousands in the steambath weeks of mid-July and August. Before that could happen, the city would have to crack down, and it would have to do so before July 4.

The Fourth of July was a predictably festive day in New York, and this year, the city had big plans for the event, especially since the war news from Europe seemed to be cooperating. France and Great Britain had just mounted a major offensive against the Germans, reclaiming five French towns, advancing as much as six miles in some places, and capturing more than 12,300 prisoners. The celebrations New York planned for the American Independence Day were well suited to such bright developments, with more than five hundred patriotic meetings to be held around the boroughs. Electric signs had been erected at City Hall and in Times Square, Columbus Circle, and City College Stadium, spelling out patriotic messages from the mayor, the governor, and President Wilson himself in incandescent bulbs that would blaze with the brightness of 55 million candles. A great deal of work had gone into planning such a day—and a great deal of it would now have to be undone.

On the afternoon of July 2, the health commissioner, Haven Emerson, known mostly for being the gentle great-nephew of author and poet Ralph Waldo Emerson, called his assistants into his office in the Municipal Building on Centre Street in Manhattan. It was a hot and gummy day, with the thermometer climbing to 84 degrees early and not showing any sign of falling. At the Polo Grounds, on the northwestern edge of Manhattan, barely 15,000 people showed up to watch the Giants fall to the despised Brooklyn Dodgers, most of them leaving early to escape the afternoon sun. As often happened when the temperature rose, the paralysis bug thrived, and throughout that day, hospitals around the city were knocked back on their heels as 72 stricken children were rushed in for care by their parents. More than 20 of those patients already seemed certain to die. Emerson reviewed the numbers from both the hospitals and the weathermen and issued a series of orders.

Of the sixty biggest celebrations planned for the night of the fourth, fifteen would be canceled. Plans for city-sponsored open-air movies would also be scrapped. Children under sixteen years of age would be banned from all places where large crowds gathered, including movie houses and theaters. Exhibitors or other businesses caught disobeying the new regulations would be stripped of their operator's licenses. More than half a million leaflets would immediately be printed and distributed, explaining, once again, how to follow the paralysis hygiene guidelines.

Emerson's rules went promptly into effect—and the polio bug slapped them aside. As the week pressed on and the temperature stayed high, 113 new cases checked into hospitals on July 5, and 87 followed on July 6. For every five cases, at least one proved lethal within the first two days, as the muscles that controlled the children's breath failed along with the ones that controlled their arms and legs. When the weekend arrived, the numbers fell and parents were briefly hopeful. But it was a false hope, a result merely of spotty reporting, as the case-counters in the hospitals took their Saturdays and Sundays off. When Monday arrived and the three-day toll was tallied, the count soared again.

In the neighborhoods, terrorized New Yorkers began freelancing solutions. Cats, many people concluded, were responsible for spreading the bug. And so cats were bludgeoned and drowned by the tens of thousands. When word got out that there was a bounty on the animals' heads, boys in Brooklyn rounded them up and brought them hissing and scratching to the Board of Health. When that word turned out to be a mere rumor, the boys killed the cats themselves. In houses where polio had already struck, the animals were murdered with special fury, flung by rage-blind parents into the rivers—sometimes when the cats were already dead, sometimes when they were still alive.

More than 70,000 cats were killed that week, but even after they were gone, the epidemic roared on. If cats weren't responsible, the people concluded, perhaps mosquitoes were. If it wasn't mosquitoes, it was rats or sewers or the always dirty Gowanus Canal. New Yorkers called, cabled, and wrote the Department of Health with all manner of other things they were certain were causing the paralysis plague, including high ground water, ice cream cones, excavations, flies, bedbugs, street dust, cornflakes, the subway, parasites in the water, alloys in cooking utensils, gases from munitions factories, the bent-over position children assumed at school desks, mercury poisoning, white clothing, earthquakes, volcanoes, electrical disturbances, sunburn, intestinal derangements, secondhand bedding, decayed food, excessive glare, unclean milk bottles, carrying coins in the mouth, and tobacco.

With so many possible sources of infection, more and more people decided to quit the city altogether. In train terminals in all the boroughs, mothers and children who had the means began fleeing in numbers that, judging by railroad ticket sales, exceeded 50,000. The actual count was probably far higher, since children under five traveled for free, meaning that there was no complete tally of just how fast the city was hemorrhaging its young. For all this, the paralysis count still climbed. In the first full week of July, 552 children fell ill; in the second week, the tally approached 1,000.

Emerson had seen enough. If the virus was going to be stopped, city physicians could not do it by themselves. Much of the burden would have to fall on private doctors, the ones who more often than not were the first to see the newly infected patients. If the doctors were to be relied on for such a job, however, they were going to have to know how to do it.

Most medical men knew little about infantile paralysis beyond what they learned from books—which meant they knew almost nothing useful at all. They knew the mossy tales of the ancient carving of an Egyptian boy with a dropped foot, a shriveled leg, and a walking stick, suggesting the disease had been around for as long as 3,500 years. They knew the great names of the great scientists who had studied the problem in modern times: the German Jacob von Heine, who had first written about the disease in 1840; Oskar Karl Medin, the Swede who had built on Heine's work, describing a local polio outbreak that claimed 44 children in 1887, and first suggesting that the disease had just the kind of contagious character that could lead to epidemics if communities weren't careful. Later came Ivar Wickman, a pupil of Medin, who studied the victims of a Swedish epidemic in 1905 that claimed 1,000 children and concluded that the disease was caused by germs associated with sneezing, coughing, and wastes from the bowel.

The New York doctors of 1916 knew too all the names by which infantile paralysis had variously been known: teething paralysis, since that was the time of life at which it so often struck; paralysis of the morning, since that was the time of day the immobility often appeared; essential paralysis, since medical men appeared to need a name that sounded more sober and well informed than the other two. They also knew the current preferred term: poliomyelitis. The name came from the Greek terms *polios,* "gray," and *myelos,* "core," and referred to the vibrant cable of gray matter that ran down the center of the spinal cord, which was the area that would be scored and scarred when a case of infantile paralysis struck.

But none of that book learning equipped the New York physicians to do a thing to help the children falling ill with polio. Emerson thus put out word to the city's medical community as a whole: An informational meeting would be held the next afternoon in the auditorium of the Polhemus Clinic at the Long Island College Hospital. Any doctors who treated children were strongly urged to attend. Emerson had no power to make the meeting mandatory, but under the current circumstances, he did not expect he'd have to.

The next day was another thick and sticky one, but Polhemus Hall was full to the walls. Doctors crowded the small auditorium, taking seats if they could find them and standing when they couldn't. On the stage facing the assembled physicians were Emerson and Dr. Louis Ager, a specialist in juvenile medicine. Joining them was Dr. Simon Flexner of the Rockefeller Institute, the man the doctors were truly here to hear. A research physician, Flexner was famous for having been the first American scientist to isolate the poliovirus. Other doctors had seen the withered muscle tissue, ruined spinal strands, and violated nerve cells the bug left behind. But Flexner had actually filtered out the virus itself, introduced it into pristine cells, and observed as those cells seized up and died—a sure indication that he had pinpointed the invisible agent responsible.

Emerson rapped the table in front of him and called the doctors to order. He read the day's infection figures: 52 new cases in all—43 of them in Brooklyn, 8 in Manhattan, and one in the Bronx. The totals were comparatively low but only because of incomplete reporting. The doctors muttered at the numbers and Emerson silenced them with a hand. With little preamble, he introduced Flexner, who walked to the podium to respectful applause and reviewed the state of the current outbreak.

Though the virus was showing its predictable preference for babies, Flexner reported, rising rates of infection among older children and even the occasional adult indicated that no one was completely safe. The mortality rate was holding steady at more than 20 percent, significantly higher than in past outbreaks. Autopsies showed that the children most likely to die were those whose medulla oblongata—a bulb-shaped area at the base of the brain—was attacked, since it was that region that allowed the body to draw breath. Parents should continue to take pains with their children: Youngsters should be regularly bathed; parents should wash their hands immediately afterward. Insects must be kept away from food; children must be kept away from insects. Sanitation, above all else, was imperative.

"Suppose a child kisses another?" a doctor asked.

Kissing could transmit the virus, Flexner explained, as could sneezing or coughing or anything else that carries secretions of the nose and throat from one person to another. Also to be guarded against were flies, soiled linens, dirty hands, and discharges from the intestines.

Was Flexner studying cures, one doctor wanted to know.

"There are no cures," he responded.

"What about wintergreen?" one doctor asked.

Flexner rolled his eyes. He'd heard about the wintergreen. "Wintergreen is not a cure or specific of any kind."

"Not by itself, no," the doctor persisted. "But mix it with Russian thyme and the oils of rosemary, cajeput, and wood and you get a paste that can soothe the muscles and promote movement." The muttering in the room rose again, shot through with a few snickers. The doctor raised his voice over it. "I've had eighteen cases that the Health Department has certified poliomyelitis and I've not yet had to sign a single death certificate." The snickering continued and the doctor, scowling, sat down.

The meeting pressed on like that for the remainder of the morning and the better part of the afternoon, with questions being shouted up and answers coming down and Flexner, Emerson, and Ager repeating their hygiene message again and again. Finally, when the alternating bits of wisdom and hooey had all been addressed, the gathering at last broke up, and the doctors—smarter for the time they'd spent in the hall—were dispatched back into their communities to do their work.

The next day, the temperature in New York soared back into the high 80s, causing at least two reported cases of heat prostration on the city's sidewalks. Nearly 60 more children, many of them with well-bathed bodies and well-rinsed throats, contracted the sickness in just twenty-four hours. Twenty-five of them were dead within the day.

By August, polio brushfires were continuing to burn across the nation. Though the coastal cities had suffered the most, the epidemic was now worsening in the West and the South, where the warm temperatures and long summers were kindest to the virus. New York, however, remained at the center of the plague, with nearly half of the nation's total number of cases. And those numbers showed no signs of falling. Just as things looked as if they might be starting to improve in one borough, a fresh pocket of disease would appear in another. The moment it did, it would be spread back in all directions by the city's arterial array of roads and bridges.

On the upper shoulder of Manhattan the paralysis circle was beginning to close tighter around Dora Salk's neighborhood. The black cars came for the McTiernan boy on 108th Street and the Zuckerman girl on 113th, the Schatzes' child and the Engles' child on Ninety-ninth and 100th and the Wisans' on 109th. Sometimes the doctors took the boys and girls away, sometimes they didn't. Always the neighborhoods were shaken in their wake.

Mothers of healthy children tried every possible preventive. Camphor, it had been said, could combat the bug, its powerful fumes protecting the nasal linings from infection. So mothers picked druggists' shelves clean of the five-cent cubes, hanging them around their children's necks like pungent charms. Other mothers, like Dora, tried more measured means. They raised the temperature of their laundry water to kill any hidden germs; they bagged the ashes from their coal stoves to keep the bug from hitching a ride on the dust; they swept their walks and the streets themselves to catch whatever danger might be hiding in ruts and gutters.

"Leave your shoes outside," Dora would remind Daniel each day as he'd return home from work.

"There are no germs on the sidewalks," he'd protest.

"Do you know that?" she'd ask.

Daniel, who had to admit he didn't, would remove his shoes.

For all such precautions, the viral tide continued to climb. As the middle of August approached, a total of 6,369 cases had been counted in all the boroughs; Manhattan—which had come to the plague late—was home to more than 1,400 of them.

Finally, perhaps inevitably, New Yorkers began to go to war with the only enemies they had yet to battle: one another. More and more children who looked suspiciously feverish were being surreptitiously reported to the Department of Health by neighbors. Money or other resources collected in one neighborhood to treat victims of the disease were not released to other neighborhoods, even if the need was greater there. Health inspectors were attacked by neighborhood groups when they came to visit homes; when police accompanied the inspectors, they were set upon too. As the fear and fury grew, the collected tension of the terrible summer, contained for so long, finally sparked and blew. When that happened, it happened not within the afflicted city but on a small spit of land out on Long Island.

If the children who had contracted infantile paralysis were going to be properly treated and studied, it would have to take place where the air was relatively free of the virus, allowing doctors to attend to the stable patients without having to manage newly sick ones. For this reason, the wealthy summer residents of the Rockaway Peninsula decided to devote a bit of their fortune and a square of their land to building a facility that could do just this kind of work. The volunteer rich raised the funds, retained the workmen, and arranged for a clean, wooden hospital building—equipped with proper electricity and proper plumbing—to be constructed before the end of August near the town of Woodmere. A medical staff was quickly recruited, lured by the promise of a tidy dormitory, a well-equipped laboratory, and the relief from the summer heat provided by the cool Long Island breezes.

As the hospital was being constructed, the year-round residents of the town began gathering at the work site and grumbling. The summer folks were building them a facility they hadn't asked for, one that would result in the town being overrun by a troop of infectious children. When the season was over, the benefactors themselves would decamp to their townhouses in Manhattan, and the people of Woodmere would be left to deal with the burden of their philanthropy.

The first patients were due to arrive on the last weekend in August, but before they could be admitted, the town board would have to meet to approve the hospital officially. That meeting was set for the Thursday evening before the weekend. When the selectmen arrived at the council hall on the appointed night, they found a swarm of locals waiting outside for them. The officials entered the hall and took their seats at the council table, and the crowd noisily followed.

The town council would be assisted in its work that evening by J. Howes Burton, a summer resident and the head of the civic group that had collected the funds for the hospital. It was Burton's job to argue for the facility, but it was Burton's type—with his wealth and his influence and his grand first initial—who most raised the hackles of the locals. The moment he took his seat on the panel, the crowd began to mutter. When he introduced himself and began to make his case for the new facility, the mutters turned to hoots. Burton tried to call out over the din, explaining—as the selectmen nodded along—that the children would be arriving only after the contagious phase of their disease had passed, thus benefiting from the care the facility could provide but posing no danger to anyone else. The crowd was not swayed. He argued that the work done in the new facility could eventually help all babies—perhaps even Woodmere's own. But the crowd was having none of it. Finally, Burton offered up the only argument he had left, and as soon as he raised it, he knew he had miscalculated badly.

"The hospital is on private grounds," he said. "And those who own the land can build what they will."

The selectmen winced and the room exploded in fist-shaking and shouts. The chairman of the panel tried to hush the crowd, but the noise only grew louder. Stepping in, the health commissioner shouted out a hopeful compromise: The hospital would be opened as planned, he suggested, but it would receive only paralysis cases that originated in the villages of Woodmere and nearby Hewlett. Children from other local communities would not be welcome—to say nothing of those from the city. Relieved at this one small concession they could make, the selectmen huddled briefly, then gaveled the proposal into law and gaveled themselves out into the night.

The crowd erupted. Streaming from the town hall, they moved in a group to the neck of land where the hospital stood, its grounds still littered with the stuff of its construction. Only a few bulbs burned inside the wooden structure, shedding just a faint light on the surrounding grounds; the waters off Long Island sloshed blackly beyond the reach of the lamps. The crowd took up positions around the building, chanting and shouting that they would stand their posts for as long as it took to ensure that not a single paralysis patient entered the facility. Sheriffs from Hewlett, Woodmere, and Hempstead, who had attended the meeting out of concern for just this kind of disturbance and remained close to the crowd as it moved, kept the people from approaching the structure too closely, but pointedly did not order them to leave.

The town selectmen sent for help, and a half dozen armed private detectives—some of whom worked as guards at the summer mansions—arrived and stationed themselves between the encircling group and the wooden building. The crowd responded by sending out runners and bringing in even more protesters, these armed with rakes and torches. The detectives responded by bringing in more of their own as well. Within a few hours, a restless ring of six hundred locals faced off against an inner ring of twenty lawmen. The crowd occasionally probed the detectives' line with a feint with their rakes. The detectives responded with lunges of their own, for now keeping their hands off their weapons. At last, the protesters lit and raised their torches.

"This building will be burned before we'll see it used," one of them shouted.

"And those who burn will be arrested," a detective answered.

A protester stepped forward. "Anyone who attempts to take a patient into this hospital will be physically restrained," he threatened.

"If an employee of this hospital is attacked, the man responsible will be shot," a detective responded.

The detectives and the protesters glared at each other across the unmarked divide. And then, slowly an unexpected thing happened: The rakes came down, the torches were lowered. Nobody was going to shoot anyone; nobody was going to burn anything. This scene on this night was less about rage than about sorrow and fear, about the swelling army of baby ghosts growing in the distant boroughs and now stalking Long Island. There'd be no reclaiming the children who had been swept away, and no saving the ones still to die.

Gradually, the rings of people began to waver and dissolve; the detectives and the mob turned from one another and straggled wordlessly off.

Late the next day, a polio patient from the town of Woodmere was admitted to the hospital. That stricken child was followed by three others from nearby Inwood, and they in turn were followed by still others from a scatter of surrounding towns. Within days, the hospital was full of children. The staff of doctors in the fine wooden building never would come up with a way to help any of them.

Jonas Salk escaped the polio bug that summer. He turned two years old in October, the same month the weather at last grew cool and Dora Salk and the other mothers could draw a breath and begin to put the season of terror behind them. In the end, the doctors counted 27,000 cases of poliomyelitis around the country, 6,000 of them fatal. More than 9,300 of the total number of victims were New York children, and of those, more than 2,200 would never see another summer. Of the ones who lived, about half would walk away from the disease with little more than a weakened hand or an unsteady leg to remind them of the scourge they'd suffered.

The rest of the survivors—some 3,500 of them—would not be seen again until late autumn or winter, when they at last came wheeling or clanking out of the hospitals, their legs and hips caged in steel-and-leather braces they would need to wear for the rest of their lives. Even the cleverest of the boys and girls would need months to master the awkward appliances, not confidently balancing back up on their bolted and buckled legs until the next spring or later. By then, of course, the air in the city would already be starting to grow warm again, and from somewhere in the sticky South—where all the wild things grew—the poliovirus would begin approaching once more.

$\sim 2 \sim$

Helen Press and her parents had been making weekend trips to visit Jonas Salk and his family in their new home in the Bronx for a few years now. But near as she could remember, she had rarely been able to get her ten-year-old cousin to come out and play.

Now and again, Helen, along with Salk's younger brother, Herman, would try to coax him into the yard for a bit of kickball or stickball, and once in a great while he would agree. But while Salk could be a serviceable enough athlete, he was also a very uninterested one. A few obligatory kicks or swings at whatever ball Helen and Herman were throwing at him that day and he'd be happily back inside the house. What Salk did do while Helen and Herman—and later, Lee, the youngest brother—were at play, was read.

Salk was, by any measure, a serious boy, troubled by sometimes curious things. Rules seemed to grate on him the most. Not that he didn't respect a good rule when he came across one. Indeed, once a law had been laid down by Dora or Daniel, he rarely needed it repeated and seemed almost to enjoy the square-cornered geometry it gave his world.

But that kind of compliance came only if the rule seemed to make sense to him. If it didn't, he'd fix it so that it would. Around the house or at school, he'd be given a project or a chore to perform, and often as not he'd change the way he'd been instructed to perform it, flipping its sequence or modifying a step, and appearing quite pleased with himself for having done so. When asked why he didn't do something the way he'd been told to do it, his answer would always be the same.

"It's better this way," he'd explain.

He'd say it not so much with cockiness as with puzzlement. It was an empirical thing, an observable fact, like saying there were seven eggs in a basket or eighteen eyelets in a boot. If someone counted them up the wrong way, you might try to explain the matter, but that person's confusion wouldn't change an unchangeable truth.

More troubling to Salk than bad rules were good rules poorly applied, as they often were in the stickball games he now and then conceded to play with the other boys on his block. While only a middling asset to any team when it came to running or fielding, he did enjoy the flow of the game and had a keen mind for the shifting, guerrilla rules that governed it. In a city filled with boys who could score runs or pitch, one who could adjudicate disputes—and do so impartially—was a decidedly rarer commodity. Jonas was thus named standing umpire of the games on his block.

Given the boy's judicious turn of mind, his mother concluded that the obvious choice when he came of age was for him to enter rabbinical school. Dora Salk had made it clear from the time he was born that while she hoped for great things from all her sons, she flat-out expected them from her first one. But it would not be easy to get him where she imagined he ought to go.

Finances remained a dodgy thing in the Salk house. Not that Daniel didn't continue to do fine design work for some of the city's finest garment houses. Now and then, however, he'd take it into his head that he ought to be doing more—opening up his own concern and hiring his own needlemen to produce the patterns he created. Once every few years, he'd give his notice and go off to do just that. While the people around Daniel would applaud his initiative, they also knew that the venture would surely come to grief, Daniel's mind for design being a far sharper thing than his mind for business. And so when the enterprise would fail, as it inevitably did, he'd always find his old job or perhaps an even better one waiting for him when he returned. In the meantime, Dora would run the household as best she could on money she had squirreled away from Daniel's paychecks in the years he was earning a living, saving it as a hedge against the months he wasn't. During those lean times, she'd reassure Jonas.

"You'll go to college," she'd tell him, pulling a chair up as he read his books at the small kitchen table. "You'll have the money."

But as it turned out, Jonas decided he didn't want to go to college—at least not rabbinical college. While the work was noble, the arena might not be big enough. Jonas didn't care if his face never became famous. But if he would never be widely known, he wanted his work to be widely felt. From his perch on the bema, a rabbi could move a congregation, perhaps even a community, but beyond that, Jonas feared, his voice would go mostly unheard. What he needed was something with greater reach that would allow him to make the most of his bigger skills.

Sharing this decision with his mother would not be easy. Going toe-to-toe with Dora over even minor things was always a losing proposition, and Salk had long since learned to finesse and nudge when he was trying to win a point with her. But there would be no way to finesse this matter.

"I don't think I'm going to go to rabbinical school," he told Dora one day as she visited him at his books.

"No?" she asked, recognizing, as Jonas did, that this was not so much a statement he was making as a proposal he was floating.

"No," he answered.

"What, then?"

"I'm going to be a lawyer."

"Lawyer!" Dora half-asked, half-snapped. "You can't even win an argument with me."

Jonas shrugged. "You have to be a lawyer if you want to be a congressman," he said. "And I want to be a congressman."

Dora looked at her son for a long, troubled moment. Lawyering was a respectable enough profession, she supposed, but a vulgar one too—at least compared with synagogue work. Serving in Congress, on the other hand, was a different matter. A congressional seat was a position with true power, true sweep; it would keep Jonas out of the garment business, get him out of the Bronx, and more important, make it clear to anyone with eyes that getting out was indeed what he'd done. Dora considered the new idea. Yes, she agreed at last, Congressman Salk was a fine idea.

The way Dora saw it, boys exceptional enough to go to Washington needed to go to exceptional schools, and she knew which one: New York City's Townsend Harris High School. Townsend Harris offered an accelerated program for gifted children who were in a hurry to finish their public education so that they could go on to university as early as possible. Jonas applied to the school and matriculated one month before he turned thirteen. He graduated when he was still fifteen. Diploma in hand, he enrolled at the City College of New York, with the state bar and the U.S. House of Representatives in his crosshairs.

Once Salk made a decision like this, he was disinclined to revisit it. His evaluation of his abilities had led him to reach one conclusion about his future, and since those talents were unlikely to change, the choice he made oughtn't either. He liked that kind of syllogistic certainty and was pleased when he could achieve so settled a state. But while his aptitudes might be fixed, his appetites weren't.

Students at City College were required to trudge through a first-year program of general courses just to make sure that the curriculum they were following was right for them. Philosophy students were thus sent off to physics classes, biology students were sent off to poetry classes, and prelaw students, with their clear-eyed plans for a seat in Congress before they turned thirty, were sent off to chemistry classes. Most of the time, the conscripted freshmen daydreamed through the required courses, but once in a while, a life changed its course.

"I don't think I'm going to go to Congress," Jonas said to his mother across the kitchen table not long after he began his time at City College. "I'm going to be a doctor."

Dora nodded warily.

"But I'm not going to practice medicine," Jonas added.

"How can you be a doctor if you don't practice medicine?"

"I'm going to go into research."

Dora looked at Jonas dubiously, but Jonas had thought this through. It was the matter of the arena again. Opening a medical practice was worthy enough, but it was also a bit of a rearguard action. By the time a person came wheezing or hacking into the doctor's office, a disease had already scored a hit. Better to take the fight straight to the illness, to develop ways to prevent people from getting sick in the first place so that they never had to call on the doctor at all. This was work that reached beyond a congregation, beyond an electorate. This was work that reached a world.

Dora began to turn the idea over in her head, but before she could determine how she felt, Jonas interrupted her. "I'm going to go into research," he said with clarity. "It's what I want to do."

The tall man left a trail of nasty scratches on the marble floor in the lobby of 120 Broadway. It was a fair bet that nearly everybody in the lobby of the giant building recognized the man's face, and knew he was Franklin Roosevelt.

It had been only two years, after all, since Roosevelt—the onetime New York State assemblyman and assistant secretary of the Navy—had been nominated for vice president on a Democratic ticket headed by Ohio governor James Cox. In the election that November, Cox and Roosevelt were shellacked by the Republican nominees, Warren Harding and Calvin Coolidge. Both of the beaten Democrats faded largely from sight—Cox to his Ohio home, Roosevelt to his townhouse in Manhattan and his snug perch in his big home overlooking the Hudson River in Hyde Park, New York. But his mere appearance still rightly turned heads.

Roosevelt arrived that morning in October 1922 the way he always had—by chauffered limousine that deposited him directly in front of the modern skyscraper where he had worked as a branch chief of the Fidelity

& Deposit Company ever since his election defeat. He had not appeared at his office for more than fifteen months, however; it was the difficulty with his legs that had been keeping him away.

That problem began in the summer of 1921, when he was thirty-nine and he, his wife, Eleanor, and their five children were vacationing on Campobello Island in Canada's Bay of Fundy. Most summers, the entire Roosevelt brood would travel up to Campobello together. This time, however, Roosevelt had business affairs to mind in Washington, as well as a Boy Scout jamboree he had promised to attend near Bear Mountain, New York. He thus shooed his family off to the island ahead of him, finishing up his Washington work and fulfilling his Boy Scout commitment before joining them there. While Roosevelt found the business in the capital something of a bother, the scout camp—with its hard exercise and good cheer—was a delight. With so many boys packed together into such close quarters, however, it did appear that a few of them might have picked up a summer cold.

On August 7, when Roosevelt at last arrived in Campobello, his family and his political aide Louis Howe met him at the Welshpool Harbor dock, where the yacht that had carried him up from New York deposited him. His arrival was a boisterous affair, with his children thrilled that he had at last been able to join them. Roosevelt himself found it hard to be so cheery, feeling somehow creaky and fatigued, as if he might have picked up a touch of whatever it was that had made the Boy Scouts sniffle.

On Wednesday, August 10, after returning from a swim with his sons, he felt even worse. After sending the boys to change out of their bathing suits, he sat down wearily to answer his mail, still wearing his own wet suit. In short order, he began to feel dizzy and hot. His temperature spiked to 102, his brain went woozy and febrile, and he began to shiver like a man struck by palsy. Eleanor sent him straight to bed.

The next day when Roosevelt awoke, things were even worse. When he tried to stand, his left leg seemed oddly wobbly. When he tried to hobble to the bathroom to shave, the leg simply buckled, causing him to collapse to the floor. Eleanor and Howe heard the crash and tore into the bedroom. They carried the frightened Roosevelt back to his bed and quickly sum-

moned the doctors. Over the next few days, the medical men visited and
each of them offered a different diagnosis.

It was a cold that would pass in a week or so, pronounced one physician brought in from across the Bay of Lubec. It was a transient spinal clot
that would be absorbed soon, assured a celebrated surgeon called up from
Philadelphia. But rather than improving, the weakness soon spread to
Roosevelt's right leg and then into his back and arms. Finally, the family
summoned Dr. Robert Lovett of Harvard University, who traveled to Campobello and evaluated the patient.

"It's perfectly clear," the doctor said with a brusque certainty. "This
man is suffering from infantile paralysis."

Inside the Roosevelt home, where the next step in Franklin's political
career was already being planned, the news went off like a bomb, but it was
a bomb the family was determined to contain. For the better part of the
next fifteen months, the public saw almost nothing of the dynamic Roosevelt and was left to speculate about his condition. Finally, a thinner, paler
Roosevelt at last reappeared in public, rolling up in front of the entrance to
120 Broadway one workday morning like any other salary man.

The long, shiny car came to a stop at the curb and the chauffeur got
quickly about the business of unloading his passenger—opening the back
door, helping him pivot in his seat, locking the knee latches on his braces
so that his legs stretched awkwardly out into the stream of office workers
hurrying by on the sidewalk. Roosevelt smiled at the people jauntily and
nodded amusedly. Wasn't this a grand bit of silliness?

The chauffeur tugged Roosevelt to his feet and handed him his crutches.
Then they made their way slowly across the sidewalk, the chauffeur holding Roosevelt's arm while Roosevelt planted his crutches and swung his
legs, planted his crutches and swung his legs. They crossed the sidewalk
this way until they reached the door of the building and entered its vast
lobby, a prairie of marble stretching a full city block to a back door opening onto Nassau Street. Carefully, they navigated a few steps, but the pol-
ished marble was impossibly slick, at least for a man on crutches. Just as they
were passing a grand marble stairway that led up to offices on the second

floor, Roosevelt slipped. His arms straining, his paralyzed legs unable to keep him upright, he toppled noisily to the floor.

The crowd in the lobby went instantly silent. Roosevelt righted himself, saluted the onlookers, and laughed easily. Such a comedy this was becoming! A husky young man hurried over and helped the chauffeur get Roosevelt to his feet. As he did, another, smaller man also approached. He was a wiry, snappily dressed fellow, perhaps ten years Roosevelt's junior. Roosevelt had often seen him around the lobby of 120 Broadway, and had even been introduced to him once or twice. The little man, so Roosevelt had been told, was a lawyer who worked on one of the upper floors; his name was Basil O'Connor. Roosevelt waved O'Connor off, assuring him that the other two men would see to him just fine.

O'Connor stood where he was and watched the hobbling group retreat. When they had at last disappeared into the elevator, he looked down at the sparkling white floor. It was then that he—and the others—noticed the trail of scratches the crippled man's braces had left behind him.

It would be months before the shaken Roosevelt would return to 120 Broadway, and he would never again attempt to navigate the lobby by any means other than wheelchair. Now and again during the time he was gone, Basil O'Connor would look for him. He admired the man he'd seen that morning, and he wouldn't half mind having the chance to work with him one day.

Jonas Salk entered New York University Medical School in the fall of 1934 and promptly became every bit the obsessive student the people who knew him expected him to be. He immersed himself in his classes and labs, studied ferociously after hours, filled his small bedroom in his parents' home with the stuff of his education. There were piles of books, stacks of notes, even a preserved pig fetus in a glass jar he had been allowed to borrow from an NYU lab when he was studying anatomy.

"Would you mind taking that thing with you?" his cousin Helen, now a teenager, would ask as Jonas surrendered his room to her during the occasional weekends she still spent with the Salk family.

"This?" Jonas would inquire, pointing with deliberate befuddlement to a paperweight or a medical text.

"That! That!" Helen would say, wagging a finger at the pickled thing while averting her eyes from it.

"Sure," Jonas would say with a shrug, gathering up the jar but somehow always replacing it within easy sight the next day.

Helen, more than most people, found her cousin exasperating; but more than most people, she also found him extraordinary. This was an acquired taste. As Jonas got older, his social skills began to look a lot like his youthful athletic skills—unremarkable things at best. The business of drawing close to people—of working through all the back-patting and small-talking and getting-to-know-you preambles other folks mastered so early—seemed to wear him out. It was hard not to notice and admire how much better Jonas's free and genial brother Herman performed in the same situations. If you had a hobby, Herman would remember what it was. If you had a dog, Herman would remember its name. Herman had a smile and Herman had charm and he'd use them both to gather up the people in a room and hold them close. Lee, the youngest Salk, did not quite have Herman's twinkle, but he did his best, learning what he could from his sociable brother, certainly more than Jonas had learned.

But there were still moments when Jonas shone. If he seemed quiet among his friends when they went to a restaurant, he was at ease with the waiter, engaging him in conversation if the opportunity presented itself and seeming genuinely absorbed by what the man had to say. If he was awkward with his parents' friends when they came by for dinner, he was comfortable with the repairman who came to fix the stove. In all of these situations, Jonas would listen more than he spoke and take in more than he gave, as if he had learned all he could from the world he inhabited and wanted to understand the ones he didn't.

There was one other situation in which the otherwise awkward Jonas exhibited something extraordinary. It showed itself mostly with the handful of fast friends he did make over the years, during the handful of dates he'd been on with girls, or in the company of family members, like Helen, with whom he truly felt comfortable. It was a thing that would occur somewhere in the middle of an intimate conversation—that elusive sweet spot in which real ideas were being exchanged and real confidences being shared. Jonas would not necessarily have more to say during such discussions than anyone else would. But when he did speak up, he would seem to refract everything that had been said so far through an odd prism of his own, casting a spangle of new lights and insights on whatever was being discussed. It was a pretty thing to watch—and it was a rewarding thing to wait for.

Lovely as Jonas's ability to re-see something could be, it could also be a liability, at least in medical school, where so much of the work involved the brute business of forcing material into memory. Only occasionally did Jonas's classwork offer him the opportunity for a flicker of true insight—most memorably during his first-year study of the science of microbiology. One of the most intriguing—and vexing—topics in the microbiology curriculum was the business of vaccines.

On its face, a vaccine was simple. In order to develop immunity to a disease, the first thing you had to do was catch a case of it—at least a very mild case. Inject a body with the weakest possible form of an illness and the system ought to have no trouble manufacturing the necessary antibodies to snuff it out. Later, if a truly wild, truly lethal strain of the same bug came along, the antibodies would be on hand, primed to recognize the pathogen and repulse it before it could gain a toehold in the bloodstream.

The trick to making a good vaccine was how you bred down your viruses, culturing them into weaker and weaker states without crossing the line and killing them altogether. The more live, spineless virus you could get into a patient's system, the bigger the flood of antibodies that would result.

Viruses, however, were slippery things. Cultivate a weakened batch of billions of them and there was always a chance that a few would muster the muscle to mutate back, finding their old infectious form and hiding out in an otherwise safe vaccine. Once in the body, they'd be free to do their pathogenic worst. No one had yet figured out a way around that problem, and most people weren't even trying. The occasional infection of the unfortunate few was the unavoidable price of inoculating the many. That, in any case, was what the great Edward Jenner believed when he developed the first smallpox vaccine in 1796, and what the even greater Louis Pasteur was said to have concluded when he applied the same technique to developing vaccines against anthrax, rabies, and cholera in the 1880s.

But Salk wondered whether the giants were right. Early in his microbiology studies, his professor mentioned that when it came to diseases caused not by viruses but by bacteria—tetanus and diphtheria specifically—it was possible to make a vaccine simply by isolating a bit of the toxins the germs produce. These chemical dog tags alone would be enough to mark the disease and allow the body to spot it should it ever appear for real. The next day in the same class, the same teacher reminded the students that while this safe strategy worked for bacterial diseases, it would not work for viral diseases, which, as science had long known, required a weakened but living version of the bug itself.

Salk copied this into his notes, but lingered after class to inquire about it further. If a mere toxic marker from a bacterium was enough to wake up the body's immune system, why couldn't a mere scrap of a virus or even its whole killed carcass do the same? It was certainly less risky than putting a load of live pathogen into a patient. Salk's professor smiled benignly. It was a very good question, but it had been a well-proven given since the days of Louis Pasteur, and untold numbers of failed vaccines made from killed viruses had proven it.

"Not knowing why it's true," the professor said, "isn't the same as it being untrue."

While unpredictable things like vaccines troubled Salk, he soon came to realize that the crisp discipline of chemistry thrilled him. Medicine might be driven as much by science as by doctrine and tradition and beliefs, but chemistry was another matter entirely. There was something about the orderliness of the science that he found appealing—the way a complex creature like a human being could be tracked back to the idiosyncratic cells that made it up, and the cells in turn could be tracked back to their sturdy, steady, predictable chemicals. You can't fully appreciate a house, Salk figured, unless you understand how to bake a brick. And he found he loved the bricks. If Salk was ever going to have answers to the kind of question his microbiology professor had left so unsatisfyingly unsettled, he'd need to arm himself with a harder knowledge than medical texts alone seemed to offer.

During Salk's first year in medical school, his analytical eye was not lost on his chemistry professor, R. Keith Cannan, who struggled to get his medical novices thinking in so clear a way—usually with little result. When he found someone who had that talent naturally, he liked to make the most of it. As the end of the second semester approached, Cannan pulled Salk aside.

"I want you to think about leaving school for a year," he said with little preamble. "I need a research assistant, and I think you'd do the job well."

"I wouldn't graduate with my class?" Salk asked.

"No. And you wouldn't receive any academic credit either," Cannan said. "Take some time if you need it. Consider it overnight."

Salk nodded, but he knew he didn't need any extra time. Risks, he'd come to think, always pay off. No matter how they work out, they teach you either what to do or what not to do. Working with Cannan was something he strongly suspected he ought to do. He'd come to medical school to learn how to conduct research, and now someone was offering him the chance to do that for real. Before he left the classroom, he'd accepted the offer.

No sooner had the year's courses ended than the professor put the student to work, and what he gave him to do was assistant's labor indeed. Cannan was studying the streptococcus bacterium, and in order to do so, he needed a lot of the toxic bugs. That meant breeding them up in great cultures and then pouring them into a centrifuge in which he could spin down the organic muck and extract the bacteria that precipitated to the bottom. But centrifuges were small, which meant a lot of pouring and spinning before enough germs were in hand. Even when they were, they were never as pure as they ought to be, carrying traces of the medium in which they'd been brewed.

Cannan wanted to find out if there was some way to do the same work chemically, with much less reliance on the centrifuge, and Salk had an idea. If he froze the culture, he suspected, the bacteria might clump together on their own, much as the solids in milk do when the liquid component freezes. Salk tried out his idea, placing a can of strep culture inside a larger container packed with calcium phosphate and ice, which together cause things to freeze quickly and predictably. The strep solution indeed froze—but the bacteria themselves weren't affected, remaining dispersed throughout the slushy mixture. Salk tried again and failed again, tried again and failed again. Then, after his final trial, as he was disassembling his little experiment, he inadvertently sloshed a little of the calcium phosphate into the liquid strep. Slowly, the state of the solution changed, with a mass of material congealing in the middle and dropping to the bottom.

Salk, surprised, drained off the liquid that remained and examined what was left in the can. It was, he saw to his delight, live and thriving strep caked around calcium phosphate crystals. All he had to do now was use a little water to dissolve the crystals away and he'd have the pure mass of germs his professor had sent him after. Salk kept his excitement in check, ran the experiment several more times, and scribbled down his notes. He looked them over and felt torn.

Salk had not been part of the medical world for long, but he was already coming to learn that it was a world that valued deference. He knew with a clean scientific certainty that he'd discovered precisely the kind of method for concentrating streptococcus bugs that Cannan had sent him after. But he was also coming to learn that if he put it so baldly—especially to a superior—what he had to say would never be heard. Instead, he affected the degree of uncertainty he believed was expected of him.

"I may possibly have stumbled onto something," he said, approaching Cannan. "But you'd better take a look."

Salk stood quietly while Cannan studied the sheets of paper and closely examined the vials of bacteria he'd collected. Then he looked at his student and gave him a nod. The method was a good one and Cannan knew it. Salk, he had reason to suspect, knew it too.

By himself, Franklin Roosevelt could never climb the 1,400 feet up Pine Mountain to the sad and collapsing Meriwether Inn in Warm Springs, Georgia. The mountain was full of rock spurs and outcroppings that could discourage even the most nimble visitor. Merely getting to the town was no simple matter either—it being too far south of Atlanta, too far north of Columbus, and too far east of LaGrange to make a handy trip by any of the easy routes. Yet people found their way to Pine Mountain and had been doing so since the original Meriwether Inn was built in 1837.

Franklin Roosevelt first came to the mountain in 1924, and like everyone else, he came for the water. People both inside and outside Meriwether County talked about the water in the town of Warm Springs—about the way it was squeezed up through fissures in the rocks with enough force to run an overshot mill a mile away; the way it splashed and broke along the mountain face, filling basins and shallows with its strange silvery glint and its odd stony smell.

The water gushed from the Meriwether rocks at a constant rate of 1,300 gallons per minute and maintained a constant temperature of 88 to 90 degrees Fahrenheit. What's more, it had a natural buoyancy that kept even the clumsy afloat. The water's lift came from its peculiar chemistry, said to include magnesium, iron, lime, and soda, as well as a touch of carbonic acid, all in such high concentrations that it sometimes left a sandy residue on the skin and the hair. Some people even whispered that the water crackled with a touch of radioactivity.

Whatever the Warm Springs water was made of, there was little doubt about its curious powers to cure. It healed skin diseases and rheumatism, liver diseases and dyspepsia, ailments of the kidneys and bladder, and even sicknesses of mood. And, it was now rumored, bathing in the pools of Warm Springs, Georgia, might also cure the crippling of infantile paralysis. At least that was the word when the recent newspaper story got around about the young civil engineer from New York City who'd contracted polio and, after three summers spent at Pine Mountain, regained full use of his paralyzed legs. It was that account that caught Franklin Roosevelt's interest and brought him to the Meriwether Inn.

Roosevelt, as his wife had learned over the last few years, was not always entirely rational on the topic of regaining the use of his legs and had embarked on all manner of travels in search of a cure. Eleanor had agreed to accompany him on many of them, but this one—a trip into the thick of a Dixie summer to bathe in magical waters—seemed like special folly. Nonetheless, at Franklin's urging, she agreed to go along.

A crowd of Georgians was waiting on the Meriwether County train platform to greet the glamorous politician and his less glamorous wife when they arrived. Mrs. Roosevelt descended from the rear car to the station platform on her own. Roosevelt was lifted from the train and deposited in the passenger seat of a touring car like just so much clumsy luggage. If he was troubled by this indignity at all, his smiles and waves certainly didn't show it.

The onetime politician was driven slowly up Pine Mountain and, unlike his wife, who saw the place for the sad backwater it was, he was thrilled—noticing less the lamentable state of the roads than the fine air; less the tumbledown condition of the Meriwether Inn than the stand of pines around it. The steep terrain crested in a rocky knob that afforded a view Roosevelt instantly loved. But when he was at last lowered into the Pine Mountain water that filled the Meriwether pool he appeared to notice nothing else at all, save the great warmth that bathed his always icy legs, the great sense of drift that suffused his lead-heavy body, the subtle tickle of the magical minerals against his long-sickened tissue. Even before Roosevelt emerged from the pool, he decided that he would return to this place—and he decided that when he did come back, he would own it.

Franklin Roosevelt had gotten such wild business notions before, and not much good had come of it. His investment portfolio was stuffed with ill-considered land deals and half-considered stock purchases—just the kind of naïve dabbling to be expected from a wealthy man who had never had to make his own money in the first place. But Warm Springs, he was convinced, had real value. More important, for this transaction he'd have Basil O'Connor looking out for him.

In the two years since he took his fall in the lobby of 120 Broadway, Roosevelt had come to rely on O'Connor for a lot. The work Roosevelt had been doing for the Fidelity & Deposit Company was, truth be told, little work at all. Preoccupied with his paralysis, he spent most of his time traveling about in search of cures. His employers did not seem to mind, evidently concluding that a Roosevelt on the letterhead was well nigh as good as a Roosevelt who actually appeared in the office, providing the firm with friends and connections and a certain landed respectability.

Basil O'Connor was a different breed of man entirely. As the second son of an Irish tinsmith, he would have spent his life in the trades himself had he not learned to play the violin, which allowed him to earn extra money in local dance bands and pay his way through college and law school. He was admitted to the New York bar on June 20, 1916, good news that came to him in the same month that so many other New Yorkers were beginning to retreat into their homes against the onslaught of that summer's polio plague.

Well lettered if not wellborn, O'Connor resolved to make up for his shortcomings by using his newly acquired legal skills to sharpen his instincts for business. By the time he was in his early thirties, he'd built himself a very small fortune. If he could form a professional alliance with a true gentleman—somebody who could attract the caliber of clients he never could—he could turn that modest fortune into a decidedly immodest one, both for himself and his new associate. Sometime after Roosevelt began reappearing at 120 Broadway, O'Connor made a congenial lunch date with him and the two passed the meal enjoyably. They made other dates after that, and eventually O'Connor made his thoughts plain.

He was looking for a law partner, he said. If Roosevelt could attract clients, O'Connor could take care of them, guaranteeing both partners at least $10,000 per year. Roosevelt would receive his share even if he did no work. If he did any at all, he would earn much, much more.

Roosevelt thought for a moment. O'Connor, he'd come to know, was an honest man; just as important, he was an exceedingly smart one. If he said he could make Roosevelt a great deal of money for even less work than he was already doing, he probably could.

"O'Connor and Roosevelt," Roosevelt said, rolling the name of the proposed firm around on his tongue. "That just might be a good idea."

"No, no," O'Connor corrected. "I think Roosevelt and O'Connor would be much more euphonious."

Roosevelt, O'Connor was not surprised to learn, agreed.

In its first year of existence, the firm of Roosevelt & O'Connor indeed generated impressive revenues for both men. When Roosevelt returned from Warm Springs, charged up with the idea of buying the place, he thus took his plan straight to his business partner. O'Connor let him know what he thought of the idea.

"What do you want with a four-story firetrap with nothing but squirrels running around in it?" he asked.

"I want it to be a spa and a rehabilitation hospital," Roosevelt said. "For polios."

The way Roosevelt saw it, he would buy the Meriwether Inn and the surrounding grounds and restore them both. The rebuilt facility would go back into the business of attracting vacationers, who would come to take the waters and pay richly for the privilege. The wealth that would be generated would be used to support facilities on the same grounds for the treatment of children and adults felled by infantile paralysis. O'Connor saw nothing but headaches in the plan, but despite his entreaties, Roosevelt pressed ahead, and over the next eighteen months he raised $200,000 from friends, business associates, and his own portfolio. He bought the entire sorry Meriwether estate, formed a nonprofit group called the Georgia Warm Springs Foundation, and set about building just the facility he had envisioned.

In 1927, the Warm Springs resort went into operation. One year later, in the summer of 1928, the New York Democratic Party found itself in need of a candidate to run for governor against the hugely popular Republican attorney general Albert Ottinger. The Democrats did not need much of a candidate—just someone who could conduct a respectable campaign and lose with grace. If that candidate had something else to keep him busy after his inevitable loss—a foundation for cripples somewhere in Georgia, say—so much the better. The local party recruited Franklin Roosevelt for the thankless work, guessing he'd appreciate even a pantomime campaign after having once harbored dreams of holding office for real. Roosevelt accepted the nomination and, as the party asked, set out to make at least a show of wooing the voters. As it happened, he enjoyed his time on the stump, and as he had noticed in 1920, the people rather enjoyed having him there. Indeed, they enjoyed him so much that three months later, on November 8, he was elected governor of the state of New York by a 25,000-vote margin out of 4.2 million votes cast. It was a surprise to Roosevelt and the party—and an even bigger surprise to Basil O'Connor.

"Take over Warm Springs, old fella," Roosevelt said when he had a private moment with O'Connor the next day.

O'Connor nodded an uncertain yes. His business sense counseled a no.

It didn't take long before Basil O'Connor's belief that Warm Springs was a harebrained idea turned out to be right—though to look at the place he and Franklin Roosevelt had built you wouldn't think so. The facility that had sprung up on Pine Mountain was, as Roosevelt had promised, first-rate, with a restored inn and a pool, a handsome dining room, and new suites and bungalows for both rich vacationers and recovering polios. In addition, there was a rehabilitation gym, a cast-and-brace shop, and even an on-campus operating room where muscle, joint, and tendon surgery could be performed.

As Roosevelt had predicted, the wealthy did come to Warm Springs to take their leisure, and the polios did come to take the cure, but before long it was clear the mix was not a good one. Lounging by the pool, the healthy guests soon turned cool to the halt and lame who hobbled or crutch-walked or dragged themselves into the water, carrying who-knew-what viruses with them. In the dining room, the vacationers put down their forks when the cripples rolled in on their wheeled beds or in their chairs, pulling up to their tables and struggling to eat with hands made clumsy by paralysis. To Roosevelt, the solution was simple: Through O'Connor, he arranged for a second pool and a second dining room to be built so that the two groups could remain apart. But this did not do the trick. The healthy guests thanked the management for its efforts, paid their bill for their time on the mountain, and went off to spend their future vacations elsewhere.

By the 1932 season, Warm Springs was a place filled with happy cripples and no one else. Without the income from the vacationers, the $47 per week that was the per-patient fee for room, board, and therapy didn't nearly cover operating expenses, especially since only about half the residents were paying that fee, the others staying for half-price or even nothing at all, depending on their need. Though O'Connor fretted the figures almost every day, his partner the governor seemed incapable of appreciating how serious the trouble was. Things only got worse that summer when the governor—borne aloft by his own charisma, an electorate grown terrified by the deepening Depression, and a party willing to take a chance— became the Democratic nominee for president of the United States. O'Connor, well pleased that his partner might be headed for the White House, nonetheless dreaded the possibility of being left entirely alone with the financial mess Roosevelt had made in Georgia. When, in November, Roosevelt was indeed elected, O'Connor's worst fears were realized.

But Basil O'Connor did not care for messes, and he had an idea of how to tidy this one up. By almost all polling measures, the new president was an exceedingly popular man, and his paralysis, once thought an insurmountable bar to his attaining office, had only endeared him more to voters, earning him the hard-luck bona fides so privileged a person could never otherwise have won. Wouldn't the American people enjoy the op portunity to thank so beloved a man? Wouldn't they like to celebrate, say, his birthday, with a series of balls around the country, and while enjoying themselves, donate a little money to fight the disease that had so cruelly crippled the man they were honoring? The events could be called— straightforwardly enough—the Birthday Balls, and the revenue they raised could be enormous.

O'Connor liked the idea, Roosevelt signed off on it, and on January 30, 1934, the first balls were held in nearly six thousand communities around the country. When the contributions were tallied over the next several days, they exceeded a staggering $1 million. The next evening, Roosevelt let the nation know just how much he appreciated every one of those dollars.

"As the representative of hundreds of thousands of crippled children," the fifty-two-year-old man with the infant's disease said in a national radio address, "I accept this tribute. I thank you and bid you good night on what to me is the happiest birthday I have ever known."

Though the revenue from the Birthday Balls fell the following two years, the amount of money they raised was still so enormous that the little Warm Springs Foundation began to seem like too small a beneficiary. What was needed, Roosevelt decided, was a larger organization with a more sweeping mission, something that would reach well beyond his retreat in Georgia—and well beyond his time in the presidency. On September 23, 1937, he signed a proclamation creating just such an institution. Warm Springs would continue to be a center of polio research and treatment, but now it would be subsumed into a far grander National Foundation for Infantile Paralysis. Medical minds would be recruited, advisory boards would be impaneled, universities and private labs would be enlisted from around the country. Money raised from donations and events would be distributed to all these scientific centers, and the greatest medical thinkers in the country would be authorized to spend it to rehabilitate the children the poliovirus had crippled. If they also found an inoculation that could protect the healthy before they ever got sick, so much the better. The nation, Roosevelt declared, was going to stomp this disease flat.

Jonas Salk's class at New York University graduated in the spring of 1938. Salk himself, detained by his time with Cannan, made it out the following year. It promised to be a busy time. Not only was he about to begin his internship, he was also just beginning life as a married man.

Salk had dated sporadically throughout college and medical school, meeting girls he liked well enough but none who fully engaged him. It wasn't until the summer of 1938, when the twenty-three-year-old Salk traveled to Woods Hole, Massachusetts, where he was earning part-time pay as a laboratory technician, that he met the tall and leggy Donna Lindsay, a young Manhattan woman studying psychology and social work at Smith College. Donna was in Woods Hole on vacation with her friends, and when the pale young man who had clearly spent too much time indoors summoned the courage to approach her on the beach, she at first did not think much of him. But the two of them quickly found they had much to say to each other and, to Jonas's delight, that they did so easily and comfortably. This was a person with whom the conversational sweet spot was always within reach, an incandescently smart person—conversant in French, Italian, Spanish, and German—with whom he could easily spend no end of time.

Donna was taken with Jonas too. She had grown up with wealth—her father's lucrative dental practice bringing in enough of an income that he could settle his family in the grand San Remo apartments on New York City's Central Park West, an ornate, two-towered building with windows that looked down on the park and a roster of residents who, for better or worse, could comfortably look down on most other families living almost anywhere else in the city. But such pampering did not spoil Donna for less genteel living. She found her family's social circle limiting, and preferred the company of people with tougher hides, a few more scars, and clearer ideas of what they wanted to contribute to the world. This was why she had decided on a career in psychology and social work, and this was one of the reasons she had taken such a liking to the young apprentice doctor.

There was one other thing that drew her to Jonas. While she found him reasonably handsome, she found his hands irresistible. They were neither too squared nor too slender, she thought, with fingers that were long but not overly tapered. These were precisely the hands a doctor ought to have, and she believed they'd be capable of wonderful work.

By the time the season was over, Jonas and Donna had spent the better part of their summer together. Before too long, they began cautiously introducing each other to their families. Soon after that, they decided they wanted to marry.

"But she's not Jewish," Dora would protest whenever the topic came up.

"She's Jewish," Salk would sigh for what seemed like the hundredth time.

"She doesn't look Jewish. Her family doesn't keep a Jewish home."

"All the same," Jonas would say, turning to Helen if she happened to be around. "Please tell her she's Jewish."

"She's Jewish, Aunt Dora. I've met the grandmother. Don't you think I'd tell you otherwise?" Dora probably did believe Helen, but she'd nonetheless simply snort and turn away, by now unwilling to yield on so important a point, even if that point was utterly lost.

Dora's objections weren't the only ones Jonas had to face. Donna's father had some reservations of his own. First, there would be no wedding until after Jonas graduated from medical school so that the honorific "Dr." could appear on the invitations. In addition, Jonas would have to do something about the rest of his name. In Dora's and Daniel's families, middle names were seen as fussy and pretentious and they thus did not give one to any of their sons. To Dr. Lindsay, a name without a middle initial was like a suit with an open collar—it looked sloppy and incomplete. Jonas, he decided, would have to have a middle initial, and since there was something commonplace about consonants, that initial should be a vowel, preferably an E. It was all right with him if Jonas and Donna picked what that E would stand for.

A man being pushed to change his mind could be stubborn; a man being pushed to change his very name ought to be flat-out unmovable. But Salk was perfectly willing to be moved. He knew what he wanted, which was Donna, and he knew what he had to do to get her. There was no reason to take the long way around if the short route caused him so little pain. There would be plenty of times in life, he guessed, that the solution would not be so easy. Jonas and Donna settled on the middle name Edward, and when the wedding invitations went out, it was Dr. Jonas E. Salk who was announced as the groom.

Dr. Salk began his internship that March at Mount Sinai Hospital on Fifth Avenue and 100th Street in Manhattan—just six blocks from where he had been born. Like most wives of interns, Donna saw little of Jonas that first year, and when she did he talked about little beyond what he was doing at work. He would study patient cases and emergency room texts, and—most satisfying to him—practice his suturing work. Donna sometimes sneaked a quiet peek as he did, watching his fine hands go and smiling to herself at the young man whose father made his living in the stitchery trade and who now, in his own way, was doing the same.

If Jonas's studies denied him free time at home, they began to do great things for his doctoring skills, particularly his ability to read symptoms and diagnose diseases. On an especially busy evening early in his tenure, the doors of the hospital's ambulance bay crashed open and a man was wheeled into the emergency room, unconscious and unresponsive. The ambulance crew had no idea what had happened to the patient, and the two interns who reached him first were mystified too. Long seconds elapsed as they checked his heart rate, respiration, and blood pressure— lethal seconds if sufficient oxygen was not getting to the brain. Salk, who was on duty as well, hurried to the gurney to see if he could help. As he approached, he thought he detected the sharp chemical whiff of acetone. Bending over the patient, he drew a deep breath, and the smell, indistinguishable from nail that of polish remover, only grew stronger.

"This man's in a diabetic coma," Salk said. "Get him some insulin."

He was right. As blood sugar rises, the body's concentration of the carbon compounds known as ketones explodes. One of the most common— and most pungent—of the ketones is acetone, and in a diabetic crisis the levels climb so high that the vapors can pass straight through the skin and lungs. The smell test was a crude method of measuring the depths of a diabetic crisis, but also an effective one. No sooner was the insulin administered than the patient's sugar levels fell and the coma broke. Such battlefield diagnosing was precisely what was needed in a good emergency room doctor—it just wasn't expected in one so young. News of Salk's quick thinking quickly spread, earning him both the admiration and the envy of the rest of the internship staff. In the hotbox of the hospital, such sentiments could be expressed only one way.

"Hey Salk," one or another intern would occasionally call out over the course of the next months. "I've got a guy with a broken tibia over here. Want to come smell him and make sure?"

Salk would wave and smile, knowing that he could expect at least a semester's worth of such needling. If it bothered him he didn't show it, but if it pleased him he didn't show that either. When the semester passed and the ribbing ended, the two dozen other interns, who were required to elect a staff president, overwhelmingly chose Salk.

Whatever professional matters the interns of the Mount Sinai emergency room had on their minds in that summer of 1940, they were nothing compared with the matters weighing on the world outside the hospital. By June, the German army had already rolled into Austria, Czechoslovakia, Poland, Holland, Belgium, Luxembourg, and—most recently and stunningly—France. The United States was so far keeping its distance, but public sentiment had begun to stir, and many Americans wanted to show their solidarity with those countries caught in the middle of yet another European brawl. At Mount Sinai Hospital, showing that solidarity came to mean wearing one of the smart little "Support Our Allies" buttons that had begun going on sale at five-and-dimes and tobacco stores around the country. At first, one intern showed up with the pin, then another followed, then a third. Finally, the hospital administrator called Salk in and sat him down. The pins would have to come off, he said. Salk asked why.

"They're not hospital issue. Suppose a patient objects."

"To the allies?" Salk asked.

"Still," the administrator said. "I want you to take care of it."

Salk could think of few things he'd less like to do. For a person with his clear sense of the right way to do things and the wrong way, he had rather less appetite for the controversy such clarity often engendered. It was not for nothing that he had avoided direct conflict with his mother, with whom few people ever won a straight-up argument. Instead, he had long ago taught himself the art of persuasive nudging—coaxing and encouraging other people to the conclusion he wanted them to reach without their ever knowing they were being pushed that way at all. By the time they got where he wanted them to go, they were convinced they had traveled there on their own. Shortly after leaving the administrator's office, Salk convened a meeting of the interns and told them about the hospital's concerns. All of the interns, particularly the ones wearing the pins, were incensed.

"What do you want to do about it?" Salk asked.

"We could write a letter of protest," someone offered.

"We could," Salk agreed.

"We could strike," someone else said.

"We could do that too. What else?"

There was a sullen pause. "I say ignore them," one of the interns wearing the pin said at last. "I'm not taking mine off."

"I'm putting one on," another intern decided.

Salk asked if anyone else felt the same. Several hands went up. "You know what?" he said. "I may just do that too."

The next morning when the intern staff arrived for work, all twenty-five of them—Salk included—were wearing shiny, new "Support Our Allies" buttons. The hospital administrator never mentioned the matter to his intern president again.

After his two years at Mount Sinai came to an end, Salk knew that by any responsible measure he ought to go to war. With the Japanese attack at Pearl Harbor having drawn the United States into the conflict the previous December, it was time for him, like all men his age, to enlist. Other people, however, had other ideas.

While he was in medical school, Salk had gotten to know and admire a Dr. Thomas Francis, the trim, mustached chairman of NYU's microbiology department and a former investigator with the Rockefeller Institute. Francis had long been intrigued by the study of viruses and had often confessed to having doubts about the very same thing that had troubled Salk in his first year in medical school: why a killed virus couldn't be used to make a vaccine that was as effective as the kind made from weakened viruses, but safer too. Francis had been studying just such a killed-virus vaccine against influenza. Salk had wandered into Francis's lab one day during his final year in school, volunteered to help out with the work, and soon found himself running virus samples from the NYU lab on Twenty-fourth Street up to the Rockefeller Institute on Sixty-sixth Street, the closest facility that had the ultraviolet irradiating machines needed to kill the bugs. Salk would then run the samples back to Francis, who would examine them to determine how well the ultraviolet light had done its lethal work. So far, the results were uneven.

Even before Salk finished his internship in 1942, Francis left New York for the University of Michigan, where he was heading up the school's new Department of Epidemiology. Francis offered Salk a job conducting research in his new lab and teaching a course in epidemiology to incoming students. But the war changed that. Salk wrote Francis a letter saying that under the circumstances, he felt he really ought to enlist in the army and serve his time, probably as a military physician. After that, he could return to private life with a clear mind. If Francis's offer was still open, he'd be delighted to accept it then.

Francis wrote back promptly. He was, he explained, still working with influenza. Now, however, he was doing it for the military. The last time the United States had entered a global war, an influenza pandemic had swept through both the home front and the armies in the field. In the United States, more than 550,000 people died at a minimum; worldwide, the disease claimed 22 million at the very least. In October of 1918 alone, about 20 percent of the American army contracted the disease; 44,000 ultimately died of it. In this new war, the army didn't want any such problems and had charged Francis with developing a vaccine. Francis, in turn, charged his staff—a staff on which he had one more opening—with helping him get the job done. Salk could join the fighting men in the field and become but a single doctor tending to single patients. Or he could come to Michigan and help save hundreds of thousands. When the matter was framed that way, Salk had no real choice. In the first full year of the Second World War, Dr. and Mrs. Jonas E. Salk packed up their New York home and went to join Tommy Francis in the unfamiliar Midwest.

~ 3 ~

Maurice Brodie began his career as such a brisk and bright figure that people were especially startled when his life came to such a dark end. They should not have been so surprised, however. Few men had been pushed more publicly to despair than poor Brodie had.

Brodie was a physician at Montreal's McGill University. He had decided in 1930 that what he wanted to do with his life was not treat disease, but study it, and the illness he wanted to study most was poliomyelitis. Like anyone interested in learning about polio, Brodie knew that the place to train was at the Rockefeller Institute in New York City, under Dr. Simon Flexner. Flexner was the same polio researcher who had isolated the bug and had become such a figure of sturdiness and smarts during the terrible plague season of 1916. Flexner agreed to meet with Brodie and instantly took a liking to him. He turned the eager young Canadian over to one of his brightest staff scientists, who would give him an intensive tutorial in the poliovirus. Brodie learned well, and after just a month went back to Canada, planning to spend the next several years practicing in the field what he'd learned in the lab. He did just that, and by 1934 was becoming known as one of the most knowledgeable polio scientists in North America. He then returned to New York, this time applying for a job on the staff of Dr. William Park, a widely respected researcher and the director of the bureau of laboratories for the New York Department of Health. Securing a position on Park's staff was a given for Brodie, since the two men had already been corresponding for some time and together had come up with an ambitious idea.

The state of polio science had advanced enough, Park and Brodie had concluded, that it might now be possible—and indeed comparatively easy—to create a vaccine against the disease. First, they would infect monkeys with polio and make sure they came down with a good, raging case of it. Then they would kill the animals, extract their spinal cords, and mash the still-living tissue down into a pulpy suspension of nerve cells and virus. Next, they'd mix that organic goo with formalin—essentially a 31 percent dilution of formaldehyde—and let it sit for ten days at refrigerator temperature. The formalin, they expected, should kill all the virus particles, while preserving their telltale molecular shape. They would then inject the preparation into children, whose immune systems, according to the plan, would recognize the dead viruses and produce a flood of antibodies that would forever protect them from the disease. The details required a bit more study: you might want to do your virus killing at something closer to body temperature than refrigerator temperature; you might want to play with the ten-day period the virus sat in the formalin. But the plan as a whole was almost certainly sound.

So confident were Park and Brodie of their idea that Park felt comfortable taking it straight to Paul de Kruif. De Kruif was a bacteriologist, the operational head of the President's Birthday Ball Commission, and a man widely celebrated as both a visionary and an artist. De Kruif was once a researcher at Rockefeller Institute himself and had done quite well in his work until 1922, when he contributed a chapter to a popular book that purported to tell all civilized readers everything they needed to know about all civilized fields of endeavor, from politics to finance to the arts to architecture. De Kruif's chapter concerned the field of medicine, and what he had to say caused an immediate sensation. Medical research, he wrote, was a sham; medical practice was a shell game. Doctors were hucksters who cured almost nothing, communicating with their patients in a language of hand-waving and quick-talking that did nothing more than take advantage of popular ignorance and earn the doctors a lot of undeserved riches.

Flexner, who was de Kruif's superior, was furious at this kind of pot-stirring, particularly when it came from a member of his staff. After reading the chapter to make sure it was as incendiary as people said it was, he marched the young agitator into his office and sacked him on the spot.

De Kruif accepted his discharge with equanimity, left the stuffy halls of the institute, and went off to write his own book, this one telling the tales of a dozen scientific giants—from Leeuwenhoek to Pasteur—and the challenges they faced on their way to being great. The book, titled *Microbe Hunters,* was damned by scientists as flip, simplistic, and sensationalized—and adored by readers as rich, gripping, and sensational. *Microbe Hunters* soared to the top of the best-seller lists, establishing de Kruif as a larger figure in literature than he had ever been in science. It was that sudden fame—not to mention that feel for the scientifically popular—that prompted the Birthday Ball commissioners to give de Kruif the position they had. He would be entrusted with the responsibility not only of directing the balls but also of helping to decide how the research money that was raised by them would be spent.

When Park came to call on de Kruif at the beginning of 1935, explaining what he and his young colleague were up to, de Kruif was instantly intrigued. The Dr. Park who was visiting him today had clearly aged: he was slower, cloudier, not always wholly present in the conversation. Park himself seemed to recognize this and made it a point to reassure de Kruif that the hands-on polio work was mostly being performed by the young and sharp Brodie, who, by the way, had already published a number of papers describing the proposed vaccine. De Kruif had read them and had frankly found them brilliant.

He asked the old man directly if the idea would work.

"This is a fact," Park answered with a flash of his old clarity. "This works."

Shortly afterward, the Birthday Ball Commission, at de Kruif's suggestion, agreed to allocate $64,000 for a vast field test of what would now be known as the Park-Brodie vaccine. The two scientists would inoculate up to 9,000 children before the polio season began and then track their health through the end of the year. Park and Brodie were eager to begin—for more than one reason.

At Temple University, physician John Kolmer was said to be working on a competing polio vaccine of his own. Kolmer wasn't trying anything so new as a killed-virus preparation. Rather, he was going to use a live virus, but one that had been weakened by sodium ricinoleate—a mildly toxic mix that could prevent the bug from causing the disease but still allow it to trigger an immune response. A vaccine containing a virus that was even flickeringly alive, Kolmer and most others knew, would always work better than one containing a dead one. Kolmer planned a slightly larger study than Park and Brodie's, hoping to inoculate 10,000 children.

Just months later, Kolmer and Park and Brodie went out into the field and ran their experiments, recruiting babies and toddlers, teens and young adults, injecting them all with their polio mix and studying them closely. At first, the results of the experiment looked exactly as good as the men had said they'd be.

"ANTI-PARALYSIS SERUM REPORTED A SUCCESS," shouted the *New York Times* when preliminary results from the Park–Brodie vaccine began dribbling out. "One Hundred Percent Success in Immunizing Human Beings."

But that dazzling figure began to fall fast. First one, then three, then nine of the Kolmer children came down with polio—developing it within a sufficient number of days after the vaccine had been administered that it was all but certain the experimental preparation was responsible. Three of the Park–Brodie subjects got similarly sick. Of the twelve afflicted children, six died. In a test group of 20,000 or so, the dozen disasters might have been tolerable, but soon other ugly problems associated with the vaccines began to surface. Many of the children who did not contract polio developed nasty abscesses at the site of the injection. It was a result, quite probably, of having been pumped up with monkey cells. Others reacted even more violently to the simian tissue, developing whole-body inflammations and allergies. Children who had been well before they received the vaccines were now very sick.

The experiments, it was obvious, were a mess. The vaccines, it was clear, were a menace. That November, just a few months after the summer field trials ended, an enraged Flexner—who had never liked rushing into the tests in the first place—exercised his considerable prestige to kill the studies, publishing a heated paper in the journal *Science* calling them entirely worthless and indefensibly reckless. The *Science* paper was reported in the daily papers the very next day.

"FLEXNER REJECTS PARALYSIS VACCINE," the *New York Times* announced. "Rockefeller Scientist Finds No Evidence That It Can Be Both Safe and Effective."

A public condemnation by Flexner was clearly a professional death sentence. But it didn't compare with a true shaming in front of a parliament of medical peers. Later in November, a meeting of the Southern branch of the American Public Health Association was to be held in St. Louis, and Park, Brodie, and Kolmer were instructed to attend.

The meeting was a large, sometimes droning event held over several days, but when the time came to address the polio fiasco, the hall was expectant and packed. There would be two presentations reviewing the failed experiments, one by Dr. Thomas Rivers, head of the Rockefeller Institute Hospital, and the other by Dr. James Leake, of the United States Public Health Service. Rivers, who knew his paper was going to be published in the *Journal of the American Medical Association,* gave a level, measured talk, laying out the facts of the studies and calling for them to be halted. Leake, unconstrained by publication, erupted.

The vaccines—if they could be called that—were disasters, Leake raged. They were irresponsible, ill considered, poorly planned, and sloppily executed. Work like this wasn't just bad science, it was practically immoral. Indeed, it was even worse than immoral. Dr. Kolmer, Leake seethed as he concluded his speech, might as well be guilty of murder.

The room fell into a stunned silence, and then slowly, not Kolmer but Brodie rose.

"It looks as though according to Dr. Rivers, my vaccine is no good," he said hoarsely. "And according to Dr. Leake, Dr. Kolmer's is dangerous."

Brodie sat down and Kolmer then stood. "Gentlemen," he said, "this is one time I wish the floor would open up and swallow me."

For all practical purposes, it did. Not long after the meeting adjourned and the scientists scattered back to their home cities, it was announced that the aged William Park and the younger John Kolmer would retire. Brodie was quietly fired from his job at the Rockefeller Institute. Too young to give up his livelihood, he found a smaller, less conspicuous position in Detroit, moved there, and retreated from the medical stage altogether.

Even as the promise of the vaccines was unraveling, there was other news from the polio labs. The very same week as the St. Louis meeting, bacteriologist Claus Jungeblut of Columbia University announced that if you really wanted to protect yourself from polio, ordinary vitamin C might be the answer. Injected in the proper dose, he claimed, it could prevent the virus from establishing a toehold in the system. If vitamins didn't lick the problem, virologists Albert Sabin and Peter Olitsky announced, perhaps nasal spray could. They had found that a good squirt of sodium alum or tannic acid at the right time could protect the body from infection. The *Times* ran ahead with these breathless stories, just as it had run with all the others, and before long everyone had stopped talking about Park and Brodie and Kolmer.

It wasn't until several years later that Maurice Brodie's name surfaced again—this time because of the news that a surprise heart attack had ended his life. Brodie was properly mourned, and the bad luck of a weak heart at such a young age was properly cursed. There were rumors that his heart hadn't given way at all, that the banished Brodie had had an active hand in his own untimely end. Out of respect for the promising man he had once been, however, no one in authority pursued those rumors further.

∾ 4 ∾

It was probably inevitable that the valor of the men of Camp Wellston would be called into question. All of them were young and in good health, after all, precisely what the nation needed when it was fighting a two-front war in Europe and the Pacific. But these men weren't in either combat theater. Indeed, Camp Wellston, located in Wellston, Michigan, was about as far from the fighting as it was possible to get.

Before the Second World War began, the men now at the camp had come to the conclusion that their convictions or beliefs made it impossible for them to engage in combat. When the fighting got under way, they argued that pacifist point before a federal draft board, and the board—with respect for the Constitution if not for the men invoking it—reluctantly backed them up, telling them they'd be permitted to go to Wellston and sit the war out. The draft board did insist, however, that if such delicate fellows found it morally impossible to pick up a gun, they could jolly well pick up a shovel or a rake. So the Wellston men had spent the last year clearing brush, chopping timber, tilling land, driving trucks, and working in hospitals—sometimes doing more than one job at a time, never receiving even a fraction of the rest or pay such labor would usually warrant.

In September 1943, word got around Camp Wellston that a Dr. Jonas Salk was coming to call on the men. Dr. Salk, so they had heard, was a scientist out of the University of Michigan who had been cooking up some formula on orders from the army. Formulas needed to be tested and the men of Camp Wellston might serve just fine.

Jonas Salk had moved to Ann Arbor some eighteen months before he and the Wellston men even began to think about each other. His first challenge when he arrived had nothing to do with inventing a formula. He and his young wife had to find a place to live.

Donna and Jonas came to Ann Arbor in a car they'd bought in New York and driven—often coaxed—the 500-some miles to their new home in eastern Michigan. The only destination Jonas knew with any certainty was the university itself, and when they arrived in town they thus drove straight to the campus to seek a referral to a nearby hotel. After checking into the little boardinghouse that was recommended to them, they promptly set out to explore the available homes in the neighborhoods closest to the campus, so that Jonas could walk to work every day and leave the car to Donna. The blocks around the university, however, turned out to be far too tony for the $2,100 per year a researcher like Salk would be making in Tommy Francis's lab. Jonas and Donna thus spent that day, the next one, and the one after that looking for homes in an ever-widening circle. Finally, they drifted out of Ann Arbor altogether and wandered into the countryside. On a narrow road near a modest farm, Jonas suddenly stopped the car.

"There," he announced, pointing out the window to a small house with an old mailbox that read "The Craigs." On the front lawn was a rental sign.

"You wouldn't," Donna said.

But Jonas would—or at least he clearly wanted to. His city upbringing notwithstanding, he had often surprised Donna with a near-reverential appreciation of the country. There was an order to nature, he'd explain to her, a cogs-within-cogs complexity that fascinated him, all the more so because—unlike the similar order that could be found in the city—it operated entirely without human intervention. His work in the lab was just nature writ small, and there was no better way to gain a feel for the workings of the tiny natural world than to immerse himself in the far larger one.

Jonas bolted out of the car and Donna reluctantly followed. The house, she found, was even worse than she'd imagined. The rumored Craigs were indeed in residence and had every intention of remaining there. It wasn't the entire house that was available at all, only the second floor—and it wasn't much of a floor at that. The quarters were small, with no central heat, just a wood-burning stove. There was plenty of fine cordwood and kindling outside, which was a good thing, since the stove would have to serve for cooking too. Behind the house, there was a canopy of trees, a tire swing, and a large garden with plenty of space for additional planting. Jonas, Donna feared, was falling for the place fast.

"This is just wonderful," he said.

She looked at him balefully.

"You at least have to admit that the price is right."

Donna sighed. Long before, she had established a simple and useful rule. When she found herself in a new or impossible circumstance, she would try to see it less as a bad turn than as a bracing one—one that would offer her the opportunity to stretch herself. When that stretching grew unpleasant, she'd shrug inwardly. "So this is what this is like," she'd say almost academically. Now, with her husband unaccountably swooning over an unheated farmhouse in the Michigan countryside and the two of them undeniably needing a place to live, she hoped the practice would work again.

"All right," she said to Jonas, "we'll take it."

The Salks moved into their new home the next day and soon found that it lived up—and down—to all their expectations. The stove turned out to have a ravenous appetite for wood, and while Donna agreed to do the stoking, it was left to Jonas to do the chopping—a job wholly unfamiliar to him and one that took a while to master. As Donna busied herself with cooking and decorating, Jonas enlarged the backyard garden.

Together, they did a respectable job of taming the house and grounds. As the year unspooled, however, they found that they could do a lot less to tame the Michigan countryside itself. Jonas and Donna slogged through springtime floods that washed out roads and kept them trapped in their home. They endured wintertime freezes that turned the ground to iron and forced Jonas to start the car by hand crank in the morning. They were smothered by periodic fogs that settled in so thick and quick that if they were out driving, they would have to pull over to the shoulder of the road and creep ahead yard by yard, Donna extending an arm out the right-hand window to guide them by feeling for mailboxes.

So this is what this is like, she would repeat to herself. *This is what this is like.*

While Donna worked to maintain both her home and her good cheer—all the while hunting for employment in her own social work field—Jonas had more than enough to keep him busy in the lab. Washington wasn't fooling when it said it wanted an influenza vaccine and it wanted one soon. Even before the Salks arrived in Michigan, the Army Epidemiological Board established an official Commission on Influenza, assuring that there would now be budgets to be maintained and deadlines to be met. Francis's team, Salk included, was formally attached to the commission, and with the second full winter—and the second full flu season—of the war approaching, the pressure was on to produce something fast.

Giving the army what it was demanding would not be easy. Salk fully appreciated how much the medical community had already learned about influenza, but he also appreciated just how much it didn't yet know. It had been only nine years since the influenza virus had been isolated for the first time. Researchers in England had collected throat washings from patients sick with flu and passed them through porcelain filters with pores so fine that nothing as plump as a bacterium could pass, though a virus—a far smaller, far less complicated organism—could. The fluid and particles that made it through that sieve were then placed in a lab dish with plenty of inert nutrients available but no living cells. If any bacteria were present, they would grow like dandelions in the fertile goo. If only viruses made it through, they would do nothing at all, since such organically simple things are incapable of multiplying unless they first enter a living cell and hijack its reproductive machinery. As the British scientists anticipated, the dishes stayed dead. When they introduced the same filtered fluids into laboratory rats, however, the animals became ill with the same disease the humans had had.

Things grew more complicated three years later when a team led by Francis himself discovered that flu could be caused by a second type of virus that was largely unrelated to the first. Now the medical community realized that there was no such thing as simple influenza, but an influenza Type A and an influenza Type B. Later, different strains of the viruses—up to 100 of them—turned up within the two types. The strains were a little like breeds within species, or states within countries. Some of them were close enough kin to offer immunity against similar strains within their larger type, but some weren't. A good flu vaccine would therefore have to be fairly teeming with bugs, with as many strains within the two types as the researchers could round up and kill and pack into a syringe.

For Francis and Salk, the first step in developing such a shot was figuring out a way to collect enough concentrated flu virus to process down into a vaccine. Centrifuging viruses out of blood and other fluids was even harder than centrifuging out bacteria, the viruses being so much smaller and lighter that they took much more spinning to get the job done. What's more, the centrifuges could hold only limited amounts of solution; it took much larger amounts than that to get enough virus for a vaccine, which meant endless rounds of filling and spinning. Clearly something better was needed and Salk had an idea: calcium phosphate. It had been his great greenhorn success during his days with Cannan, and here, perhaps, it would work again. Salk tried it and found that the technique did work— but only sort of. The calcium phosphate was able to pull virus out of solution, but it left far too much behind to be truly useful.

The alternative was blood cells. The influenza virus was known to have an odd affinity for red corpuscles, attaching itself to the cells' sticky outer coat. Since scientists already used the white part of chicken eggs to grow flu viruses, Salk wondered what would happen if midway through the three weeks that it took an embryo to develop in the egg, the growing chick was killed and its blood was allowed to flow into the surrounding fluid. If the virus stuck to the blood cells as it ought to, and if the cells were then put through just the right process of warmings, washings, and salt treatments—a process Salk proposed to figure out himself—all the virus the scientists needed could be concentrated out and purified.

Salk went promptly to work inventing such a method, and after countless trials, developed one variation that worked. He and Francis wrote the research up and submitted it to the journal *Science,* which—to Salk's delight if not his surprise—published it. Salk was exhilarated by the recognition, and faintly annoyed by it too. It was in Francis's lab that the work had been performed and under Francis's tutelage that he had learned much of what he knew. But it was Salk's own hand that had done the most to develop the technique. At the bottom of the *Science* paper, Francis's name was nevertheless listed first. Salk—like a mere scientific aide-de-camp—appeared second.

Not long after, Francis and Salk completed a follow-up paper to submit for publication, also based on work Salk had principally conducted. The twenty-seven-year-old apprentice approached his middle-aged mentor and explained, carefully, that he'd very much appreciate it if this time around, the sequence of their names could be reversed.

"You want your name before mine?" Francis asked, scarcely able to believe the brass of the boy.

"Everyone already knows who you are," Salk said. "It doesn't really matter if your name comes first or last."

"You know that's not the way things are done."

"I know."

"And yet you'd want it done that way here."

"Only if I really earned it," Salk said, careful to keep his tone respectful and his pose deferential.

Francis pursed his lips. He was paying Salk a fair wage to come into the lab every day and do his work, and while that plus the satisfaction of a job well done might have been enough for many, in this case it apparently wasn't. Francis wasn't a man who admired ambition by itself, but ambition coupled with ability was another matter. He had always known that Salk had real talent. He had also always suspected that he might require a lot less leash than most men in his position. What he was betting on was that the young man might also accomplish a lot more if given that freedom.

"Salk," he said, "why can't you do things the way everybody else does?"

Salk smiled. Francis, he understood, had just agreed to give him what he wanted.

Over the next year, Salk startled Francis with his energy, teaching his required epidemiology courses and then tearing back to the lab, where his research output fairly exploded. As he cultured multiple colonies of healthy flu virus and categorized them by type, he began pouring himself into the job of figuring out how to make them safe for use in a vaccine. Had he been working on a live-virus formula, his technique would have involved passing the virus from one animal to another and another, selecting bugs that got weaker with each such transmission until they became so enfeebled that they would stimulate antibody creation without causing disease. But Salk did not want weakened viruses that were unlikely to get anyone sick, he wanted stone-dead viruses that were certain not to.

Heat, he found, killed the bugs easily but not uniformly, always seeming to let a few viruses slip through. The ultraviolet method he and Francis had used in New York worked reasonably well too—the high-energy pulses lethally scrambling the genetic guts of the virus. But here, too, some of the heartiest bugs managed to survive. A third, if inelegant, option was the crude chemical known as formalin—the same diluted formaldehyde Maurice Brodie had used. Brodie's failed polio vaccine might have been a disaster, but the fault, Salk suspected, didn't lie with the formalin. Handle it properly and he just might be able to accomplish with the influenza virus what Brodie had failed to accomplish with the poliovirus.

Salk began experimenting with formalin, playing with dilutions, temperatures, and times of exposure, and indeed found that properly mixed and balanced it killed viral cultures consistently and completely. Before long, he had enough dead cultures to begin picking the right ones to use in trial vaccines and injecting them into laboratory mice. Most of the time, the protovaccines failed. But after repeated trials, Salk hit on the odd formulation that would actually cause the animals' antibody levels to rise significantly. After still more trials, the refined vaccine indeed protected the mice from influenza infection. By the fall of 1943, Salk and Francis had precisely what the army had asked the Michigan team for: an inoculation against flu that actually worked—albeit only in rodents. Next it had to be tested in humans. The army pointed them to Camp Wellston.

The procedure Salk envisioned for the test was a straightforward one: After recruiting a handful of Wellston volunteers, he'd inject them with the vaccine, then send them off for a while to let their immune systems cook up antibodies. After a few days, he'd call them back and draw a little blood. If a good load of antibodies was indeed present, he'd then swab the men's throats and nasal passages with cotton saturated with live flu. If, after a few more days' incubation, they resisted becoming infected with the disease, Salk and Francis would know that their vaccine worked.

On September 15, 1943, Salk arrived at Camp Wellston and was promptly shown to the classroom building where he'd be conducting the test the following day. He set up a little card table in the hallway and instructed that a blanket be nailed up nearby, screening off two classrooms and a bathroom where the men would be quarantined throughout the study so that no stray virus could escape the group and cause an off-season flu epidemic on the base. While the volunteers were in residence, nobody would come within 20 feet of the blanket, except Salk himself and a messenger who would leave trays of food on a table near the boundary line three times a day and then hurry away, calling an all-clear when one of the participants could emerge to collect them.

The next afternoon, when all the volunteers had been chosen, Salk arranged his syringes and vaccine vials on a sterile cloth on the card table, then called to an officer, who called to the men to come in and take their shots. Salk watched as the twenty or so men—boys, practically—trooped down the hall toward him. Salk respected the way they stepped forward to test his unproven brew, but he was also grateful to them for giving him the opportunity to be administering any kind of injections at all. Salk had struck a costly bargain when he decided to spend his career in research, understanding that he was committing himself to live his life as a doctor who would no longer get to care for patients. For this one morning, however, he'd be doing that hands-on job.

Salk looked toward the first boy in line and summoned him forward. The boy's name was on the card Salk had in his hand, and his hometown—Pontiac, Michigan—was too. He asked for the information all the same. When the boy mentioned Pontiac, Salk reacted as if it were far and away the nicest town he'd ever visited. He asked the boy about himself and listened closely as he described the philosophy degree he was pursuing at the University of Michigan and the part-time work he used to do delivering milk for the local Borden Creamery branch. Salk complimented the boy on his obvious sense of initiative. All that information had been on the card too.

Finally, Salk turned to the syringes. He explained the preparation he was testing and what he hoped the results would be. The boy, who had heard it all before, nodded.

"All right if we begin, then?" Salk asked.

The boy offered up his arm. Salk swabbed it, injected the vaccine, and withdrew the needle. The boy turned toward the quarantine rooms. Before he could walk off, Salk caught his eye.

"Thank you for helping us out," he said.

The boy disappeared behind the blanket.

By the end of the afternoon, Salk had injected all the boys and seen them all off into the isolation rooms. Then he returned to his own room on the base, pulled out his memo book, and started writing up his notes. After a time, he stopped, turned to a clean page, and did something he never did: he began to compose a story.

It was a little tale, just a couple of pages long, about a group of peaceable men who had agreed to assist a group of peaceable doctors, allowing them to fill their bloodstreams with a decidedly unpeaceable virus. True to its nature, the virus went promptly to war with the men's red blood cells. The cells responded in kind, fighting fiercely back. In the bloodstream, however, there was also another class of cells—white blood cells—that weren't given to fighting wars. Instead of doing battle with the viruses, these cells would simply approach and absorb the invaders, surrounding them with their globular arms and subduing them with nothing more hostile than an embrace. The pacifist strategy worked so well that before long the viruses were contained, the hostilities stopped, and antibodies showed up, to make the temporary peace a permanent one.

"Soon," Salk wrote, "all of the cells forgot what the fight was about and, true to pacifist tradition, a synthesis of opposing forces was established. The synthesis was called 'immunity.'"

Salk looked at what he had written—a piece of silliness entirely at odds with the hard-edged writing with which he typically filled his research notebooks. The science of his Wellston work he would have to share. His little story was more properly tucked away somewhere.

Three days later, Salk called his volunteers back out of isolation, drew their blood for sampling, and at the same time exposed them to the live flu virus. A few days after that, he had his results. The boys' blood fairly brimmed with protective antibodies, and they had not gotten sick with the flu itself. Francis and Salk's influenza vaccine worked—and worked spectacularly. More important, the principle of the killed-virus vaccine worked. Immunity to viral diseases was possible, and it didn't take a live-virus vaccine to do it.

Ecstatic, Salk returned to his quarters, gathered up his belongings, and prepared to go home to Ann Arbor to report the good news to Francis. Before leaving the camp, he made a final trip to the building where the boys had been quarantined. He tacked his little story up on the bulletin board. At the top, he added a dedication.

"To All Guinea Pigs," he wrote. "And to Science."

In all the time Franklin Roosevelt had been in the White House, he'd never lost the pleasure he took in his visits to Warm Springs. Lately though, the trips had begun to wear him out. By April 1945, Roosevelt was in the thirteenth year of his presidency, and by any measure, he appeared wrung-out. His skin was crepe-like, his face was gaunt, and the already limited time he could spend on his feet with his heavy steel braces stiffening his legs had dwindled to almost no time at all. More troubling still, his blood pressure—something that had been giving his doctors fits for a while now—had exploded out of control, due mostly to way too much work and way too many cigarettes. Just months earlier, Roosevelt had been elected to a fourth term in the White House, meaning four more years heaped on that disintegrating frame. Letting a man in such shape travel was out of the question, and Roosevelt's doctors had made it clear that he should remain in Washington and let the people he needed to see come to him. Roosevelt mostly complied, but he drew the line when it came to Warm Springs.

It had been a long time since Roosevelt had had much of a direct hand in the operations of the Georgia facility. Basil O'Connor had been managing both Warm Springs and the National Foundation for Infantile Paralysis as a whole for years and had been doing so extraordinarily. Sometimes, it seemed, the foundation could barely figure out how to spend all the money it raised.

Since the very first of the Birthday Balls, donations had never quit pouring in for the fight against poliomyelitis. The money came from drives and dances, from collection cans passed around in theaters and donation baskets passed around at fairs. When it slowed down, there was always a new idea to get it moving again. Celebrities like Bud Abbott and Lou Costello were recruited to film public appeals. Corporate and political leaders like Edsel Ford and Averell Harriman joined the foundation board to lend it clout and cachet. Showman Eddie Cantor was signed on as a consultant and quickly proved his worth. Each year, the NFIP sponsored what it called a Mother's March, during which the people in a community would be told that on a given day, local mothers would be walking up and down the streets collecting donations. Families interested in contributing were supposed to indicate their willingness by turning on their porch lights. Porches flared in towns all over the country, but the name of the event—suggesting only mothers need participate—soon seemed too narrow. Cantor suggesting nicknaming the event after the *March of Time* newsreels that played in movie theaters, calling it instead the March of Dimes.

The public loved it, offering up handfuls of dimes during the drives and stuffing even more of them into envelopes or taping them to penny post-cards and mailing them directly to foundation headquarters or even the White House. Cities took to launching their own Mile O' Dimes cam-paigns, calculating that it took about 90,000 dimes laid end to end to stretch a mile, and if local folks could be encouraged to start a dime line running down a sidewalk or along a series of curbside booths and keep contributing coins until a mile was reached, $9,000 could be raised in no time at all.

"How many dimes in a mile?" asked a sample radio ad the NFIP sent to dozens of cities. "A new type of measuring, you say? No, a new type of good Samaritan." When listeners grew tired of hearing one ad, the cities could rotate in any one of seven others the foundation had scripted for them, conveniently adding their own town's name in the spot left blank in the text.

As the funds streamed into foundation accounts, they streamed straight out both to rehabilitation facilities and to over fifty universities and re-search labs each year. There was the generous endowment the NFIP pro-vided to help physicians learn the newly touted Kenny method—a regimen of massage and hot packs created by Sister Elizabeth Kenny of Australia, which showed promising results in keeping paralyzed muscles limber and paralyzed limbs straight. There was the $15,000 grant to Long Island Col-lege in New York to try to develop a live polio vaccine that could be tested in animals, and the $4,800 grant to the Michael Reese Hospital in Chi-cago to determine if the disease could be treated by electrical stimulation. There was the $12,000 grant to Johns Hopkins University in Baltimore to investigate how to manage the aftereffects of paralysis, and the $500 grant to the Edward J. Meyer Hospital in Buffalo to look for ways to protect the spine with strychnine. There were big and small grants, promising ones and long shots. There was even a massive $161,350 grant to the Tuskegee Institute in Alabama to build an aftercare facility for Negro polio sufferers, a class of patients who had long received only spotty treatment for the dis-ease, suffering the twin indignities of paralysis and neglect.

For all that basic research, the mission of the NFIP remained far less de-voted to preventing polio and far more to restoring strength to the children who had already been felled by it. Vaccine research would not be forbidden or officially discouraged—indeed, it would even be financed now and again. But the much preferred goal would be to develop a reliable treatment for the disease, a way to revive the ruined muscles of children already paralyzed. Master that kind of therapeutic magic and you could restore mobility to any polio victim without exposing others to the unnecessary risks of a vaccine.

No matter how the NFIP chose to spend its money, the disease itself seemed heedless of its plans, surging when the weather and the whim seemed to seize it. In 1939, a comparatively modest 7,343 people in the United States contracted polio. In 1940 and 1941, the number crested to over 9,000. By 1943, it was up to 12,450; in 1944 it soared to 19,029. The virus, targeted for extinction by so many, seemed to care little for the effort being made against it.

Roosevelt's own case of paralysis still benefited—or so he continued to believe—from his trips to Warm Springs. During his visit in April 1945, he would be encamped in his so-called Little White House, a green-shuttered cottage he had had built on the grounds shortly before he became president. The cabin was decorated modestly, with a simple mohair sofa, parchment-shaded lamps, twin beds in the two bedrooms, and a small writing desk. Near the flagstone fireplace was a well-worn leather club chair, a nest of side tables, and his always at-hand penguin-shaped cigarette lighter. Roosevelt loved the privacy of the place and would be receiving few official visitors there this time, devoting himself to answering his mail, attending to paper-work, and sitting for a portrait that he'd been putting off having painted for a while now. On the afternoon of the twelfth, he also planned to take in a minstrel show the patients were putting on for him, then join the cast and the audience—most of them children—for an early-evening picnic of Brunswick stew. The show was set to begin at four P.M. At about one-thirty, shortly before his lunch was to be served, Roosevelt was sitting in his leather chair near the stone fireplace, while the society artist Elizabeth Shoumatoff—known in her circles as Mopsy—worked on his portrait. As she painted, he signed his memos and bills.

"Here's where I make a law," he announced casually, scribbling his name on a finance bill. Shoumatoff laughed agreeably. On the other side of the room, a waiter, a young Filipino boy, began to set the table for lunch.

Roosevelt noticed him and signaled to Shoumatoff. "We have fifteen minutes to work," he said.

Moments afterward, Roosevelt raised a hand to his head. "I have a terrific headache," he said, slumping forward.

Margaret Suckley, a cousin who was helping attend him that day, looked confusedly at his bent form. "Have you dropped your cigarette?" she asked.

Roosevelt looked up at her. "I have a terrific pain in the back of my neck," he said.

With that, he slumped again and lost consciousness. His porters rushed in and carried him to his bed. The presidential doctor was summoned and examined his patient. The blankness in Roosevelt's eyes and the depth of his unconsciousness told him all he needed to know: the already sickly man had suffered a massive cerebral hemorrhage, just the kind of disaster his medical team had feared was coming when the president's blood pressure took the turn it had. This type of brain burst was wholly untreatable, and the doctor could do little more than sit with the stricken Roosevelt for nearly two hours, watching as his breath grew weaker, his color grew purplish, and his skin grew cold. Finally, at three thirty-five—longer than the doctor would have imagined so frail a man would have lingered—the president slipped away.

At the moment Franklin Roosevelt lay dying, the cast of the Warm Springs minstrel show was assembling backstage, the performers wearing the familiar blackface. All the minstrels tonight, of course, would be in wheelchairs, except for Graham Jackson—a popular Negro pianist out of Atlanta, and a Roosevelt favorite.

At about quarter to four, the audience began rolling and hobbling into the theater. No sooner were they in their places than they began sneaking looks to the back of the hall, where the president was supposed to arrive in his own chair—Warm Springs being the only place in the public world he wheeled himself about openly as opposed to having aides whisk him into position before the crowd arrived at an event. Backstage, Mabel Irwin, the director of the show and the wife of the facility's chief surgeon, looked about worriedly for Jackson, who had been expected to arrive some time ago, bearing the bright red roses he always presented to the president when he performed for him. Suddenly, Jackson did appear, sweeping through a backstage door, wearing a long black duster. He carried his flowers limply under one arm and an oversized prop cigar in the other. He was crying.

"What in the world is the matter?" Mrs. Irwin asked, shocked.

"We can't go on," Jackson said.

"Why not?"

"The president is dead," Jackson answered, choking back tears.

"That isn't a bit funny," Mrs. Irwin scolded.

Jackson seized her hand. "I'm sure it's true," he said. "I just heard it over the radio as I changed my clothes."

"Which station?"

"All the stations. It's on every one on the dial."

Jackson and Mrs. Irwin bolted to a window and looked out at the parking lot adjacent to the theater. The area that had been roped off for the president was filled with cars, as it should have been. But the president's own car—and, more tellingly, the radio car that would have preceded his arrival—were missing. Mrs. Irwin looked at Jackson wide-eyed, then collapsed against his chest, weeping. Jackson let his funny cigar and his presidential flowers fall to the floor.

A few minutes later, Mrs. Irwin stepped through the curtains and announced to the children that the president who had so easily wheeled among them had died. The children who were old enough to understand what they were being told cried. Those who weren't old enough cried because the other ones did.

Not long before Franklin Roosevelt succumbed to cardiovascular disease, the scientific world learned that the influenza virus had succumbed to Jonas Salk and Tommy Francis. The success of Camp Wellston proved that the flu vaccine could, in theory, control the disease. In order for the matter to be settled with scientific certainty, however, a far larger study would be needed, one in which a whole population of people could be inoculated, then sent back into the world in the teeth of the flu season to see how they fared with wild virus coming at them from all sides. Just two months after the Camp Wellston work, in the winter of 1943–44, Salk and Francis conducted just such a massive study, inoculating 12,500 students on nine college campuses with their new flu vaccine, and another 12,500 with an inert saline solution. Then they sat back and waited to see how the real formula would perform compared with the ersatz one.

They were thrilled at the results. An astounding three and a half times as many people who had received the saline got sick as those who had gotten the real vaccine. A difference of 50 percent could have been explained away as mere statistical noise. Even 100 percent would have left plenty of room for uncertainty. But 350 percent was hard, clear proof that the flu could be prevented. Francis and Salk announced their findings, and the newspapers—the local ones at least—leapt on the news.

"Flu Preventive Developed Here by Francis and Salk," boasted the *Ann Arbor News.*

"Influenza Vaccine Developed at U-M," announced the *Detroit Free Press.*

Far more important to Salk was the report that appeared in the esteemed pages of the *Journal of the American Medical Association.* "A Clinical Evaluation of Vaccine Against Influenza," read the title. The work was credited simply to the "Members of the Commission on Influenza," which Salk knew was precisely the attribution so institutionally sponsored a study called for.

"Just wondering if you saw this," a delighted Salk said with forced casualness as he brought his copy of the journal to Francis's office only moments after he received it.

"I did," Francis said levelly, unfooled by Salk's cool. "But there's still a lot of work to do."

Salk didn't have to be told. By some measures, the young scientist and his mentor had entered the golden circle of medical researchers—a circle shared by Jenner and Pasteur and the other scientific giants who had learned how to beat a lethal disease. As a result of their work, the influenza pandemic of 1918 need never occur again. But that didn't mean flu could be eradicated entirely. The virus that caused the disease was an especially protean one, mutating from year to year and place to place. The vaccine

Francis and Salk had developed, impressive as it was, contained only three strains of influenza—two of Type A and one of Type B. With the world swimming in ever-changing flu viruses, there would never be a perfect shot to beat them all. Rather, the beginning of each influenza season would require epidemiological reconnaissance work in which the approaching viruses were isolated in the first few people they infected, then processed into a vaccine that would stop the spread before it went much further. Francis and Salk hadn't developed a conclusive answer to flu as much as a conclusive strategy, one that would have to be pursued year after year and generation after generation for as long as the virus existed. Learning how that viral scouting ought to be conducted meant Salk would have to go on the road.

For the better part of the next two years, the army sent him traveling the country and the globe investigating outbreaks of influenza. He visited Buckley and Lowry fields in Colorado when the soldiers there fell ill with a Type A epidemic. He visited Camp Edwards in rural Massachussetts and the Hampton Roads Camp in central Virginia when a similar outbreak struck in the East. He traveled to Camp Atterbury in Columbus, Indiana, where German prisoners of war who had survived the battle of the Huertgen Forest—the warm-up clash for the Battle of the Bulge—were confined, living 75 at a time in 50-man barracks, and greenhousing a strain of Type B flu. He accepted the temporary rank of army major so that he could travel to occupied Europe after the war and conduct his studies in the bomb-blasted towns of Heidelberg, Munich, Wiesbaden, Frankfurt, Landsberg, Stuttgart, Salzburg, and elsewhere. He set up advance monitoring posts at all the hospitals he visited so that local epidemiologists could spot the flu bug if it appeared and track its advance. He was practicing the kind of high-stakes medicine he wanted to practice, seeing to the health of whole nations, and working in an arena a continent wide. And it started to wear on him.

Salk knew the value of this kind of viral reconnaissance work. "Every case of disease poses several questions to those engaged in controlling it," he would lecture the students he taught at the University of Michigan. "What is the source of the infection? How is it spread? Who else may have acquired it?" It was a speech he had written and delivered every semester since he'd arrived in Ann Arbor, and he knew that it represented the very nuts and bolts of epidemiology. But he also knew the cost of such work. Conducting research in the field kept him away from the lab, where there were other viruses and bacteria to be studied and other vaccines and cures to be invented. More important, it kept him away from home, where he was increasingly needed.

Over the course of the previous two years, the modest farmhouse in the Michigan wild had started to grow cramped. In January 1944, the Salks' first son, Peter, was born. Even after he arrived, Jonas and Donna did a fair job of convincing themselves that the little home was perfectly adequate for their needs. Jonas's mother, Dora, did not quite see things that way, and when she came to visit, she made it clear that she would prefer to see her son—to say nothing of her grandchild—settled down in a more prepossessing place.

"That's a closet?" Dora asked on her first tour of the house, passing by the small bedroom Jonas and Donna were decorating for Peter.

Dora's objections notwithstanding, Donna and Jonas managed to stick it out in the Craig house until the middle of 1946, when they learned that Donna was expecting another baby. Before it arrived, they moved to a larger home—still a rental, but one they would at least have to themselves. Two weeks before the baby was due, in March of 1947, Jonas was sent back on the road by the army. The youngest of the Salk brothers, Lee, thus had to be summoned to sit with Donna in case an emergency arose. One arose indeed when Donna went into early labor the same day a late-season blizzard hit, meaning that it was left to Lee to gather up both her and Peter, get them into the car, and drive them to the hospital over the snowed-out roads. Jonas, reached by telegram, fought his way home through the same storm, arriving at the hospital well after the baby—a boy they named Darrell—did. Jonas spent the next few days alternating his time between visiting Donna and Darrell in the hospital and caring for Peter at home, making him plate after plate of scrambled eggs and ketchup—a meal that had the dual advantage of being something Peter loved and something Jonas knew how to prepare.

It was in the midst of all those changes in his family life that Jonas decided his work life would have to change too. He'd been with Tommy Francis for a long while now and had learned a lot—so much, in fact, that he wondered if that might be all there was. It could, he thought, be time to take the next step.

"You know," he told Francis soon after Darrell's birth, "if an opening were to become available for the directorship of another lab—"

"—you'd take it," Francis finished his thought.

"I might," Salk answered.

"You should," Francis said. "You've been ready for that for a while."

In May 1947, just such an opportunity presented itself. The director of the virus lab of the California Department of Public Health had just stepped down, and the state was looking for a replacement. California invested heavily in its health programs, and Salk already knew that the facilities of the lab would be first-rate. What's more, after five years in the Michigan cold, he suspected a move to Berkeley would delight Donna. Salk applied for the job, exchanged a series of encouraging letters with the committee doing the hiring, and, when they were requested, shipped out a thick stack of his research reports and published papers. The fact that one of those papers included the triumphal announcement of the influenza vaccine could not, he reckoned, hurt his cause any. But there were a lot of other investigators seeking the glamorous Berkeley billet as well, and as spring of 1947 edged toward summer, the periodic letters he received from the West grew vaguer and vaguer. Before long, the correspondence stopped altogether.

A short time later, another letter arrived. It offered an opportunity Salk had been half-expecting and, truth be told, half-dreading. For several years, the University of Pittsburgh had maintained a virus laboratory that had earned a well-deserved reputation as a perfectly awful place to work. The lab was barely a lab at all—just a basement space in one distant wing of the city's Municipal Hospital. There was little staff, less equipment, and no funding at all to speak of. The director of the lab was a Dr. Walter Schlesinger, a man Salk had met and befriended at numerous conferences over the years. Schlesinger, he knew, was a scientist with wonderful plans for interesting research who was getting slowly fed up with the indifference the Pittsburgh administrators were showing to any of his proposed projects. Finally, he up and quit. Word of Schlesinger's resignation spread quickly across the academic gossip wires, and it thus did not surprise Salk when a letter arrived for him bearing a University of Pittsburgh return address.

"Dear Dr. Salk," wrote Max Lauffer, the head of the medical school's research branch. "You have probably heard by now that Dr. Schlesinger has resigned his position as the head of our virology laboratory. The board wondered if you might be interested in considering the opening created by Dr. Schlesinger's departure."

Schlesinger clearly had mentioned Salk as his possible successor. He didn't know whether to thank him or curse him. He read on.

"Our plans are to maintain the laboratory but reorganize it. Lab space will be expanded and new equipment will be provided. All work in the labs will be conducted under the umbrella of the medical school, but independent work will be encouraged. We are looking for the sort of man who has his own interests and will want to pursue them."

Salk regarded the letter suspiciously. Pursuing his own interests with the backing of a major university was precisely what he wanted—provided the Pittsburgh administrators really intended to mend their ways and were not simply looking for a quick replacement to cover up the black eye Schlesinger's resignation had given them. Nonetheless, all Lauffer asked in the close of his letter was that Salk consider the position and perhaps come for a visit—at the university's expense, of course—to see for himself what the school had in mind.

Salk accepted Lauffer's invitation and within two weeks made the trip to Pittsburgh. When he arrived on campus, he was surprised—and impressed—to find that it wasn't Lauffer who was there to greet him at all but William McEllroy, the dean of the medical school as a whole. McEllroy took him on a tour of the campus, leading him first to the forty-by-forty-foot dungeonlike lab space Schlesinger had so despised. Salk could see why he'd loathed it so. The room was shadowy and half-empty, set between an abandoned darkroom on one side and a morgue on the other. The ventilation was poor and the overall atmosphere was grim. The only advantage

Salk could see was that the windowless space was at least free of the industrial soot he had noticed hanging in the air and clinging to his clothes the moment he arrived in town. He looked around dubiously.

"It's not much now," McEllroy admitted. "But it will be. We could annex the darkroom or the morgue if you wanted. There's also space in the hospital building next door."

Salk looked at McEllroy skeptically, but if the dean was just blowing smoke, he was doing so expertly. He repeated his promise that Salk would have the freedom he'd need to hire a staff and pursue the work he chose. As a further inducement, he mentioned that the job would come with a salary of $7,500 per year—better than a 50 percent increase over what he was earning in Michigan even after periodic raises.

"We're serious about this lab," McEllroy said. "We want it done right."

Salk thanked McEllroy for his time, promised to think about the position, and returned to Michigan. He told Francis of the trip and confided that he was seriously considering leaving soon.

"For Pittsburgh?" Francis asked. "But there's no real lab there."

"No," Salk agreed, "not yet. Just empty rooms and promises."

"You don't want to wait for something better?"

Salk knew the Pittsburgh facility was wholly inadequate, but that very fact meant it was also wholly his. He wouldn't merely be moving into the lab, he'd be building it. He looked back at Francis with a shrug. "I think I fell in love with the place," he said.

Francis gave Salk a long look. "Try it for a year," he said at last. "If you don't like it there, come back here."

Salk thanked Francis for his understanding and agreed he might well return one day, all the while knowing he probably wouldn't. On a hot morning at the beginning of August, he packed his family into his car and set out for Pittsburgh. He spent much of the two-day drive contemplating just what kind of work he'd like to undertake once the new facility was operational. Viruses continued to intrigue him, particularly measles, the common cold, and even polio. Before long, he'd go gunning for at least one of them.

Cutting hay on a murderously hot day in Daisytown, Pennsylvania, was never easy work. Jimmy Sarkett had been out in his family's fields with his uncle Lou since morning, and though he'd expected to feel wilted and exhausted, he hadn't expected to feel sick as well.

What Sarkett noticed first was a bone-deep fatigue and a feeling of whole-body heat that went far beyond what the sun was causing. He cast a long eye toward his uncle Lou, who was far enough off that he was unlikely to see him, then staggered over to a fat bush where he could lie down in the shade. If Uncle Lou did spot him there, he probably wouldn't call him for loafing, but he would insist that they quit for the day and go back inside, where the boy, who was only ten after all, could rest up some. That, Jimmy figured, was worse than being called a shirker.

So he remained hidden under the bush for that whole hellfire afternoon, trying to doze when he could, but keeping one ear tuned for the moment his uncle clicked his tongue for the horses, tossed his tools into the back of the wagon, and prepared to ride back to the house. When, late in the afternoon, Jimmy did hear the sounds of the workday ending, he struggled up from beneath his bush as if he had just retrieved a dropped tool, gave a weak-armed wave, and hurried over to the wagon—or as much as he could hurry with legs suddenly gone wobbly. When he got there his uncle took a single look at him and frowned with concern.

"We're going home, boy," he said.

The uncle could readily see that something was gravely amiss with Jimmy, and Jimmy himself could feel it. What neither of them knew was just what it was. At some point within the last two weeks, Jimmy had ingested a few flecks of poliovirus passed on to him by someone he would never know. The bug might have been entrained in the airborne mist released by a cough or sneeze; it might have been lingering on a bathroom fixture or a privy door, the invisible intestinal residue of an unknown person who had been there before. Wherever the virus was waiting or floating, it made its way onto Jimmy and into his nose or mouth and then into his throat—exactly the warm, rich, wet environment it was built for.

Once there, it took up residence in the tonsils and nearby lymph tissue, and within two hours began reproducing itself. With each passing hour, more and more copies of the virus were invisibly and painlessly manufactured, swarming through the infected tissue. With each innocent swallow, Jimmy transported some of that virus down his throat and into his stomach, where it encountered more lymph nodes. There, the virus population exploded, multiplying not only in the lymph tissue but inside the white blood cells that lived there as well, causing them to swell and burst, splattering still more virus to healthy cells and tissue nearby.

This multiplying and bursting, multiplying and bursting, played out for up to ten days, and still Jimmy had no idea of what was taking place in his innards. Finally, in the second week of his infection, a very unlucky thing happened. In up to 95 of every 100 people the polio bug bit, the virus never moved much past the lymph nodes. In a few of those 100, however—and Jimmy was one of them—it breached the nodes and poured into the bloodstream. There it multiplied further and streamed everywhere in the body the blood would touch, including the anterior horns of the spinal cord. The horns, a pair of projections in the gray matter along the front edge of the spine, convey signals from the brain out to all the muscles in the body. Sometimes the virus didn't stop at the horns, swimming up the bloodstream to the medulla oblongata, the bulb-shaped area at the base of the brain. Once inside either brain or spine, it slipped inside the nerve cells, chewing them up—and blowing them up—the same way it had the white cells. When it did, the signals traveling to the muscles began to sputter and die. With them, the muscles themselves did too.

That was what was happening in the body of Jimmy Sarkett. He and his uncle rode in the hay wagon back to the house, where the boy's mother packed him off to bed, and called the doctor in nearby Vestaburg. The doctor arrived in the early evening, by which time Jimmy's fever had soared, his wobbly legs had grown altogether still, and his arms had begun to fail him too. To the degree that he could move at all, it was only to thrash with the pain that now clawed at all the muscles in all his limbs. It was no secret, to the doctor at least, what the febrile boy had contracted, and that it might steal his very breath next.

The doctor summoned an ambulance, which raced to the farm, collected Jimmy and his mother, then raced back toward Pittsburgh. They were heading, the woman and boy were told, to Municipal Hospital, the finest medical facility the city had to offer, and one with a first-rate ward for children felled by muscle sickness. It was only when he learned that news that Jimmy Sarkett fully realized what he had. When he did, he began to cry.

Jimmy cried as the ambulance pulled up to the hospital, as he was wheeled into the building and up to the boys' and girls' ward, and as the grim-looking doctors bent over his bed. He was ten years old, had never left the Daisytown farm, and was now in a bright room in a strange place feeling a terrible pain in all his limbs that wrung a primal howl from him if he moved so much as a flicker. And he knew—just knew—that his mother would have to leave him here. When he realized all that, he cried some more.

Jimmy Sarkett cried for the better part of the first twenty-four hours he was in Municipal Hospital, as the poliomyelitis settled deeper into his tissues, leaving fewer and fewer of his muscles working. It would be days before the fever would break, weeks before his muscles would stabilize, and months before he'd leave the hospital—rolling out in a wheelchair with ruined legs and weakened arms. Even then, he would not go home, but would instead be installed in the well-regarded D. T. Watson rehabilitation home in nearby Leetsdale, Pennsylvania, for schooling and care and to determine what function, if any, could be restored to his wasted limbs.

Before Jimmy Sarkett finally did leave Municipal Hospital, a nurse drew a sample of his blood and, as she was supposed to do, labeled the vial with his name. Because of overwork or oversight or perhaps mere unfamiliarity with the uncommon surname, she slightly misspelled it, writing it as Saukett, not Sarkett. Before long, that wrong surname would become a very familiar one, particularly to the young doctor formerly of Michigan who was now setting up shop down in the hospital's basement.

The epidemiological lottery of 1947 tapped 10,827 people for paralysis or death. The virus made its choices randomly, cherry-picking babies and toddlers, adolescents and even some adults, with no discernible pattern to the contagion. For all that arbitrariness, however, it was not an especially terrifying summer—not, at least, compared with the one before.

In 1946, a staggering 25,698 Americans had been sickened by polio, nearly double the 1945 total and the most in more than twenty-six years. No part of the country was spared the viral onslaught, but a few states—Minnesota, Florida, California, Utah, Colorado, Alabama—were fairly swamped by the sickness. In Minneapolis alone, 942 children fell ill, a huge gash in the childhood ranks of even so big a city. In Florence, Alabama, 112 children were infected in a county where the population numbered barely 20,000. Everywhere in the country, the season ran hot and late, and it wasn't until deep in the drizzly fall that it at last ended.

Basil O'Connor and the National Foundation for Infantile Paralysis entered 1947 well staffed with some of the best scientific minds in the country for whatever the season might throw at them. But when an epidemic was raging, what was also needed was hands-on health-care workers who could look after the sick and help teach the healthy how they could stay that way. For that kind of on-the-ground attention, there was nothing to touch the NFIP's women.

Early on, O'Connor had given little thought to the women of the foundation. The country's growing network of March of Dimes chapters were run by civic leaders and supervised by local doctors, nearly all of whom were men. Women had a role in the work, but it was a minor one, limited mostly to small-bore labor like holding teas and rolling bandages. This was a worthy contribution, and O'Connor was content to leave things that way. Not long ago, he had even approved the hiring of a woman to work in the New York offices and oversee the ladies' modest activities. The new woman's name was Elaine Whitelaw, and it would be weeks before he would actually say hello to her; when he finally did, he would not forget the experience.

Whitelaw was a child of privilege who grew up in a comfortable apartment on West End Avenue and Eighty-seventh Street in Manhattan. She had learned something of the terror of illness in the summer of 1916, when her parents swept her out of that tony home and carried her away from a polio plague that would have no regard for the elegant addresses of the children it might strike. As she was growing up, her parents made it a point to teach her more about hardship. Though her father had amassed a modest fortune in the international diamond trade, talk around the dinner table was not of wealth and privilege but of class struggle and worker exploitation and the global changes that could be wrought by the socialist revolution blossoming in the East. Cocktail parties in the Whitelaw home were filled with similar chatter. Names like Eugene Debs, Nicola Sacco, and Bartolomeo Vanzetti came up often in the conversations.

When Whitelaw was old enough to find work, she took a job with the Spanish Civil War Organization, raising funds and circulating literature on behalf of the armies of the Republic. Later, after the outbreak of the new World War, she accepted a similar position with America's National War Fund. It was while she was in that post that she received a call from the National Foundation for Infantile Paralysis, offering her a job in the newly created position of Coordinator for Women's Activities. Hypnotized by anything related to or even touched by Franklin Roosevelt, she accepted.

Whitelaw was hired by Peter Cusack, the foundation's executive secretary, and worked with him and most of the other NFIP staffers on the eleventh floor of 120 Broadway. Basil O'Connor worked above in his old law offices on the twentieth floor, often entirely out of sight for days at a time. When Whitelaw arrived at her new job, the first thing she did was review the limited portfolio of activities she'd been hired to manage. She was not pleased with what she saw.

If the NFIP really wanted the help of women, she concluded, there were countless ways to do it better: Recruit mothers and wives to collect donations in movie theaters—a reliable source of funds that had flagged of late, since all the ushers had gone to war and taken better-paying jobs when they came home. Enlist other women to conduct local education seminars, court wealthy donors at community lunches, hold sales and swap meets to raise other funds. More important, women could be trained to set up neighborhood and emergency-care groups and even help purchase equipment and recruit staffers for local hospitals. To coordinate all these jobs and undertake new ones, entire women's divisions—under the oversight of women directors—could be established within all the local chapters.

Whitelaw wrote her suggestions up and passed them on to Cusack, insisting that Basil O'Connor—isolated in his office aerie or not—needed to read them. Cusak passed the memo up to O'Connor. The next day, Whitelaw found a note on her desk, written in a tidy, nasty-looking hand.

"Don't do anything," it read. It was signed, "B. O'C."

Whitelaw stared at the note with displeasure, then marched into Cusack's office. "I want to meet Mr. O'Connor," she announced.

Cusack reluctantly phoned O'Connor's secretary to request the meeting and was surprised when it was granted—for a few days later at precisely four P.M. He hung up, informed Whitelaw, and then warned her, "Be there at ten of four. Mr. O'Connor keeps his clock five minutes fast so that if he's feeling ornery he can yell at you for being late."

Three days later at precisely 3:50, Cusack and Whitelaw appeared on the twentieth floor, passing first by the shrine-like office of Franklin Roosevelt, which had been left untouched since the day in 1928 when he went to Albany to be sworn in as governor of New York. They presented themselves to O'Connor's secretary and were shown into his office. The foundation chief was seated behind his desk, apparently indifferent to their arrival. He was a shiny, stylish, now plump man. His clock read 3:55. O'Connor looked up and motioned to Cusack to sit; he did not extend the same courtesy to Whitelaw.

"Mr. O'Connor," Cusack said, "this is Elaine Whitelaw."

O'Connor regarded her without much expression. "Well?" he asked unpleasantly.

Whitelaw drew a breath and plunged into her pitch, repeating the plans she had described in her memo, but with much greater passion and far greater detail than she had been able to express on paper. She spoke as she had learned to speak at her parents' table and in their salons—succinctly, persuasively. When she finally paused in her stream of speech and looked again at the clock, she saw that nearly a quarter of an hour had passed. Neither O'Connor nor Cusack had made a sound in that time. She leaned forward and looked at O'Connor directly.

"Well?" she said.

The foundation chief stared back at her, unsmiling still, but unoffended as well. "That's all very interesting," he said. "I'm sure it's a lot of baloney, but it's interesting baloney."

Then, O'Connor did what Whitelaw had hoped he'd do: He invited her to sit and—with a flicker of surrender—asked her to tell him more. For the next three and a half hours, Whitelaw spoke and O'Connor listened, then O'Connor spoke and Whitelaw listened. When they were at last done, O'Connor told her to return to her office. He asked Cusack to stay. Whitelaw left, so wrung-out from the high-tension session that she needed to support herself against the cold marble wall of O'Connor's anteroom while waiting for the elevator. Half an hour later, a happy Cusack joined her in her office.

"Come out for a drink," he instructed, "then be in early tomorrow. All Mr. O'Connor could say was, 'Don't lose that girl. She fights for what she believes.'" As of that night, the Women's Activities Division of the NFIP became a far larger, far more powerful body than it had ever been before.

With the help of Whitelaw and public affairs director Dorothy Ducas, the NFIP quickly raised and deployed a national army of volunteer women. In the summer of 1947, in Utah alone, March of Dimes planners divided the state into community-sized polio districts and recruited fifty to sixty women in each to be trained as emergency volunteers during epidemics. In bigger communities in other states, those teams were commensurately larger.

Equally pleasing to O'Connor, the women under Whitelaw's command were able to throttle up NFIP fund-raising dramatically. In 1947, foundation revenues soared and the money was poured into the states that were hungriest for it—$363,300 in hard-hit Colorado, $377,013 in Illinois, a staggering $531,850 to care for just 352 paralysis victims in Idaho. While the money was being collected and disbursed, Whitelaw and Ducas schooled O'Connor in how to raise even more, instructing him to quit spending silently and instead begin publicizing in detail just what kind of care all the donated dollars were buying.

"The public can't see you only when you come to them with your hand out," they'd scold. And so the foundation's seasonal advertising campaigns expanded to year-round campaigns, touting the $161,000 given to Dade County, Florida, alone to fight an epidemic and the $2.48 spent to mend the braces of a seven-year-old girl in Alabama; the $138,400 granted to the University of Pennsylvania to study abnormalities in muscles and nerves and the $20 provided a child in Illinois to settle a doctor bill.

By the time 1947 was out, the foundation had the welfare of the 10,000 children who had been struck sick that summer as well in hand as possible, with hospitals and doctors and therapy programs in place to care for nearly all of them. Already it was printing up 30 million informational brochures for the 1948 season, planning to have them in parents' hands before the spring. When the literature was ready, Whitelaw's women would see that it got where it needed to go.

Deep in the autumn of 1947, Jonas Salk was still carrying an entirely useless key on his keychain. It belonged to the distant door of Tommy Francis's virus lab at the University of Michigan. Salk had been more than ready to quit his Ann Arbor job when the time came, but to make the leave-taking easier he had told himself—only half-jokingly—that he was really just out on field duty, as he had been all the other times he'd taken to the road to conduct his influenza work over the years. He had not expected to feel such mistiness over a job in a lab he was convinced he'd outgrown, yet it had been his first lab, and it was a jolt to move so far away from it.

"I am not too surprised to learn that you are missing Ann Arbor," wrote Stella Barlow, a former colleague with whom he maintained an occasional correspondence. "Most people do even when they hadn't thought they'd liked it so well when they were here. And you always liked it." Salk, who had liked it indeed, would thus keep his Michigan key where it was for a time—a reassuring charm he'd discard only when he felt he'd fully settled into his new position in Pittsburgh.

There were a lot of things that made that settling in difficult, but this time finding a house wasn't one of them. By now Donna knew what it was Jonas wanted in a home and, more important, Jonas knew what Donna would abide. There would be no wood-burning stoves in the family's next house, no washed-out roads or landlords downstairs. Donna wanted a comfortable place and she wanted it to be her own. Jonas, for his part, was certain only that he still wanted a home in the country.

The couple compromised on a big, airy, comparatively modern house on a plot of land at the intersection of Perry Highway and Maple Drive in Wexford, Pennsylvania, a lush rim of country not far from the dense crush of the city. Dora set up housekeeping and Jonas got straight to work planting a garden, planning to grow the odd flower in his backyard plot, but mostly looking forward to raising vegetables. It was an artifact of the war years—when Victory Gardens kept plates full at home and freed up precious resources to be sent to soldiers overseas. Salk found that he took great pleasure in coaxing anything at all from the soil, but even more so if what he cultivated had come practical use.

While getting settled in the Wexford house was a quick and comfortable business for the Salks, things were far less pleasant on the morning of October 1, when Jonas arrived for his first day of work at his new and largely empty laboratory in the basement of the University of Pittsburgh's Municipal Hospital. Dean McEllroy had been telling the truth when he promised that Salk would have the money and space he'd need to build the lab he wanted—but it was an incomplete truth. The whole story came slowly clear in a series of letters Salk exchanged with McEllroy and Max Lauffer in the months between the time he accepted his new position and the time he actually moved. Space, the administrators made clear in their correspondence, would indeed be made available—provided Salk himself took the initiative to court the right faculty members, make the right friends, and wheedle the right empty office from the professor or administrator who currently controlled it.

Money would be available too, but only some of it would be provided by the university directly. The rest would have to come in the form of independent grants from outside foundations—outside foundations Salk would have to woo himself. Chasing after endowments meant learning to become not just a scientist but a salesman too, writing up descriptions of the work he hoped to pursue and the results he hoped to obtain, then submitting the proposal to administrators and philanthropic groups as if it were some sort of investment prospectus. It required the kind of predictive certainty that good science—with all its unanticipated turns and switch-backs—almost never allowed. And yet, as countless lab chiefs before Salk had learned, it was precisely the level of certainty he'd have to sell.

Arriving in his half-lit lab that first morning on the job, Salk sat down at his empty desk, uncovered the well-worked typewriter Walter Schlesinger had left behind, and began to peck away.

"Subject or subjects of investigation," he typed. "To conduct studies in the field and laboratory of both a research and applied nature."

Salk looked at what he'd typed. He was starting to sound like a bureaucrat already. All scientific study took place either in the field or in the lab, and all of it was either pure research or practically applied. The sentence said absolutely nothing. He turned back to the keyboard and got more specific.

"Program of Research," he typed out. "Poliomyelitis."

Ever since Salk had decided to come to Pittsburgh, the problem of polio had continued to tease at him. Influenza research remained a possibility, and had he wanted to continue to devote himself to that line of work, he could have done so easily. The officers in the army's medical division still had real fondness for the young man who'd helped whip the flu. They'd already awarded him ongoing grants for his work, charging him with the job of maintaining the influenza listening posts he'd help set up around the world and researching new ways to speed up vaccine production.

Salk was happy to be offered the assignment and accepted it gratefully, but with the disease for the most part contained, the work would demand only moderate effort—and almost no imagination. Studying the common cold had a lot more appeal, if only because it was such a universal affliction, had stymied so many researchers before, and could probably attract no limit of charitable grants. Measles also had promise—a common illness as well but one that was more often lethal than most people realized. Despite all this, Salk found that it was polio that increasingly engaged his thinking.

There were a lot of ways to begin a program of polio research, mostly because there was so much that remained a mystery about the disease. For one thing, polio appeared to be an illness that was impervious to good hygiene. From cholera to colds to familiar influenza, the rules were simple: Stay clean and you stay healthy. Come too close to open latrines, unguarded coughs, and the infectious aerosol of airborne sneezes and you could pick up any bug at all.

But polio turned at least some of that dictum on its head. The scattered cases of infantile paralysis that for millennia occurred only here and there first began to nucleate into epidemics in the nineteenth century—just the era when indoor bathrooms and sealed plumbing were keeping hands cleaner and sewage more contained than ever before. Yet not only did polio outbreaks become more common, they became particularly so in places like Sweden and New York, where homes were especially well piped and people were especially well scrubbed.

The counterintuitive explanation was that while the poliovirus in human waste and elsewhere could spread the disease, it could also inoculate against it, exposing infants and young children to frequent mild infections that caused few if any symptoms but provided a lifetime load of antibodies. Remove that low, slow background exposure and you'd be completely helpless against a strong, wild strain of the bug that might hit you later.

Also surprising was how resilient the body could be even when it was under a full-blown polio attack. In just the last few years, David Bodian of Johns Hopkins University had studied the spines of polio victims and found that at least 60 percent of the nerve cells associated with a particular muscle had to be damaged or destroyed before any paralytic symptoms appeared at all. This remarkable neural tenacity helped explain how seemingly healthy but profoundly infected people could serve as viral couriers, spreading either paralyzing polio cases or protective, symptomless ones, depending both on the strain of the virus they were carrying and the constitution of the person they passed it on to.

Salk had lately made it his business to catch up on all the work being done in the field and had selected several possible roads that might carry him into it. At the moment, the best way to diagnose the presence of polio was simply to watch for its telltale fever and paralysis to make their appearance. This was a bit like waiting for a forest to burn down in order to determine that there had been a sloppy campfire smoldering somewhere. Any number of scientists had been working to develop a polio blood test, guessing that if you detected the presence of the virus early enough, it might be possible to block it from ever reaching the spinal tissue. Salk found this problem especially ripe for study.

In addition to wanting to develop a test for the virus, he was also interested in the problem of growing the virus easily in the lab. For all the ferocity polio exhibited once it got inside the body, it was a rather frail and fussy bug, growing only in human beings, certain species of monkeys, and if you knew how to manage it, cotton rats. For researchers accustomed to growing their cultures in antiseptic flasks and petri dishes, this made for messy—to say nothing of expensive—work. What's more, if you hoped to develop a polio vaccine, where you got your virus could make a very big difference, as the hapless Kolmer, Brodie, and Park had learned a dozen years earlier when they injected children with monkey cells to such awful effect. Salk, who had grown flu viruses in chicken eggs, wondered if it might not be possible to do the same with polio. Eggs weren't as elegant an answer as sterile dishes, but they didn't require cages, food, and full-time handlers either, which was a lot more than you could say for a clattering lab full of monkeys and rats.

Finally, Salk wanted to learn more about the life cycle of the poliovirus itself. The fact that polio was a summer bug had never really been questioned, but the reason for such seasonal selectivity was another matter entirely. Some suspected that the virus might survive cold climates when winter hit by establishing a living reservoir in animals that were themselves yearly migraters. Others suspected that the virus simply went into some kind of hibernation. Salk suspected something else. Was it possible, he wondered, that polio was actually present year-round, but needed a cofactor, such as a seasonal allergen, to become dangerous? Perhaps the virus could not successfully invade the body unless it was able to sneak through some sort of biological crack when the immune system was busy protecting itself against pollen, ragweed, or one of the season's other nuisances. Close that crack somehow and you might shut the paralysis entirely out.

All these possible courses of research fascinated Salk, and he spent several days typing them out in careful detail. He submitted them to Lauffer and McEllroy as he was supposed to—expecting, quite reasonably, that they would be impressed, and hoping, less reasonably, that a flood of funding would follow. While he awaited their response, he turned his attention to the business of hiring a staff.

Drawing what he knew from the labs with which he'd been associated in the past, Salk penciled out a rough idea of the number and nature of employees he'd need for the work he envisioned doing, including technicians, secretaries, glassware cleaners, and animal handlers, to say nothing of the physicians, Ph.D.'s, and other learned researchers he'd need to chart and conduct the actual research. The junior staff alone might cost him $13,000 per year in cumulative salaries; the senior staff would run much more.

Salk placed advertisements for the lower-tier positions, and soon found himself interviewing hopeful-looking applicants in his hopeless-looking basement. The university had already informed him that any candidate he chose for however lowly a post would have to be approved before he could formally offer the position. He quickly became skilled at composing the kind of letter that would persuade his superiors that he'd made the right choice.

"Dear Dr. Lauffer," he wrote in one such letter, "I have enclosed for your consideration the application of Mrs. Beatrice Sampson to provide us with the necessary services for cleaning and maintaining glassware. Mrs. Sampson is the kind of person I would like to have from the point of view of interest and intelligence and reliability as well."

Salk went on for one or two more pitchman's paragraphs, then concluded with a final, pointed aside about his badly undersupplied lab. "I regret," he wrote, "that we had only a single application form for her to fill out." If Lauffer noticed his barb, he never acknowledged it.

At the same time Salk was hiring his junior staff, he was also trying to coax more lab and office space from the other faculty members who currently controlled it and, often as not, didn't really need it. Here, too, the art of obeisance would be one of the most important skills he could bring to the job. Salk spent his days in his lab typing uncounted solicitous letters pleading for the resources he'd once imagined would simply flow to him. He spent his evenings at home, trying to forget he'd done it.

"I've become a bureaucrat," he'd lament to Donna.

"That's part of the job," she'd answer.

"But I'm supposed to be conducting research."

"That's the other part."

Salk plodded through the autumn this way—slowly accumulating staff and space and continuing to wait for approval of his proposed work—as his first Pittsburgh October darkened into November, and November gave way to December.

Finally, not long before the holidays, a hinge in Salk's world unexpectedly turned. He received a call from Dean McEllroy's secretary, telling him that a Dr. Harry Weaver from the National Foundation for Infantile Paralysis had recently phoned. He hoped to visit the university sometime the next week and had specifically requested permission to drop in on the virus lab and meet its new director—the young man who had done such a fine job with Tommy Francis and the flu vaccine out in Michigan. Salk, like anyone in the virus field, was at least passingly familiar with most of the NFIP's higher-ranking names and had heard much about Harry Weaver.

Weaver had been chosen as the foundation's director of research just the year before, and it was an appointment that angered many. Part of the problem was Weaver's credentials—particularly the fact that he didn't have any to speak of. To be sure, he was known as *Dr.* Weaver, but his advanced degree was a Ph.D. and it had been awarded in perhaps the softest of all imaginable fields: philosophy. Weaver *had* earned some scientific stripes as a professor of anatomy at Wayne State University, in Detroit, and had both conducted and overseen a fair amount of basic medical research. But his diploma marked him a doctor of letters, and nothing in his body of work would ever change that.

Then, too, there was the very nature of his new position. Basic research, as everyone knew, was essentially a hermit's game, carried out in the privacy of the laboratory with a small circle of collaborators and a narrow-eyed suspicion of anyone else out there who might be conducting similar work. You didn't so much as whisper about what you were doing until you'd actually done it, publishing your work in a paper that would clearly mark it yours and yours alone. That rule held true even if you were part of a national foundation of scientists, all fighting the same disease and all answerable to the same bosses. The very idea that the leaders of the NFIP would bring in a person to force them to cooperate was galling.

Yet Weaver and the foundation knew what they were up to. Their work would never come to anything if all the scientists laboring in the NFIP's vineyards weren't talking to one another—or at least to a single overseer—to make sure efforts weren't being duplicated and dead ends already abandoned by one lab weren't still being pursued by others. Almost immediately upon being named to his new post, Weaver thus lit out from the NFIP headquarters at 120 Broadway and spent much of his time paying calls on the men in the field, working to win their trust or at least their grudging tolerance.

At every one of the labs Weaver visited, his performance would be essentially the same. He'd look slowly around at whatever outfit he was inspecting that day and then nod and smile appreciatively. He'd seen a lot of polio research in the last year, he'd say, but this setup—here in Baltimore or Chicago or Long Island or Buffalo or California or Alabama—was truly impressive. In fact, though he wouldn't mention this to the other labs, the national headquarters was holding out special hopes for the work being conducted here.

The investigators would beam at Weaver's attentions and allow that yes, they were mighty proud of the research they were doing here. When Weaver would then happen to mention that the foundation was holding a conference in the next month or two and he hoped he could count on the scientists to come and talk candidly about every scrap of their work, they'd say they'd be happy to.

Weaver did a splendid job not only of appeasing the scientists he already had in his pen, but of corralling new ones. He kept his eyes open for promising new talent, and when he found it, he did what he could to make it his own. When he learned that young Salk was half-idling in the base-ment of Pittsburgh's Municipal Hospital, he decided he ought to pay a visit. He arrived as planned just a week after his initial call. Salk welcomed McEll-roy and Weaver to his lab, and with barely concealed self-consciousness showed him around the dreary space. Weaver seemed unaccountably im-pressed by what he saw.

"It's quite a setup you've got here," he said. Salk looked back at him oddly. "Or it could be quite a setup," Weaver amended.

Salk thanked him.

"In fact," Weaver added, "it might be just the place to do some work we're considering."

The foundation, he explained, was looking to round up three or four labs to conduct an extensive study—perhaps the most extensive it had ever undertaken. The labs would be kept busy for up to three years and would be backed by generous research grants. McEllroy asked how much those grants would be.

Weaver shrugged. "Maybe a couple hundred thousand dollars per year." Salk and McEllroy widened their eyes. "It has to be a lot," Weaver said. "It's for virus typing."

That, of course, made sense. For a long time now, researchers had known that just as there were two different types of influenza virus, there were three different types of poliovirus, with many different strains within each type. Determining the type of every possible strain would be essential if you ever hoped to develop a polio vaccine, since even the strongest im-munity against one type would still leave you vulnerable to the other two. Worse, even if an effective three-virus vaccine—a so-called trivalent—could be invented, there was no way of knowing if among the thousands and thousands of polio cases reported each year there was not a fourth or fifth or sixth type of virus drifting about.

The NFIP had by no means settled on the development of a vaccine as one of its principal objectives, but if it was ever going to, it was essential to begin a comprehensive typing program now, scooping up a large, repre-sentative sample of strains and taking their immunological measure to make sure they all belonged to one of the three groups. It was the kind of slow, repetitive, mind-numbing research that ambitious scientists dreaded, but it was what was now needed to move the state of knowledge forward. Salk had not come to Pittsburgh to do such oarsman's work, and if anyone had been offering him anything better, he'd have taken it. But no one was. Moreover, he knew that any lab that did get involved in the typing program would be helping the foundation take an enormous step on the road to wiping out the disease. The first scientists on that road would probably be the first ones to make it to the end.

"We'd be happy to take it on," he said to Weaver. Weaver smiled, then extended his hand and shook Salk's vigorously.

Within days, a check for $148,000—with a promise of more to come—was on its way from 120 Broadway in New York to the little virus lab at the University of Pittsburgh. Not long after that, the Sarah Mellon Scaife Foundation, Pittsburgh's largest philanthropic group, got wind of the endowment and weighed in with a $35,000 grant of its own. At City Hall, Mayor David Lawrence, recognizing a public relations plum when he saw one, stepped in too, making a few calls and twisting a few arms and seeing to it that the scientist who'd just been tapped for such important national service would get every square foot of additional lab space he deemed necessary. The empty morgue next to his laboratory would be his, as promised. The empty darkroom would be annexed too. Other space in other buildings would be granted as requested. What Jonas Salk needed would now be his—and he would not have to write any more letters asking for it.

One of the first things a scientist had to do when he was accepted into the embrace of the NFIP was get to know the other, more senior scientists already there. Salk learned that his opportunity to meet the foundation elders would come on January 7, 1948, at the Statler Hotel in Washington, D.C., where the details of the virus-typing project would be discussed and planned. He had little idea of what to expect of the gathering, but one thing he was absolutely certain of was that while he was there he was going to keep his mouth mostly shut.

Scientific conferences were hierarchical and competitive affairs, with seniority measured by a lot of yardsticks—age, number of published papers, length of affiliation with whichever organization was sponsoring the event. By all of those measures, Salk was a comparative pup. More important, he was one who had little taste for going up against wolves.

The glittery list of other attendees gathering at the Statler—the senior war council in the long fight against polio—had been battling the poliomyelitis virus since Salk was a mere student. He himself had joined the campaign a matter of weeks ago. Staying quiet in the presence of such viral veterans was almost certainly the best way to go. If he had any scientific differences to take up with them at all, he'd not come at them squarely, but obliquely—as was his preference in any conflict.

The Washington meeting had been planned for some months, with the scientific business set to be conducted on January 7 and 8. The following night there would be a gala dinner celebrating the tenth anniversary of the NFIP. Salk looked forward to the first part of the three-day event but not the rest. The idea of an anniversary dinner celebrating the tenth year of an organization with which he had been associated for only twenty-some days left him feeling like a bit of a pretender.

Whatever Salk's feelings were, he knew that the meeting was essential to the work he was about to undertake. The virus-typing program would be far and away the most sweeping research project in the history of polio work. If the study was to have a chance of succeeding, the leaders of the foundation would have to coordinate the efforts of everyone involved.

Salk arrived in Washington on the evening of the sixth—his train ticket purchased for him by the foundation—and checked into his room in the Statler, which had been prepaid too. The morning of the first session, he rose early, dressed, and arrived in the designated conference room, where a coffee service had been set up and many of the other scientists were quietly milling about. Of the people so far present, he knew only a few—among them Weaver, who was lost in conversation with a small group of other men, and Tommy Francis, whose Michigan lab had done some limited work for the NFIP even when Salk was there, and now, with the lion's share of the influenza research done, had taken on more polio chores. Salk had known that Francis would be attending, and happy to see a face he recognized, he hurried over to say hello to his onetime boss.

Across the room, Weaver broke from his conversational circle and began waving to the group at large, calling the meeting to order. A conference table had been arranged with twenty-one places, each set with a notepad, water glass, and name plaque. A secretary's table was positioned nearby for the stenographer who would be taking down the minutes of the meeting. A projector was set up in the back of the room and a white screen in the front for anyone who would be giving a talk that would require lantern slides. Salk approached the table, took his seat, and looked around at the other people settling into their designated spots. Now that he could put name plaques to faces, he was impressed anew with the company he was keeping.

Seated a few places away at the oversized table was John Paul of Yale University, one of the foundation's earliest grantees and one of the first men to demonstrate—a full seventeen years earlier—that an animal that had been infected with one type of poliovirus could still be made sick with another, early proof that the hydra-headed disease could be stopped only with a hydra-headed vaccine. Also present were David Bodian and Howard Howe of Johns Hopkins University in Baltimore, who had shown that chimpanzees could be fed the poliovirus and come down with the disease, proof that oral infection was at least one route the bug took into the body. Joining Bodian and Howe was Isabel Morgan, also of Hopkins. Morgan, the only woman present, had gotten a head start on typing work already, screening numerous strains and continuing to find that they fell into one of only three distinct groups. Morgan did not regularly attend NFIP gatherings, and her presence here was one more indication that this meeting was more important than most. Also in the room was Charles Armstrong, a researcher at the United States Public Health Service who was admired for having found the one strain of polio that could be grown in cotton rats, a more expendable and affordable reservoir than monkeys and chimps. One other person in attendance today was Albert Sabin.

Barely eight years Salk's senior, Sabin had been a virologist with the Rockefeller Institute and was now with the Children's Hospital in Cincinnati. He had been associated with the NFIP for five years already and had made an enduring impression on almost anyone who came into working contact with him. Salk had met him only once or twice before, most notably in 1946, when Sabin had come to Ann Arbor for a conference and Salk had helped him secure a room at the local Hotel Hollenden. Sabin had also borrowed a nickel from Salk when he needed pocket change. Upon his return to Cincinnati, Sabin promptly wrote Salk a thank-you note and enclosed five cents' worth of postage stamps to repay the debt. Their respective books, as far as Salk could tell, had been balanced ever since. That did not mean that he did not still find Sabin a little bit larger than life.

Tall, mustached, and surpassingly fond of his always present pipe, Sabin had a profoundly sharp medical mind, and an equally sharp way of expressing it. A Sabin opinion was a well-formed thing, incisively thought through and unshakably held. He'd explain it to you if he absolutely had to, but if he did, he'd expect you to get it in a single go. If you needed the point repeated—either because you didn't understand it or, worse, because you didn't agree with it—he'd treat you not so much with exasperation or impatience as with something closer to weary pity. Such displays of disdain would be intolerable if it weren't for the fact that he was right so much of the time—and when he wasn't, he still seemed so sure of his position that he'd easily rattle you in yours.

One thing about which Sabin was particularly certain was the whole business of polio vaccination. Unlike some of the other foundation members, he did not get skittish at the mere idea of massive immunization programs with a mass-produced vaccine. Indeed, since first affiliating himself with the NFIP, he'd given a lot of thought to the problem of how an effective inoculation could be developed, and was convinced that the job could be accomplished only with a live, weakened bug. Sabin had heard the occasional talk about the potential of killed-virus vaccines and frankly had not had much use for it. Stimulating the immune system with a dead virus was a dubious idea—a little like trying to get a healthy hound to hunt a dead fox. The dog might nose about at the thing, but it certainly wouldn't mount a vigorous attack.

Live vaccines, on the other hand, had proven themselves again and again—stimulating the immune system to provide fast, robust, reliable protection against all manner of diseases. If you absolutely had to fool about with such unproven methods as a killed-virus vaccine, you might do so when you were studying a low-stakes illness like the common cold. Polio deserved a more reliable—to say nothing of a more responsible— approach. People who had spoken to Sabin before this week's meeting reported that he had similarly strong ideas about how the virus typing ought to be conducted too. If he did, there was little doubt he'd make those thoughts known as soon as Weaver called the gathering to order—which the research director soon did.

"Gentlemen," Weaver said, either overlooking Johns Hopkins's Isabel Morgan or extending her the complicated compliment of including her in that form of address. "In case we don't happen to know everybody," Weaver went on, "I think we might go around the table and identify people. Starting on the far side is Dr. Paul from Yale, Dr. Howe from Johns Hopkins, Dr. Salk from Pittsburgh, Dr. Wenner from Kansas, Dr. Sabin from Cincinnati, Dr. Armstrong—I don't know where he's from, the Health Service I suppose, but he works for so many people."

The scientists laughed obligingly. Weaver completed the other fifteen introductions, smiling easily at the faces that were so familiar to him, and then proceeded to business.

"Now, the purpose of this meeting is to permit the National Foundation to ascertain your judgment on the following matter: Do you believe it is important to undertake a program to determine the number, characteristics, and geographical distribution of the poliomyelitis virus?"

This, of course, was not a question at all. If the scientists didn't feel it was important to conduct the typing study, they wouldn't be here at all today. Being trained in science, however, meant being trained in the experimental method—a method that demanded that no premise, however self-evident, be assumed to be true without first being framed as a hypothetical. "If it is indeed important," Weaver went on, "have the methods been developed to permit a solution to these problems?" That question was a different matter.

The three types of poliovirus were very different bugs, distinguished by their very different behaviors. Type I was the most common of the three, the one most likely to lead to epidemics and paralysis of the limbs. Type II was a milder virus than Type I, the likeliest to lead to asymptomatic cases, though in the weak or unlucky, it could still paralyze or kill. Type III was the rarest of all and that was a very good thing, since it was the one most likely to lead to bulbar polio, the infection of the medulla oblongata, the lower bulb of the brain, leading to paralysis of the diaphragm, destruction of breathing, and so often death. The only hope for these cases was the feared iron lung, a horizontal, tanklike device into which the body was slid up to the neck. Rising and falling pressure within the machine then expanded and contracted the chest, forcing breath into and out of the lungs. Only the patient's head protruded from the tank, the mouth and nose forcibly drawing in and expelling room air.

Before a virus sample's type was known, it was identified in a less scientific but decidedly more poignant way—by the name of the unfortunate child in whose blood it had initially been identified. Over the years, scientists had identified and logged hundreds of so-named viruses. There was the Grabowski strain, for nine-year-old Janice Grabowski, who was admitted to Los Angeles County General Hospital in August 1943 complaining of a high fever and pain in her shoulder and legs. Her sister, Virginia, was admitted at the same time with similar complaints. Janice eventually walked away from the disease; Virginia was paralyzed. There was the Korpisz strain, for twenty-one-month-old William Korpisz, who was admitted to the Harriet Lane Home at Johns Hopkins Hospital with a fever and sore throat that proved to be polio. His ten-month-old brother and three-year-old sister also had the disease. There was the Farabaugh strain, for ten-year-old Robert Farabaugh, also of Baltimore, who came to the hospital on July 25, 1944, with a fever and a cough—a cough made weak by a dying diaphragm. By July 26 he was unable to swallow; by July 27 he was in an iron lung; by July 28 he was dead. There were untold numbers of other strains, drawn from untold numbers of other children, some of whom had died, but from each of whom a bit of blood or stool or tissue had been saved.

All these samples would have to be studied and typed. And though the method for doing so had long been established, it was monstrously complicated.

At its most basic, typing a virus involved infecting a monkey with a strain of polio whose type you already knew—say, Type I. When the monkey recovered—no sure thing—it would then be immune to all strains in the Type I group. You would next infect it with an unknown strain—say, the Greer or Bonnet or Randolph or Plum or Berg or who-knew-what other bug you had on hand. If the monkey resisted the new virus, it meant that that one was Type I too. If the monkey succumbed to the new infection, it meant the virus was either Type II or Type III. By now your monkey ought either to be dead or so sick it was no longer any good to you. This meant destroying that animal, moving on to another one that had been made immune to Type II, and repeating the experiment with the same unknown virus. If the virus still failed to match, you'd need yet another monkey, this one immune to Type III.

Making things even harder, all of the untyped viruses had different levels of lethality. One strain might be so powerful that a mere hint of it could knock a monkey flat; another might be so weak it would require a huge and concentrated slug of the bug to do any harm. If you didn't know the power of each unknown virus, you might think a monkey that exhibited no reaction to it was immune when in fact you had simply administered an underdose. This meant that before the typing work could even begin, thousands more monkeys and countless more months would have to be spent administering slowly increasing concentrations of virus to animal after animal to determine when the symptom-triggering threshold of each strain was crossed. This hit-or-miss method could require as many as 140 monkeys to determine the strength of a single strain before the typing itself could even begin.

That was the work most of the people in the room assumed confronted them. Planning such a vast research project would be a hard and often prickly business, at least in some measure because of Sabin.

Shortly after the discussions got under way, John Kessel, a researcher from the University of Southern California, presented some findings on the poliovirus's well-studied Lansing strain and its relationship to the equally common MV—or multivalent—strain, a combination of various strains first mixed together in 1914 and stored at the Rockefeller Institute

ever since to be used as a sort of viral constant with which all the best polio research up to then had been conducted. Kessel felt that the MV strains
and the Lansing were closely related, though two years earlier he had published a paper concluding just the opposite. Reserving the researcher's right
to rethink his findings, he had recently written an updated paper containing his new research, and had drawn up a checkerboard chart to illustrate
the known history of the two strains and many others. The chart was set
up at the front of the room; Sabin disagreed with many of its conclusions.

"Dr. Kessel," he said during the presentation, "a good many people,
like you, have indeed found that MV and Lansing are quite similar. But I
was wondering whether you had any data that might contradict that."

Kessel looked cross. Sabin was referring to his disavowed paper, making
it clear to anyone at the table who happened not to know it that Kessel had
already had to reverse his own mistaken conclusions once. Could his current theories be any more reliable?

"I have no more data," Kessel said crisply.

"It was clear from your paper—" Sabin began.

"Are you going back to that old paper?"

"That was published in 1946, if you consider that to be old."

Kessel pointed to his chart, filled with its new, revised data. "The findings
are different now," he said. "The Lansing serum did neutralize MV in mice.
That is it at the bottom of the checkerboard in the right-hand corner."

Sabin regarded the chart with a thin smile. "It is a nice table," he said.

Kessel started to answer and Weaver cut in. "Gentlemen," he said, "I
hate to cause this discussion to be temporarily suspended, but I notice a
few of you getting a little uneasy."

From his safe seat between the combatants, Salk took the bickering in
and, as he had promised himself he would, stayed mostly quiet. On the second day of the conference, however, a far more important conflict emerged.

Thomas Turner, another Hopkins scientist, had long been known to
have reservations about the monkey typing procedure, worrying that it was
simply too cumbersome to produce results in anything like a reasonable
time. He had been said to be considering an alternative method, but there
had not yet been a suitable opportunity to raise his idea. Early in the second

morning's proceedings, when Sabin was holding the floor with a broad discussion of the accepted typing technique, Turner seized his moment.

"Your premise is that you'll infect the animal first with a known virus
and then test an unknown type against that, correct?" Turner asked—a bit
rhetorically, since that was the only known way the work could be done.

"Yes," Sabin replied.

"I see," Turner said. "That is one way of doing it. But you could also do
it the other way around."

Salk jolted up in his chair. That was precisely the thought he had been
mulling. Since well before this morning's session began—since before he had
been formally invited to the Washington event, in fact—he had been toying
with a way to turn the entire, awkward typing technique on its head and, in
the process, simplify it dramatically. He broke his self-imposed silence.

"In line with what Dr. Turner points out—" Salk said.

"I want to get clear what Dr. Turner meant myself," Sabin interrupted
dismissively.

Salk immediately fell quiet. But what Dr. Turner meant was evident.
The thing that made the typing procedure so time-consuming, to say
nothing of monkey-consuming, was the business of testing the strength of
each virus first—measuring the so-called infectious titer. But while viruses
could be weak or strong, highly infective or just barely so, one thing about
which they did not differ nearly so much was their ability to generate antibodies—their so-called antigenic titer. A particular polio strain might be
too feeble to cause symptoms at anything but the highest doses, but as long
as there were enough virus particles present for the body to detect at all,
the immune system would still produce a flood of antibodies, no fewer
than it would produce in the face of a far more powerful strain.

Suppose—Turner, Salk, and a few others had wondered—you reversed
the typing work, infecting a healthy monkey with a small dose of an unknown polio virus first—a dose less likely to make it sick. Whether or not
the animal did come down with the disease, it would surely muster its antibody response. You could then challenge the monkey with a standard,
disease-causing shot of a known virus, say a Type I, whose precise infectivity level was already well established. If your animal resisted infection, the

unknown type was also Type I. If not, you would have to repeat the experiment, to determine if it was II or III. This work would still be tedious, but at least you could start right in on it, skipping all the infectivity testing and saving the 140 additional monkeys per strain. Salk's own back-of-the-envelope calculations suggested that the typing program the NFIP was considering, which would take three years using the original technique, might take just a single year with the reverse method.

"I want to get clear what Dr. Turner meant," Sabin now repeated. "You test a known virus against an unknown inoculation without having to determine your infectious titer first?"

"Yes, essentially," Turner said. "It could make things much easier."

"It could," Salk agreed, jumping in again. "In view of the fact that it makes very little difference how much virus you use to infect the animal at first—"

"It makes a great deal of difference," Sabin interrupted.

"But the question isn't how much virus is present in the blood," Salk persisted, "it's how much antibody. That's the relevant measure, isn't it?"

"Now, Dr. Salk," Sabin said airily, "you should know better than to ask a question like that."

Salk said nothing. There was an awkward shifting in the room as the other men watched him to see if he'd answer. But Salk maintained his silence. It wasn't scientific reasoning that would hold sway in this exchange, but scientific swordsmanship, a game for which he had little affinity. He would concede the moment, but in his own mind, he wouldn't concede the scientific point. The foundation's typing work was vitally important, and he'd be honored to perform it. But he'd perform it the way he thought best. The results he achieved—better, faster, more reliable—would prove him right.

Jonas Salk kept his eyes fixed on Albert Sabin and then dipped his head slightly. Sabin nodded back and the debate resumed—this time with Salk merely listening.

The typing committee concluded its meeting later that afternoon, resolving, ultimately, that either the direct or reverse typing method would be acceptable, with each of the four labs participating in the work free to try either one. There was nonetheless little doubt that three of the labs would choose the traditional technique—nor much doubt about who the exception would be.

After most such high-level gatherings, the NFIP headquarters circulated minutes of the discussions to make sure all the particiants agreed with the way they'd been quoted. Since the transcripts would become part of the foundation's permanent records, and since this had not been a sworn legal proceeding, it was understood that the scientists should comb through those records, eliminating any awkward or impolitic moments. The scientists themselves were expected to do that combing, and while the foundation officials provided no specific guidelines, they did make it clear that they'd be disappointed if any transcripts were returned to them with the unpleasant bits still remaining.

Salk received his minutes in the mail, opened the envelope, and pulled out a sheaf of papers that included all the times he had spoken up during the meeting. It was a small stack—certainly smaller than Sabin's or Weaver's or even Francis's would be. He riffled through sheets and stopped at the point at which he and Sabin had had their exchange. He read his first remark.

"In view of the fact that it makes very little difference how much virus you use . . ." he had begun his argument. That, he knew, was precisely the kind of directness the foundation might not want from its newest member. Dr. Sabin was a veteran, Dr. Salk a conscriptee. Salk scribbled his proposed change.

"In view of the *possibility* that it *may* make very little difference how much virus is used . . ." the new, more diffident Salk said.

Flipping quickly through the transcript, he found one or two similarly barbed bits and smoothed them over. Then he slid the amended transcript into a fresh envelope addressed to the foundation, and turned back to his more pressing work. Science was a nonnegotiable business, but politics was evidently something else entirely. Only one of the two held any appeal for him.

There was no real reason for John Enders to keep poliovirus in his
freezer. He certainly didn't plan to do any work with it and might
not even have remembered that he had it at all. One day, however, someone reminded him it was there. When that happened, Enders
changed the world.

The research lab Enders ran at Harvard University's Boston Children's
Hospital was known for turning out first-rate work. It was hard to pick up
a journal or textbook without seeing a chapter, a paper, or at least an interesting letter Enders had contributed. It was even more of a delight to listen to him speak. Given the precision scientists had to bring to their work,
they were not an especially lyrical bunch. Not so with Enders.

A trim little man favoring tweed coats, bow ties, and vests, he'd earned a
master's degree in English from Harvard in 1922 and then, at age twenty-

five, set about pursuing a Ph.D. in philology, the study of languages. He was well suited to that discipline. When Enders spoke, he held you fast—his words sometimes ice-like in their clarity and glint, other times playful little puffs of meringue. In either event, they were extraordinary.

But philology, he soon discovered, was too arcane to keep him engaged, a narrow field with no real impact on the world around him. "I mouth the strange syllables of ten forgotten languages," a dispirited Enders wrote to a friend shortly after embarking on his new career, "letting my spirits fail, my youth pass."

Finally, in 1927, all that changed. That year, Enders befriended the widely admired Hans Zinsser, a professor of bacteriology at Harvard and one of the school's finest instructors. Zinsser recognized in Enders a crackling intellect that he was convinced was less suited to the humanities than to the sciences. Enders—restless anyway—agreed, and with a suddenness that surprised even him, turned his attentions away from language and toward bacteriology, earning a Ph.D. in the field.

Enders's professional transformation—"this antipodal revolution of my studies," he liked to call it—excited him as language never had. From 1931 to 1946 he worked with Zinsser, principally studying how to grow pathogens and other microorganisms outside the body. In 1946, he set up his own Harvard lab to continue that line of work.

The research Enders was doing was vitally important. Since so many of the known viruses grew only in the living bodies of humans or animals, the accepted method for cultivating the bugs for study was exceedingly complex and time-consuming, requiring scientists to breed or buy a lot of rats or monkeys or dogs, infect them, kill them, and then drain their blood or tease out their tissue for the pathogenic samples they needed. How much simpler it would be to grow your viruses in a sterile glass, as you could with most bacteria.

To help come up with ways to do that, Enders had hired two promising young physicians, Thomas Weller and Frederick Robbins, both also of Harvard. Weller and Robbins had been classmates and roommates in school and then gone off to serve in the war, Robbins in a virus lab in Italy,

Weller in a similar facility in Puerto Rico. Afterward, they returned to Harvard hoping for a topflight research post, and were thrilled when Enders provided one.

One of the more common viruses Enders and his two assistants decided to tackle was varicella—ordinary chicken pox—trying to determine if it might be possible to grow it in a mixture of skin and muscle tissue taken from miscarried fetuses. Mixing the right growth medium was the key to the work, and one afternoon as they were preparing it, Weller raised an altogether different—and altogether surprising—idea.

"Suppose we tried a little polio too?" he asked. "We've got some Lansing strain in the freezer. Might as well use it up."

Even coming from a greenhorn researcher, this was an unexpected suggestion. Poliovirus, as everyone knew, not only couldn't grow outside the body, it couldn't even grow outside of nerve tissue within the body. Polio cultivated in the laboratory could grow only in tissue taken from the spines of monkeys, humans, and occasionally rats. In 1935, no less a pair of researchers than Peter Olitsky and Albert Sabin of Rockefeller University had proven this point. They extracted tissue from pristine human embryos and tried growing samples of the MV polio strain in cells taken from the brain, spinal cord, lungs, liver, kidneys, and spleen. The virus failed entirely in all but the brain and cord material. So painstakingly conducted was the experiment and so well reported were the results that Sabin and Olitsky's conclusion—that poliovirus could grow only in nervous system tissue—became one of the unshakable bits of polio dictum.

This was problematic for any researchers dreaming of one day developing a polio vaccine, since whatever virus they used in their work would have to be absolutely pure, uncontaminated by the extraneous monkey tissue that helped make Kolmer's and Park and Brodie's preparations such disasters. Even if a pure vaccine was somehow developed, you'd still need to figure out a way to mass-produce it, something that would require untold gallons of pure virus, enough to manufacture inoculations for tens of millions of children and still have plenty left over for all the new babies who would ever come along. You couldn't do that growing polio in monkey spines.

Enders, who had no reason to believe the accepted polio wisdom was wrong, nevertheless figured there was no harm in letting his subordinates look into the question, giving them the go-ahead to try to grow a little poliovirus using the same medium they had prepared for chicken pox. With Enders overseeing, they first mixed the virus with the culture, waited a few days, and then injected the mix into healthy monkeys. If the animals got sick, the virus had indeed grown in the culture. If they stayed healthy, it hadn't. To the researchers' astonishment, the monkeys indeed came down with a full and florid case of polio.

To confirm their findings, Enders slid a sample of the cell culture under a microscope. The virus itself would be invisible even under the most powerful magnification, but the infected cells wouldn't be. Any of them that had been sickened by polio would be misshappen and swollen, filling with multiplying virus particles until they finally burst and spilled their toxic mess out to the healthy cells around them. Enders peeked into the scope, and to his astonishment, spotted just that spreading contagion. Trying to contain himself, he nodded to Weller and Robbins and uttered just one word: "Cytopathogenicity."

Robbins smiled at the word. It meant nothing more than cell sickness, but until this moment, it had not existed. It was one of Enders's linguistic confections and Robbins thought it delightful.

Quickly, the three men expanded their experiment. They tried growing polio on fibroblasts—the precursors of the body's connective tissue—and it worked. They then tried fully mature, nonreproductive tissue, seeding human kidney cells with live polio, and once again the virus held and grew. Finally, they turned back to animal tissue, using a kidney once more but this time harvesting it from a monkey. While simian spinal tissue had caused such severe reactions in children receiving the Park and Brodie and the Kolmer vaccines, simian tissue from other parts of the monkey's body might, the Harvard team speculated, be tolerated a little better. Once more, the experiment succeeded.

Now the problem was nailed. Pure poliovirus could be farmed, and it could be done in a predictable way with safe tissue taken from animal donors—far, far fewer of those animals than had been needed before.

Sabin and Olitsky had been wrong—tripped up, it seemed, by a peculiarity of the MV strain of polio. That strain could indeed not grow outside of nervous tissue, but other strains could. A polio vaccine might still be the stuff of fantasy, but any research team that chose to undertake the job would now have a far easier—and safer—time of it.

The three men would write up their findings and publish them as quickly as they could. Even Enders would probably not be able to find much room for poetry in the paper. But the scientists who read it, they trusted, would see the elegance all the same.

The monkeys easily outnumbered the chickens in Jonas Salk's virus lab. The mice, to be sure, outnumbered the monkeys. And any one of those species outnumbered the humans. That was saying something, since by the middle of 1948, there were easily two dozen scientists working in the busy new laboratory, and that number showed every sign of growing even further.

In the few months since the Pittsburgh team was tapped by the NFIP for the polio-typing project, the lab had exploded with activity. Mayor Lawrence had made good on his promise of more space, providing Salk not only with all of the square-footage he might need in the hospital basement but also with bigger, brighter, airier quarters on the hospital's bustling first floor. Thanks to the money that suddenly seemed plentiful, all that work space was stuffed with animals, new equipment, and even modest new decor.

The coveted morgue was now wholly Salk's and hummed with sterilizers and incubators. The room itself had been completely restored to accommodate all the new hardware. Freshly run wiring snaked behind the walls, new lights blazed overhead, new plumbing pumped water to lab stations. A little cookstove and a small refrigerator were installed in the suddenly cheery place so that the technicians could take their lunch breaks at a tidy little kitchen table where the autopsy tables used to stand. The only thing kept just as it had been was the great bank of morgue drawers that had once held human remains and whose prodigious capacity now made them handy places to stash supplies, spare parts, and documents. The rest of the basement was similarly well restored and equipped, as was the new first-floor space, which had been mostly given over to offices for Salk and his senior staffers.

It was Salk himself who oversaw the restoration of the entire facility, spending his days with painters, plumbers, electricians, and carpenters. He supervised as walls were demolished and built, partitions were configured and installed. He drew up budgets and met them, drew down funds and spent them, all under the scrutinizing eye of the NFIP, the Mellon Foundation, and the university itself. All those benefactors wanted to ensure that the money they were providing was being well used, and Salk devoted hours every day to the tedious business of demonstrating to them that it was.

"Dear Dr. McEllroy," he wrote to the dean early in the restoration work, "You will recall that steel partitions ordered last spring through the kindness of the university were to cost $4,058. The cost of the partitions will now be $4,481 due to problems with supply and delivery. I regret any inconvenience this $423 adjustment might cause you."

After a day filled with such dime-and-dollar detail, Salk noticed that even when he was at home at night, he had trouble turning his mind purely to leisure. His family noticed too.

"What are you doing?" Donna asked him late one evening as she came into the kitchen and found that he had pulled the oven away from the wall and was busy cleaning the back of it, using a toothpick to scrape away years of accumulated grease from the grooves in the screwheads.

"Cleaning the oven," he answered. "You've been after me to do it for weeks."

"The inside," she said, "you only had to do the inside."

Salk shrugged. "This side was dirty too."

Even when the improvements in his lab—and the tidiness of his home—were well in hand, Salk had untold other chores to occupy him. Foremost on his mind was the job of hiring his senior staff. Salk may have cared little for the institutional politics of running a lab, but he found himself actually looking forward to the prospect of hiring and managing his team. His sometimes awkward social skills would be less likely to cause him trouble in the context of the laboratory, where the rules were well established and the lines of authority were clear—particularly when he was the first in that line.

The most important if least scientific of the vacant positions Salk would have to fill was that of administrative manager, someone who would handle the operation of the lab, overseeing every aspect of it except the scientific research itself. Salk placed an ad for the job and after interviewing only a handful of candidates believed he had found precisely the person he was looking for in Lorraine Friedman, a tall, young Pittsburgh woman who projected a rare and appealing blend of confidence and deference from the moment she walked in the door. Friedman impressed Salk with a crispness that never seemed brittle, a whimsy that never seemed frivolous, a true interest in the clerical nature of her prospective work, but a clear eyed understanding of the manifestly larger goals the lab was trying to achieve. To Salk's own surprise, he offered her the job before she even left the office. To his greater surprise, she hesitated, saying that she'd have to go home and discuss the matter with her parents.

That night, the phone rang in the Salk home. It was Lorraine Friedman's mother calling to speak not to Dr. Salk but to Donna Salk. Jonas looked perplexed, but Donna shooed him away from the phone, understanding better than her husband could that if a mother wanted to get a feel for the character of a man who might be playing such an instructive role in her child's life, it was another mother she needed to talk to. The two women spoke at length, and before the call was done, Donna had invited the young Lorraine for a get-acquainted dinner. The girl came to dine that very weekend, and during the course of the meal it became clear that the inquisitive nature of Lorraine's mother had been inherited by the daughter.

"I'm fascinated by your polio work," Lorraine said to Salk, an opening conversational bid that was clearly meant to be less a declaration than a gentle question. Salk obligingly described the typing project.

"Your Michigan work sounds interesting too," Lorraine said next. So Salk described his influenza studies.

"What must medical school have been like?" the girl asked as well. Salk gave her an accounting of his years at NYU.

Finally, when the evening was over and Friedman was gone, Salk turned to Donna with a smile. "That went well, don't you agree?" he asked.

"Yes," Donna said. "I think you got the job."

More challenging than finding administrative talent was the job of finding scientific talent. One of Salk's earliest, best, and least likely recruits was Byron Bennett, a brusque, stocky army major and lab technician he had met during his influenza days. Bennett, who worked both in flu and typhus control during the war, never went by the title doctor, principally because he wasn't one, and he never boasted of his scientific degrees, principally because he didn't have any. What he did have was one of the sharpest scientific minds and the best set of natural lab skills Salk had ever encountered. He also had a fierce appetite for alcohol. The drink and the smarts were always at war within Bennett, but Salk figured the good far outweighed the bad, and with close supervision and lots of hard work he could help Bennett bring his single weakness under control while bringing his considerable strengths to the polio project.

Salk called Bennett to Pittsburgh and offered him the position, and Bennett accepted. Salk was still uncomfortable with the business of currying favor among his superiors at the university, but he seemed to have an intuitive feel for cultivating the trust of his subordinates. It was the same careful attention he extended to the waiter in a restaurant or the workman in his home, though in the workplace it could pay much higher dividends. With the fragile Byron Bennett now in his employ, Salk decided that within the walls of the lab, his new hire would always be addressed as Major Bennett, a respectful tip of the hat to a man who otherwise had no honorific in the scientific world.

Also joining Salk's inner circle was Julius Youngner, a twenty-eight-year-old M.D. he'd met at the University of Michigan who had made it clear to Salk that he'd be happy to move East with him should a spot in the Pittsburgh lab ever open up. Youngner had a reputation for generosity in the lab, showing more willingness than the average ambitious researcher to share what he knew with other ambitious researchers.

In addition to Youngner, Salk hired zoologist and microbiologist Elsie Ward, who had been working as an industrial chemist before answering Salk's ad. She'd impressed him with her breadth of scientific knowledge and a near-gardener's understanding of the critical business of coaxing tissue cultures and virus colonies to grow. Francis Yurochko was hired as a senior technician who would help oversee the care of the animals. Salk also took on Percival Bazeley, an M.D. and onetime tank commander in the Australian army whom Salk also knew from the war and who showed not only a physician's feel for medicine but a magician's feel for hardware—a skill that would be essential in a laboratory that would be so dependent on its machinery.

Finally, Salk hired James Lewis, a bacteriologist with a Ph.D. in philosophy and biology. Lewis had worked in the pharmaceutical industry over the years and would now be overseeing all of the virus lab's animal experiments. On Salk's team, there might be no position more important.

The precise population of animals that would take up residence in Lewis's part of the lab was not certain at first, but the jobs they would do had been well planned. The chickens, rats, and mice would be used principally for experiments in viral culturing and chemical toxicity. The monkeys would be used for the far more complicated typing business. Most of the monkeys that would live—and die—in the virus lab would be Java monkeys, which the scientists more properly knew as cynomolgus monkeys. They were quick, curious, personable animals, bigger than a large cat but not much. The rest would be rhesus monkeys, just as valuable in the kind of research Salk was doing but a little harder to come by. Both types would cost about $35 per animal, not including delivery, depending on where you bought them, who had shipped them, and whether they'd been bred in captivity or caught in the wild.

Such a huge population of monkeys would be required by all four labs conducting the typing study that even before the work began, the NFIP established its own monkey farm in Pritchardville, South Carolina. The new facility would be a place where the animals could be bred, fed, and carefully raised. Then when they were grown, they'd be disease-tested and tattooed and shipped out to the labs that would put them to work.

That work would be unpleasant. Whether you favored the reverse-typing technique Salk advocated or the traditional method Albert Sabin and others preferred, getting a polio bug into a monkey would have to be done the same nasty way. The animal would be placed on a scale and then anesthetized with a fixed bit of Nembutal for every five pounds of body weight. When the monkey was unconscious, it would be stretched on a board. Its head would be shaved and a chin strap affixed to keep it stationary in the event of an involuntary flinch. A small hole would then be drilled in the skull and the virus would be injected directly into the brain. The head would be cleaned and bandaged and the animal would be returned to its cage, where it would be observed and kept warm while it remained under sedation.

In the week or two that followed, the scientists would watch the animals for signs of sickness. All labs measured the extent of the infection in their own way. Salk had developed his own system for grading monkey paralysis on a scale of 0 to 5. A score of 5 represented a normal limb; 4 meant that an arm or leg appeared weak but could still be used for jumping or climbing; 3 indicated a limb that could be used only poorly; 2 was a limb that could still be raised against gravity but could do little else; 1 was a limb that displayed only flickers of movement at the joints; 0 was complete paralysis. Each monkey's limb-by-limb score would be recorded on its chart in the order of right arm first, then left arm, then right leg, and finally left leg. A card in the door of each animal's cage would be updated as the disease worsened—a score of 5-4-1-3 giving way perhaps to a 3-2-1-1 and then a 2-1-0-0—a clinical way of recording a deeply unsettling process. When the workmen arrived to install the cages—with doors that opened and closed with a cold metal rattle—the place began to look equal parts lab and jail, an appearance that would only grow sharper when the monkeys were in residence and began to jump around in the clattering boxes.

There was, Salk knew, a cure for such anticipatory remorse. Now and then, when he had an idle moment, he would leave his lab and go up to the hospital's third, fourth, and fifth floors, where the wards of polio children lay. The children too were well and truly jailed—some in iron lungs, all of them in enfeebled bodies that had quit working as they should. It was the zero-sum nature of the virus game that the only way to prevent more blameless children from streaming into the upper floors was to sicken and kill the blameless monkeys in the basement. Somewhere, perhaps, was the person who could tease out all the moral threads of that arrangement, but polio scientists, as a rule, could not turn their minds to the task. Once the virus was beaten, all the creatures—the ones upstairs and the ones below—could be left in peace. Until someone offered a better deal, this was the one they would have to take.

Returning to his lab, Salk did resolve that there was a tiny kindness he could do for the animals in his care. All researchers performing NFIP work were required to buy not only their monkeys from the Pritchardville farm but their monkey feed too. The mix came in 25-pound bags that cost $2.50 each and consisted of a combination of seed wheat, soybean, milk powder, table salt, bonemeal, and vitamins. The dry preparation would be mixed with water and pressed into a half-pound cake that would be presented to the animals once a day. The regimen was guaranteed to keep the animals well nourished, but nothing more.

As some labs had already learned, cynomolgus monkeys—far and away the most common ones that would be used in the labs—were a bit less hearty than rhesus monkeys, and often needed a little more than the prescribed portion of feed so as not to lose weight. There were any number of ways to make up the difference, but in Salk's lab the extra calories would not be provided with a dry biscuit or an extra dollop of food paste but with bananas, melons, and other fresh fruit—a small adjustment of the moral scales but an adjustment nonetheless.

John Troan was a journalist who knew a good story when he saw one. Jonas Salk, he feared, was nothing of the kind.

Troan was an inexhaustible science reporter for the *Pittsburgh Press* who, in the ten years he'd been with the paper, had made himself something of a lay expert on any medical topic that had even a shred of newsworthiness and a lot that didn't. Given what he'd had to overcome in his earlier life, what he'd accomplished professionally was that much more impressive.

Troan was the son of an Austro-Hungarian immigrant who worked in the Pennsylvania coal mines and began each day with a jigger of Prohibition moonshine, a morning tonic that would allow him to hack just enough of the miner's asthma out of his lungs to make him fit for another day in the pit. As the head of the house, he worked hard in the hole, but no harder than his wife, who brought nine babies into the world, only to see six of them die in infancy. She nonetheless had the scrap to produce a tenth, John, who was born in 1918.

John found early on that he loved both the written word and the idea of steady pay, and at age twenty figured that a job in journalism was a happy way to satisfy both appetites. He was hired by the *Press* in 1938, and on December 19 of that year he published his first story, an account of a comparatively ordinary gypsy wedding—ordinary, that is, except for the fact that the groom had died of pneumonia two days earlier. The deceased, who had loved his intended fiercely, had declared at the time of his engagement that if he should somehow not live to see his wedding day, he would want the ceremonies to proceed anyway. And so they did, with eight bridesmaids, six ushers, three trainbearers, and a twenty-five-piece gypsy band trooping into the church for a thirty-five-minute ceremony. When it was done, the wedding party trooped back out, leading a hearse in a slow march to a nearby cemetery, where the groom was lowered into the ground and the bride tossed her bouquet onto the coffin top. John Troan—then known as John Troanovitch—was there to cover it all, filing a thirty-sentence story that, to his delight, the *Press* published almost exactly as he'd written it. If the editors found sufficient space for the entirety of Troanovitch's prose, however, they did not find it for the entirety of his name, which they shortened to John Troan, promising it would make him both more memorable to readers and more popular with typesetters. Whether it did or not, the name stuck fast.

Troan's way around a sentence and his feel for the human condition convinced his editors that he'd be best suited to covering the sciences, particularly medicine. While such a beat initially struck Troan as comparatively soft, he soon came both to love it and to work hard at it. He made himself an indefatigable presence at fifteen area hospitals, three regional universities, and a research clinic in the Pittsburgh vicinity. The stories he collected there captivated his readers.

There was the one about the habitual burglar who, faced with a possible life sentence as a repeat offender, elected instead to have the frontal lobe of his brain partially severed to extinguish the criminal compulsion, a cure that worked only for a few years before he returned to the business of burgling—his reconfigured brain evidently working just as well, or just as ill, as it ever had. There was the one about Jock Sutherland, the coach of the Pittsburgh Steelers, who vanished suddenly from his home and was later discovered wandering in a stupor in northwest Kentucky between the towns of Bandana and Monkey's Eyebrow, suffering from an inoperable brain tumor. There was the story of the sixteen-year-old girl at the Western Psychiatric Institute who inadvertently swallowed a needle while she was sewing, requiring doctors to send to the Westinghouse Research Laboratories for a specially milled magnet on a string, so that the girl could swallow that too and doctors peering into her stomach with a fluoroscope could fish out the menacing needle before the mindless process of intestinal peristalsis could move it even deeper into her gut.

Troan was pointed to a fair number of his scoops by tipsters he cultivated, none more valuable than Campbell Moses, assistant dean of the University of Pittsburgh Medical School, who liked and respected the young reporter. In the spring of 1948, during one of Troan's routine Friday afternoon visits to Campbell's office, the assistant dean offered him an unremarkable-sounding lead.

"Why don't you go see Jonas Salk?" he recommended.

"Who's that?" Troan asked, fairly certain that if the man were anyone at all he'd have heard of him by then.

"He's the young whiz the dean brought in from the University of Michigan. He's doing some work for the polio foundation. How about you say hello to him and tell him Moses sent you?"

Troan did as the assistant dean suggested, trudging over to the hospital lab and presenting himself to Salk's secretary, a serious-looking Miss Friedman.

"I'm here to see Dr. Salk," he said.

"Who are you?"

"John Troan."

The secretary seemed unmoved.

"From the *Pittsburgh Press.*"

Still nothing.

"Moses sent me," Troan added, with a roll of his eyes.

Friedman nodded and showed him into Salk's office.

John Troan liked Jonas Salk from the moment the two men shook hands. The doctor did not leap up to greet him with that excess of enthusiasm he'd learned to recognize in ink-hungry researchers. Nor did Salk remain unnaturally cool, glowering at Troan from under his brows as scientists did when they were so protective of their research they wouldn't even tell you whether they were practicing cardiology, hematology, or physics—much less just what sort of project they were engaged in at the moment.

Before Troan could even ask about the polio research Salk's lab was pursuing, Salk began describing a little mopping-up work he was performing for the army's influenza board. It was a project that might not seem exciting to most folks but one that Salk himself found fascinating. Troan asked if he might hear about it.

One of the problems with his influenza vaccine, Salk explained, was that it sometimes failed to stay in the body long enough to do much good. Get even a high dose of the potion into the hard currents of the bloodstream and it would sometimes be cleared out so fast it would have no time to wake up the immune system as it was supposed to. The answer to the problem was something known as an adjuvant. Thicken the vaccine with a benign substance like mineral oil, and the more viscous mix would not be able to break down so easily in the blood. What's more, the oil would act as a sort of intentional irritant, a cinder in the eye of the immune system that would cause it to churn out even more antibodies than it normally would.

Salk, as luck would have it, was traveling to Fort Dix, New Jersey, just this weekend to try out a flu vaccine fortified with a mineral oil adjuvant on 15,000 soldiers. The results of the experiment could have implications not only for influenza but for any other disease for which Salk or anyone else might later try to develop a vaccine—including polio. Would Troan be interested in writing about the impending trip and the vaccine science behind it? Troan allowed that he would.

"My only condition," Salk said, "is that I'd like to see what you write before you publish it."

Troan frowned. The doctor might have his rules, but the reporter had his own.

"Look," Troan said, "I'll make you a deal. I'm going to report this in the Sunday edition. You get a copy and read it when it comes out. If I foul it up, you never have to talk to me again."

Salk, dubiously, stood and shook his hand.

Two days later, while driving back from New Jersey, Salk took a detour to Atlantic City, the only nearby town big enough that it might carry a newspaper from distant Pittsburgh. He walked the boardwalk until he found a newsstand that indeed had a copy of the Sunday *Press*.

The next day, a telegram arrived for John Troan at his desk in his Pittsburgh newsroom. "You did a splendid job," the telegram read. "Jonas E. Salk."

Troan was pleased. He suspected that the young doctor might have at least a few more good stories in him.

Occasional detours into influenza work notwithstanding, the typing project in the Pittsburgh virus lab took little more than the year Jonas Salk had predicted it would, getting under way in earnest in the late summer of 1948 and wrapping up in the early fall of 1949. But it was a year that took a lot from the staff.

Most nights, the lights of the lab burned until well after dark, with Salk and his team regularly clocking twelve-hour days over the course of six- or seven-day weeks. All the scientists involved in the research exceeded even

Salk's high expectations. Lewis, who had plenty to do overseeing the autopsying and tissue-culturing of monkeys, also assumed iron control of the day-to-day operation of the animal quarters as a whole: Cages were regularly inspected and compulsively cleaned; the health of the monkeys was meticulously monitored; meals were prepared strictly according to specifications, with Lewis often running spot checks on consistency and freshness.

Bazeley brought similar care to the lab hardware, modifying chick incubators so that they could double as culture incubators, designing and building new flash evaporators and culture agitators from the ground up. Bennett too—with a little deft handling from Salk—excelled. If the Major occasionally showed up for work with the rheumy eyes and mottled face of a man who had fairly poisoned himself with alcohol the night before, he never once had so much as a whiff of fresh drink about him while he was on the job. Salk would keep a close watch on him on his bad days, look forward to his skill and his company on his good days, and do what he could to see that the second exceeded the first.

Most impressive of all was the gentle whip hand Lorraine Friedman took to the day-to-day operations of the lab. From the moment she arrived, Friedman began studying the politics of the place and learned who required the most access to her boss, who required the least, and who Salk himself most needed or wanted to see. She familiarized herself with vendors, donors, and administrators. Before supplies needed to be ordered, she anticipated it; when Salk double-booked appointments, she knew whom to cancel. She learned too about her boss's other inconvenient quirks: When a lab assistant appeared with a scientific problem that needed solving, Salk would often puzzle out an answer on the spot, then take the assistant's notebook and scribble out whatever solution they had reached. He would then tear out the sheet of paper, hand it over to the young scientist, and absentmindedly keep the notebook. Over that year, many a timid technician forlornly watched a valued notebook vanish into the cluttered top drawer of Jonas Salk's desk. It was left to Friedman to collect the accumulated notebooks from the drawer at the end of each week and make a walking tour of the lab, returning them all to their rightful owners.

With extraneous administrative matters off his mind, Salk was able to concentrate wholly on the typing work, overseeing an operation that was as efficient as it was scientifically precise. Virus strains would come into the lab under a gaggle of meaningless names, undergo the reverse-typing technique Salk favored, and leave identified as poliovirus Type I, II, or III. No sooner would the team finish one batch of bugs than Salk would receive a letter from Weaver containing new ones.

"I am attaching hereto a list of viruses that I should be pleased if your laboratory would titer at your convenience," Weaver would politely write.

Salk pleased Weaver indeed, and within thirteen months had exhausted all the strains the national headquarters had set aside for him to study. There might still be more to come as more suspicious strains were drawn from more boys and girls around the country, but so far, the results were promising: Not one of the viruses Salk or anyone else had studied even hinted at the presence of the feared fourth type of polio. The toll in monkeys all this work exacted was fearful, of course: In Salk's lab, more than 1,800 animals had been infected and killed so far. This, however, was just a fraction of the total of 17,000 that the foundation projected for all four labs participating in the typing program. Salk's comparative economy of animals—far fewer than his allotted 4,250—was a direct result of the reverse-typing method.

Salk's speed was such that by the middle of 1949, he and his lab staff once again found themselves with little to do. The NFIP was no doubt favorably inclined to bankroll future studies they might want to undertake. But it was not the foundation's responsibility to recommend what those studies ought to be. It was the prospective grant recipients themselves who were expected to dream up interesting avenues for work and present them to the New York headquarters for approval. If Salk didn't come up with one such avenue soon, he could easily slip from the funding queue. Almost immediately, an entirely new project suggested itself.

Isabel Morgan, whom Salk had met at the typing meeting in Washington, had been busying herself at Johns Hopkins University with what was being described as a first formulation of a possible polio vaccine—and a killed-virus vaccine at that. Morgan's work generated only mild enthusiasm among NFIP members, representing a stress fracture in the foundation's belief that live vaccines held an advantage over killed ones—not to mention the advantage therapies or cures could hold over any vaccine at all.

Nonetheless, what Morgan had done was intriguing. Exterminating poliovirus cultures with doses of formalin, she injected them into chimpanzees and found that the preparation indeed boosted the animals' antibody levels and appeared to protect them from subsequent infection with a live virus. That ought to have been big news, but nobody—Morgan included—believed it was the entire story.

First of all, polio was not a natural sickness of chimpanzees, and anything that happened in the systems of such unintended hosts was not necessarily directly translatable to humans. What's more, any immunity that did develop could be a fleeting thing, protecting the chimps against a later dose or two of live virus but failing altogether as a permanent shield. Finally, while formalin was undeniably lethal to poliovirus, the power of that toxicity and the best ways to take advantage of it remained a mystery. Nobody knew how much of the poison you'd have to use to kill the bug or how long and at what temperature the virus would have to soak to ensure that all of the pathogenic particles were indeed dead. If Morgan's crude vaccine worked at all, it might simply be because weakened but live viruses survived the formalin and were waking up the immune system. Still, there was no denying the fact that the work was worth investigating further.

More important than Morgan's study—and far more certain—was the announcement out of Harvard about the remarkable achievement of John Enders and his lab: growing poliovirus in culture. If Morgan was making even possible progress immunizing animals with viruses isolated the old way—from the minced spines of afflicted monkeys—what might it be possible to accomplish trying similar animal experiments with Enders' pristine viruses? Salk wondered. The key was getting ahold of Enders and petitioning him for a bit of his culture material.

Salk returned to his typewriter to compose an appeal not to Enders himself—who would probably ignore a voice shouting out from the NFIP wilderness—but to Weaver, who had far more ability to move scientific resources from place to place. Summoning up the blandishment skills he'd had to hone in two years of administrative work, he drafted a request that he hoped contained just the right balance of by-your-leaves and if-I-mays.

"If you could arrange for us to get some of Dr. Enders' material," he wrote after explaining his basic idea, "we would very much like to immunize some monkeys with it. You appreciate this is something we could do very easily along with the other work we are doing for the Foundation. Indeed, I believe you had mentioned something like this yourself in the course of a conversation we had some time ago, but we never did get back to it to arrange anything definitely."

Salk posted the letter to Weaver, and five days later he received a response. The research director wasn't biting.

"This is in response to your kind letter of September 7," Weaver wrote. "I feel certain Dr. Enders would be very happy to furnish you some tissue culture virus if you would care to ask him for it. Why don't you write him at the Children's Hospital?"

Salk winced. This was so much more than the mildly helpful advice it pretended to be. This was foundation code for no, for take a seat, for remember your place, please. Salk might be a promising player in the polio war, but he was only a single player—one of hundreds of game pieces Weaver had to arrange on his national map almost every day. The research director could not begin sliding one token ahead of the others simply because a scientist got itchy to try something new, particularly something as unproven as a killed-virus vaccine. Weaver's letter was as resounding a refusal as Salk was likely to get, made worse by the fact that he nonetheless invited Salk to go straight to Enders and seek an even more resounding one. Despite his better judgment, Salk did just that.

"Dear Dr. Enders," he wrote, "I do not want to intrude on any things you yourself might be doing or want to do with your new culture. I would like to offer, however, whatever help we can provide in determining its immunizing capacity in monkeys. If this sort of thing would interest you, I would be very happy to plan with you something that might be a joint study."

Enders was no more moved than Weaver. "You may be sure that all of us greatly appreciate your interest," the Harvard man sniffed to the Pittsburgh man, "but we are engaged in some pilot experiments of our own and I would prefer to have the results in hand before wishing anyone else to undertake any investigation. Should the results be encouraging, we might well be anxious to accept your kind offer."

Salk did not need to be told a third time. He was keeping very big company now, stalking very big game, and even with the collegiality Harry Weaver sought to foster, there was only so much help he could expect in the hunt. The NFIP might fund any reasonable project he chose to undertake, but it would be a project he and his team would have to conduct largely on their own. With the sting of the refusal from New York and Harvard fresh, he found himself more rather than less committed to try.

Shortly afterward, Salk wrote two more letters. The first was to Enders, thanking him for his prompt response and implicitly assuring him that he would not be troubling him again. The second was to Hamlin and Company Insurance Brokers in New York City. What, he wondered, would be the cost of life insurance for himself and a laboratory full of scientists working with the poliovirus? Hamlin wrote back promptly, informing him that such insurance would indeed be available, but the policies would be priced at a premium rate—about 20 percent above the usual charge. The company trusted Dr. Salk understood the risk in insuring people who would be so exposed to the possibility of lethal infection.

Dr. Salk assured Hamlin that he did understand. His team had spent the last year wading deep in the polio pool and he knew precisely how deadly it could be. He had sought a little assistance to wade deeper still, but it had not been forthcoming. Nonetheless, plans he was formulating now might provide another way. A little insurance somewhere down the line would probably be a good idea.

9

I t took more than 250 miles for Bill Kirkpatrick to lose his legs. But by the end of that long ride from his grandmother's home in Sunbury, Pennsylvania, to his own home in Pittsburgh, they were undeniably failing. Kirkpatrick didn't realize what was happening to him at the time. He felt fatigued and stiff, certainly, but that was to be expected, given all the exercising he'd been doing lately to bulk himself up for his school's football team.

Now, getting out of the car with his parents, the sixteen-year-old wondered if he might have overdone it. Not only was he feeling a creeping creakiness—especially in his neck and back—he also noticed that the skin of his abdomen had begun to feel strangely prickly, almost as if he'd been sunburned.

If Bill's problem wasn't an excess of exercise, he knew it might be a touch of typhoid fever. He had had a bout of the illness once before, when he was ten years old, and it had started much the same way. Until he was certain, however, he wouldn't mention the matter to his mother, who would surely make an unnecessary fuss. Instead, he'd simply climb into bed to see if he might be able to sleep the problem away.

Sleep, however, did not come easily. Bill sweated and thrashed, and when he did briefly doze off, he'd awaken feeling more, not less, fatigued. In the middle of the night, when he got out of bed to go to the bathroom, he found that his legs felt improbably weak.

When morning at last broke and Bill's mother did not hear the bustle of her boy getting ready for school, she came in to make sure he was awake. She was stunned at what she found. Bill was lying flat on his back, hot, damp, and struggling for breath. His eyes were rolled back in his head.

Terrified, she phoned the doctor, who promptly ordered an ambulance to take the boy to Municipal Hospital. Bill was listening to his mother's half of the conversation from down the hall. He wanted to tell her the problem was typhoid, except it was a terrible struggle merely to draw a breath, much less convert that breath into speech. So the boy stayed mostly silent as he was carried out of his bedroom and into the ambulance, the jouncing of the high-speed ride that followed sending jolts of pain through his frame. If this was typhoid fever, it was a savage case of it.

Bill held fast to the fiction of his typhoid for as long as he possibly could. He held to it as the emergency room doctors took him in hand and poked a long needle into his spine so that they could draw off fluid and see for themselves what the problem was. He held to it as they hurried him into a private room and attached a mask to his face that drizzled air into his lungs—air that did little to roll away the boulder that seemed to have settled on his chest. He held to it even as the weakness spread from his legs and chest to his arms and hands and his fever rose and broke and then rose again. Bill lived for three weeks in and out of that fever-cloud, until at last the storm in his system subsided and he emerged spent and gaunt—his breath weak and ragged, all of his limbs but his left arm paralyzed.

Kirkpatrick was eventually wheeled from his private room into a far larger, brighter Municipal Hospital ward. It was filled with children and other adolescents, held upright largely with the aid of leather and buckles.

Only then did Kirkpatrick fully accept that his typhoid was instead a case of infantile paralysis—one that had ridden the road of his nervous system straight up to the base of his brain, not only crippling his limbs but nearly taking his breath. Of all the ruined bodies in the ward, his was one of the most ruined of all.

It would be months before Bill Kirkpatrick would leave the polio ward. When he did, he, like others before him, would be sent to the D. T. Watson rehabilitation home in nearby Leetsdale, Pennsylvania, to see if the resident doctors might be able to give him back some of what the virus had taken away. He expected the disease would probably keep his legs. His lungs and his arms he'd fight to get back.

10

Public speaking was never something Salk looked forward to doing. And addressing a group of fretful parents filled with questions about the dawning polio season—questions he couldn't answer without leaving them more fretful still—was the worst kind of public speaking of all.

The arrival of June meant the arrival of the heat, and in 1950 it looked as though the steamy months would bring some nasty numbers with them—at least if the previous two polio seasons had been any indication. In 1948, during a summer that was otherwise unremarkable, 27,726 American children had been struck by the disease, nearly triple the figure from the year before. In 1949, that already alarming toll exploded again, to 42,033. It was a number that was almost impossible to contemplate— equivalent to filling every seat in Chicago's Wrigley Field with children, adding 3,000 more standing in the aisles, and then paralyzing them all.

Now, in early June of 1950, before summer had even truly begun, the first feverish children were already starting to stream into doctors' offices and emergency rooms, portending a terrible July and August. The Schenley High School parent-teacher association thus called the young polio researcher who'd been covered by the local papers and asked if he could offer some encouragement.

Salk had no idea how to reassure the families in the short term. But he was actually feeling a lot more optimistic than he ever had before about where all his polio work might be taking him over time.

When Enders turned down his request for polio culture, Salk decided he would simply have to make his own. The Pittsburgh team would need the proper equipment for work of this kind, and the most important piece of all would be the clumsy hunks of rotating hardware known as roller tubes. Essentially large, drumlike devices with holes for holding hundreds of test tubes, roller tubes were essential for keeping polio cultures properly mixed and incubated, rotating the samples in a slow rotisserie of ten to twelve revolutions per hour for eight straight days at a constant temperature of 95 to 96 degrees.

Salk guessed he'd need a lot of roller tubes for the work he had to do and expected they'd cost at least $7,500. Shortly after receiving his refusal from Weaver and Enders, he thus went to Dean McEllroy, hoping that the university would be willing to cut the necessary check. McEllroy looked surprised at Salk's request. The NFIP had already pumped more than $300,000 into the Pittsburgh lab. Surely so large a bounty could cover so small a charge. But Salk made it clear that that money was off limits.

"The foundation isn't sponsoring this research," he said.

McEllroy was almost certainly pleased. The dean had been only too happy to have a group as glamorous as the NFIP aligning itself with an operation as homegrown as Salk's. But there was always the risk the relationship could get overly cozy. Let the virus lab and the foundation become too closely linked in people's minds and the University of Pittsburgh could get shut out of the public relations windfall altogether—a mere landlord providing space for other people's research. It would be nice, at least this once, if Municipal Hospital had its name over whatever bit of sparkly science came from Salk's team. McEllroy promised Salk he'd see what he could do, then contacted the trustees of the Spang Foundation, another local philanthropy, and requested the funds for the equipment. The Spang group promptly complied.

The following month, Weaver swung through Pittsburgh on one of his periodic tours of the local grantees and paid a call on Salk. The first things he noticed when he arrived were the banks of shiny roller drums, spinning and churning throughout the lab.

"What's all this?" he asked.

"We're culturing virus," Salk answered.

"With New York money?"

"Local money."

Now it was Weaver's turn to sweat. He didn't mind a little initiative on the part of his grantees, but too much of it could spell trouble—the first sign of a good scientist getting restless in harness. If Salk could raise money so easily, the foundation would have to act fast to protect the investment it had already made in him. Weaver returned to New York a few days later, and not long after that, Salk received a letter from NFIP headquarters informing him that there would be a $7,500 check forthcoming to pay for the equipment the Spang Foundation had already bought. From now on, it would be the NFIP that would be supporting any tissue-culturing work Salk might do. Salk was more than happy to agree.

With his battery of roller drums and his rough knowledge of Enders's methods, Salk was soon incubating virus that was as pure as any the Harvard lab could make. Now he had to decide what to do with it all or, more precisely, what Thomas Rivers would let him do. Rivers, as overall chairman of the NFIP's committee on research, was Weaver's boss in the New York headquarters. As anyone associated with the foundation eventually concluded, Thomas Rivers could be a coarse son of a bitch. That, as it happened, was just fine with Rivers, because a coarse son of a bitch was precisely how he thought of himself.

Rivers was born in Jonesboro, Georgia, and came out of that place as raw—and unselfconscious about it—as the town itself. From the time he was a boy, he'd been known as someone who said what he pleased, cursed when he wanted, spat where he liked. This might not have destined him for the genteel world of scientific research, but he also happened to have been born with an absolutely incandescent medical mind. Rivers recognized his own gift and in 1909 enrolled at the Johns Hopkins Medical School in Baltimore. After barely a year, however, he noticed that his body was suddenly starting to fail him—his hands going weak, his arms going heavy, his shoulders drooping, his head dropping. The Hopkins doctors properly diagnosed the affliction as Aran-Duchenne atrophy, a neuromuscular disorder that usually disabled its victims utterly and permanently.

Rivers, more piqued than self-pitying, left Baltimore and slouched off to Panama to work as a medical assistant in a modest hospital. He'd reckoned that so wild a country wouldn't be terribly choosy about the condition of the people it hired, and in the event that his physical strength somehow returned, he'd have a little clinical experience with which to return to Hopkins, complete his education, and talk his way into a job later on. As it turned out, Rivers's Aran-Duchenne, not expected simply to go away, did just that. Shortly afterward, he came back to Baltimore and got his degree, then began a loud, profane, and stellar career. He conducted field research for the Army Medical Corps during both world wars, studied viruses at Rockefeller University during the interregnum between hostilities, and eventually went to work for the NFIP, setting overall research policy and supervising the administration of any eventual treatments.

In the foundation's quiet New York headquarters, Rivers tempered his exuberant vulgarity not a whit, freely dispensing opinions, obscenities, and even ethnic affronts with an almost blissful indifference. When he first met Albert Sabin, he remembered him both for his brains and his religion and, so it was said in polio circles, took to referring to him as The Smart Jew, a moniker that passed for a compliment when it came from Rivers's lips. When he met Jonas Salk, he labeled him The Young Jew.

For all this, Rivers rarely gave anybody true offense, if only because his stunning bluntness always seemed equal parts affectation and impulse. And when presented with the opportunity to do real damage to a scientist or his reputation—as he was back in 1935 when he accepted the job of speaking out against the deadly Park–Brodie and Kolmer vaccines at the public health convention in St. Louis—he generally pulled back, preferring to rely on the measured tones of the sober scientist rather than the braying tones of the country cutup. Nonetheless, the NFIP researchers were pleased that when they sent grant proposals up for official approval, the smooth and artful Harry Weaver would act as gatekeeper to Rivers, judiciously deleting the researchers' most extravagant ideas and thus sparing them the research chairman's ebullient disdain.

When Salk sat down in the late spring of 1950 to map out what he wanted to do next, he thus tailored his pitch for an audience of one. It was a pitch he'd been composing in his head for a long time.

"Dear Dr. Weaver," he typed, "Some time ago I promised to write to you to share my thinking about the research we would like to undertake. My orientation at the moment is to see if we can develop a satisfactory procedure for the prevention of poliomyelitis by immunologic means."

This was a dangerously direct—even reckless—bit of phrasing. "The prevention of poliomyelitis by immunologic means" was, of course, just a mush-mouth term for a vaccine. The foundation had not yet even grown comfortable with the idea that a vaccine was the ultimate answer for polio, much less that the still green Jonas Salk, who had been shooed off less than a year ago when he suggested such work, was the man to develop it. But Salk felt differently. For one thing, he now had his own stockpile of virus, thank you very much. For another, the fact remained that rookie or not, he and Tommy Francis were the only ones among the foundation scientists who already knew what it took to invent a successful vaccine, having successfully done just that against the flu. With one virus scalp hanging from his belt, he was confident he could bag another.

Salk hammered out his thoughts in dense, blocky paragraphs filling single-spaced page after page, describing a huge, multifront assault on polio that he proposed not only to help plan but to help lead as well. He wanted an exhaustive, open-ended hunt for new strains of the virus; he wanted sweeping field studies of epidemic pockets to determine how the bug worked, where it hid, why it paralyzed some people and spared others; he wanted to study new ways to inactivate the virus so it could be used in a vaccine, and new ways to fortify that vaccine with adjuvants. He wanted comprehensive tests of any vaccine he might develop, first in monkeys and chimpanzees and then—sooner rather than later—in humans. This last part of his proposal he knew was radical, but he was in no mood to hedge.

"I have investigated the local possibilities and find that not too far from here there are institutions for hydrocephalics and other unfortunates," he wrote. "I think we may be able to obtain permission there for a study of immunization. This is more of a dream than a reality," he conceded. "All the same, the time has come for initiating the critical experiments, and the time has come for those experiments to be carried out in man."

Salk sealed his letter and mailed it out before the audaciousness of his proposal could give him pause.

Harry Weaver read the proposal when it arrived in New York and barely knew how to respond, there was so much wrong with it. He slashed through the paragraph about human testing; he crossed out the idea for studying how to kill the poliovirus. He read over the grand suggestion for sweeping field studies with exasperation. Salk hadn't even used the proper forms necessary to submit an official grant request.

Weaver answered Salk's eight-page manifesto with a mere page and a half. For at least the next year, he ordered, he didn't want to see much more than the ongoing typing work coming out of the typing labs. If Salk had run out of strains to type, he'd be pleased to provide him more. Thereafter, Salk might be allowed to pursue some of his other ideas, but he'd have to dial them back dramatically. He would not be permitted to try killed-virus studies, though he could work with live viruses. He could use animals to test any preparation he might develop. Human tests would be out of the question. If Salk promised not to exceed the limits Weaver imposed and to exhaust those lines of research fully before even considering moving on, the research director might be able to get the plan past Rivers—provided Salk typed the damned thing up properly.

Salk complied, submitting his scaled-down ideas as instructed, and before long, approval of the limited plan and the pledge of a limited grant came back from New York. To Salk's own surprise, he was philosophical about this half a research loaf. If the foundation needed the old ways—the live virus—to be disproven first, he'd be willing to do it. If headquarters wanted him to go slowly on human testing, he'd comply. Soon enough, any sensible scientist would see that the plan he was proposing was the only way to go, and when that happened, he'd be ready.

It was with that easy combination of patience and hope that Salk accepted the invitation to go to Schenley High School on a hot evening in early June to talk to the parents who would be gathered there. If he could share a bit of his optimism with them it would be worth the time and exertion.

Salk appeared in the rear of the auditorium on the evening of the meeting and tried to remain as inconspicuous as he could. While his reserve and his decidedly unmedical attire didn't give him away, his very unfamiliarity—a new face in a roomful of people who knew all the old ones—did. He hurried to the front of the room and climbed the handful of steps to the lectern before he could be stopped with questions. The crowd quieted. The PTA president introduced him, and Salk started in, looking out over an audience of worried faces and waving fans.

"An epidemic," he said with as much authority as he could, "is not likely this summer." The crowd slumped in relief and Salk gently shushed them. "But the fact is, there wasn't an epidemic last summer either. There were only seventy cases here in Allegheny County. In a community this size, that's not an epidemic. Even the one hundred thirty-nine cases back in 1944 didn't technically qualify."

The crowd began to mutter. Salk had misjudged the mood in the room. What he was giving them were case-counters' numbers—cold figures that did nothing to address the flesh-and-blood idea that 70 or 80 or 139 children in the local community might end the summer without the use of their legs. Salk quickly shifted course and began addressing the crowd not as scientists, but as parents.

"I do believe," he said more softly, "that a solution to the polio problem will be forthcoming within our lifetimes—perhaps much sooner. Meantime, people have been doing a lot of unnecessary worrying—and even some foolish things—to protect themselves. A lot of this concern about insects, for example, just isn't necessary."

"Are you working on a cure?" someone called out.

"There may never be a cure. But there will be a vaccine. That I believe. A vaccine won't make sick children better. But it will keep healthy ones safe."

This, of course, was what the parents wanted to hear. The evening went on for a long while after that, with worried questions getting tossed up and level answers coming back down, but that single, fragile promise was why the parents had shown up at all tonight.

Well before the month of June 1950 was out, the true heat of summer settled in around Pennsylvania and the rest of the nation. The season spun out slowly, and before autumn arrived, 33,300 American children were struck with poliomyelitis, nearly four times the battlefield deaths incurred during the Revolutionary War, the War of 1812, the Mexican-American War, and the Spanish-American War combined. A disturbing and disproportionate 134 of those afflicted children lived in Allegheny County.

When John Troan first started getting to know Jonas Salk, there were a lot of things the reporter wanted to know about the doctor, but one of the most important ones was where he ate his lunch. Troan knew how to get a scientist talking, and he knew that asking him questions in his office could be the surest way to pry nothing out of him at all. A man behind a desk was a man who was on his guard. But slide up next to him at a lunch counter or a bar, when he was relaxing with his burger or his beer, and he might tell you anything you wanted to know.

Troan realized it would be a while before he could get that cozy with Salk, but he quickly set about trying. His once-a-week visits to the Pittsburgh medical school now became twice-a-week visits, with a standing appointment with Campbell Moses on Fridays and a less formal drop-in on Dr. Salk on Mondays. Lorraine Friedman remained the gatekeeper of Salk's operation, and Troan knew enough to present himself at her desk each week before even thinking of penetrating deeper into the lab.

"Is Dr. Salk free today?" he'd ask, perfectly happy to accept either answer, or at least hoping to appear that way.

On some occasions Lorraine would shoo Troan off and on some occasions she'd show him in. On those days when he did get an hour or so with

Salk, he'd make it a point to let the scientist determine where the conversation ought to go. More often than not, Salk had no special news to share and instead simply wanted to talk about the little cogs of his work—how you coaxed polioviruses to grow, how you titrated antibodies in blood, how you told a Type I bug from a Type II or III. Troan did get the occasional, minor story out of these meetings, and Salk, he supposed, was pleased with a little mention in the papers. But mostly the doctor appeared more interested in educating him about the science behind the bigger headlines that might be coming someday. Troan allowed himself to be so schooled. One quiet Monday, as their tutorial approached its end, Salk had a suggestion.

"Why don't you wander around the lab?" he said. "There are very good people here. I think you ought to get to know them too."

Troan did as he was told, and with the approval of Lorraine Friedman, embarked on a self-guided tour of Salk's growing shop, paying calls on Byron Bennett, Julius Youngner, Elsie Ward, and all the rest. Finally, he wound up in the animal lab with Jim Lewis, spending the better part of the afternoon chatting with the scientist Salk had good-naturedly labeled "our monkey man." At the end of the visit, Troan had a question.

"Does Dr. Salk take his lunch in the office?" he asked.

"No," Lewis said. "He eats out."

"Does he have a particular place?"

"Very particular," Lewis said. "The Bamboo Garden. It's out the door and half a dozen blocks down the hill to the left. You like Chinese food?"

"I'll learn to," said Troan.

Troan let a few days go by and then, one lunch hour, wandered into the Bamboo Garden. It was a spare-looking place, decorated in a vaguely Eastern style and dense with the smell of Chinese cooking. As he expected, Salk was there. He was seated at a table, working on a plate of food and a pot of tea, while reading through a stack of papers. Troan wandered by and affected surprise when Salk looked up and noticed him.

"You eat here too?" Troan asked.

"Every day," Salk said.

Troan chuckled at the remarkable coincidence and took a step toward another table. Salk—perhaps moved by collegiality, perhaps merely by manners—cleared his papers away and waved him back. Troan offered an obligatory gesture of demurral and then, before Salk could accept it, took a seat. The waitress brought him a menu and he scanned it confusedly, finally ordering tea, because that's what Salk was drinking, and egg foo young, because that's what he recognized.

Troan searched for something sociable to say. In May 1950, he knew, Donna Salk had given birth to the family's third child, a boy named Jonathan.

"So," Troan said, "you have three boys in the house now."

"We do."

"That must keep you busy."

Salk laughed. "John," he said, "you didn't come here to talk about my boys."

"No," Troan admitted, "I didn't."

"I didn't think so," Salk answered. "So why don't we discuss something else."

Salk pushed his papers aside and leaned forward, assuming a posture he'd never before assumed in the lab. He then proceeded to talk to Troan in a whole new way, describing not just the scientific minutiae of his work, but also the larger picture, the grander goals. Salk had a clear sense of the great arc he would have to follow to get from where he was in his study of polio to where he wanted to be. And for the first time, he seemed willing to share that vision with Troan. The reporter listened quietly, took notes carefully, asked questions only when necessary. And as the lunch hour played out and passed, he allowed himself an inward smile. More and more lately, he'd noticed that Salk had been addressing him by his first name. That, he knew, was at least as important as any of the science he was learning here today.

With the grudging permission of Thomas Rivers and the go-slow warnings of Harry Weaver, Salk immersed himself in the circumscribed research program the NFIP had approved for his lab. Much of the work he truly wanted to do might have to wait, but the hands-on job of inventing a vaccine—rough and wrongheaded as the NFIP's prescribed methods might be—had at last begun.

The first thing Salk would need to do if he was going to develop a true polio preventive was to track down a strong, stable, gold-standard sample of each of the three types of virus. A vaccine would do no good at all if any of the viruses from which it was made grew erratic or unpredictable as the preparation was being manufactured. Most researchers studying the trio of polioviruses preferred to work with the Brunhilde strain, named for the chimpanzee it had been taken from; the Lansing strain, named for the city in Michigan in which it had been isolated; and the Leon strain, named for the human children in whom it had first been found. Salk wanted better, even steadier strains to serve as templates for his work and quickly identified what he considered an ideal trio.

The first of them, a Type I virus, had originally been isolated by Tommy Francis himself, working under one of his early NFIP grants in the few free hours he had while still battling flu. Francis had harvested the bug on September 10, 1941, from Patricia, Mary, and Fred Mahoney, three siblings living in Akron, Ohio, who had been exposed to a patient suffering from paralytic polio and had picked up the virus themselves but had never gotten sick. Type I, for the purposes of Salk's work, would now be known as the Mahoney type.

A clinically perfect Type II bug turned up in a sample that had been isolated in 1942 by doctors working with the United States Army's Middle East Forces stationed in Egypt. As was its fashion, the military simply applied an antiseptic acronym to the virus: MEF. A yardstick sample for Type III polio, the least common of the group, was the hardest to find, but Salk discovered one in an especially nasty bug that had been taken from ten-year-old Jimmy Saukett—though some now said his name was really Sarkett—who had spent a spell in Pittsburgh's own Municipal Hospital. Whatever the boy's name was, he was fortunate to have survived his illness, given the power of the particular Type III he'd caught. He was now well past the acute stage of the disease and living at the nearby D. T. Watson rehabilitation home, working to regain some of his preinfection strength. Salk could not help feeling a flicker of proprietary interest in a bug that had been harvested under his own professional roof and that would now become such an important part of his work. In Salk's lab, the Saukett type henceforth became the family name for the Type III line.

Had Salk gotten his way, he would have treated these bugs with no greater courtesy than that with which he'd treated his flu bugs back in Michigan, which is to say he would have begun to murder them with formalin. But he had been ordered to pursue first the daintier path of merely weakening the viruses. In 1935, John Kolmer's discredited vaccine relied on sodium ricinoleate to do this job—with famously unsatisfactory results. Most researchers now preferred a less toxic and more tedious attenuation method, passing the virus through successive generations of chimpanzees or other animals, counting on the fact that even the strongest strains sometimes lost their pathogenic oomph as they went along.

This was the work the NFIP had in mind for Salk, and this was what he would do. But it wouldn't be his only work. Deep in a memo to Byron Bennett and Jim Lewis, he vaguely suggested a few ideas for other studies the lab's staffers could conduct if they found themselves with some idle hours. Perhaps they'd conduct some experiments in viral mutation; perhaps some in the duration of the antibody response. As an apparent afterthought, he also tossed out a third option: "Inactivation by chemical methods."

Bennett and Lewis knew the man they worked for and they knew what it was he wanted. "Inactivation" meant virus-killing and "chemical methods" meant formalin. They would conduct their live-virus studies just as they'd been instructed to. But in their free time—time Salk would surely make available to them—they would get a quiet, under-the-table killed-virus program going too. When the time came to bring it out into the light, they wanted to be prepared.

Few people in the NFIP pretended that the idea of a vaccine didn't scare the living daylights out of them, and that, given the chance, they wouldn't do precisely what anxious bureaucracies always do when they're feeling that way—which is to say they would table the thing. Foundation scientists got their first real opportunity to reconsider the idea of a polio vaccine the following May, when the NFIP's Committee on Immunization met at the Hotel Commodore in New York.

As its name suggested, the Committee on Immunization concerned itself not with polio cures but with polio preventives—everything from vitamins to diet to sanitation to the elusive vaccine. Albert Sabin had been a member of the committee for a while, and Jonas Salk—in a nod to his persistent interest in vaccine research—had recently been appointed too. There were twenty other members of the panel, including Harry Weaver and Thomas Rivers, as well as Hart van Riper, the foundation's medical director. Van Riper had been a pediatrician in Florida who eventually joined the NFIP after his wife was stricken with polio. His role in the foundation was to oversee the practical application of whatever it was the research teams developed, but his influence went beyond that well-defined portfolio. He was smart, sharp, and opinionated, and he was coming to wield increasing influence in the foundation's highest councils.

Van Riper and the other men gathered and got down to business straightaway. What they wanted to talk about most, they decided, was not how to eradicate the poliovirus with the take-no-prisoners strategy of a vaccine, but how to rein it in more gently with the far less permanent tactic of passive immunity.

Vaccines provided what scientists thought of as active immunity—with the bloodstream of the person who had received the inoculation learning how to cook up antibodies whenever they might be needed. Doctors had also long known that a person who wasn't immune to an illness could borrow the resistance of someone who was, simply by receiving a donor shot of that person's gamma globulin—the liquid component of blood in which antibodies are found. Soldiers and overseas travelers routinely relied on this passive approach, lining up for gamma globulin shots before visiting unfamiliar parts of the world that could be home to unfamiliar pathogens. In some cases, the shots helped. What's more, they were relatively risk-free, since it was protective antibodies alone that were being injected into the body, not temperamental viruses.

But such good-health-on-loan was temporary. Injected gamma globulin was washed from the body in a matter of weeks, and even during the time it lingered, there was no certainty it would work at all. Transient, imperfect immunity, however, was better than no immunity at all, and during the great polio epidemic of 1916, panicky New Yorkers had scrambled to receive scarce shots of whole serum—a less refined blood preparation than gamma globulin—drawn from people who had survived polio. If New Yorkers could try passive polio immunity with serum in 1916, couldn't contemporary doctors try it with gamma globulin in 1951?

The majority of scientists attending the Commodore had taken no formal position on gamma globulin trials, but a handful of others, Salk included, were cool to the idea. Certainly, passive immunity was not without merit. Salk himself had been wondering what might happen if cows could be inoculated with high doses of poliovirus so that antibodies would form and flow into their milk—milk that could later be fed to children. But this was a modest strategy, a backstop bit of research that would do nothing to control the disease completely and forever. A few other researchers, however, led by Dr. William Hammon, a foundation grantee who had previously done his work at UCLA and had recently assumed a faculty position at Salk's own University of Pittsburgh, had gone on record as wanting to make passive immunity a centerpiece of the foundation's work—and a major consumer of its funds. After Weaver called the meeting to order, Hammon rose to make his pitch.

"I think we are all agreed that gamma globulin contains considerable antibody for all major polio types and probably for any as yet unrecognized types," he said. "To put this to the test, human populations will have to be used to determine how long this protection lasts and how big a dosage is required."

Hammon proceeded to lay out his plan for such a study, and it was clear he had given the matter exhaustive thought. He proposed a sweeping experiment in any one of a number of communities that were at historically high risk for polio epidemics. Half of the children in the study would receive real gamma globulin shots and the other half—what the researchers called the control group—would receive an inert gelatin preparation so that the results could be compared at the end of the summer. The size of the doses would be determined by the size of the child. The smallest boys and girls would receive 5-cubic-centimeter injections; bigger ones would get 10 cc's; the biggest of all—80 pounds or more—would receive 15 cc's. Hammon spelled out when the study should begin, how long it should be run, and how the children should be recruited. For consistency's sake, he specified how he wanted the shots to be administered.

"The injection," he said, "should be in one buttock."

Including so much detail in any proposal could be a smart thing, but it could also be a dangerous thing. Twenty-two scientists closed in a conference room could spend most of a day arguing about a single cc in a dosing suggestion. Give them an entire field trial to debate and they'd probably rip it to shreds. What troubled these twenty-two scientists was less the quantity of the gamma globulin that would be administered than the problem of determining which children would actually receive the protective shots and which would receive the control material. If you really believed passive immunity worked, could you morally deny it to any child who willingly stepped up to participate in your experiment?

"You'll lose the support of the public if you give something to one child and another thing to another," Albert Sabin warned. "And for that matter, we don't even have a way to figure out which child gets which."

"You do it on a random basis," said Thomas Rivers. "Every other person who comes to your front door you shoot with the real stuff."

"Can you really send every other child home with nothing at all?" asked Norman Topping of the National Institutes of Health.

"They should at least be given a piece of candy as a reward for coming in," said John Paul of Yale University.

As these and other debates played out, Salk stayed largely quiet. Gamma globulin was by any measure a half-measure, and what the men in the room were doing was yielding to the scientist's impulse to halve those halves. There was only so long even the reticent Salk could abide such dithering. Openly clashing with colleagues was something to be avoided, but not at all costs. And the costs of delaying now would simply be too high. For the first time in his dealings with the NFIP elders, he could not merely nudge or coax the conversation, waiting for it to flow his way. If the committee members were going to avoid making a grave mistake, he'd have to force them to avoid it himself.

"We could argue from now until the end of the afternoon about details and it won't get us much further," Salk said, surprising the other men with his directness. "I think the experiment should be done, but it should be done with the very definite reservation that if it does not work, we will have to find another way of solving the problem. We may have to abandon the idea of passive immunity altogether."

The men in the room looked at Salk in a rare moment of general agreement. What he said made both scientific and political sense. Crude experiments like Isabel Morgan's chimpanzee tests had shown that a vaccine could be carefully explored without calamity, but the Park and Brodie and the Kolmer tragedies still—and forever—cast long shadows. A compromise involving a major gamma globulin trial could provide a way out for both sides, at last providing a route to the long delayed vaccine work. Those scientists reluctant to pursue vaccines could take some satisfaction from the idea that studies of active immunity would be deferred until there could be at least one good passive-immunity study. Those who saw the vaccine as the true way to go could make this final concession to the passive camp before heading full-tilt into active immunity. Salk may not have been the first in the room to consider this conciliatory ground, but he was the first to give voice to it. The debate in the Commodore ballroom ground on for hours more, proceeding straight up until its scheduled 4:15 adjournment, but by that time the decision was not in doubt.

The gamma globulin study was overwhelmingly approved and would begin as soon as possible. Thousands of children in a city yet to be selected would soon be injected with a preparation that could give them the rare chance to live through summer without the fear of being crippled before winter. If it failed, the foundation knew where it would have to turn next.

The people of Utah County got their gamma globulin shots shortly after Labor Day. It had been a nasty summer across the entire overheated state, and even while some parts of the country began to look forward to the arrival of autumn, the disease was still raging in the West. William Hammon knew this would be a perfect place to try out his shots.

Hammon arrived in Salt Lake City on August 29, requested an audience with the county medical society, and made an extraordinary offer: There were at least 12,000 children between the ages of two and eight living in Provo and two smaller towns, and he wanted to inject a fair percentage of them with a dose of something that might let them survive the viral fire that was raging in the rest of the state. Already poised to roll in behind Hammon was a field team from the NFIP that would conduct the work. The scientific detachment was a big one—twenty nurses, five nursing supervisors, six pediatric residents, one research associate, one physical therapist, and not incidentally, four representatives of the foundation's public relations department to help explain the project to the populace. If the county medical society gave the go-ahead, the team would set out for Utah immediately.

Much of the board, as it happened, was away for the holiday, but the ones still in town heard Hammon out and unanimously approved his plan. This rump council then cabled the members who were away, informing them of the action they had taken. Telegrams came back approving the approval.

The Tuesday after the holiday, Hammon's team arrived, and he and the local medical committee held a press conference announcing and explaining the injection program. The state's communications web leapt on the news. Notices were read in Mormon churches; physicians hurried to radio stations to endorse the plan; local women's groups, prodded by the foundation women, sent out calls for volunteers to help administer the shots. Makeshift clinics were established around the county, and rental cars were made available to medical workers. The Provo Hotel threw open its doors to serve as a temporary headquarters.

The clinics went into operation at nine A.M. the following day and promised to remain open until nine P.M.—provided supplies held out. Parents and children swarmed to the sites, each of which was equipped with two inoculating tables so that injections could be administered as quickly as possible. Even with that, lines of fidgety children and anxious parents snaked out the doors. When the boys and girls at last reached the tables, they were injected in the buttock, then given a lollipop, which they were encouraged to begin eating on the way out, the thinking being that the children still waiting in the queue would feel less dread of the injection ahead if they could catch a glimpse of the reward that would follow.

At the end of the first day, more than 2,000 children were injected before the supplies on hand ran out. More gamma globulin would have to be brought in and unpacked overnight. Meantime, the 2,000 needles that had been used had to be rinsed and soaked, then driven 45 miles to the closest major hospital so they could be sterilized in an autoclave and returned for reuse before sunup. The injections resumed the following morning and ran until the middle of the fourth day, when the supplies of gamma globulin and inert gelatin were exhausted for good. The doctors counted 5,731 boys and girls who were ultimately injected, or about half of the target population at risk of contracting the poliovirus.

Then Hammon and most of the rest of the NFIP army decamped. They left behind a mop-up team to live among the locals for the remainder of the fall, tallying the number of polio cases in the gamma globulin group, comparing them with the control group, and sending those figures back to New York. By October those numbers were in.

Of the 2,871 children who received the true gamma globulin, only one contracted paralytic polio. Of the 2,860 who received the counterfeit shot, four got sick. Those numbers were so tiny as to be almost meaningless. But when extrapolated out to an entire summer and multiplied up to the population as a whole, they told a different story. Out of every 100,000 untreated children, 140 would contract polio; out of every 100,000 treated ones, 35 would get sick.

Gamma globulin was indeed a barrier to polio, albeit an imperfect one: Even in the children in whom the passive immunity apparently worked, it vanished in as little as five weeks—far less than a single polio season— leaving them once again vulnerable to infection.

Dr. Hammon had gotten his experiment and he now had his results. Gamma globulin was a small port in the polio storm. But it offered only passing sanctuary, and that was not good enough.

In the same hot week in which William Hammon was traveling to Provo
for his gamma globulin study, Jonas Salk was heading in the opposite
direction, aboard the ocean liner *Stockholm,* en route to Copenhagen.
Of the two men, Salk clearly had the sweeter deal.

As trans-European liners went, the *Stockholm* was a glamorous one,
particularly since Salk's previous trips to Europe had all been in the service
of—and on ships owned by—the United States military. For this journey,
Salk would be traveling in a single room with a private bath on the vessel's
breezy boat deck. The cabin-for-one would set the NFIP back a tidy $395.
Salk's trip home would be more elegant still: a first-class, $485 room
aboard the celebrated *Queen Mary.*

Salk was sailing to Copenhagen for the Second International Poliomyelitis Conference, an event that would be even flashier than the ship in
which he would arrive. Queen Ingrid of Denmark would preside at the

opening of the conference's first session. Niels Bohr, the Nobel physicist and head of the Danish Academy of Scientists, would be seated as conference president. Polio researchers from throughout Europe, Asia, and North and South America would be streaming in too. The United States delegation alone would exceed two dozen scientists and, in addition to Salk himself, would be made up of most of the NFIP's unofficial College of Cardinals, including Thomas Rivers and Basil O'Connor.

Though Salk was still among the lower-ranking NFIP members making the trip, he would have the highest profile. Each delegation that attended the conference was invited to present one scientific paper, and the foundation had decided that its contribution would be a report on the organization's three-year virus-typing program. Since Salk had shown such speed and efficiency in performing his own typing assignments, he'd been chosen to present the findings. His selection as the project's point man had so far not prompted any grumbling from the scientists in the other three labs involved in the project—a sign either that those researchers genuinely respected his skill and bore him no ill will, or that they bore him plenty but simply decided not to say anything about it. Either way, there was no discernible griping.

Even for people completely new to the typing work, the basic findings of the study were straightforward: Of all the samples tested, 85 percent fell into the Type I category, the most common paralytic type; 12 percent fell into Type II, the milder, more often asymptomatic type; and just 3 percent were Type III, the often lethal type that paralyzed breathing. But if those findings were easy to understand, their implications—including what they meant for future typing work as well as for treating polio or vaccinating against it—were far more complicated. For that reason, Salk had been assigned to prepare the Copenhagen presentation in collaboration with David Bodian and Albert Sabin, both of whom would be attending the conference too.

Working with the relaxed Bodian did not cause Salk any real concern; working with the temperamental Sabin was something else entirely. Before the two even began to compose their report, they began exchanging a series of letters that served less as genuine foundation work than as weather balloons to measure each other's mood. They shared their thoughts about the science of typing, the theory of vaccines, the conduct of field tests—in the process getting a sense of just how great their differences actually were and just how fiercely each man might defend his positions if forced to do so.

Salk's principal difference with Sabin, of course, concerned the merits of a live polio vaccine versus a killed one. But while that was a white-hot issue, it was not something they were required to address immediately. Other, lesser differences did come up right away, one of them a new theory Sabin had floated that there might be a whole category of polioviruses called subtypes—bugs too specialized to be a true type unto themselves but too broad and changeable to be a sharply defined strain. Salk thought this was mostly smoke. When it came to polio, a type was a type, and if you went into the wild looking for a whole new kind of viral beast, you'd do nothing more than waste both your time and your resources. In an especially long letter to Sabin, he mentioned this conviction—and did so in a decidedly tone-deaf way.

"I note your continued enthusiasm for the notion that there may exist subtypes of poliomyelitis virus," he wrote. "After working with influenza viruses in which the existence of subtypes was quite clear, I am quite unimpressed by the difference among the poliomyelitis viruses indicating the existence of subtypes."

Salk almost certainly knew better than to talk to Albert Sabin this way. The passage was a comparatively short one in a letter that was otherwise stuffed with objectively expressed science, but it was precisely the kind of seemingly snide aside that might set Sabin off. Not only was Salk suggesting that Sabin's ideas were based less on science than on a mere unreasoned *enthusiasm,* but he was also reminding the senior scientist that he, the young Salk, had already trod this ground before when he and Tommy Francis invented their splendid influenza vaccine. Perhaps when Albert Sabin too had a vaccine of his own, the passage suggested, he could speak with true authority. Whether Salk was simply, preemptively, trying to put Sabin in his place before they set to work on the Copenhagen paper, or whether he merely had a scientific point to make and did so as straightforwardly as he could, was impossible to determine from what was on the page alone.

What was certain was that Sabin didn't like it. He received Salk's four-page letter and that same day fired back a four-line response, acknowledging that the two men had philosophical differences and suggesting that Salk choose a "more dispassionate" way to express his view. "I do not have what you call 'enthusiasm for the notion that there may exist subtypes of poliomyelitis virus,'" he concluded. He signed the letter with a small and angular "Albert."

Salk, given the chance to appease Sabin, chose not to. "Dear Albert," he wrote in response, "Thanks for your note. I look forward to seeing you soon."

Oddly, this exceedingly poor start yielded good results. With a better sense of the lines each man had drawn in the sand, Salk and Sabin now took care not to step over them. Their subsequent letters were genteel, filled with so many polite preambles and asides that there was no chance anyone's toes would get trod on again.

"It is a pleasure to read Jonas Salk's beautiful diction," Sabin wrote, after receiving an early draft of Salk's conference report. "Having said that much, I would like to proceed with several suggested changes."

"Your suggestion with regard to the wording of the first sentence is much better than the way I stated it," Salk responded to one of Sabin's recommended changes. "I think this improves the paragraph considerably."

With Bodian's help, the two men produced a report that cogently captured what the typing study had yielded. Once in Copenhagen, Salk did the paper justice, delivering it confidently and authoritatively.

Salk's presentation took place early in the conference—the 9:30 A.M. session on just the second day of meetings—meaning that he was free to spend the rest of the week attending as many of the other presentations as he could without his public-speaking duties weighing on his mind. A number of the other delegates, particularly those who had brought their families along, set aside at least a few free hours to enjoy the museum trips and city tours the conference sponsors made available. Salk, however, had come to the conference without Donna and the boys, and for him the week was thus entirely business. He stayed until the very last paper was delivered, and once the final gavel fell, he checked promptly out of the hotel and hurried back to the docks for his scheduled boarding on the *Queen Mary*. He was anxious to return both to his lab and to his family, and he was equally anxious for a possible shipboard audience with Basil O'Connor.

During the sail east on the *Stockholm*, O'Connor had not been much in evidence, preoccupied as he was with the work that lay ahead. The trip home, however, was a different matter, with all the foundation delegates free to enjoy six languid days. Such unscheduled time was a rare thing for NFIP scientists, and it allowed a sense of playfulness and ease, especially at the large table in the ship's dining room where Basil O'Connor held court each evening.

In the manner of his onetime partner, Franklin Roosevelt, O'Connor always enjoyed a good meal and a good crowd, and during the dinners aboard the *Queen Mary*, he took it upon himself to keep the conversation moving and the good cheer flowing. Even in such a convivial atmosphere, however, he appeared troubled—and with good reason. Accompanying him on his trip overseas was his well-loved daughter Bettyann, a thirty-one-year-old mother of five. In a darkly ironic turn, Bettyann had been struck by her own case of polio just over a year earlier. In 1950, the plague had hit especially hard in Virginia, her home state, where more than 1,200 people fell ill, more than four times greater than the state's caseload the previous summer. In Richmond, the Medical College of Virginia alone was overwhelmed by 410 paralysis patients during that searing season, including the prostrate Bettyann.

"Daddy," she said in a telephone call to her father after she was admitted to the polio ward, "I think I caught some of your disease."

Now, thirteen months later, her recovery was slower than her father—who knew a thing or two about infantile paralysis—had promised her it would be. Her disappointment and despair were beginning to show. O'Connor's idea that she join him on this trip was an attempt to buoy her spirits both with the glamour of Europe and with the same kind of hopefulness he always felt in the presence of so many wise scientists devoted to defeating the scourge.

With Bettyann's mood on his mind, O'Connor worked even harder than he usually did to keep his own mood and that of the people around him as light as possible. During mealtimes, he found that one of the best ways to do that was to use the too-serious scientists at his table as foils, needling them playfully about everything from their schooling to their lab work to a gobbledygook grant request they might have submitted the year before, which O'Connor himself had had the pleasure of rejecting. Mostly, the scientists laughed agreeably at the foundation chief's tweaks, certain that they ought to play along, but uncertain about whether or not they ought to tweak back.

Salk, however, did tweak. He liked O'Connor and saw nothing in the folksy Irishman's demeanor that suggested he would not tolerate a little reciprocal ribbing. And so when O'Connor teased Salk about the wild ideas in the grand proposal he'd sent Harry Weaver the year before, Salk teased back about the miserly way O'Connor had financed the work he did approve. When O'Connor poked Salk about some contrary position he'd taken at a meeting, Salk poked back about O'Connor's excessive devotion to doctrine. The feints were kept light and the two men enjoyed them. More important, Bettyann, who by chance had been seated next to Salk, seemed to be amused too. Apparently, there were few better ways to brighten her up than to take a mischievous swipe at the man who played as large a role in her life as he did in the scientists' own.

Later on, when the food arrived and the diners broke off into quieter, semiprivate conversations, Salk and Bettyann had a chance to talk about more serious matters. After they had exchanged some obligatory pleasantries, he asked her, gently, how her rehabilitation was going. She allowed as how it was not going well.

Salk told her that that was evident, if not in her weakened limbs then in her troubled mood. Did she know that it was an entirely natural thing for her to be feeling as bleak as she did, that it would in fact be a surprise if she didn't?

Bettyann answered with a shrug.

Salk asked further if she also knew how resilient even the most severely stricken polio patients could be; how their bodies seemed to remember how to work, and with effort, could regain a surprising degree of the strength and mobility they'd lost.

Salk may or may not have believed that was true, but he had met enough polios and read enough research to be certain that their believing in it was an essential first step in achieving any recovery at all. Salk couldn't give Basil O'Connor's daughter terribly much, and his imagined vaccine would never give her anything at all. But he could share his genuine hopefulness.

Watching this and other conversations between Salk and Bettyann unfold, O'Connor liked what he saw both in his daughter's frame of mind and in the man who was working so hard to improve it. Over the course of the return journey, he and Salk found themselves increasingly drawn together—on the deck, in the pool, at the rail, looking out at the Atlantic and talking about what it was they hoped to accomplish with the National Foundation in the years to come. O'Connor was studiedly agnostic on the subject of how to attack polio—perfectly happy to fund gamma globulin if that proved the best approach, equally happy to bankroll either a live or a killed vaccine if they proved more promising. On the long float home, Salk found himself with Basil O'Connor's ear and with the rare chance to share many of his ideas. O'Connor paid close mind to what the young scientist had to say. And what O'Connor paid close mind to, the NFIP as a whole did as well.

At about the same time Jonas Salk was getting to know Basil O'Connor, Bill Kirkpatrick was getting to know a pretty, paralyzed, redheaded girl. Kirkpatrick knew the girl was paralyzed, of course, because otherwise he'd never have met her where he did. Whether she was in fact pretty and had red hair he had to accept as an article of faith, since he had never actually set eyes on her.

Kirkpatrick's body, trained for football, failed him so completely that for the entirety of his stay in Pittsburgh's Municipal Hospital he never emerged from isolation. On the overcrowded polio ward, "isolation" was a loose term. Kirkpatrick was installed in a large, sunny room with four other boys in four other beds—all five of them waiting for the early stages of the disease to pass so that they could see which muscles, if any, still had a spot of life in them. Stronger patients were able to explore the lounges and sun parlors and the long, smooth hallways, teaching their seditious limbs how to move with the aid of wheelchairs and crutches. Kirkpatrick was nowhere near ready for such activity.

Confinement to bed was a tedious prospect for any five boys, paralyzed or not, but the polio ward did provide some distractions—including the five paralyzed girls in the room across the hall. While the boys and girls might never walk across that wide divide to have a look at one another, they could certainly shout across it. Once they felt strong enough and brave enough, they'd call out names, make introductions, then talk, tease, laugh, and flirt, growing oddly fond of one another based on the sounds of their voices alone.

Kirkpatrick found he had taken a shine to one voice in particular. He liked what she had to say, he liked the sound of her when she said it, and he tried—subtly, he hoped—to make that clear to her. He'd be the first to answer when she called out and the first to laugh when she tried out a joke, and she began extending the same attention to him. They went this way for a week or so, until finally, on a sleepy evening when the other boys in his room were dozing, he stopped a nurse as she was making her rounds and asked her what she could tell him about the girl. The nurse smiled.

"I know she's fifteen."

"Anything else?" the sixteen-year-old Kirkpatrick asked.

"You want to know if she's pretty?"

Kirkpatrick shook his head yes.

"She is. And she has red hair."

A few days later, when Kirkpatrick's mother came for a visit, she brought him a vase of flowers. After she had gone, he stopped the same nurse and asked her if she might select a rose from the vase and carry it across the hall to the red-haired girl. The nurse agreed, chose a rose, and vanished from the room.

A moment later, the girl called out. "It's beautiful!" she said. "Thank you, William."

Weeks later, when Kirkpatrick had regained enough of his strength to be released from the ward, he was sent off as planned to the D. T. Watson rehabilitation home. In keeping with hospital policy, he was not taken into any of the other rooms to say goodbye to any of the other children, for fear that the idea of being left behind would shake their fragile spirits. The girl across the hall would thus have to remain nothing more than a remembered voice.

Once Kirkpatrick got to the Watson home, it would have been easy to forget about Municipal Hospital. The Watson students attended classes, exercised outside, used canes and tennis balls to play makeshift games of wheelchair hockey in the hallways—and got scolded for the noise they made. Kirkpatrick worked hard to make the most of such freedom. When he did have time shortly after his arrival, however, he made it a point to write the red-haired girl a letter, telling her how he was doing and asking how soon she'd be released. He addressed the letter to Municipal Hospital, guessing that it would be given to her if she was still in residence and forwarded to her home if she wasn't.

Kirkpatrick mailed out the letter and waited several days for a response. He waited several more after that and then more still. Finally, during mail call one afternoon, a nurse brought him an envelope. Even from a distance, he could see that it did not have the familiar shape of the mail he routinely received from his mother, a sign that it might be from a decidedly more exciting sender. The envelope was, however, familiar in a different way. It was the very one he'd sent the red-haired girl, creased and smudged from the trip it had taken back to him.

Kirkpatrick took the unopened envelope in his hand and looked at the front, where he had carefully written the girl's name. There was now an additional word printed there: DECEASED.

After the International Poliomyelitis Conference adjourned, the members of the NFIP's Committee on Immunization decided that it was a good idea to gather for a final December meeting before the end of 1951. There were a lot of questions the scientists needed to address before the calendar turned, not the least being how they should spend their research resources in the year about to begin. Gamma globulin had been ruled out as a final answer for polio, but the limited protection it did offer made it appealing all the same. Basil O'Connor thus decided to use millions of dollars of foundation funds to buy up as much gamma globulin as the organization could afford, then distribute it free wherever epidemics struck—the better to prevent the panic and price-gouging that often accompanied such outbreaks. It was time, however, to start making real plans for the vaccine work that had been implicitly agreed to at the last meeting.

This Commodore Hotel meeting would be attended by more or less the same twenty-two men who had attended the previous one. The question of vaccine work would be listed third on the day's agenda, behind such narrower matters as a refined test for detecting poliovirus in the blood and a further analysis of the gamma globulin field trials. Even before he arrived at the hotel on the morning of the meeting, however, Harry Weaver, who would once again be presiding, knew he wanted to reshuffle things.

"With your permission," he said as the other scientists took their seats, "I would like to take up item three first."

Weaver certainly expected debates when the vaccine question came up, and he seemed to want to get them started and over with while everyone was fresh. Even before the arguments got under way, it was clear how the camps would line up. Albert Sabin would take the lead in favor of the live-virus principle, along with Joseph Smadel of the Army Medical Center, who had always been vocal in his support of the idea. Jonas Salk would line up in favor of the killed vaccine, along with Norman Topping of the National Institutes of Health. The other eighteen men were wild cards.

As the discussion began, it played out precisely that way, but subtly, sometimes inadvertently, some of those wild cards revealed themselves. When the committee found itself debating the beside-the-point issue of whether the virus in a killed vaccine should actually be described as killed, or whether a softer, more scientific word like "inactive" should be used, Thomas Rivers tried to settle the matter quickly, calling for a term that seemed awfully friendly to the Salk-Topping camp.

"Why don't you avoid both 'killed' and 'inactive' and stop a lot of argument?" he asked. "Say 'safe for use,' which is an entirely different proposition."

Then the debate turned to how the scientists could be sure that a virus in a killed vaccine was indeed wholly dead—the critical question that had to be convincingly answered before skeptics could ever be persuaded. The brusque Rivers tried to blow right by the problem.

"I think we will all have to admit that there is no test to be sure the stuff is inactive," he said. "Why not just accept that? Why kid ourselves? Just say it won't produce disease and that is all there is to it."

Sabin and Smadel leapt on that uncertainty. How could you ever say something did not present a danger when you might be injecting even a few particles of living, unweakened poliovirus directly into the arm of a child? Where was the "safe for use" in that proposition? In case anyone doubted the danger in what Salk and Topping were proposing, Sabin was prepared to remind them where such killed-virus folly could lead.

"The situation of formalinized vaccine was what was used by Brodie," he said. "His experiments on human beings fell into the same category as this dubious procedure."

Merely mentioning the name Brodie was a perfect poison pill. Sabin went on for a sentence or two more, though he needn't have bothered. "I am one of those people who simply believes that if it is possible to infect an individual with an attenuated virus, you ought to try," he said.

Rivers, however, at last seemed to have exhausted his patience for all the jabbing and hand-wringing. Unique among the men in the room, he knew what it was to have his own body fail him, as it had when Aran-Duchenne atrophy took hold of him so many years earlier. The committeemen had come here today to pick a vaccine, not just pull their beards and wave their hands, especially when summer was now just 180 days away.

"Gentlemen," Rivers said sharply, "let's come down to the only truly important matter, and that is trying to do away with poliomyelitis. We are fast approaching the time when we must get this work over into human volunteers. That is admittedly hazardous, but I am in favor of doing it as soon as possible in as cautious a manner as possible." He looked around the room at the fractious men staring back at him. "It's time," he said, "that this committee got ready to go somewhere."

That, it seemed, sealed it. The year was over, the gamma globulin trial was done, and the options were exhausted. The Committee on Immunization had been around long enough to know what true immunity was and how it could be achieved, and a vaccine was it.

The meeting pressed on for several more hours until its scheduled end, but even before it got there, the new position of the Committee on Immunization was clear: The formal barricades against vaccine development would be swept away. Those scientists inclined to try to invent an inoculation against polio would be permitted to do so. Whether it was made from a killed virus or a live virus did not much matter. The first vaccine that worked would be offered to the world.

Before the scientists adjourned, they reached consensus on one other matter as well. Just two years earlier, the Nuremberg war crimes trials had come to an end. The judges had heard four years' worth of evidence on all manner of atrocities, but among the most horrific had been the reports of the medical experiments carried out on unwilling prisoners. Determined that men of medicine should never again so abuse their art, the governments that had sponsored the trials issued ten-point guidelines by which all future medical research would have to abide. Under the new rules, scientists would be required to ensure that the participation of all their subjects was truly voluntary, that a study's potential risk did not exceed the humanitarian importance of its goals, that all unnecessary physical or mental suffering would be avoided. Most important, the work would have to stand a fair chance of yielding happy results for the overall good of society—results that could not be obtained in any other way.

"I think," said Norman Topping, as the meeting was drawing to a close, "that it might be very well for those people here contemplating human experiments to get a copy of the Ten Points." The committee agreed.

∞ 12 ∞

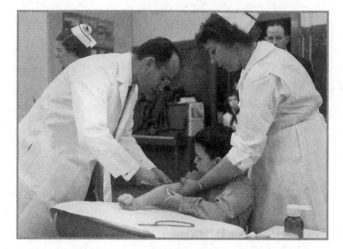

A t least fifty technicians and scientists now reported for work each
day at Salk's lab, with many others dropping in to lend a part-
time hand as the need arose. What struck Salk more than the
swirl of people at work, however, was the swirl of folks around him at home.

Jonas and Donna never intended to have more than three children, and
after Jonathan came, they indeed succeeded in holding the line at that. But
that didn't mean the property in Wexford wasn't becoming a busy, boisterous place. In addition to the Salks, the Dize family was in residence on the
grounds, leasing the apartment over the freestanding garage near the main
house from the same owner to whom the Salks paid their rent. Tilford
Dize was a trolley car driver, Helen was his wife, and Saundra was their
four-year-old daughter. Tilford and Helen were a quiet and pleasant couple, and Saundra was a good-natured girl who quickly became one of
Jonathan's preferred playmates.

On either side of the Salks' home were two other properties, one home to a family far richer than theirs, one to a family so poor they relied on a privy for their sanitary needs. Children from both those homes and others often came to visit the Salk boys and Saundra, and all of them would tear through the house or into the surrounding woods from morning to sundown.

Now and again, Jonas's parents, Daniel and Dora, would come from New York for a visit as well, occasions that would generally delight Jonas and the boys but could go a bit harder on Donna. Dora, as was her nature, would police the house with an unpleasant eye, commenting on any shortcomings she spied, which often as not involved what Donna put on the table each evening, particularly if it did not pass kosher muster. Of late, Peter, the oldest boy, had taken an insatiable liking to bean-with-bacon soup—from the can—and demanded it at almost every evening meal, including the meals Dora shared with them. On those occasions, Donna had to be careful.

"If you want soup," she would remind Peter before his grandmother arrived, "just ask for bean soup. Whisper the bacon part to yourself. I'll know it's there."

Salk did not mind looking out for the possible skirmishes between his mother and his wife, wrangling the boys when they needed wrangling, shoveling snow and sweeping walks and even checking the coal furnace in the garage when he came home late, refilling it if it was empty so the fire wouldn't go out overnight and leave the Dizes chilled. And for a short while he continued to have at least a bit of free time in which to handle those affairs. But that changed fast.

With the NFIP having at last having lifted its objections to a poliomyelitis vaccine, the world of the virus lab was turned upside down. Months of quiet vaccine research conducted with loose coins left over from earlier grants were now over. In their place was a rush of new foundation funds and a new encouragement—indeed a new requirement—that every nickel of it be spent on vaccine development. The NFIP's 1952 grant to the Pittsburgh Virus Lab amounted to a load of nickels indeed—$211,420 worth. Of that, $73,500 was paid directly to Okatie Farms to provide the monkeys Salk and his team would need for the year's work. Such a huge population of experimental animals was one sign of the kind of results the foundation expected from the lab. The war chest of cash Salk would have left over to conduct those experiments was the other. But the mere availability of money did not mean the work would be easy.

Developing a killed vaccine would not be a linear process that moved neatly from one goal to the next, but rather a broad, multifront effort, with the Pittsburgh team breaking down into a handful of smaller teams, each working simultaneously to develop the different techniques that would be essential to getting an effective polio preventive made. Some of the researchers in Salk's lab would take on the job of figuring out how to use the Enders technique to grow even better, cleaner poliovirus in culture; others would be working to perfect the tricky business of killing the virus with formalin; others would focus on developing the best possible adjuvant to increase the punch of the vaccine; still others would be responsible for testing the preparations in animals and developing the protocols for later studies in humans.

The first of these hurdles—improving on the Enders technique—turned out to be more complicated than the Pittsburgh team had imagined. Monkey kidneys still appeared to be the best medium for cultivating polio. The virus simply loved kidney tissue, growing easily, cleanly, and nonallergenically. The key was knowing how to prepare the organs and then coax the most virus to grow in them. It was not a simple procedure to master.

After a monkey was sedated and killed, the kidneys would be removed, then washed, minced, and chemically pureed. The thick solution that resulted would be strained through cheesecloth and spun in centrifuges, causing the individual cells to separate from the other debris. The cells would next be treated with a bit of streptomycin and penicillin to kill any errant bacteria, and then left to grow in a rich goo of nutrients known as Medium 199. A sort of cellular chow made up of amino acids, minerals, proteins, and vitamins, Medium 199 was developed by Connaught Medical Research Laboratories in Toronto, where—as the name of the product suggested—chemists had tried out 198 other formulas before hitting on just the right one to keep hungry cells thriving. With the help of the Canadian mix, comparatively small populations of purified kidney cells would roar to life, multiplying speedily in their flasks and dishes until they coated the sides in a healthy gray film. When the colonies were big enough, the Pittsburgh team combined them with live poliovirus. Then something nasty would happen.

Over the course of weeks, the monkey cells would begin to die, the gray film growing ragged and the cells swelling and bursting as the virus multiplied inside them. Eventually, the mixture would turn quiet and clear—a sure sign that the once-roiling colony of cells was entirely dead. The liquid would then be filtered once more to remove any cell scraps and other debris. What remained in the flasks was pure, vicious poliovirus—much more than what the scientists had begun with.

Incubating the virus, of course, was only the first step in the vaccine process. The next step—killing it—was left to another of the Pittsburgh subteams. Polioviruses intended for use in a vaccine had to be murdered gently, dispatched in such a way that there was no doubt they were dead but that their tiny remains were kept perfectly preserved. Formalin did the the job splendidly, congealing some of the virus's proteins while at the same time keeping its outer coat intact. But that was only if you handled the toxin just so. Use too little and you'd leave living bugs behind; use too much and you'd wad up the virus entirely, making it unrecognizable to the immune system and therefore useless. The Pittsburgh researchers thus had to adjust and readjust a wealth of variables in the formalin bath they drew for the bugs, modulating concentrations, temperatures, exposure times, and more, all in pursuit of a quick, clean kill that could be counted on to leave no survivors.

Even if you did succeed in balancing the formalin just right, it was still possible some stragglers would escape the chemical's toxic effect. Viruses in solution tend to clump and precipitate. When even a small scrum of the bugs drift together in the mix, the ones on the inside of the cluster are shielded from the liquid in which they're floating, protected from any toxins like formalin that may be present too. The same thing happens when the viruses and other tiny solids rain down out of the fluid, settling on the bottom of the container in a submicroscopic silt that keeps the most deeply buried ones protected. In both cases the answer was for the scientists to agitate the liquid periodically, then run it through a series of finer and finer filters, breaking up the viral clumps and straining away the rubbish.

Assuming you could manage all this and did brew yourself up what you thought was a pure batch of utterly dead bugs, it was still necessary to test what you had. One way was simply to draw off a sample of the mix, neutralize the formalin, and inject the killed viruses into a monkey. If the animal didn't get sick, you could be reasonably sure the viruses were indeed all dead. But was it all the viruses in your entire batch that had died or just the ones in the syringeful you captured? The only way to be sure was to draw off another dose and then another and another, until the entire supply had been injected into monkeys and none of them had fallen ill. That gave you the satisfaction of knowing that you had done your work well, but at the price of your entire virus sample, leaving you nothing with which to develop your vaccine.

The adjuvant problem was a tough one too. Few doubted that a polio vaccine ought to be mixed with some kind of immune-system irritant that would prod the bloodstream to produce the greatest number of antibodies possible. And few doubted that that adjuvant should be some type of mineral oil. But which type? Too viscous an oil would gum up the vaccine; too thin an oil would simply disperse. The answer turned in part on how you hoped to inject the vaccine.

If there was any advantage the live vaccine had over the killed, it was that the live could be taken orally. Since at least one of the disease's natural infection routes was the mouth, the wild virus would eventually multiply in the stomach. From there, it would cross over into the blood, hitching a ride in the circulatory slipstream until it reached the nervous system, where it would do its paralytic damage. Live, weakened virus in an oral vaccine mimicked that life cycle, flourishing in the digestive tract, where it would stimulate antibodies and set up a so-called gut immunity. Killed viruses couldn't do that, since by definition they had no life cycle. Instead, they would have to be injected into the body, setting up their line of antibody defense directly in the bloodstream, where they could nab a wild virus infection while it was en route to the nervous system.

But performing the actual injection took some practice. Firing the shot straight into the bloodstream seemed to make the most sense, since it was there that the vaccine would have to do its work. But the riptides of the circulatory system could be murder on a vaccine, breaking it up and washing it clear before it had a chance to do the immune-stimulating work it was built to do. What's more, injecting even a light adjuvant into the blood could be dangerous, forming a lethally oily clog in the arteries and veins. Injecting the contents of the syringe into the muscles was a better choice, allowing it to linger longer and work better before it was absorbed. But muscles are still blood-rich tissue, shot through with microscopic capillaries that take up the vaccine and adjuvant and hand them off to the bloodstream almost as quickly as if they had been deposited there in the first place. The best choice was to inject the preparation just under the skin, where a properly balanced mix of vaccine and oil would form a sort of reservoir that would be absorbed at a slower pace. While the development of the vaccine would thus rely on an incalculable range of finely calibrated scientific steps, the eventual delivery of the solution would depend on something as fallibly human as a light touch and good aim.

These problems kept Salk and his staff busier than they had ever been before, away from their families and locked to their lab benches for what were turning out to be steadily lengthening workdays. Salk himself found he was having to spend more and more of his time acting not just as research director but as shop steward too, both planning the direction of the lab's work and monitoring his staff as they went about trying to get it done.

"How's that culture look to you?" he'd ask a young technician as he stopped on one of his frequent lab prowls, peering over her shoulder at a petri dish that appeared to be growing more than just the polio culture it was supposed to be growing.

"It looks like there might be some mold," the technician would admit.

"Looks that way to me too."

"It's only a little."

"Which is already way too much."

Salk would instruct that the culture be discarded and the dish be cleaned and the technician would comply—both of them sharing the unspoken understanding that she would never grow mold on her polio again.

If the lab began falling behind on minor housekeeping jobs, Salk did not hesitate to let his Ph.D.'s, masters, and bachelors know that none of them, himself included, was above a little rote work.

"Assignments for the Week," he'd type on a list he posted every Monday. "Lewis and Youngner will bleed and dispose of the paralyzed animals. Bennett will separate and file the serum. Yurochko will see that cage trays are cleaned and oil is applied to the wing nuts by Tuesday." At the bottom of the page, he'd often add a less technical aside. "Ann will try to keep her personal space neater, please," he'd scribble.

As lunches were skipped and vacations were put off and clouds of cigarette smoke—courtesy of a new habit even Salk had picked up—began rising like thunderheads over offices and cubicles, the administrators of the University of Pittsburgh couldn't help noticing all the hard labor, and couldn't help being thrilled by it. With the NFIP pumping the kind of money it was into the work, Pittsburgh had arguably moved into the lead among the competing institutions racing to crack the polio problem. The world outside would surely want to know about this development, and the administrators decided to begin issuing a regular wave of press releases.

Salk, for one, wanted no part of such premature tub-thumping. The relative freedom he and his staff enjoyed from the newspapers and television stations was a direct result of keeping their mouths comparatively shut and, when they did talk to the media, talking only to folks like John Troan of the *Pittsburgh Press,* who appeared to understand in a visceral way how complex the science was and how long the road to a vaccine would be. Stirring up other, less sophisticated reporters would only stir up the public too. Salk, however, was not the one who made decisions about the press, and when the university officials made it clear to him that they were going more public with his work, he asked only that he be given a chance to look at any announcement before it went out. The university agreed.

A few days later, the first press release arrived on his desk. To Salk's surprise and relief, it turned out to be well balanced, trumpeting the amount of the NFIP grant a little too loudly and a little too crudely perhaps, but at least getting the figure right. It then described in detail how the money would be used and the challenges that lay ahead. It concluded with a self-evident summary sentence.

"What Dr. Salk and his associates are primarily concerned with," it read, "is developing a practical method of preventing poliomyelitis that is both safe and effective."

Salk read the release and added little more than a punctuation mark here and there. Before he signed off on it, however, he went back and pointedly scratched out the word "primarily." If the press people were committed to going public with his work, that was all right. But there would be no *primarily* about the lab's research this year. Salk and his team were setting out to invent a polio vaccine and they would undertake virtually nothing else until that job was done.

To the unacquainted eye, the Polk State School in Polk, Pennsylvania, seemed like a surpassingly pleasant place. It was located on 2,100 acres of pretty Pennsylvania farmland, dotted with administrative buildings, schoolhouses, and airy residential cottages. The great green expanse was almost entirely self-sustaining, with 600 acres set aside for dairy herds, 100 acres for corn, 75 acres for garden crops, and dozens more for oats, potatoes, and apples. The dairy farm produced an average of 30 ounces of milk each day for every one of the 3,400 children who lived on the grounds.

But not everything at Polk was as pastorally pleasing as it seemed. The children who lived here were what the state of Pennsylvania loosely called mental defectives, a term that, according to lawmakers, included idiots, imbeciles, and the more broadly defined feebleminded. Medical men preferred more finely drawn terms than legislators did, variously diagnosing the boys and girls who lived at the school as hydrocephalics, congenitally retarded, or simply luckless babies who had suffered severe oxygen deprivation at birth or cerebral injury later on. The worst-off of the patients were little more than warehoused here—kept clean, healthy, and well fed and as stimulated as they were capable of being. The better-off were examined for what the 650 staff members called correctable defects, and then trained up to whatever their level of trainability was. The children would stay at the Polk School for an average of twelve years—some a good deal longer. With all that, it was no wonder the place gave outsiders such a sense of melancholy. For a scientist conducting polio work, however, the Polk School also offered irresistible promise.

All polio researchers dreaded the day a vaccine would have to be tested in humans. The facts of the experimental transaction you were proposing, after all, were simple: You would be presented with a group of healthy children and would knowingly infect them with a virus, albeit a killed or weakened one. If the test went well, the children would have performed a great service to science; if the test failed, they would be crippled; if it failed catastrophically, they would die.

Even the most committed researcher could be easily frozen into inaction by such a set of choices had there not been more to the equation—and there was. No matter what happened to the boys and girls in your study, there were still millions of other children at large, children living in a world aswirl with wild poliovirus. What if the relative handful you used in your work could help prevent tens of thousands of others from falling ill or dying each year? Wasn't an experiment like that not only defensible but morally mandatory? The question ultimately turned on the icy arithmetic of body counts, and when things were added up that way, it became at least a little easier to proceed with any human trial. Certainly it helped if you had absolute faith in the safety of your vaccine, though Kolmer and Park and Brodie had had that faith as well. It helped too—though you wouldn't dare think it, let alone say it—if the children you used in your work lived in a place like the Polk State School, a place set aside for boys and girls who had no real chance of making any contribution to the larger world other than the one you were offering them.

In early January 1952, just as the NFIP grant was arriving and the vaccine work was picking up momentum, Salk wrote to Dr. Gale Walker, the superintendent of the Polk School, to share the thoughts he'd been having about his work and about the role the Polk children could play in it. He explained what his vaccine was, how he hoped to test it, and what he hoped it might achieve.

"We regard what we are doing as the introduction of a new immunizing procedure with the 'opening night,' so to speak, being held at Polk," he wrote. "Although some may look upon this with reluctance, others may look upon it as an opportunity to fulfill the wish we all have to contribute something to posterity."

Walker received Salk's letter and liked what he saw. As it happened, just the previous September there had been a frightening flurry of cases in the Polk infirmary. It was only by a stroke of luck that the close-quarters living of the institution hadn't led to a schoolwide epidemic. If Salk's experimental vaccine could help prevent that from happening in the future, he'd be willing to present the proposal to the children's families.

Before Walker could begin to approach the parental guardians, however, he had to approach the governmental guardians. His first step, he explained in his return letter to Salk, would be to send out a feeler to the state's attorney general and secretary of welfare to determine if human trials were even legal, never mind moral. The prospects for any such tests would depend entirely on their answer. That seemed like a reasonable, or at least predictable, precondition to Salk, and he agreed to let the matter perk with Walker and the state for a while. In the meantime, he turned his attention to another children's institution altogether: The D. T. Watson Home in Leetsdale, Pennsylvania.

The Watson Home had been in operation for thirty-six years, ever since the death of David T. Watson, a Harvard-educated attorney who had been one of the most successful legal advocates in the state—and indeed the nation—representing the likes of John D. Rockefeller, Andrew Carnegie, and the United States itself in its boundary dispute over the territory of Alaska. Watson and his wife had never had children of their own, but other people's children enchanted them. Strolling down the sidewalks of Europe, Watson would toss coins to the boys and girls he passed. While visiting London, he and his wife grew fond of a waiter who had taken especially good care of them in their hotel restaurant. When they learned that the man had a granddaughter suffering from a bone disease, they arranged for—and paid for—her treatment at a Swiss hospital, providing her the finest orthopedic care available on the continent.

When Watson died in 1916, it thus came as no surprise that he bequeathed his entire 68-acre, $1.8 million estate to the state of Pennsylvania, with instructions that it be turned into a home where poor, crippled girls between the ages of three and sixteen could receive care and rehabilitative treatment. The timing was good for such philanthropy—what with the paralytic carnage left behind after that year's polio plague—and by the summer of 1917, two dozen eligible girls had enrolled at the new D. T. Watson Home.

The black iron gate at the opening of the estate and the long driveway flanked by pin oaks gave no clue to the restorative nature of the huge, bright house that awaited the patients. The place had been re-equipped with ramps and rails to make navigating its long halls and at least its low stairways possible, as well as an array of new classrooms, gymnasiums, and play areas. Soon word of the wonderful Watson facility got around, and summer after summer, more and more girls sought admission. By 1934, a new 200-room building—containing a hospital, school, and dormitory rooms—had to be built on the grounds. By 1942, an uncharacteristically light polio season, the home decided to open its doors for the first time to boys.

Now, in 1952, the D. T. Watson facility was rivaled only by the legendary Warm Springs in Georgia for the good name it had earned in the polio community. And that, in addition to its handy location, caught Jonas Salk's interest.

Before he could safely inject any vaccine into the veins of children who had never had a clinical case of polio, he knew he would have to try it out on those who had already been hit by the disease. What Salk envisioned doing was recruiting a group of polio survivors and drawing their blood to read their antibodies. This would tell him which of the three types of poliovirus each child had contracted. He could then inject all the boys and girls with a vaccine made from their type only. If the antibodies in the blood rose above their existing levels, he'd know the shot was a good immune-system stimulant. If any rogue live viruses happened to make it into the mix, those same existing antibodies would be more than able to round them up and exterminate them. Only if the vaccines proved themselves in this cycle would Salk feel truly comfortable trying them out on the unprotected Polk children in the next.

Salk thus began another round of correspondence, this one with Dr. Jessie Wright, the Watson chief of staff, to see if the home might be willing to participate in such a study. Wright was celebrated in the field not just for her fine work with the children in her care, but also for the development of the increasingly popular polio rocking bed. Designed to tip a paralyzed child slightly forward and slightly back, the bed allowed gravity and the shifting weight of the body's viscera to expand and contract the chest rhythmically. For polio children with respiratory problems that were comparatively minor, this could mean permanent freedom from the iron lung. As Salk had hoped, Wright responded to his proposal as positively as Walker had, even going so far as to send back a list of fifty-two potential subjects.

While waiting for the attorney general and the secretary of welfare to weigh in on the idea of human trials, Salk had to write one more letter, once again looking into insurance coverage, but this time addressing his request to the Medical Malpractice Company of Fort Wayne, Indiana. Even if the Polk and Watson parents agreed to the polio studies, little would protect the virus lab and Salk himself from an avalanche of lawsuits should something go wrong. Salk thus inquired about just what kind of liability insurance the company provided for the sort of work he was contemplating. The insurers wrote back promptly, pleased to inform him that they indeed offered the kind of protection he was looking for. The premium would cost him $13 per year, renewable annually. The protection such a payment bought him would be generous but fair, imposing a limit of $5,000 on the claims of any one plaintiff, with an absolute ceiling of $15,000 worth of payouts in any twelve-month period. Surely no physician could be contemplating more than three claimants in a single year. Salk considered the fifty-two names Jessie Wright had sent him along with the as-yet-undecided number of other children at the Polk School. For now, he put the insurance man's letter aside.

❧

The University of Pittsburgh had been entirely convinced that issuing a series of press releases had been a first-rate idea—but that was before the sheriffs from upstate New York began calling the virus lab. They were safeguarding an important delivery, they said, one that was already on its way to Salk's lab. They had no idea what was inside the package, but they did know it was urgent—at least that was the way the New York physician who had sent it to Dr. Salk described it. The problem was that "urgent" was an increasingly loose word these days, one a lot of people were using when they contacted the Pittsburgh lab.

Even before the press releases went out, Salk had been hearing from growing numbers of people who had learned of his research through one means or another and simply had to get in touch with him. Some called or wrote with advice, some with questions, some with insights they were certain would help the busy doctor in his work. There was the housewife from Toronto, Ohio, who wrote to say that cat's milk was the answer to polio since, as everyone knew, polio might be caused by cats, so why shouldn't the animal hold the cure too? Simply draw off a nursing cat's milk, reduce and concentrate it to a state in which it could be injected into the body, and it would almost certainly stop paralysis in its tracks.

"This if you choose it will be your work," she wrote. "If not, I am going to send it to a well-known New York researcher." She then added, "It might be well to point out that I have my name protected as the originator of this cure."

There was the far more poignant plea from the Pennsylvania man with severe multiple sclerosis who had heard of Salk's work and mistakenly believed he already had a successful vaccine in hand. He wanted to know if it might treat his illness as well. "If you think that this vaccine or anything else that you wish to try for M.S. could help," he wrote, "I am willing to try it at my own expense."

After the press release was issued, things only got worse, with letters and calls pouring in from journalists who hoped to talk Salk into sitting for interviews, entrepreneurs who hoped to talk him into a vaccine-marketing partnership, parents who desperately hoped to buy a vial or two of vaccine before the next polio season arrived. Salk wrote back to as many of these petititoners as possible, reassuring the ones he could, offering his regrets to the ones he couldn't. But the calls from the sheriffs were another matter entirely.

It was early in the morning when the lawman from Greene County, New York, first phoned with the news of the package for Dr. Salk, explaining that it had been placed in his hands personally by a local doctor who had asked him to see it safely south to the Ulster County line and there to hand it off to that county's sheriff. Lorraine Friedman, who took the Greene County sheriff's call, thanked him for his help and passed the message on to Salk, who seemed only mildly interested. An hour later, the Ulster County sheriff phoned, saying that he was now in possession of the package and was shepherding it one county farther south. An hour after that a similar call arrived from the Orange County sheriff, then the Rockland County sheriff. Finally, the sheriff of Queens County phoned in. He now had the box and was driving it straight to New York City's Idlewild Airport, where it would in turn be flown as cargo on a small commuter plane to Pittsburgh.

By now, even Salk was interested. It would take at least a few hours for the plane to be cleared and the flight to be made, and Salk waited impatiently. Very early in the evening, word arrived from Pennsylvania's Allegheny Airport that the package had landed safely. It was no less than the pilot of the plane himself calling, promising that he would make the drive from the airport personally to ensure that the box arrived and Dr. Salk's work wouldn't be disrupted. By now, word of the pending delivery had gotten around the lab, and more than a few technicians found themselves casting curious glances toward the front door.

Finally, less than an hour later, the door of the lab opened and the blue-uniformed pilot walked in, carrying a small brown box in his hands. A cluster of lab workers gathered around as Lorraine accepted the box and called back to Salk. He emerged from his office and took the package. As

the technicians and the pilot craned forward, he picked up Lorraine's letter opener, slit the brown paper wrapping, lifted up the top of the box, and
peered inside at a small glass container and a note from the doctor. Then
he dropped his head and laughed.

"It's a stool sample," he said. "He thought we might want to culture
the virus."

The lab workers erupted into laughter of their own and peeked forward
for a glance at the unlovely thing. The flask was then duly carried to a
freezer and catalogued with dozens of other stool and tissue samples await-
ing polio culturing. The staff soon went back to work, but not before resolving that from now on, they would inquire far more closely into the
contents of any package being sent. It went without saying that there
would be no more press releases for at least the immediate future.

The long hours Salk's researchers were putting in at the virus lab paid
off even faster than they'd hoped, as riddle after riddle surrounding
the preparation of the polio vaccine was cracked. They found the proper
thermometer setting at which to inactivate the virus, discovering that a
body-temperature formalin bath would kill the poliovirus within 7 to 9
days, and a temperature of 77 degrees would extend that time to 56 days.
Any other time in between could be achieved simply by dialing the heat up
or down. Salk developed a logarithm that allowed him to track the disap-
pearance of the virus as it died off, reliably projecting ahead to precisely
when the last particle would wink out so that the vaccine could safely be
used in humans without wasting the entire batch in animal testing first.
The staff tried out samples of the vaccine in tissue and it appeared to be
safe and effective; they tried it further in monkeys and it seemed to work
there too. By the spring of 1952, the time was approaching when they
could at last take the step of testing it in human children—provided the
state of Pennsylvania said they could.

As it happened, the state's attorney general and secretary of welfare responded comparatively promptly to Dr. Walker's letter of inquiry, and

their reactions were mixed. While they had grave reservations about any tests involving human beings and the poliovirus, they were inclined to approve them—provided the doctors could show that the work might in some way benefit the children in the study themselves. It was easy for Salk to satisfy that condition when it came to the Polk children. After all, none of them had ever had a clinical case of polio before, and if the proposed vaccine worked, it would ensure that they never did. In the case of the Watson children, things were a little trickier. The whole purpose of Salk's study was to inject them with a type of polio they already had and to which they were thus already immune. The initial injections would therefore avail the children nothing at all. Since most of them had presumably contracted only one type of polio, however, they were still vulnerable to the other two. Subsequent injections with successful vaccines against those types could protect them from getting sick again, preventing their already poor physical state from one day growing worse.

With the state grudgingly willing to allow the work to go ahead, Salk, Walker, and Wright, along with lawyers for Polk, Watson, the NFIP, and the University of Pittsburgh, had to draft and redraft a waiver letter the parents of the volunteers would be required to sign. The letter had to be stuffed with warnings and disclosures of all the countless things that could go wrong, and yet somehow persuade the parents not to run screaming from the very idea of the study. Ultimately the parents of 47 Polk patients and 40 Watson patients did sign the form, and with those letters and the approval of the state in his pocket—not to mention his trial vaccine—Salk began making final plans for his fieldwork at the two schools.

It was in May and June of 1952 that he actually began the studies. The initial trips to both institutions would not be terribly interesting, at least scientifically. All Salk needed from each Watson patient was a preliminary blood sample so that he could read the antibodies and type the virus. For now, that was all he required from the Polk patients too. Even though those children had never been sickened by polio, it was entirely possible that any number of them had been struck by a symptomless, subclinical attack at some earlier point and would thus be carrying antibodies of their own. Only if Salk tested the blood of both groups would he be able to establish a baseline from which to measure the antibody boost his vaccine might later provide.

Salk set out for the eighty-mile drive to Polk on the morning of May 23, with Lorraine Friedman accompanying him. It was a pleasant day to make the trip. The seasonable springtime weather that had broken out over most of the state meant that the Polk grounds would be in bloom. Nearly all the resident children would probably be outside, enjoying one of the uncounted parties that were routinely held on the lawns—picnic parties, birthday parties, good-conduct parties for the older girls who helped the nurses with the babies, wading parties for the younger children when it was warm enough to use the little pools.

Almost all the children would be invited to the parties, the only exceptions being the so-called no-productive patients, the ones whose minds flickered on so low a burn that they typically did little but stay in their cottages. And even they had recently been eased into a training program, going outside in work teams to pull up the large weeds and turn over the flat stones that often proved such a nuisance to the gardeners. It provided them with a little sun and a little exercise and maybe even a sense of having accomplished something, though the doctors could never be certain on that point.

The only thing that made this comparatively happy picture especially hard to take was that not all of the children at Polk—no-productives or not—were young children. There was a reason the patients spent so many years at the school, and that reason was that many of them would simply never have the wherewithal to leave. With families willing to pay for their care for as long as the state would have them, they would slowly grow into their teens and beyond, moving into dormitories built especially for older patients, until the idea of holding them in a school meant for children simply became insupportable.

Salk was prepared for the older patients when he arrived, but Lorraine wasn't. She fell quiet at the sight of the near-adults clumsily playing at the children's games; she seemed rattled by the ripe and unavoidably unpleasant wards, where patients who could not care for themselves were cleaned and tended to in a manner meant for babies. She turned away at the sight of the no-productives doing pretty much nothing at all. Whatever wonders the lab back in Pittsburgh might one day produce would do nothing for what ailed these patients.

For his part, Salk pressed gently ahead with the work he came to do. In his everyday life, he sometimes displayed a curious awkwardness with boys and girls other than his own. He never seemed to know precisely how to calibrate his behavior to a child's age, leading him to address the three-year-old, eight-year-old, and twelve-year-old with the same sort of undifferentiated condescension. Children under his care, however, were a different matter. In that situation, the boys and girls did need more or less the same thing from him—a soft tone, a gentle touch, a nudge of encouragement if they seemed frightened. This applied whether the children were toddlers or teens, and whether they were simple or quick.

Today, Salk took the Polk children carefully in hand and drew their blood as painlessly as he could, joking with the boys and girls who appreciated jokes, smiling at the ones who understood only that. He gave each child a lollipop from a box he'd brought with him and promised he'd bring more whenever he returned. When necessary, he'd remove the candy's wrapper for them. Throughout it all, he'd cast the occasional glance to Lorraine, nodding his encouragement.

Later, when they were in the car driving home, she spoke up for one of the only times that day. "If this were all there was to the job," she said, "I don't think I could do it."

Three weeks later, as the Polk blood was still being tested and titered, Salk set out for his visit to the D. T. Watson Home, this time accompanied by a pair of Municipal Hospital nurses in place of Lorraine, who had elected to stay home. Though the parents of all the children in the Watson study had willingly signed the carefully drafted waiver, most of them had decided to be present when the doctor from Pittsburgh arrived so that they could have a final talk with him before letting him get about his work. The parents, Salk had been told, would be assembled with their children in the school's auditorium. Those boys and girls who could get around on crutches and canes would struggle into the auditorium's seats next to their parents. Those who could not walk at all would pull up beside them in their wheelchairs.

Salk and the nurses arrived in the auditorium at the appointed hour, the nurses attired in proper white uniforms, Salk in tie and white lab coat. Salk walked to the front of the room alone, shook hands with the superintendent and the other doctors, and smiled at the students and parents—all of whom remained silent. He reached for a metal folding chair, pulled it over to where the families had gathered, and addressed himself to the children first.

"As your parents and the doctors have told you already," he said, "there are three types of polio, and each of you got one of them. We can't tell which kind just by looking at you, but there are markers in your blood that will let us know. So what we need to do today is take a little bit of blood out of your arm so we can carry it home with us and give it a good, close look."

The children nodded and Salk went on to explain what would come next—how he'd return in a few more weeks with a particular kind of shot for each child; how that shot would make even more of the markers appear in their blood; how he'd have to take other samples after that to watch the markers rise and fall.

"I can't say that any of this will make you any better, because it won't," he said. "But it might help other boys and girls not get as sick as you were."

He asked the children if they had any questions and none of them did. The parents, however, had plenty.

Could the shot bring the disease back? a mother asked.

"Drawing blood can't," Salk assured her. "And as long as we give the children a vaccine made only from the virus they already have, that shouldn't hurt either."

Could the vaccine prevent the children from getting sick again?

"No," Salk admitted. "A vaccine against the two types of virus they don't have might do that. But we're not at that point yet."

"I got a yellow fever shot when I was in the army and it made me sick," one father said. "Why couldn't that happen here?"

"Again," Salk answered, "we're injecting the children with a type of virus they already had, and a killed virus at that. It should be safe."

Salk and the group spoke for a while longer, until, at last, the questions were exhausted. Then he nodded to the nurses in the back of the room, who came forward with kit bags of syringes, vials, adhesive bandages, and alcohol. Collapsible tables had been opened up for them and they arranged their tools on sterile cotton cloths.

The children had each been given a registration card that they would hand to the nurses when their blood was drawn so that the dates of all samples and inoculations could be recorded. Bill Kirkpatrick—the onetime high school football player and friend of a lost redheaded girl—held one of the cards. In the upper right corner was a "W-1." He suspected that the W stood for Watson; he knew that the 1 meant he was to go first. Farther down the list was twelve-year-old Jimmy Sarkett, a boy who had been paralyzed by an especially virulent Type III virus.

At the request of the teachers, the children came forward, according to the number that appeared on their card. Salk cast his eyes over the fidgety group, then looked toward the front and gave Bill Kirkpatrick a nod and a smile. The boy struggled forward with the aid of a back brace, a leg brace, and two canes. He eyeballed the bristle of needles on the table.

Salk followed his gaze. "They look nasty, don't they?" he asked.

Bill nodded.

Salk inclined his head toward the other, younger children. "Hope they're not afraid of them," he said in a whisper. Bill smiled and Salk looked inquiringly at the needles.

"Okay to proceed?" he asked.

Bill nodded, Salk took up a needle, and slid it into a vein in the boy's arm. He withdrew a vial of blood, he regarded the vial closely for a moment, then labeled it carefully.

"Thank you," he said, "for going first."

Bill shrugged. "I have two nephews. I don't want them to get what I had."

Over the course of the next two hours, the thirty-nine other children came forward. Salk greeted Jimmy Sarkett familiarly, nodding to himself when he noticed the properly spelled name on the card. When Jimmy was done, the remainder of the children trooped up, some regarding the needle blithely, some with terror, all tolerating it admirably.

After the last of the children had come ahead and the last of the samples had been drawn, Salk offered his thanks once more, packed up his tools, and along with his nurses, made the drive back to Pittsburgh. He would spend the next twenty days typing and retyping the antibodies in all the blood. On July 2, he would return to the D. T. Watson Home. This time he would bring with him a poliomyelitis vaccine. Once again, Bill Kirkpatrick would be the first to get the shot. The others would follow him. Whether 46 million more children in the United States would follow after that was, for the moment, impossible to know.

After a time, it became hard to defend the virus lab against all the reporters trying to shoulder their way inside. As the summer of 1952 unfolded, however—an especially hot summer that looked as though it was going to be a growth year for polio—Salk continued to deny almost all of them access. On those occasions that he was inclined to talk to any reporter, it was mostly to John Troan of the *Pittsburgh Press*.

Salk increasingly respected Troan's lay understanding of all matters polio and his ability to explain what he knew in a smart and comprehensible way. Just four days before Salk made his first trip to the Watson Home, Troan published a long story entitled "Where Do We Stand on Polio?," walking his readers through the thicket of such arcana as epidemiology, cross-immunity among viral types, the function of antiviral medications, and the various stopgap therapies researchers were still using to treat polio symptoms, such as curare nerve toxin or priscolene blood-vessel dilator to relax affected muscles. With all that, he did not even mention the possibility of a vaccine until the last column of the long, nine-column item. Salk's name did not come up at all until the fifty-seventh of the story's fifty-nine paragraphs, well after the likes of John Paul, David Bodian, and Albert Sabin.

It was this kind of lost-in-the-swarm anonymity both for himself and for vaccine research as a whole that Salk craved. That, more than anything, was why he allowed Troan such frequent—often exclusive—access. All the same, Troan could not always keep the unfolding drama to himself.

One of the other *Pittsburgh Press* staffers who had a keen interest in polio was Bill Jacobs, the paper's assistant city editor and, not incidentally, Troan's boss. In his spare time, Jacobs moonlighted as a stringer for both *Time* and *Life* magazines. Filing an exclusive from inside the virus lab would be a true coup for Jacobs, especially if he'd be allowed to bring along some of *Life*'s celebrated photographers. Jacobs buttonholed Troan in the newsroom and asked him to help broker the arrangement. He would need just half a day of Salk's time, not an hour more. Troan thought for a moment, weighing a request from his editor against the reticence of his source. There was no good answer, but the editor was the one standing directly in front of him.

"I'll see what I can do," he said.

Later that day, Troan called Salk and made his case straightforwardly, explaining Jacobs's request and adding a small plea of his own. "For *Life*, Bill may be just a stringer," he said, "but he's my boss here in Pittsburgh."

"Okay," Salk said. "Have him come."

Jacobs made the necessary arrangements, and several days later he appeared in the lab as agreed, escorted by a watchful Troan and accompanied by a three-man photo team from *Life*. Jacobs had been telling the truth when he said that they would need only half a day, and Troan had been telling the truth—at least as he knew it—when he passed that estimate on to Salk. But no one told the cameramen that. There were a lot of reasons *Life* photography was so widely acclaimed, and one of them was that the photographers themselves took their time. In Salk's lab, that meant devoting the better part of the morning to positioning lights, adjusting blinds, moving furniture to new and unlikely positions that made it useless for lab work but evidently pretty in a picture.

Salk did as little grumbling as he could as his laboratory was turned upside down, but he was sorely tested. Since it was he who would be the subject of most of the pictures, he could not simply go about his work until the photographers were ready for him. Rather, he would have to stand idly in frame while fine adjustments in lighting and staging were made. Troan and Jacobs both read his darkening mood and offered what appeasement they could.

"Only a few more minutes," they'd promise unpersuasively. "Almost done now."

Finally, early in the afternoon, the preparations were all made and the photographers proceeded to shoot. They coaxed Salk into all manner of contrived poses—peering through a microscope at nothing, talking on the phone to no one, reviewing what appeared to be data on a clipboard that actually contained blank sheets. Finally, the photographers spotted a small rack of test tubes filled with blood serum and poliovirus.

"How would you examine those if you were going to?" one of the photographers asked.

"I'd lift the rack up and look underneath," Salk answered.

"Would you mind?"

Salk sighed, lifted the rack up to the light, and peered through the tubes.

"Higher, please," said the photographer, and Salk obliged. "Higher," the photographer repeated. "No, higher still."

Salk did what the photographer asked, holding the rack at an increasingly acute angle, until all at once a test tube slipped from its slot and fell to the floor. The glass shattered into tiny shards and the culture and serum splashed about everywhere.

The photographers froze, looking at the live virus as if they could practically see it squirming at their feet. As a group, they slowly lowered their cameras and began backing toward the door. Troan remained in place and Jacobs, with some effort, did the same. Salk, nodding wearily, placed the rack back on the lab counter, plucked up a formaldehyde-soaked rag, and carefully swabbed up the mess. When he was done, he stood and looked at Troan.

"Half a day?" he asked, not entirely pleasantly. "It's a good thing this is leap year. I can make up the day I lost."

∞ 14 ∞

Half past seven in the morning was the time Elsie Ward usually set aside to feed her babies—or that was what she liked to call them, at least. In truth, Ward's babies were merely cells—monkey, mouse, sometimes human cells—but she nonetheless cared for them dearly. In her small corner of the Pittsburgh virus lab, she protected them, fretted over them, kept them nourished with warm helpings of nutrient whenever they needed it.

Even by the standards of the best and cleanest labs, Elsie Ward was a stickler. Her workstation was always both furiously busy and fastidiously tidy. She kept a large supply of mercuric towels on hand and always went through them fast, since she demanded an antiseptic surface for all her work, even when the experiment she was conducting didn't strictly call for one. She never seemed troubled, as most researchers were, when an errant spore or bacterium would contaminate an experiment, since if one of them landed in a laboratory dish, it would serve as an early warning that more of them were floating through the air. "I want to know what's contaminating my lab," she'd say as she discarded the culture in the dish.

In the summer of 1952, Ward's station was a more important place than it had ever been before. Jonas Salk and his team had needed most of the months of June and July to complete the preliminary analysis of the blood they'd drawn at the Polk School and the Watson Home, then return to inject the children with vaccine, then return again a few weeks later to draw more blood that would tell them if the dead virus had indeed prompted live antibodies to bloom in the children's systems.

Determining whether that had happened would not be an easy thing. Since antibodies were even smaller than the already invisible viruses they were designed to attack, it was impossible simply to look at a blood sample under a microscope and take a census of what was there. Instead, viral researchers had to make their determination indirectly. First, a test tube that had been seeded with healthy human or animal cells would be mixed with poliovirus with an appetite for those cells. Serum drawn from the children's blood would then be poured in too. If antibodies had grown in sufficient numbers and sufficient strength, the viruses would be snuffed out and the cells would thrive. If the antibodies were too weak or didn't exist at all, the viruses would be free to bloom and the sacrificial cells would be the ones that would die.

Whichever direction the experiment went, there were a few ways to monitor the progress. Healthy cells, which were visible under the microscope, would have a characteristic plumpness, with a sound-looking nucleus and intact cytoplasmic guts. Unhealthy cells would grow swollen and misshapen and develop vacuoles where the cytoplasm was degenerating.

The color of the tubes would be an even more direct signal of the health of the cultures. Mixed in with the cells, virus, and antibody was a small amount of pinkish dye that was sensitive to acidity. If there was no metabolic activity in the solution—that is, if the children's blood cells had died—the fluid would be low in acids and the dye would turn red. If live, healthy cells were present, they'd churn out carbon dioxide, converting the solution from neutral to acidic, and the color of the dye from pinkish to yellow.

In a typical polio experiment, up to 128 test tubes would be placed together in a rack, with the concentration of blood serum decreasing from left to right. If the vaccine had done its job in the human subjects, each tube should thus turn a tiny bit yellower than the one to its immediate right, indicating that the cells in that brighter tube were faring just a tiny bit better. Getting a good look at all the test tubes usually required lifting the rack to peer at them from underneath—a dangerous nuisance that could cause the kind of virus spill that had so frightened the *Life* photographers. Just recently, Salk had gotten around this problem by placing his racks on a transparent surface and rigging a mirror angled at 45 degrees beneath it. This allowed the whole sweep of the experiment to be read at a glance.

One morning in mid-September, Elsie Ward came to the lab even earlier than usual to look in on her babies. She had been incubating cells for most of the summer, growing the healthy cultures that would be mixed with the Polk and Watson serum when Salk determined the time was right. Just the morning before, he had made that determination, and the first batch of serum had been stirred into the first rack of test tubes. It would take at least twenty-four hours for the experiment to begin playing out and the tubes to change—or not change—their telltale color. Ward, better than anyone, knew that there was no sense rushing to check on the progress of the work before it was ready, since cultures died or thrived at their own patient pace. That sensible truth, however, did little to stop her from coming to the locked and darkened lab so early that September morning.

She opened the main lab door on the first floor of the hospital building, flipped the lights on, and made her way down the black-and-white-checkerboard hallway. Salk's empty office was just two doors from the entrance, with Lorraine Friedman's unmanned workstation positioned protectively outside of it. Private offices belonging to Byron Bennett, Julius Youngner, and the other senior staffers lined the walls farther along. So did larger, open spaces shared by more-junior members of the team. A small group headed by Don Wegemer worked in a communal area on the left. Ward worked in a smaller, double lab off to the right, one she shared with Angela Laurent, a research fellow assigned mostly to the influenza work Salk's lab still pursued on the side.

Ward entered the room, threw on the light, and immediately cast her eyes to her spotless workstation, with its big rack of 128 test tubes. The first thing she noticed was an unmistakable scream of yellow flashing back to her from inside the tubes—many shades of yellow actually, each tube brighter than the one that preceded it and all of them brighter still than the pink or red ones to the right. This was precisely—*precisely*—the color pattern the experiment had been designed to produce, with the borderline between red and yellow marking the spot at which the concentration of antibodies in the serum was sufficient to kill the virus. In the small sample group of Polk and Watson children, Jonas Salk's polio vaccine had worked perfectly.

As a rule, Ward was not one to exclaim much when she was either pleased or chagrined. "Oh my!" was all she would typically say, and "Oh my!" was what she said this morning.

Ward spent the next hour bent over her workstation, peering at the tubes under her microscope. The cells in the yellow fluid indeed exhibited the shape healthy cells ought to; the ones in the red fluid had indeed assumed the sorry shape of those gone dead. Before long, she heard more doors opening in the lab and footsteps approaching. She looked up and saw Laurent enter their joint work space.

"You might want to see this," Ward said levelly.

Laurent looked at Ward's tubes, beamed, and poked her head out into the hall, calling to the scientists in the nearby offices. Wegemer, Bennett, and a handful of others hurried in, saw what Ward and Laurent had seen, and let out a whoop. Soon others arrived at work and streamed in too. Finally, Salk himself appeared.

As a rule, Salk didn't begin his workday until he performed a little ritual, stopping in his office to remove his sport jacket and slip on his white lab coat. He had rarely been known to take the coat off during the work-day and had never been known not to have a second one handy when the first was being laundered. Today, however, he was unaccustomedly out of uniform, clad in his jacket with the lab coat nowhere in sight. Knowing what might await in the test tubes even before he arrived at work, he had apparently made a straight path for Elsie Ward's lab.

"How do they look?" he asked.

Ward pointed to the rack. "It worked!" she exclaimed.

Salk made his way through the group toward Ward's microscope. He peered into the eyepiece at the shapes of both the living and dead cells, glanced at the test tube pattern of red to pink to yellow. His work, he now knew, had turned a corner from which it would never turn back. On more than one occasion he'd told his staff that what they were looking for in their polio studies was a *yes* from nature—some irrefutable confirmation that the path they were pursuing was the correct one. What he saw at Elsie Ward's workstation was that *yes*. He looked up at her and smiled.

"Good for you," he said. "Well done."

Salk appeared more wholly happy than anyone in the lab could recall having seen him before, and yet he seemed subdued too. It was less as if there were something troubling him than as if he'd almost known what was coming. One or two of the senior staffers—the ones who knew Salk best—flashed a look at one another and exchanged suppressed smiles. It would not be beyond Salk to have slipped into the lab even earlier than Ward had this morning, sneaked an impatient peek at her cultures, and then re-treated for a cup of coffee somewhere off campus so that his technician could arrive and enjoy her discovery. Salk was lab boss enough to know the value of such defining moments for young researchers, but not actor enough to fake his own surprise when he returned. In either event, he would never tell and none of the senior staffers would ask.

Regardless, it was almost certain he was already thinking ahead—to the hundreds and hundreds of other blood cultures that would have to be run to confirm the meaning of today's results and the thousands of other times the antibodies would have to prove themselves. The experiment that had worked under Ward's hand would now have to work repeatedly and reliably when other scientists tried it too. Then, of course, it would have to work in the world at large.

"Okay," he said to the room. "Now let's do it again."

The summer of 1952 turned out to be a very good time to develop a polio vaccine. The ugly clump of molecules that made up the poliovirus was a mindless thing, with no volition or will, but as Salk and his team began to circle it more closely, it almost appeared to begin fighting for its life.

The paralysis season began in early June that year, in the warmer, wetter parts of Texas and Louisiana. The disease took hold in that steamy pocket in a few lethal weeks and then ranged out through the entire gulf and bayou region. It saturated the southern part of the map, then turned north and raced up along the vein of the Mississippi River, pulsing through the valley states and seeping up to the Great Lakes region beyond. With the country cut in two, the virus then pivoted east and west, racing simultaneously to the Atlantic and Pacific Coasts. By midsummer, there wasn't a state in the nation that didn't have the sickness—in most cases at epidemic levels.

The numbers, no matter how they were added and re-added, stunned the epidemiologists. The summer of 1951 had been the third-worst polio year on record, with 28,386 children and adults sickened, crippled, or killed. The 1952 season more than doubled that, with a disease count of 57,879. By the middle of August, more than 3,000 children were being swept up by the illness each week; the second week in September, the figure topped 4,000. During one peak stretch between September 16 and 20, doctors diagnosed 4,191 cases in just five days, more than double the polio total in the entire year of 1938.

The terror that took hold of New York in the long-ago summer of 1916 this time seized the entire nation, with summer camps slamming their gates, movie houses closing their doors, parents sealing their children into their homes. Pittsburgh's Forbes Field was located close enough to the University of Pittsburgh Virus Lab that on good days the polio scientists could hear the roar when Pirates left-fielder Ralph Kiner launched another of his increasingly frequent home runs. Attendance at Forbes dropped from 956,590 in the 1951 season to 686,673 in 1952, despite the fact that Kiner himself was leading the National League in homers, a rare achievement for the always awful Pirates.

The NFIP's March of Dimes drives did what they could to rise to the challenge, pulling in a staggering $28 million—more than a 33 percent increase over 1951—and yet every dollar of it would come too late to help a single one of the illness's newest victims. The success in Salk's lab had been met, blow for blow, by the worst epidemic in the recorded history of infantile paralysis.

Salk and his staff grimly followed the plague throughout the summer and into early fall. News from their lab of the progress they were making would go a long way, they knew, toward easing the nation's growing panic—and yet it would do so misleadingly, implicitly promising a solution to the disease that was nowhere near at hand. For now, Salk thus kept as quiet as possible about the Polk and Watson findings, informing Basil O'Connor and Harry Weaver, and assuming that Weaver in turn would tell Thomas Rivers. Beyond that, he was not yet prepared to discuss his work even with the rest of the NFIP, much less with the world as a whole.

Before Salk could consider taking so public a step, he and his team would have to expand their studies dramatically. With the help of Jessie Wright and Gale Walker, the superintendent of the Watson and Polk homes, they recruited other volunteers among the patients of the facilities, and more still stepped forward from the adult staffs. The new subjects were typed and inoculated as the first group had been.

As the pace of the work increased, Salk spent even less time at home, and the burden of his workload soon began to show. To Donna's distress, he'd not yet given up the smoking habit he'd picked up from his team, and when he'd come home late in the evening, it was often with heavy eyes, a lined face, and the ghost of tobacco smoke clinging to him. Inevitably, he'd have one or two small scraps of paper tucked under his tie clip, each bearing a scribbled phone number or some other reminder. It was a practice he'd established lately when there was a call he absolutely had to make or a chore he absolutely had to do, reasoning that he could never get undressed at the end of the day without removing his tie and seeing the notes. Even before that happened, Donna was likely to notice the slips and implore him to do whatever he had to do and throw the silly things away.

But if the work was taking a toll, it was also paying off. By the time 1952 was almost at a close, Salk's sample group of inoculated children and adults had grown to 161. For the sake of thoroughness, he had been testing both an aqueous vaccine—a watery preparation that included no adjuvant—and a creamy white one fortified with mineral oil. The aqueous variety, used in 71 of the subjects, triggered antibody production against the Type 2 virus only; the adjuvant version, used in 91, provided protection against all three types. Better still, a December reading of the blood of the first 87 subjects showed that their antibody counts were holding at about the same levels they'd registered in September. The five-month stretch from the July inoculation to the December readings hardly represented lifetime immunity, but it did match the length of a long polio season—and the antibodies showed no sign of flagging.

This was precisely the kind of milestone the NFIP as a whole would want to know about. It was time, Salk decided, to open up about his work, and the place to do it would be at the upcoming meeting of the foundation's Committee on Immunization, set for January 22, 1953, at the Hotel Hershey in Hershey, Pennsylvania.

The hotel was a palatial building constructed in 1933, with a vaulted lobby reminiscent of an Italian palazzo, a great circular dining room, and sweeping views over the grounds. The NFIP favored the pleasant place because it seemed to encourage the scientists to be pleasant themselves— opening up more about their work and restraining their most heated exchanges, almost as if they were trying to live up to the gentility of their surroundings. Whatever the reason for the good behavior, the foundation preferred it that way.

Though none of the other NFIP grantees who would be in attendance knew for certain what Salk had developed, they had an idea that something was afoot, if only because of the money he was receiving. When grants for 1953 had been announced, Salk was again high up on the funding heap, with an endowment of $255,472—for a total of more than $1.25 million of NFIP money over the last five years. Even if the budget didn't hint at what was going on in Pittsburgh, the members of the lab staff themselves occasionally did. John Troan, by now a familiar and well-trusted figure in the lab, had been told nothing explicitly by Salk, but he could read moods and he could count hours and he knew the kinds of days the team was putting in.

"How are things going?" he'd ask Jim Lewis, both men knowing that the question was more than a casual one.

"They're going well," Lewis would say, "but keep the lid on." Troan, true to his unspoken compact with Salk, did. But if Lewis was leaking—even if only by tone and smile—others in the lab surely were too.

Among the most curious of the outsiders looking for nuggets from Pittsburgh was Albert Sabin. For more than a week in mid-January, Sabin had been on the road, touring East Coast polio labs to get a sense of the work that was being done there. By pure coincidence—at least as he described it—he would be passing by Pittsburgh about two days before the Hershey meeting and phoned Salk in advance to inquire if he might drop by for a courtesy call. Perhaps, he suggested, the two of them could then share a train to Hershey. Salk agreed and even invited Sabin to have dinner at his home. He also asked Lorraine Friedman to book Sabin a room at the Hotel Schenley, and to reserve both men a parlor car on the eleven A.M. train from Pittsburgh to Harrisburg the day before the meeting, arriving at 4:18 that afternoon. Two full days, one full meal, and five hours and eighteen minutes on a train with Albert Sabin should, Salk guessed, finally warm him to the man or cool him entirely.

It did neither. Sabin was a gracious guest in both Salk's lab and in his home, flattering his work and his staff and, later that evening, his wife's fine food. But he also had questions—a lot of them—both in Pittsburgh and on the train. What was Salk working on? How far had he gotten? Was he really as committed as he seemed to be to this idea of a killed-virus vaccine or was he considering trying the live approach? Salk answered Sabin's questions guardedly.

"Frankly," he said, in the only flat fib he told that whole two days, "I'd be glad to go either way. I'll try the killed and if it doesn't work, I suppose we'd be able to work with the live."

Salk was knowingly misleading Sabin, but it was a lie with little consequence. The truth would come out within a couple days, after all, and it seemed somehow wrong to share what he knew with one scientist before revealing it to all the others. Besides, Sabin had already made his disdain for the killed-virus technique known. His seeming interest in it now was motivated either by collegial pity for a fellow researcher who was devoting himself to such a scientific dead end, or competitive relief that Salk's pointless work would clear the field for Sabin's own live-virus studies. In either case, whatever information Salk might share now could not possibly affect the direction of Sabin's work.

Once the scientists convened at the Hotel Hershey, Salk needed to play cute no more. There were a number of recently completed studies that would be reported during the course of the gathering, and many of them would precede Salk's. Burying the Pittsburgh results that way was no accident. O'Connor knew that it was Salk's research that would most excite—or inflame—the group, and he wanted the other studies to get a fair hearing.

When Salk at last rose to speak, he did so with a studied flatness. He was here, he explained, to describe his progress with "various formalin-inactivated polio preparations"—perhaps the most oblique way imaginable of saying the words "killed vaccine." These preparations, he explained, had been developed in his lab and injected into a tiny sample group of 161 children and adults. It was so far impossible to say that the potion had fully proven itself, but it had produced high and steady antibody levels almost immediately. Permanent immunity would probably require three injections, each shot containing killed samples of all three virus types. The first two injections would come a week or two apart, the third would come two months later. Before it was possible even to contemplate that, numerous variables would have to be studied further, including questions of doses and adjuvant formulations, to say nothing of the problem of scaling up production techniques so that the vaccine could be mass-produced.

Salk's presentation was one of the most cautious he had ever made, a caveat accompanying nearly every claim. The scientists, however, looked straight through all the qualifications to the nub of what he had accomplished and were suitably stunned—and predictably torn.

Tommy Turner of Johns Hopkins rose to congratulate Salk on his vaccine—no point in calling it anything else—and said he wanted it used as soon as possible. If the NFIP justified its large-scale gamma globulin trial in Utah with the argument that the mere act of testing the serum could help prevent at least some cases of paralysis, surely the same case could be made for Salk's protovaccine. Joseph Smadel of the army's Walter Reed Hospital agreed.

"When are you going to do your Provo test?" he asked.

Sabin saw things differently. Having spent the last two days believing that the cards Salk was showing him in his left hand were the only ones he held, he was completely surprised when the scientist from Pittsburgh turned over the one in his right. He responded by declaring the card worthless. The study, he announced when he had the floor, was badly incomplete. Salk's adjuvants were questionable, the kidney tissue from which he cultured his virus was dangerous, the Polk and Watson sample groups were far too unrepresentative of the population as a whole to be of much value at all. Even if Salk could address these flaws, it went without saying that the inconvenience of a killed vaccine—repeatedly administered by injection instead of popped into the mouth the way a live vaccine could be—was a problem Salk could never overcome. There were many studies to be done—probably years' worth of them—before a sweeping field trial of any killed vaccine could even be considered.

O'Connor, whose opinion was the only one in the room that truly mattered, was of two minds. He had been in the polio game longer than anyone there and he understood both the science of the work and the parliamentary machinations behind it. Salk's vaccine was now the leading contender in the vaccine race, but a race it still would be, at least until Salk could test his preparation further.

The Hershey meeting still had a day to go, but as far as O'Connor was concerned, it had done its job. The men in the room now had the information they needed, and even as they continued to argue about what that information meant, he was certain that no consensus for a Provo-scale test would yet emerge—nor should it. While the other men debated their way to that inevitable conclusion, O'Connor was already contemplating how to get word of Salk's work out to a much more exclusive group of NFIP officials: its board of trustees.

Ever since the days of the Birthday Balls, O'Connor and Roosevelt had relied on a core group of industrialists and Wall Streeters to keep the NFIP solvent through even the hardest economic times. The trustees were men who might not know a virus from a bacterium, but they surely knew where money could be found and how other wealthy men like themselves could be persuaded to donate some of it when the need arose. In 1953, the board was made up of thirty-eight powerful men, including Thomas Watson, the chairman of the board of International Business Machines; Robert Woodruff, chief of the executive committee of the Coca-Cola Company; Arthur Kirsten, Jr., president of the West Indies Sugar Corporation; and David Sarnoff, a retired brigadier general and now the president of RCA.

Getting news of Salk's preliminary success to these much prized moneymen as quickly as possible was vital, if only so they wouldn't find out first from some other source and take offense at being left in the dark. But the information they were given would be selective. O'Connor wouldn't mention Salk by name, protecting what was left of his lab's privacy. Nor would he mention many specifics about the vaccine, figuring the fewer details he gave these influential laymen, the fewer they could misunderstand and erroneously pass on. He'd tell them only what they absolutely needed to know, which would be more than enough.

O'Connor wanted to convene the trustees' meeting as early as January 26—just three days later. With the exception of Harry Weaver, there would not be a single scientist invited to the gathering. O'Connor asked Weaver to deliver the address explaining the Polk and Watson findings; he told Salk to stay over in Hershey an extra night to help Weaver draft the presentation. He also expected both men to understand that he, O'Connor, would edit the remarks as he saw fit, speaking the language of moneymen far more fluently than the two scientists ever could.

Three days later, the meeting convened at the lush Pierre Hotel in Manhattan. Weaver, who had not had much time to rehearse his talk but was gifted at working even a difficult room, decided he would open his presentation the way he knew powerful men liked to be addressed: humbly. After explaining that his purpose this evening was to provide them with an overview of the progress polio research was making, he immediately conceded that he might not be up to the job.

"I am very conscious that it is impossible for any one individual, myself included, to totally comprehend the program of research against poliomyelitis," he said. "There is more truth than humor in the remark of that unknown sage who once said, 'He who can do research does it; and he who wants to but can't is made the director.'"

The trustees, assured that no mere doctor would be talking down to them tonight, laughed appreciatively. Then Weaver, who understood every shred of current polio work better, perhaps, than any man on the planet, walked them through a long and rich history of the last two decades of research, from Kolmer, Park, and Brodie through Enders, Weller, and Robbins through the triumph of the typing program, the gamma globulin trials in Utah, and the terrible epidemic of just the past summer. Finally, he came to the current news.

"Some very exciting tests are now under way," he disclosed, "on a new killed-virus vaccine, one that is administered in conjunction with certain potentiating oils. I would like to be able to announce that field trials for such a vaccine will take place in 1953. This I cannot say with complete assurance, but I can say that tremendous progress has been made—in fact, the kind of progress one is accustomed to seeing prior to the taking of an important step forward."

Weaver, as planned, did not name names, but no trustee could have been fooled. Salk, this had to be Salk. It was his name that had been so liberally sprinkled throughout the foundation newsletters and the occasional newspaper, and Salk himself who'd been so liberally sprinkled with yet another generous endowment from the NFIP. And while the idea of "potentiating oils" sounded a lot like sorcery, it also sounded an awful lot like the adjuvants the foundation had been touting of late.

The trustees would not press the point of the scientist's identity today, allowing Weaver and the overworked Salk this bit of sensible secrecy. But Weaver ought to know—or perhaps O'Connor ought to tell him—that men who ran companies might not be scientists, but they were surely pragmatists. These men had been backing the National Foundation for Infantile Paralysis since 1938. They would surely know who was responsible when that support began yielding results.

The storm that blew through Salk's world following the Hershey meeting gathered slowly, but powerfully. Nobody pretended that the news from the Polk School and Watson Home could be completely contained, not with the families of the subjects whispering to other families and the University of Pittsburgh whispering to the press. Already, the requests for information from reporters and parents were increasing. After that, industry came calling too. The Lilly Pharmaceutical company wrote with a friendly inquiry into the progress of Salk's work and happy congratulations on any success he might have had so far. Lilly added that in the event that the NFIP didn't plan to mass-manufacture Salk's potential vaccine itself, the company would be more than pleased to talk about taking on that complicated job. That it would also be an enormously lucrative job went without saying. It was all but certain that other pharmaceutical companies would soon be making similar offers.

Things would only heat up more in March, Salk knew, when his paper on his work—an obligatory step for any study even a fraction as meaningful as the Polk and Watson trials—was published in the *Journal of the American Medical Association*. Weaver anticipated this and called yet another meeting of the NFIP brass for February 26, 1953, at the Waldorf-Astoria, in the hope of resolving just when a Provo-style field trial should be held. If anything, however, the question only grew more contentious.

"My feeling," said Thomas Rivers, who had come down firmly in favor of a trial, "is that between now and January of 1954, Dr. Salk might want to go ahead and vaccinate, let us say, 25,000 children in the Pittsburgh area, mainly to be sure the vaccine is safe."

"I don't know that we even have a vaccine yet," Salk protested, wincing at the premature use of the word. "We have preparations which have induced antibody formation."

"I think you have a vaccine, Jonas," Rivers said with a wave.

"If every vaccine that was ever used on human beings had been put through half of this," said Joseph Smadel, "we wouldn't have any preventive measures at all. If the army had had to go through half this to get a vaccine for soldiers in Japan or Korea, the war would be long over before—"

"Joe," O'Connor interrupted, "in the army you're working with essentially captive people."

"*You're* working with captive people!" Smadel snapped back. "These are four-year-olds! Somebody picks them up and brings them down and they get a shot."

"Somebody has to decide to pick them up and bring them down voluntarily," O'Connor said evenly.

The meeting adjourned, as the last one had, with no decision at all, and Salk returned to Pitttsburgh, looking forward to the publication of his paper—a determinedly sober work titled "Studies in Human Subjects on Active Immunization Against Poliomyelitis: A Preliminary Report on Experiments in Progress." That leaden headline alone was meant to discourage lay readers, and the cautious phrasing of the body of the paper should have had a similar anesthetizing effect on the scientific community.

But that was not to happen, thanks to Earl Wilson. Wilson was the hugely popular and widely read theater writer for the *New York Post.* A Midwesterner by birth, he had originally written his column under the starry-eyed title "An Ohioan on Broadway." But so vital a part of the theater community did he become that he was soon an Ohioan no more, and the column name was shortened to the cleaner, more urbane "On Broadway." As it turned out, even Broadway was too narrow a paddock for Wilson to wander, and he began looking farther afield for his stories—sometimes into the world of medicine. Recently, he had gotten wind of a possible new vaccine or cure for polio someone was said to be cooking up. While he didn't know much about the science itself, he had once heard that a fellow named Howard Howe of Johns

Hopkins University was something of a polio expert. If anyone was behind the new potion, it had to be him. Wilson called Howe and asked him directly.

"No," Howe said, "that's not me. It's Jonas Salk."

Wilson coaxed from Howe everything he knew, which was more or less everything Howe wasn't supposed to say to the press, and the next day—less than two weeks before Salk's paper was scheduled to appear—the "On Broadway" column carried the news:

"NEW POLIO VACCINE!" the headline screamed. "BIG HOPES SEEN!"

Salk, who did not regularly read even the best New York papers, never mind the *Post,* learned of the story third- or fourth-hand. He promptly called the NFIP headquarters to see if it was true. When he learned that it was, he raced to New York to see Basil O'Connor.

"This is a huge embarrassment," he said.

"I know it is," O'Connor responded.

"This makes it look like I was hunting for press. It makes it look like we've got the vaccine."

"It does," O'Connor agreed. "What do you want to do about it?"

Salk knew exactly what he wanted to do. "I think I should go on the radio."

O'Connor liked the idea immediately. Now that the public relations damage was done, there was nothing to be gained by returning to the lab and hoping the storm would subside. Only a measured plea for caution and patience—a plea coming directly from the scientist doing the work—might dissuade people from believing that polio was already beaten. The proper rules of the scientific game made no provision for a researcher going public this way. But Earl Wilson had already changed the rules, and Salk and O'Connor would now have to play within the new ones.

O'Connor would have little trouble arranging a radio show for his scientist. With all the courtesies he'd exchanged with New York's media types over the years, it was a small matter to phone up friends at CBS radio, explain what it was he needed, and secure a time slot for the following week—Thursday, March 26, at 10:45 P.M. Salk would have fifteen minutes to speak, and CBS would beam whatever he said across the nation.

Salk returned to Pittsburgh and spent the better part of the following week doing nothing but composing his address. Fifteen minutes seemed a fantastically long time to fill, and though O'Connor would use two or three minutes to introduce Salk and a CBS announcer would take thirty seconds or so to introduce them both, that still left the scientist—whose last major speech had been to a few hundred scientists in a Copenhagen conference room—more than eleven minutes to talk to 149 million people.

On the morning of March 26, 1953, Salk returned to New York and spent a restless day with O'Connor waiting for night to fall. Well before ten P.M., the two men hired a car to take them from the NFIP's downtown office to CBS's midtown headquarters. They were shown into the studio and then into the broadcast booth. The room was claustrophobic—small, stuffy, and oddly isolated from the vast audience it could reach. When the on-air light went on, however, Salk was anything but alone.

"The Scientist Speaks for Himself!" the announcer intoned. "The public affairs division of the Columbia Broadcasting System has arranged this special program because we feel it will be of interest to everyone in America. The scientist who will speak for himself tonight on the subject of a polio vaccine is Dr. Jonas E. Salk, of the University of Pittsburgh's School of Medicine. Basil O'Connor, president of the National Foundation for Infantile Paralysis, will introduce our speaker. Mr. O'Connor?"

O'Connor nodded to the announcer, leaned into the microphone, and spoke with an easy calm. He thanked the listeners for tuning in that evening and thanked them too for all the help they'd long offered the foundation—"*your* foundation," he stressed. It was that kind of help, he said, that had brought them all to so remarkable a pass tonight.

"The many scientists whose investigations you support recognize that their progress depends on your sympathetic understanding of the work they do. Dr. Jonas Salk is one of those scientists and he will speak to you tonight about research he is conducting under a grant from the National Foundation. It is a dramatic and inspiring story. So it is with great pleasure that I present Dr. Jonas E. Salk."

Salk looked down at the triple-spaced radio script in front of him and began reading aloud.

"Thank you, Mr. O'Connor," he said. "There will appear in the March 28 issue of the *Journal of the American Medical Association* a preliminary report of studies that are in progress on vaccination against poliomyelitis. This topic has been featured prominently in the news and there has been much speculation about it. For this reason I welcomed the opportunity to speak directly to you."

Faithfully following his well-rehearsed plan, he offered a brief lesson in the long arc of polio research, a review that would consume two-thirds of the time he had to speak. Only by providing the decades-long context for his work, however, could he be clear about where it now stood. When that ground had been laid, he at last said what he'd gone there that night to say.

"Experiments are now under way," he disclosed, "showing that an experimental vaccine that appears to be safe is capable of inducing in human subjects antibody formation to all three types of poliovirus. These experiments are still in progress and many are quite incomplete. Nevertheless, the results provide justification for optimism. We are now faced with facts and not merely theories," he said. "With this new enlightenment, we can move forward more rapidly and more courageously."

Salk concluded his remarks without a good night, since he was told that that would be left to the announcer. Instead, he simply leaned back from the microphone and breathed a sigh. The announcer leaned in and made his sign-off remarks, and the on-air light went dark.

The next day, Salk suspected, everything he knew would change, as the country reacted to what he'd done that night. His colleagues—or at least those who'd disagreed with his killed-virus strategy in the first place—would be furious, outraged at what they'd consider the nakedly self-promotional thing he'd done. But Salk and O'Connor had done what they'd believed had to be done, and the next day Salk would once again be focusing his mind exclusively on his work.

Salk left CBS the moment the broadcast was over, taxied straight to Pennsylvania Station, and caught the first available train back home. He slept as well as he could during the long ride in his jouncing seat, arriving in Pittsburgh early in the morning. Without a change of clothes, he went directly to his lab. A short time later, at a somewhat more human hour,

John Troan, who had listened to the broadcast the night before, phoned Salk's home, hoping for an early quote for the story he was filing. It wasn't every newspaperman who was trusted with Salk's home number—indeed, Troan was the only one—and it wasn't a privilege he abused. But this story seemed to be one that was worth a call. The phone rang in the Salk kitchen and Donna answered it. She and Troan exchanged their good mornings and he then asked for Jonas.

"Oh, he's at the lab," Donna answered.

"Already?" Troan asked.

"No, no. He never came home."

Troan whistled, then remarked that he didn't expect that kind of dedication even out of Salk.

"John," Donna said with a laugh, "then you don't know Jonas."

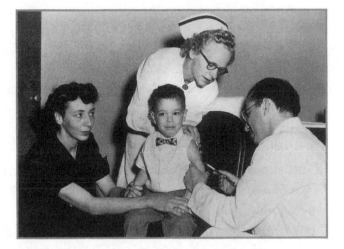

15

No matter what Darrell Salk said, nobody in his family believed that he was hiding under his bed because he wanted to read a book. Certainly, Darrell liked his books, but five years old was still five years old, and reading was still not the first of his passions—particularly not on an evening when his father was home unexpectedly early from his lab. Darrell had visited the lab any number of times, and while he knew that the work his father did there was important, he knew mostly that it was home to a lot of monkeys, mice, and chimpanzees, good enough reason for anyone to want to stay there late. Tonight, however, his father had returned well before dinner, and since that was an increasingly rare event, it was not one to be missed by staying in his room.

The problem, as their mother had explained to them earlier in the day, was that their father was coming home early all right, but he was also bringing shots along with him. Darrell's father had given his sons shots any number of times before—mostly penicillin when they were suffering from earaches—and they had never much cared for the experience. But as they grew out of babyhood, the boys found that somehow the prospect of a needle seemed even worse. Now they could not only feel it but anticipate it, dreading its sting for hours before it actually happened. Lately, their father and mother had taken to giving them the odd flu shot or other injection they needed when they were sleeping, rolling up a pajama sleeve or skooching down a pajama bottom and getting the thing done so deftly that the boys never knew it had happened at all.

Tonight's encounter with the needle, though, required drawing blood, which was a job their father had no choice but to do when they were awake, lest they twitch in their sleep during the comparatively delicate procedure. Not only that, tonight they'd have to get yet another shot afterward, one that contained the preparation their father had been working so hard to invent. The whole idea unnerved both Peter and Darrell, though it was lost entirely on the toddling Jonathan.

Darrell and the other boys weren't the only ones in Jonas Salk's close circle who'd been getting shots of late. Salk himself had gotten one, using his right hand to inject himself in his left arm with the vaccine he'd been developing in his lab. Donna Salk too got a needle. So did the technicians, doctors, and other researchers who worked for Salk. This was partly to protect them from the risk of a stray virus that might splatter from a dropped or broken test tube—a risk they'd simply had to live with until now—and partly because taking the vaccine was the right and proper thing to do, given that they were planning to ask whole populations of children to do the same. Salk was convinced the vaccine was entirely safe; nonetheless, he made it a point to do all the injecting himself, wanting his staff to be secure in the knowledge that if anything did somehow go wrong with the preparation, he alone would be responsible.

If Salk's confidence in his vaccine was as great as it seemed to be, of course, iron logic alone demanded that his next step be to inoculate his sons, if only to protect them from the approaching polio season. Donna needed surprisingly little convincing—in fact, almost none at all—of the wisdom of this reasoning. She had long since learned to decipher Jonas, and when it came to his work, that job was especially easy. His belief in the scientific process was so utter that it was well-nigh impossible not to believe what he believed. Donna could easily boil away his enthusiasm, his pleasure, his pride in a thing he'd invented and tested. What was generally left was a hard stone of scientific truth, and with that in hand, she'd trust him with anything.

Salk brought his kit bag of syringes home and set them up on the kitchen table. He placed a small rack of sterile blood-sample tubes next to them. He called out to Peter and Jonathan, while Donna went upstairs to coax Darrell out from under his bed. The youngest and oldest sons entered the kitchen and stared wide-eyed at the needles; when Donna brought Darrell in, he did the same.

Ordinarily, the moments before an injection were the moments Salk would use to begin calming and reassuring the child who'd be on the receiving end of the shot. While he had schooled himself in that art when he was inoculating boys and girls he didn't know, however, he found he reflexively steeled himself against it when the children were his own, leaving the job to Donna. It was a phenomenon common to physicians when the patient was simply too close for the clinical distance that was necessary in medicine. Salk noticed the feeling not only when he was injecting one of his sons, but when he was doing something as simple as extracting a loose tooth.

"Let me have a look," he'd instruct, then reach in a finger and pop out the tooth with a single flick. There would be plenty of time to applaud the boy's courage when the tooth was in his hand. Not before.

Donna thus reassured the boys tonight while Jonas quietly prepped the first blood-sample vial. It was an ugly, vacuum-sealed test tube that literally sucked blood from the vein when the physician attached a needle and broke a seal in the rubber neck that connected it to the tube.

Jonas asked Peter for his arm first, swabbed it with alcohol, tapped out a vein, and plunged the needle in. All three boys winced once, then again as they heard the vacuum pop. As the pain turned out to be less than what Peter had imagined, his crumpled face slowly smoothed out and his tight-closed eyes slowly opened. Salk finished drawing the blood and withdrew the needle.

"That was very good," he said to his son. "Very, very good."

Darrell and Jonathan followed. Darrell squirmed more than his older brother had, Jonathan howled and thrashed. After the bleedings were done, Salk produced three far smaller needles and injected all three sons with a creamy, mineral-oil-fortified vaccine against all three types of poliovirus. Those shots took only a happy instant. Salk didn't mention that two more would follow over the course of weeks.

The boys, relieved, went off to play. Donna, satisfied, went off to finish making dinner. Her husband had made her an implicit promise tonight, and she believed it: No son of hers, she now trusted, would ever contract a case of poliomyelitis.

16

It was hard to imagine that the polio plague could get worse in the summer of 1953 than it had been in the summer of 1952. Disease trackers could not be certain, but they knew an epidemiological fluke when they saw one and 1952 was almost certainly it; they would not be likely to see such a freak statistical storm again.

But 1953, if anything, started out even worse than 1952—a lot worse. During the very first week in June, a fortnight before summer even got under way, 250 cases of infantile paralysis were reported nationwide. The number, though tiny in absolute terms, was shocking, more than twice the 119 cases documented in the same week the previous year. Project that out over the entire season and at least 115,000 boys and girls would be sickened or killed. It was always possible that that first small report was itself a statistical aberration, but that hope was dashed the following week when the case count grew to 305, compared with 218 the year before. Pennsylvania nearly tripled its 1952 total, jumping from 36 cases in that two-week stretch to 98. In New York, the early count was equally terrible, with 318 cases reported, compared with 147 in the same period the year before.

The NFIP, which had scrambled to meet the emergency the previous summer, now found itself ginning up again. From their headquarters at 120 Broadway, foundation epidemiologists tracked the weekly infection tallies, determined the hardest-hit communities, and immediately began shipping their limited stockpiles of gamma globulin to the still healthy children living there. NFIP operators manned foundation phones around the clock, fielding calls from cash-strapped chapter chairmen pleading for iron lungs or medical teams or just one spare carton of gamma globulin to treat a terrified neighborhood where a child had just taken sick. Doctors and public affairs officers were dispatched from New York to the worst viral hot spots, instructing local health-care workers in ways to stabilize the sickest patients, contain the spread of the contagion, and educate the uninfected public about what they could do to stay that way.

Returning from the field, headquarters staffers brought back tales of desperation and dedication in the sickened communities. There was the local volunteer in rural Missouri who drove panicky parents and their feverish child 100 miles through the night to bring them to the only available community hospital able to treat polio patients, then drove the same 100 miles back so he could open up his gas station for business before dawn. There were the local volunteers who would stay on call for reports that another stricken boy or girl was being brought in to a local hospital, then race ahead to the emergency room to make sure one more bed could be found and made ready in wards already overflowing with the ill.

As the summer wore on, the number of polio cases slowly eased back to more typical levels, but the NFIP and the local chapters remained twitchy about an outbreak that had already whipsawed one way and then the other. The scientists in Salk's lab were equally anxious, their moods rising and falling with the infection reports. But they had other things on their minds as well.

From the moment Salk went on the air that March, the lab came under siege. Few people who made their lives in the quiet community of medical researchers were prepared for what would happen when they—or their lab boss—crossed the line from anonymity to national celebrity, but as reporters who covered this sort of thing could have told them, events always played out the same way. At the first whisper that your lab was closing in on a new treatment or cure, four things would happen: The desperate would descend on you, the moneymen would woo you, the media would hound you, and the fanatics would despise you. Of all these developments, it was the fanatics who surprised the lab the most. And of all the fanatics, it was Duon Miller of Coral Gables, Florida, who seemed the most unhinged.

Miller was a wealthy marketer of what people called patent medicines: nonprescription pills and potions made of more or less anything at all. There was no limit to the illnesses the preparations were said to treat—easy claims to make, since there was no requirement that the ingredients be listed on the label. In his free time, Miller also bred oversized boxer dogs, well-muscled animals he was willing to sell to almost any buyer—provided his customers were neither Negro nor Jewish. If Miller billed himself as an authority on dogs and medicines, however, he considered himself even more of an expert on one other topic: polio. His beliefs were decidedly unorthodox.

Pouring a fair share of his considerable wealth into handbills, mailing lists, and magazine ads, he promoted the idea that infantile paralysis was not caused by a virus but rather by malnutrition. The disease could be avoided entirely if you'd swear off colas, refined sugars, and any other processed foods. The National Foundation for Infantile Paralysis, which was responsible for spreading the virus fiction, was a menace, devoted to brainwashing the public with a lot of theories and promises that would raise money for doctors but do nothing for patients. As for Basil O'Connor's gamma globulin stockpiles? Nothing short of an attempt at intravenous miscegenation.

"When a child's bloodstream is polluted with gamma globulin, how do you know if it is from a white person, a Negro or a Jap?" his handbills asked. And as for Jonas Salk's much touted trial vaccine? "Monkey juice, a sneaking attempt to violate the bodies of innocent children."

Miller howled so loudly and defamed Salk so freely that a Miami judge finally stepped in, fining him $1,000 and placing him on probation for mailing libelous and scurrilous materials. But the prohibition against public drum-banging did not prevent him from private hectoring, and he used that freedom to contact the men he considered most responsible for the massive fraud—including Salk.

"The article in the Miami Daily News on your polio research is as pathetically amusing as your title: 'a leading scientific authority,'" Miller wrote in one of his frequent letters. "You cannot PROVE polio is spread by a virus. Do you honestly believe the public will believe $18,000,000.00 in March of Dimes money was spent on this project? Basil O'Connor must be getting ready to holler for more dimes and dollars . . . what a racket . . . IT'S CRIMINAL!!!!"

That letter, like most of Miller's letters, spluttered on for pages, a bristle of all-capital letters and multiple exclamation points. Salk knew the manner of man he was dealing with the moment he opened the first letter, but he was disturbed by him nonetheless. Miller was part of an increasingly vocal, increasingly troubling subculture of pamphleteers, a group that included Morris Bealle, a Washington, D.C., publicist who claimed that a cure for cancer had been developed but was being suppressed by the "Jewish-controlled American Medical Association"; Royal Lee, a nonpracticing Milwaukee dentist who rabidly attacked chlorination, vaccination, pasteurization and—for reasons known only to him—aluminum cookware; and W. D. Herrstrom, a leader of a growing community of extremists that claimed fluoridation was part of a larger socialist and Zionist plan.

"I'm going to answer this man," Salk said to Lorraine Friedman after reading Miller's first letter.

"Don't do it, Dr. Salk," she said. "All you'll do is encourage him."

"He sounds encouraged already."

"Then you'll only dignify him."

Salk responded to Miller all the same and did what he could to maintain his own dignity. "I am sure that your objective and ours is the same," he wrote, "the ultimate prevention of polio. I must add that were your criticisms based on sound scientific data, you could afford to be more gentlemanly in your remarks." Salk sealed the letter and mailed it out.

Harder for Salk to deal with than rants from the fringes were the pleas from the parents of polio victims who'd learned of his work. "I am the mother of 13 children," wrote a woman from Rome, whose letter, like many others, had been routed to the university's Department of Modern Languages for translation before it could be passed on to Salk. "I beseech you to give me information to cure my little one"—*mio piccolo,* she called him. "He is two years old and was struck in October in both of his legs. Help me cure him and make him walk again as his brothers and sisters and you will do a good deed."

Salk received similar letters in Portuguese, Spanish, badly broken English, and some languages he didn't even recognize. His response was always more or less the same.

"It is extremely difficult to have to say I'm sorry," he'd write, "but I can be of no help even though I would like to be. Should the vaccine you have read about be all we hope it can, the best it can do is prevent attacks of poliomyelitis. Nonetheless, I am sure that your child is in capable hands and that the doctors will do all they can."

Francis Pray, the University of Pittsburgh's public affairs director, did what was possible to shield Salk from this growing deluge, instructing his staff to be ready to answer all personal appeals, press requests, and hate mail. Basil O'Connor helped out too, circulating a twelve-page fact sheet through the New York headquarters and all of the NFIP's state and local chapters containing everything any reporter could possibly need to know about both gamma globulin and the Salk vaccine. There ought not to be a single inquiry even the most probing journalist could ask that couldn't be satisfied by the gracefully quotable answers, freeing Salk and his staff from having to respond themselves.

But if such measures put a speed bump in the path of the press and the parents, they did nothing to slow down the drug companies. Pfizer, Wyeth, and Parke, Davis pharmaceuticals had already joined Eli Lilly in making overtures to the NFIP and to Salk personally, letting them know they'd be available to mass-produce the polio vaccine whenever it was ready. Of all the firms, it was Parke, Davis that had at least a slight edge. Salk had worked with the company on the development of the adjuvant for his flu vaccine years earlier and was continuing to do so with his polio adjuvant. So satisfied was he with the Parke, Davis professionalism that he even accepted an offer to serve as one of the company's paid consultants, allowing him to weigh in on other projects he found interesting and, not incidentally, supplement his modest research income with a small corporate stipend. But Parke, Davis evidently saw the relationship as something more than that. Not long after Salk's radio appearance, the company issued a press release making it clear that, in its opinion at least, the recent achievement in Pittsburgh had not been Salk's or the NFIP's alone.

"Parke, Davis has been working jointly for many years with Dr. Jonas Salk who developed the vaccine," the release claimed. "Dr. Salk also developed the adjuvant used exclusively in the flu vaccine made by the company. When the new vaccine meets the tests of safety and effectiveness in field trials, Parke, Davis will be in a position to make it available at once."

The text was careful not to say explicitly that Salk was conducting his vaccine work in the employ of Parke, Davis, or that a deal was in place to manufacture his trial vaccine. But it left that impression.

"Dr. Salk works for Parke, Davis as a consultant and received financial aid from the company," claimed a Detroit newspaper in an article the next day.

"Parke, Davis announced that there is close cooperation with Dr. Jonas Salk who announced the discovery of a new polio vaccine," the wire services echoed.

Salk and the NFIP learned of the release and they were outraged. Basil O'Connor had so far raised and spent $18 million to beat polio, and he wasn't about to let a corporate bit player seize credit now. The foundation issued an angry press release denying Parke, Davis's claims. Salk fired off a telegram to the company president, condemning the Parke, Davis press release as disturbing and misleading, and summarily resigned his consultancy position. The president cabled back within hours, apologizing for what he called a "gross misunderstanding." He promised an investigation and hoped that the problem would "not adversely affect our longstanding cordial relationship."

Salk, however, would not be moved and considered that relationship at an end. Parke, Davis would continue to be included on the list of prospective bidders for the mass-production work still to come, since neither Salk nor the NFIP was inclined to allow personal pique to get in the way of the development of the vaccine. But for the present, the manufacturer would be allowed to worry that it was now nothing more than one of many in the queue of companies hoping to earn the foundation's favor.

Peter, Darrell, and Jonathan Salk could not be certain, but it was just possible the pressure had at last caused their father to lose his marbles. At least that's how it seemed one night over dinner in the summer of 1953.

The younger two boys still did not have an absolutely clear idea of just what it was their father was doing at his lab those last months. Peter, now nine years old, knew what polio was and that their father was developing something to fight it. He understood that a cure made sick people better but a vaccine prevented them from ever getting sick in the first place. Darrell, age six, grasped all those facts, though imperfectly. Jonathan, age three, was entirely in the dark.

What all three boys did understand at a far more primal level was the toll their father's work was taking on him. If the polio problem was keeping him away from the house for longer and longer stetches of the day, it also appeared to be claiming his mind even when he wasn't at work. Every summer, the family would take a two-week vacation at Oberlin Beach on Lake Erie's Ohio shore. The boys loved the swimming and sailing, and even Jonas generally seemed to relax—sunning, reading, and passing the evenings playing Scrabble and Jotto, a brain-numbing game that involved guessing a five-letter word by comparing the frequency and pattern of the letters it shared with other words. This summer they'd made the trip as always, but for the first time, their father seemed not to be enjoying himself—restless, distracted, reading only fitfully, and playing his word games only half-interestedly. Much of his time he spent on the phone, taking calls from Pittsburgh or New York.

When the family got home, things were no better. Recently, Salk had delighted Darrell and Peter by agreeing to drive them to school each day in the family Studebaker, freeing Donna of the early-morning job. The Salks did not listen much to the radio in their home, and Salk at first abided by that rule in the car, instead using the time to ask his sons about what they planned to do in school that day. He asked more or less the same question the next few times they made the trip, and it thus came as a wonderful surprise one day when he flipped on the radio instead, seeming to want to share with his two older sons a subversive little pleasure that their mother and baby brother didn't have to know about. It was only after several such morning trips that Darrell noticed that his father wasn't listening to the music at all and instead had a familiar not-here look in his eyes—the look that was a sure sign his mind was back in the lab working on his polio problem. It was that always distracted, never-at-peace seriousness that made Jonas's performance at dinner one night such a surprise.

"I heard the funniest joke today," he said, barely getting the sentence out before beginning to laugh at the recollection of the thing. Salk didn't tell jokes that often or that well, but he certainly knew enough to realize that the laugh comes at the end, not at the beginning.

"Seems that way," Donna said, smiling. The boys began to giggle with him.

"There are three doctors on a golf course," Jonas began. "One's an orthopedist, one's a rheumatologist, one's a neurologist." He stopped for a moment, suppressing another laugh.

"Dad!" Peter said. "Tell it!"

"Okay, okay," Jonas went on. "So there's this guy in front of them with a limp. They make a bet as to what his problem is. The neurologist says it's a peripheral neuropathy associated with a spinal lesion. The orthopedist says it's a bony problem. The rheumatologist says it's a joint problem."

The language was lost on the boys, but they got the general idea. "Finally," Salk went on, "they go up to the guy, tell him they're physicians, and ask him which of their diagnoses was right. 'Beats me,' the guy says. 'I thought it was gas!'"

With that, Jonas erupted in tears of mirth and the boys, unsure what was so funny but delighted all the same, joined in. Donna nodded happily, pleased to see her husband so splendidly out of control. It took Jonas a while to collect himself and try to resume his dinner. As soon as he did, the boys asked him to tell his joke again. Jonas dissolved anew.

It was not until the cusp of summer that much of the stress and turmoil that ensued in the wake of Salk's radio appearance at last passed and he was able to focus fully and clearheadedly on his work. His first priority was also his most scientifically important one: expanding the size of his tiny sample group so as to improve the reliability of his findings. Both Gale Walker and Jessie Wright of the Polk and Watson homes pitched in, seeking out new recruits in the ranks of their unvaccinated children. Salk sought new volunteers at the Industrial Home for Crippled Children, another Pittsburgh institution with a long history of caring for polio patients. He also approached—warily—the headmasters of the Sewickley Academy, a pricey prep school located just northwest of Pittsburgh.

Sewickley enrolled children from kindergarten through twelfth grade, covering a large arc of the polio-vulnerable population. Like the Polk patients, these boys and girls would have no greater or lesser likelihood of having been exposed to polio than any other children, thus providing a pristine testing population. Unlike the Polk patients, the Sewickley students had not already been damaged by some other unlucky circumstance. Indeed, they were among the best-bred, best-fed children the community could produce. If Salk's vaccine was ever to be universally used, he knew, he'd have to begin testing it on such well-treasured boys and girls sometime. To his delight, both Sewickley and the Industrial Home agreed to participate.

Mustering his lab for this four-school fieldwork, Salk organized his technicians into rotating teams that would be out on the road almost constantly, taking blood and performing inoculations. Percival Bazeley took the lead in this project, designing mobile sterilizing ovens the investigators could carry with them so they could clean their syringes between uses—a job made especially tedious by the fact that the tolerances between the rubber plungers and the glass bodies of the shots were never very precise, meaning all the parts had to be matched up by code number in order to fit properly. Bazeley was also dissatisfied with the test tubes the lab used, always bothered by the paper seals that came with the Bakelite caps. The things worked well enough for routine experiments, but the polio field studies were not routine. With agitators and fermenters and flash evaporators to maintain in the lab, he nonetheless took it upon himself to tweeze all of the little paper disks out of the caps himself, hand-cut new rubber seals, and glue them carefully in place.

As the work progressed, Salk's sample group slowly grew to 200, then 300, then up toward 600 children. As it did, his vaccine began showing itself to be a more complex thing than he had imagined. For one thing, the difference between the aqueous formulation and the creamy, oil-fortified one did not appear to be as great as the earlier findings had suggested. When the vaccine was mixed with the proper adjuvant, it continued to produce a far superior immune system kick than it did when it was administered in the watery medium alone, raising antibody levels higher and keeping them there longer. But a funny thing happened to the blood of patients who had been inoculated with the aqueous shot. If Salk waited out the initial antibody response, allowed the levels to drop back to the point at which they were nearly undetectable, then stirred fresh virus into the test tube of the patients' blood, an entirely new flood of antibodies would appear. It was as if the blood had developed a sort of immunological memory of its first contact with the bug—a memory powerful enough that it could do without even a small standing army of antibodies, instead producing them and pouring them forth only if it needed them.

This was huge news for a number of reasons. First of all, even Salk, who had lived and died by the adjuvant-fortified formula when he and Tommy Francis were developing their flu vaccine, knew that injecting oil into the body of a child was not a completely risk-free business. The paraffin adjuvants used at the beginning of the century sometimes caused localized cancers at the site of the injection—tumors referred to interchangeably as paraffinomas or oleomas. The adjuvant Salk preferred for his vaccines was far lighter stuff—mineral oils supplied to him and Parke, Davis by the Standard Oil Company and the Pennsylvania Refining Company, according to the formula he had worked out in his lab. Despite these decidedly nonmedical manufacturers, he was all but certain that these adjuvants would not pose the same risk the older ones had. All but certain was not the same as absolutely certain, however. If it was possible to eliminate the oil from the vaccine altogether, the cancer concern would vanish with it.

More important, the idea of immunological memory went a long way toward answering the question the doubters raised about whether a killed-virus vaccine could ever provide immunity that was as long-lasting as the live variety was. Critics had always cited the undeniable fact that antibody levels often fall sooner in people who have been inoculated by killed viruses than by live viruses. If it turned out that the antibodies had simply retreated into the tall grass, to come roaring back at the first sign of a virus in the bloodstream, it would do a lot to silence Albert Sabin and the rest of his live-virus school.

But Albert Sabin, it appeared, wasn't about to go quietly. Immediately after Salk's paper on the Polk and Watson studies was published, Sabin wrote him a letter decorously damning it. He had read the paper with great interest, he explained, but was struck less by how well the vaccine worked against polio Types II and III than by how poorly it had fared against Type I. The shot appeared to trigger a true Type I immune response only in people who already carried some antibodies to that type—the very people who would need protection from that particular virus least. If this was as well as the vaccine worked, it was no vaccine at all. Sabin then congratulated Salk on the studies, signing off with all his good wishes and his kindest personal regards, and said that he looked forward to discussing other concerns he had about the paper at Salk's convenience.

Salk accepted the criticism with as much equanimity as he could. His work did not claim that the immune response to all of the viral types had been identical, and Type I had indeed shown the poorest results. But it wasn't the insoluble problem Sabin clearly seemed to want it to be. All three vaccine formulations would take a lot of refinement before they were ready. There was a reason, after all, that Salk had stressed the word *preliminary* in his paper's title.

Sabin wasn't through, however. In the summer, the American Medical Association held its annual convention in New York. This was the signature event of the professional year for the association's 38,500 members, and while not all of them could possibly attend, those who weren't there would at least read the papers that were presented. Sabin had booked himself time for one of those presentations.

John Troan attended the meeting, which was held in a ballroom at the New York Hilton. Troan had seen Sabin speak before and had always been impressed by the man's native smarts and his flat-out brilliant way of expressing what he believed. But that very manner also made Troan uneasy. Sabin projected such confidence that he could convince you of just about anything he wanted—a power that was easy to abuse. When Sabin's turn to speak came, he strode to the podium and quickly made his agenda clear.

"Since there is an impression," he began, "that a practicable vaccine for poliomyelitis is either at hand or immediately around the corner, it may be best to start with the statement that such a vaccine is not now at hand and that one can only guess what is around the corner."

For all the recent hopeful chatter, he explained, even the man who invented the supposed vaccine admitted in his study that his potion was grievously flawed—arguably useful against the Type II and III viruses but utterly useless against Type I. Worse, it was probably dangerous as well.

"The Type I Mahoney virus used in Salk's preliminary work is a good example of a virus that should not be used," Sabin said, "because in minimal doses it produces paralysis readily." Even if that weren't the case, the inherent shortcomings of the entire idea of a killed-virus vaccine, particularly the brief duration of the protection it provided, disqualified it from serious consideration. "Unquestionably, the ultimate goal for the control of poliomyelitis is immunization with a living, virulent virus which will confer immunity for many years or life."

Watching from the back of the hall, Troan whistled softly to himself. This was as thorough a shelling as one scientist could inflict on another in so public a venue. Troan had read Salk's paper many times over, and he recognized immediately the lines of reasoning Sabin had used to make his attack. The Mahoney virus was indeed an especially lethal strain. The vaccine had indeed been less effective against that type. The supposed short-term immunity of the killed-virus vaccine was a point that had by no means been settled. That Salk knew these issues needed to be addressed and fully believed they could be was nowhere mentioned in Sabin's address. There wasn't a single whole truth in the presentation, but there wasn't a single untruth either. That was the genius of it—and that was precisely what Troan had feared.

He wrote his story for the next day's newspaper, but before he filed it, he phoned Salk, both to prepare him for what would be on the newsstands and to give him a chance to comment on the record. He did not look forward to the call.

"I'm running a story on Sabin's AMA speech and you ought to know what's going to be in it," he explained when Salk answered the phone.

"Go ahead," Salk said warily.

"Your vaccine's not ready for testing and there's no telling when it will be," Troan recited, reading from his notes. "Only a living virus can provide long-term immunity, not an inactivated one."

"That's it?" Salk answered.

Troan bulled ahead. "He also said the vaccine doesn't work against Type I and that the Mahoney is too deadly to use anyway."

"That bastard!" Salk exclaimed, using both a tone and a word Troan had never heard out of him before. "He knows better than that!"

"It's what he said," Troan answered. "I have to report it. You want to respond?"

Salk fell silent for a moment. "No," he said crisply. "No comment."

Troan filed his story as promised, and the next morning it appeared both in the *Pittsburgh Press* and across the wires. Had there ever been any question about Albert Sabin's views of Jonas Salk's work, there was no more. The Cincinnati scientist had now decided not merely to raise doubts about the vaccine; he had apparently decided to go to war against it.

∞⊖

There was never a time when Jonas Salk considered pulling rank on Harry Weaver. That Salk was an M.D. and Weaver wasn't went without saying. That Weaver was the NFIP's research director and Salk wasn't went without saying too. The two men rarely found themselves with differences worth arguing over, but on the odd occasion that they did, the counterweights of their respective positions kept them in balance. In the summer of 1953, Weaver kicked the fulcrum out from under them.

With the polio season still boiling throughout the country, Weaver was becoming increasingly convinced that the foundation had to get to work field-testing something more than gamma globulin, and had to do it soon. Nobody—Salk least of all—denied that a massive field trial would be necessary before a vaccine could be fully and finally approved, but the question was when. More and more, Weaver had grown convinced that that time was now, though Salk did not agree. Working by himself in his NFIP office, Weaver nonetheless set about drafting a memo about the next direction in which the NFIP would need to go.

Titling the document simply "Plans for 1954," he began outlining a grand field trial to begin within a matter of months. On the first of the year, Weaver declared, a vast research team bearing up to half a million vials of the Salk polio vaccine would head for 100 communities around the country with populations between 50,000 and 200,000. All the communities should include at least 5,000 polio-susceptible children in a narrow age range of, say, five to six years old. Starting with the towns farthest south and drifting north along the course the poliovirus traveled, the doctors would proceed to vaccinate every one of those targeted boys and girls. All the injections would be completed no later than June 15, before the majority of the wild virus alighted for the summer. The children would then be monitored throughout the season.

The job would be a staggering one, requiring dozens of epidemiologists in New York to war-game the study, and hundreds—indeed thousands— of doctors, nurses, and technicians in the field to execute it. If it worked, however, the disease would truly be on its way to being licked.

Weaver promptly circulated the memo throughout the NFIP, making little effort to control who saw it within the organization, or for that matter who saw it outside—including the press.

Salk received a copy of the plan at the same time most other people in the organization did and was stunned. He had so far dosed barely 600 children with his experimental preparation, and now Weaver would have him passing it out to half a million more by winter.

At the same time Weaver was blindsiding Salk from the left, he hit him from the right as well. With the approval of O'Connor, he announced the formation of a new executive panel within the foundation that would be known as the Vaccine Advisory Committee. As its name suggested, the committee would be devoted to the single, narrow job of quickly implementing some kind of large-scale field trial—probably a variation on Weaver's own—for the final assault on polio. The new group, which would begin meeting immediately, would be made up not of the theoreticians who had long dominated the Committee on Immunization. Sabin, Hammon, and even Salk himself would be swept aside in favor of pragmatists and implementers like David Price, U.S. assistant surgeon general; Norman Topping of the National Institutes of Health; and Ernest Stebbins of the Johns Hopkins School of Hygiene and Public Health. The Committee on Immunization would continue to hold its meetings and make its suggestions. But it would be marginalized, a beast from an earlier age when a true vaccine was not so teasingly close.

Salk wanted no part of all these plans, which he was convinced were both impatient and imprudent. He was not about to allow himself to be turned into the Kolmer or Brodie of his era. If he was going to wrest control of his vaccine back, he'd once again have to call on Basil O'Connor.

O'Connor was well regarded for knowing both how to talk and how to listen—a critical skill in the days when he used to vet the dreamy ideas of the voluble Franklin Roosevelt. The moment he heard Salk's voice on the phone, he spoke appeasingly. "Jonas," he said, "why don't you come see me."

Salk did as O'Connor said, booking the first available train to New York. He walked into the foundation chief's office and unburdened himself.

"You've got to get some of this pressure off," he said. "You've got people planning logistics before the basic research is even done."

"I know," O'Connor said.

"You've got committees planning trials before a vaccine is even in hand. We can't work at this pace. *I* can't work at this pace."

O'Connor allowed Salk to speak for as long as he needed to, describing his worries about the press, the drug companies, the letters from the parents, and now Harry Weaver. Finally, O'Connor broke in.

"Jonas," he said, "nobody's going to rush you into releasing a vaccine you're not happy with. That doesn't mean you're going to like everything you hear coming out of this office. But do me a favor: Pay attention to what I'm saying to you now, not what you read in the papers. They're not always going to be the same things."

Salk nodded.

"Now," O'Connor said, "let me ask you one thing in return: Is it at least possible that you'll have something ready for a field trial by the end of 1953 or the beginning of 1954?"

Salk thought about it. "Yes," he said, "it's at least possible."

"Good," was all O'Connor answered.

O'Connor now asked his secretary to send for Harry Weaver. He quickly appeared in the office as if he'd been waiting for the call—which he may well have been. Weaver listened as O'Connor filled him in on everything he and Salk had just discussed. He readily concurred with all of it, particularly the part about the iron reliability of Basil O'Connor's word. With that reassurance, Salk returned to Pittsburgh.

Three weeks later, the wire services released a breaking medical story under the boldface headline, "Mass Field Test Slated for Polio Vaccine." Only the night before, Basil O'Connor, the president of the NFIP, had delivered a speech in San Francisco in which he made the surprise announcement that before the next paralysis season arrived, over 1.2 million children would be inoculated with an exciting new polio preventive that just might be able to knock out the disease for good. "If the vaccine comes out the way we want," O'Connor said, "the polio problem will be solved."

Salk read the story and chewed over his thoughts. *Pay attention to what I say to you, not what you read in the papers,* O'Connor had instructed him. He decided to heed that advice.

Before that summer was out, Basil O'Connor sprang one more surprise on the National Foundation for Infantile Paralysis: He fired Harry Weaver.

Though not everyone outside the foundation's headquarters knew it, the research chief's overreaching had become a problem, extending well beyond the release of the too ambitious field-trial memo. More and more, Weaver had begun exercising authority he did not strictly have—countermanding directives from O'Connor, Rivers, and Hart Van Riper; overruling the decisions of his scientists and grantees; conducting long-range planning meetings and shutting out the other senior members of the foundation when they tried to participate.

Weaver's decision to circulate his field-trial idea was a bit of institutional presumption O'Connor had been willing to tolerate, particularly since it reflected both his own and Rivers' view of things. But as part of a larger pattern, it was becoming intolerable.

"Either he goes or I go," Van Riper had warned.

O'Connor, who could calculate a man's value to an organization down to the last scrap of work he did, knew that Weaver's administrative and motivational skills had been indispensable in getting the NFIP to where it was today. But what O'Connor needed most now were not organizational men but medical men—rigorously trained, fiercely disciplined ones. And that wasn't Weaver. Just before setting off on a working vacation to Europe, O'Connor settled the matter. He told Van Riper to try to salvage the situation as best he could, but he was free to do anything he thought best.

Both men knew what that would be, and within days Van Riper quietly did it. Not long after, during the first week in September, an unsuspecting Jonas Salk received a letter in his Pittsburgh lab.

"It is with considerable regret," Harry Weaver wrote, "that I must advise that my association with the National Foundation for Infantile

Paralysis has been terminated. I could not take this step without expressing my profound thanks for the work you've done in helping to achieve the real progress that has been made in the field of poliomyelitis. I trust that you realize it was not easy to write this letter to you. Sorry, but it had to be."

Salk was taken wholly by surprise. Weaver, for the time being, could be reached at his home in Bedford Village, New York, and Salk would certainly call to commiserate with the man he'd grown to admire so much. But things, he knew, had changed forever. His first patron in the NFIP was gone. All that remained now was the work Weaver had recruited him to do.

∾ 17 ∾

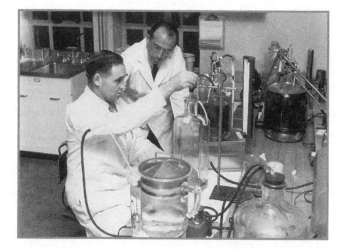

It was almost inevitable that the United States Congress would eventually get itself involved with Salk's vaccine. It was a safe bet too that Albert Sabin would get himself involved with Congress's involvement.

Of all the branches of government that should have had an interest in the progress of the vaccine, Congress was near the back of the line. The National Institutes of Health had been a player from the start, with Norman Topping representing Washington on a number of NFIP committees. The United States Public Health Service had a role as well, helping to coordinate epidemic control and plan field trials. Even the secretary of the Department of Health, Education, and Welfare, Oveta Culp Hobby, was keeping an eye on things from a distance, ready to step in and license the vaccine for manufacture once it was approved. But Congress had no real dog in the fight.

That was not a comfortable role for Congress, and so it invented itself a role, courtesy of the House Committee on Interstate and Foreign Commerce. The committee did not have particular expertise in medical matters, but the fact was, any vaccine that was invented in a place like the Pittsburgh Virus Lab would eventually have to be shipped out of its home state to the forty-seven other states, and if that wasn't interstate commerce, nothing was. The committee thus decided that hearings on the polio vaccine would be in order.

Since the developer of the vaccine could not hope to be objective about what he had invented, Salk would not be called as a witness. The committee would request his research findings and answers to specific questions if they came up. The congressmen would instead call the well-regarded Dr. Albert Sabin of Cincinnati, a clear-eyed researcher with a reputation for good science. Dr. William Hammon of Salk's own University of Pittsburgh, who had been so involved with the much-publicized gamma globulin studies, would be summoned too, as would Hart van Riper, the medical director of the NFIP.

The congressional committee was satisfied with this trio of researchers, but for the Pittsburgh Virus Lab, it was a nasty trifecta. Van Riper had never voiced full-throated support for the vaccine, nor could he, given his informal role as peacemaker within the foundation. Hammon's heart was still with gamma globulin and his head was easily swayed by live-virus arguments. And Sabin was singularly Sabin. He had been warning about the perils of Salk's misguided vaccine for years, and now he would have a chance to make his case before a panel of lawmakers.

The hearing was called for October 14, and while Salk was made aware of the date well beforehand, he did not really have time to give it much thought. He and most of his staff were now working full seven-day weeks, frequently reducing the time they spent at home to its almost irreducible essence—just the hours needed for a short night's sleep, a shower, and a change of clothes. Even that brief stretch often wasn't possible. The culturing and inactivating experiments the staffers were running required attention at precise intervals throughout the day and night. If a roller drum needed to be warmed or cooled every four hours, the person conducting the experiment had to be there for each of those maintenance chores. If a culture had to be checked every three hours, the person had to be present at ten P.M., one A.M., four A.M. and so on throughout the twenty-four-hour cycle. Requesting help from another researcher was always possible—but unlikely to yield anything, since the other staffers were on different three-hour leashes of their own.

With time spent outside the walls of the lab dwindling, the staff of fifty soon became a default family. More and more, meals were taken communally at the little table in the morgue lunchroom. Sibling-like rivalries would sometimes break out when the lab, which was grinding out a growing number of research papers, was preparing a new one for publication and the list of researchers who would receive credit was scrutinized like a batting order. Eccentricities began to emerge too. One of Jim Lewis's cynomolgus monkeys gave birth in captivity to a tiny, healthy male. The team developed an instant attachment to the little creature, dropping by the animal lab for visits and delighting when Lewis brought it around for walks and play. Lewis called the animal Corky—a name that instantly stuck—and as monkeys continued to be shipped into the lab, injected, killed, and processed down into parts and tissue, it was universally understood that Corky, alone among the nonhuman creatures in residence, would remain forever unharmed.

For Salk, the demands of the lab were matched by demands at home, as the family planned a long-in-coming move from its Wexford house. Salk's love of the country remained undiminished. But the trip into and out of the city each day—which took at least forty-five minutes, and that only if the weather was good and the traffic was light—grew to be more and more of a burden.

Instead, he and Donna had their eyes on a lovely, almost grand house near the university, with pillars on the front porch, stained glass in the stairway landings, and elaborate wallpaper in the dining room depicting a pleasant little country scene. Swapping the real country for a teasing mural of it seemed like a poor bargain, but the seven-minute commute from the new home to the lab sweetened the deal considerably.

It was in the midst of all this that the Commerce Committee's hearings were held. The session was scheduled to be a short one, lasting just a single day—appropriate enough given the make-work nature of the proceedings. When the hearing was gaveled to order, the committee chairman—Charles Wolverton, a powerful New Jersey Republican who had been a member of Congress since 1926—nonetheless began with a fair bit of oratorical throat-clearing, lauding the work of the NFIP, thanking the scientists for taking the time to visit Washington today, and tipping his hat to the one man who was not here for the event.

"In some respects I have noticed that Dr. Salk has been modest enough not to claim too much," Wolverton said. "And yet even to claim a little gives much encouragement to laymen who have a natural interest in the polio problem."

Wolverton yielded the floor to Sabin, and the Cincinnati doctor quickly made it clear that if Jonas Salk was being modest, it was only because he had much reason to be. "Dr. Salk's process of inactivating virus is not new," he charged in his prepared remarks. "It is not different or patentable."

Worse, he went on, even if the vaccine provided some weak protection, there was no telling how long it would last or whether it was even safe. And while the congressmen might not be aware of it, the very idea of building a vaccine from a killed virus was not even an established one—a bit like constructing a house from rotten wood.

Van Riper came next and tried to be more measured in his remarks, but he didn't reveal a great deal more enthusiasm than Sabin had. "Dr. Salk has demonstrated that the vaccinated individual would indeed have protection," he condeded, "but it would last only about a year. I think none of us believes Dr. Salk's vaccine, if it is in fact a vaccine, is the final answer. Still, if this inactivated virus can produce immunity that does last a year, then I think socially we should consider its use."

To Sabin, however, that was a politician's position—and he was no politician. If you were certain you were pursuing the right vaccine, you could perhaps go ahead and plan something as ambitious as the field trial. If you weren't, you didn't. He called for recognition to speak.

"I for one, would strongly oppose large-scale work on hundreds of thousands of children based on the work of any one investigator," he said, "no matter how eminent, how great he may be."

The testimony proceeded through the afternoon, but the acid tone of Sabin's denunciation stayed in the air. There was never a risk that the committee wouldn't endorse the NFIP's position on the field trial, but now that position seemed at least a little less clear. A vast polio experiment might be taking place soon, but if it indeed happened, it would be with only the most grudging support from some of the foundation scientists long assumed to be behind it.

Salk did not learn about the goings-on at the hearing until the next day, when he, like any uninvolved party, read about it in the newspaper—and then he said little about it. Such public sniping at so late a date was not doing anything to push the field trial forward. There was an enormous amount of work to be done before any formal test of any final vaccine could hope to begin. That work would not get done in a congressional committee room.

Whatever progress the NFIP was making in rolling out its new vaccine, it was making a lot less getting the story told properly by the press. There was John Troan, of course, along with a few other reporters who understood the science thoroughly and explained it clearly. But that list of quality journalists, to Salk's mind at least, was a short one, and he continued to do his best to avoid almost the entire press corps. Troan, who never minded having the competition eliminated, was nevertheless troubled that Salk wasn't doing a better job of communicating with the public. When the chance presented itself, he shared that concern with his friend.

"I had a call from Bill Jacobs today," he told Salk when he phoned him at the lab one morning. Jacobs, of course, was Troan's editor at the *Press* and the man who had arranged the picture session with the photographers from *Life*. "He told me that you had a visit this week from *Time* magazine."

Salk did not sound pleased. "That reporter," he practically spat.

"Gil Cant," Troan said. "He's very good."

"He didn't seem very good to me. He came in here like a burglar, asking me over and over if the vaccine is safe. So I threw him out."

"It's a question everyone's going to ask."

"And I answered it. But once ought to be enough. I never should have agreed to see him."

"It's *Time* magazine, Jonas." Troan realized that if hundreds of thousands of children were going to submit to the new vaccine, the inventor of the stuff had better be willing to introduce himself to those children's parents. A magazine like *Time* could help that happen.

"How about if I talk to the reporter for you?" Troan offered. "You let him send me a list of questions. I'll read them to you over the phone and write down your answers."

"I wouldn't have to speak to him?"

"Not a word."

Salk thought. "All right," he said. "Have him mail you his list."

A week later, Troan received Cant's questions—a good sixty of them—and phoned Salk. The first dozen or so were strictly about science, and Salk answered them willingly, if brusquely. Then came the rest.

"How many bedrooms do you have in your house?" Troan read.

"What?"

"Does your wife make you breakfast every morning?"

"John!" Salk snapped. "Do I have to answer these?"

"No, Jonas, you don't."

Troan scanned the rest of the list, bypassing any questions that didn't deal strictly with medicine. Salk answered the remaining ones and concluded the call. Troan wrote up the answers and mailed them to Cant, figuring his fellow reporter could hunt up the personal details about Salk's life on his own. Later that week, Salk sat down at his desk and began drafting and redrafting a formal request to the NFIP public affairs department. When he was satisfied with it—after three longhand versions—he had Lorraine Friedman type it up and send it out.

"There are just so many hours in the day that my associates and I have at our disposal," he wrote. "At the risk of being regarded as uncooperative, I must ask that the laboratory and I be forgotten for the next six months. We make this request in the public interest since it is in this way that we and the press can be of greatest public service."

The memo was passed up the line to O'Connor, who read it and promptly ordered that a directive be issued to the foundation at large. It was sent under the name of a lower-level administrator in the New York headquarters, but it was clear whose orders he was carrying. "I am instructing every member of the staff that they are not to communicate with Dr. Salk by telephone or by letter without direct approval of Dr. Van Riper," the memo read. "Neither are members of the staff to refer or direct calls to Dr. Salk from people outside the Foundation."

After that, a curtain dropped around the Pittsburgh Virus Lab, with few outsiders beyond John Troan getting a glimpse of what was going on inside. Troan was pleased at his ongoing access, and pleased too that he'd arranged for Salk to spend some time with *Time*—even if the scientist himself didn't understand why.

The researchers in the virus lab were under no illusion that they'd heard the last from the folks at Parke, Davis—and that was all right with them. The drug giant might have played fast and loose with the truth in its press release, but the fact remained that there weren't a whole lot of other companies out there that had the manufacturing muscle and the distribution reach Parke, Davis had—something that would be essential in getting the vaccine where it needed to go for any eventual field trial. Of course, saying that few companies had Parke, Davis's power was not the same as saying no companies did, and particularly after the press-release dustup, Salk was inclined at least to consider working with them all. What he didn't know was that the matter had largely been settled, thanks to an arranged marriage between Parke, Davis and the virus lab, brokered by the now absent Harry Weaver.

Earlier in the spring, the then-research director reached an oral agreement with the company's bosses, promising that when a final formula for an adjuvant-fortified vaccine was at last settled on, the recipe would be delivered to Parke, Davis first. There was no money in such a deal for the NFIP—and certainly none for Harry Weaver. Basil O'Connor and Franklin Roosevelt had always made it clear that the public had paid for the NFIP's work many times over with all the donations it had made since the very first Birthday Ball. Any vaccine that came of that work would thus not be the NFIP's to sell. Rather, it would simply be turned over to industry for mass manufacturing.

But it wasn't money Weaver had in mind; it was speed. Reluctant to go fumbling with a laborious bidding-and-vetting process when there was at last a vaccine for manufacturers to make, he took it upon himself to shake hands with Parke, Davis and give the company an advance chance to start tooling up. That handshake helped explain one, if not all, of the liberties the company had taken in its press release. Since Weaver had acted with the full authority of the foundation, the foundation was bound to honor the deal. If the arrangement didn't work out, the mess would no longer be Weaver's to clean up. The way things looked now, a mess might indeed be in the making.

When Basil O'Connor learned about Weaver's deal, he decided to give it a chance and arranged for a visit by Parke, Davis representatives to the Pittsburgh Virus Lab, so that Salk could walk them through his methods and give them as much of his final recipe as he had. The corporate scientists came in early fall of 1953, and after their time with Salk was done, O'Connor asked them to get to work straightaway trying to manufacture an initial 30-liter lot of the vaccine. In early November, Salk visited the Parke, Davis plant to check on how their work was coming. He was appalled at what he saw.

The Detroit operation was, to his eyes at least, huge and unwieldy, with redundancy and inefficiency all along the line. There were work teams with up to eleven women reading cultures and scanning test results, despite the fact that less than half that number—rigorously trained and closely supervised—might do much better. There were not enough people in the truly skilled, truly senior positions to oversee the work of the less trained employees. Unions protected the jobs of poorly qualified workers, making it hard to discipline or fire them when the need arose. For a manufacturing process with a margin of error measured in individual virus particles, this was utterly intolerable.

Worse, Salk believed, for all Parke, Davis's apparent lust for the vaccine, the company wasn't entirely sure it wanted it—at least not the way Salk was making it. Whatever else the vaccine might be, it was also a product—and a seasonal product at that—and Parke, Davis had a responsibility not just to customers but to stockholders as well. Selling polio vaccine in, say, the fall, was a little like selling Christmas decorations in summer—possible, but nowhere near as profitable as moving the merchandise when demand was greatest. For that reason, Parke, Davis wanted to get something safe and effective into the hands of parents and doctors as soon as possible, and if Salk's formula wasn't it, the company might try to invent its own. No strangers to vaccines, the corporate scientists had even spoken of scrapping the formalin inactivation technique altogether and turning back to ultraviolet methods.

Given both the manufacturing problems and this institutional ambivalence, Salk was not surprised when the first 30-liter batch of vaccine the company did manage to produce was not even remotely ready for use. Centrifuge times had been off, oven temperatures had been wrong, the fluids in which the virus floated were not even sufficiently clarified—a disastrous error if you hoped to prevent the bug from hiding out from the formalin behind specks of debris. No one expected this trial lot to be perfect, but Salk had expected it to be better.

Even if Parke, Davis managed to perfect its manufacturing method, there was no certainty that it could manage to turn out the enormous quantity of vaccine the foundation would need for the field trial. A lot depended on just what that quantity would be, and that, in turn, depended on the Vaccine Advisory Committee. One of the most difficult questions with which the group had begun to grapple was whether the field trial should be conducted with full and formal double-blind controls or with simpler, so-called observed controls. It was a question of scientific ideology that could crack the group wide open.

William Hammon's gamma globulin trials had been a model of good, double-blind protocol, with some of the subjects in the study receiving real serum and some receiving the immunological equivalent of soda pop, nobody knowing which was which until the labels were revealed on the vials at the end of the polio season. This method prevented biases from contaminating the study as participants were evaluated.

For the vaccine field trial, this would be more important than ever. Not only would investigators have to be able to diagnose polio cases properly, they would also have to screen the vaccine for side effects, something that would be difficult without a control group to help distinguish vaccine-related ills from other ones. Finally, double-blind placebo controls were simply the gold standard for good science. If you wouldn't use the most rigorous methods possible when testing a vaccine that contained a potentially lethal virus, when on earth would you?

But many people wanted no part of the double-blind method—most notably Salk. It wasn't just that he was convinced his vaccine worked and that such controls were thus unnecessary. It was that, given that belief, it seemed flat-out immoral not to make the preparation available to as many children as possible. Somewhere in the sample group would be at least a handful of boys and girls who would step up for the field trial the NFIP was proposing, offer up their arms and immune systems for foundation science, and still come tumbling out of summer without the use of their legs, all because they had been shot up with an ersatz injection instead of the real thing. This was indefensible—a "fetish of orthodoxy," as Salk thought of it—and he simply couldn't abide it. What he preferred instead were simpler observed controls, a study in which as many boys and girls as possible would be inoculated with real vaccine and then be compared with similar communities in which the children had not been dosed with anything at all. The difference in disease rates between the two groups would be the measure of the vaccine's success. Let the luxury of double-blind controls be saved for other studies, when someone was testing a vaccine against an illness like the common cold.

From his office tower in New York, Basil O'Connor viewed all this argument and uncertainty with continued impatience. With the clock ticking down to 1954, he was plain fed up with catfights among his scientists and manufacturers, thrashing out matters that ought to have been settled already. If the field trial was going to take place in 1954, the injections had to begin before the onset of the polio season, so that a fresh infection that started incubating in a child just before the vaccine was administered would not be mistakenly blamed on the virus in the shot. That meant that injections would have to commence no later than March and perhaps as early as February. Disputes over protocols and problems at the factories were not the way to get this done.

O'Connor decided to settle things himself and to tackle the Parke, Davis problem first. The way to do that was simply to scrap Harry Weaver's deal. As a Wall Street man with a healthy respect for free markets, he understood both the invigorating effect of competition and the stultifying effect of monopoly. This particular monopoly had not had a chance to harden yet, and before it did, he was determined to bust it apart.

With the growing influence he now wielded in the pharmaceutical world, O'Connor scheduled a meeting for November 11 at New York's Commodore Hotel on the corner of Lexington Avenue and Forty-second Street. He invited representatives from ten major drug companies: Lederle Laboratories, Pitman-Moore, Eli Lilly, National Drug, Upjohn, Sharp and Dohme, Wyeth, Squibb, and the lesser known Cutter Laboratories in Berkeley, California. He also, of course, invited Parke, Davis. All ten firms attended.

O'Connor called the meeting to order in a conference room in the hotel precisely at noon on the scheduled date, and made it clear from the start that for all the industrial firepower the men in attendance represented, they were here to learn, not to speak. O'Connor first invited Salk to step up and describe his new vaccine to the companies that weren't intimately familiar with it yet. Salk did so, giving the men a quick overview of his methods. Then O'Connor reclaimed the floor and reviewed the kind of field trial the NFIP was imagining and the preparatory work that was already under way at Parke, Davis. Finally he came to the nut of the matter, describing the magnitude of the job that would be expected of any company that decided to join the project. The numbers he cited were stunning.

In the three or four months that might remain before the trial began, the foundation would require between 1.3 million and 1.9 million doses of polio vaccine, depending on how many injections each child received and whether all of the boys and girls would be getting the genuine preparation or some would receive a placebo. The vaccine would be a trivalent preparation, containing killed samples of all three types of poliovirus, so that even a single shot could get all three types of antibodies going.

According to Salk's data, it would take 10 days to inactivate the virus, 18 days to conduct safety tests in tissue culture, 10 more days for safety tests on animals, and 28 days for safety tests on human volunteers. Samples from all of the vaccine batches would go through their testing in three places: the manufacturers' own labs, Salk's lab, and the National Institutes of Health in Bethesda, Maryland. Since the tests on the animals and humans could be run simultaneously, the work would take a total of 56 days. But since prudence required that a further cushion be built into that schedule, Salk added two more weeks, bringing the production time to 70 days. And none of that included all the preliminary days or weeks it might take the manufacturers to study Salk's vaccine recipe and tool up their labs with any needed equipment. As of that afternoon, there were 95 days to go until the middle of February.

Salk and O'Connor were under no illusion that all ten companies would want to participate, nor could the foundation manage so many diverse manufacturers even if they did. Some of the companies might be dissuaded by the fact that they could expect to make no money at all on the field-trial work, though if the vaccine proved successful they would be in an ideal position to sell it on a national, even global, scale. During a break, when a few of the representatives approached O'Connor to say that they were indeed intrigued by the work, he posed a question: How effective, he wanted to know, would the vaccine have to be for the companies to want to market it?

Effective, of course, wasn't the same as safe. There'd be no compromising on the foundation's requirement that the vaccine cause no harm. But assuming a 100 percent safety level, he wanted to know, what would the preparation's success rate at actually preventing polio have to be before the companies would be willing to sell it?

"Maybe twenty-five percent," one representative said.

"Perhaps fifteen percent," offered another.

O'Connor was shocked. Fifteen percent effective meant 85 percent useless—or a huge majority of children who would sit still for the vaccine only to receive no protection at all from it. If that was the best the foundation scientists could do, they'd have no business calling their preparation a vaccine at all.

The meeting adjourned with no firm commitments from any of the companies, but it was clear that at least six of them—Lilly, Wyeth, Pitman-Moore, Cutter, Sharp and Dohme, and Parke, Davis—were interested. They would not be given much time to contemplate their final decision.

As the drug executives returned to their home cities and Salk returned to Pittsburgh, an energized O'Connor turned his attention elsewhere, scheduling one more meeting for just two days later, on November 13, this time at the Plaza Hotel with the Vaccine Advisory Committee. There were three lingering questions the panel had to address before mass production of the vaccine could begin: Was the Mahoney virus indeed safe to use in the Type I vaccination or was it, as Sabin insisted, too wild for the work? Was the aqueous vaccine indeed as effective as the adjuvant-fortified one? Finally, would the foundation adhere strictly to the double-blind protocol or would a looser, observed control standard be acceptable? O'Connor did not intend to adjourn the planned meeting until his scientists had answered all three questions. Nor would they be allowed to go home until they had agreed on a firm date for the beginning of the trial.

The committee members met as O'Connor ordered. With mountains of data from the Pittsburgh lab in front of them and with the foundation chief keeping them properly focused on it, they found—at last—that they were able to move through their work with near-corporate efficiency. The Mahoney matter they disposed of quickly, agreeing that none of the data so far suggested that when properly processed into a vaccine, this strain was any more dangerous than any other Type I. If it was also the one Salk found the most stable and effective, he would be permitted to continue using it.

The debate over the aqueous and oily formulations was settled with equal certainty. After refining their methods further and further, the Pittsburgh researchers at last appeared to have developed a version of the aqueous preparation that was nearly as potent as the adjuvant-fortified one. Since it also carried none of the carcinogenic risk the oily formula did, it would be the committee's vaccine of choice.

Finally—and unexpectedly decisively—the committee also settled the double-blind matter. Given the suffering caused by even a single case of polio and the enormous number of children who might be spared that torment if the vaccine proved effective, it was decided that it would be—as Salk had argued—simply unethical to inject any child with nothing but sugar water. The placebo control would thus be done away with; instead, field-trial doctors and nurses would inject second-graders in selected communities with all the genuine vaccine the manufacturers could make. First- and third-graders would be used as observed, uninjected controls.

With those matters so clearly settled, the committee did insist on a concession to those inside and outside the NFIP who felt uneasy about taking such an enormous experimental leap—going from 637 inoculated subjects to hundreds of thousands in just a matter of months. A small pilot trial would be scheduled for just after the first of the year, the committee decided. Salk would inject between 5,000 and 10,000 school-age volunteers in Allegheny County, in and around Pittsburgh, with his vaccine. If it proved both safe and effective in this dry run, the field trial would get under way on the morning of Tuesday, February 9, 1954. O'Connor would make the official announcement of all this within a few days. Salk would be expected to get straight to work planning the pilot study.

On November 16, O'Connor did make the announcement. Now sixty-one years old and a seventeen-year veteran of the NFIP, O'Connor clearly saw the endgame in front of him. His friend Franklin Roosevelt had not lived to see that game play out. The foundation chief, though not willing to push the vaccine further than it was ready to go, clearly did not want to miss the finish too.

Several days later, Salk was having lunch in the Bamboo Garden with John Troan, who had stopped by for tea and egg foo young—the only dish he'd really learned to tolerate—and for Salk's thoughts about the work that would soon begin.

"John," Salk said, nodding wearily over his food, "I'm beginning to think Basil just wants to make sure this thing gets done in his lifetime."

It was always late in November, when the polio season was well and truly over, that the disease toll from the previous summer could finally be determined. The 35,592 cases of infantile paralysis that struck the country in 1953 came as something of a relief compared with the 57,879 who had gotten sick the season before—especially given the virulent way the season had begun—but it was a numbing number nonetheless.

Worse, as the caseload grew, so did the number of months in the year in which children appeared to be getting sick. Even as the epidemiologists watched, the poliovirus seemed to be slipping the traditional bonds of the calendar, arriving earlier in the season and staying much later. It was not at all uncommon for children to begin falling ill as early as April and continue coming down with the disease as late as the cold, wet days of November.

The Municipal Hospital polio ward, upstairs from Salk's lab, was no exception to the community of health facilities that had to cope with the problem. From April 17 through November 24, 1953, fully 391 patients, almost all of them children, were carried into the Municipal emergency room suffering from fresh cases of polio. On 12 occasions, two siblings were brought in; on one occasion, three were. Of the 391 patients, 323 were paralyzed. Sixty-one of the 391 were younger than three years old. Nine were infants, less than twelve months old.

Children from no fewer than thirteen Pennsylvania counties were represented in the Municipal Hospital polio ward, but just one county, Allegheny, with its high population and dense urban center, had contributed 52 percent of them. Salk had not been pleased that the Vaccine Advisory Committee had suddenly instructed him to test his vaccine on 10,000 children in that suffering county. On the other hand, if there was ever a community that needed the protection his vaccine could provide, this was it.

Raising such a large militia of boys and girls would be far harder than recruiting the mere 637 volunteers he had used in his studies so far. To succeed, he would have to cast a very wide net, and the public schools of Allegheny County would be the obvious, perhaps the only, place to begin.

Salk himself drafted letters to the schools. The appeal would be distributed to the children and, in turn, carried home to the parents, and would explain the purpose of the preliminary field trial and invite any interested volunteers to participate. Salk took pains to avoid actually using the word "volunteer" in the letter. Volunteers were people performing some unpleasant duty. The participants in this study were being offered something much different—and much better—and ought to be required to *request* participation in the project. This wasn't merely the language demanded by lawyers who wanted to protect the university and the NFIP in case something went lethally wrong—though it pleased the lawyers all the same. This was the exacting language of a scientist who'd invented something he was certain was safe and who would not have it presented any other way.

"We're providing a good thing," Salk would tell his staff. "We ought to say it that way."

As Salk was tooling up for his little local trial, the NFIP as a whole was preparing for the far larger, million-person event that would follow. The most important job the foundation had to do before it could begin was find somebody to analyze all the results when the study was done. Even a modest piece of lab-bench science needed a single objective investigator to sort through the findings and determine—coldly, clinically—what they meant. A study that would be national in its scope and global in its implications needed such a figure all the more.

Basil O'Connor, of course, was not qualified for the job. He was not a scientist, and even if he had been, he was already openly and hopelessly biased in favor of the vaccine. The other senior members of the foundation's senior committees—Rivers, Smadel, Hammon, Topping, Paul, Bodian, Howe, even the ostensibly fair-minded van Riper—were too touched as well by the ideological arguments that had led the foundation to this point in the first place. Salk, obviously, was out of the question.

What was needed instead was someone who was familiar with the foundation but not politically enmeshed with it; who knew the personalities involved in the trial but was comfortable enough to exercise absolute authority over them; and most important, who understood in his very marrow how the complex business of vaccine science worked. What was needed was Tommy Francis.

Salk's onetime mentor and collaborator on the flu vaccine had been quietly continuing his work on viruses and infectious diseases at the University of Michigan for years, turning out well-regarded research and avoiding the shrillness of scientific debate. On occasion, he'd be asked to serve as a sort of elder NFIP statesman, sitting in on the odd committee or offering the odd opinion but never getting involved in matters more deeply than that. In this capacity, he had made a lot of friends and won almost universal respect—something few of the other, more partisan NFIP men could claim. The risk always existed that a former supervisor could never judge a former apprentice's work objectively, and that Francis would be biased in favor of whatever conclusions Salk hoped he'd reach. But that very familiarity also made Francis uniquely qualified to see any holes that might exist in Salk's work and to call him on them if he found them. Francis, it seemed clear, would be perfect for the new post. The only problem would be getting him to accept it.

For months now, Francis and his wife had been touring Europe on a working vacation, stopping in labs and universities around the continent and then visiting the sights in their off-hours. In the early winter they arrived in London, their final stop before coming home. With the help of the University of Michigan, van Riper located them there. He placed an overseas phone call to Francis and described the work the foundation was offering—and Francis turned him down flat. The scale of the project was overwhelming, the politics were poisonous, and if he could be perfectly honest, the observed controls the NFIP was planning were junk. He would not be interested in the work in any event, mind you, but if the NFIP was going to conduct the study, it should at least conduct it right.

Van Riper and O'Connor saw a glint of light. When Francis returned to the United States, O'Connor called him in for a meeting in New York and pressed him again. Francis refused again, once more citing both the politics and the cursed observed controls. O'Connor answered that it hadn't been easy lining up states whose health directors were willing to consider the field trial. The only sweetener he'd been able to offer was that all the children who participated in the study would at least receive a real vaccine that the foundation really believed would protect them from poliomyelitis. With that promise—not to mention endless phone work and in-person glad-handing—he'd been able to recruit an impressive thirty-three states. He couldn't go back on his pledge now without the risk of losing them all.

Francis acknowledged O'Connor's bind, but insisted that he'd still have to pass. O'Connor implored him at least to think about it overnight. If he had the time, he might even want to talk to Salk, one of the foundation's most passionate observed-control zealots. Perhaps he could persuade Francis of the indefensibility of the double-blind.

Francis took O'Connor up on that suggestion, but as it turned out, he was the one who did the persuading. Salk's zeal was nothing compared with Francis's steady conviction, and in the course of a long telephone conversation, Salk eventually saw that if denying some children the real vac-

cine was morally questionable, conducting so important a study in anything less than the very best, most rigorous way was equally wrong. If
Francis, of all people, said a double-blind trial was the best possible one he
could conduct, Salk would accept that.

Francis carried that news back to O'Connor, and O'Connor, in turn,
managed to strike a compromise: The thirty-three states that had been
promised observed controls would still get them, but eleven more would
be added to the mix, and there the study would be rigorously double-
blind. With so many children now involved, the work would certainly produce reliable results.

Francis accepted the new plan and asked for a few more significant con-
cessions before he'd finally accept the position. As long as he stayed within
the broad outlines to which he and the NFIP had agreed, he'd have to have
utter authority over the entire project: He'd make all decisions, resolve all
disputes, and oversee all the data collection himself. What's more, not a
soul—not Salk, not Van Riper, not even O'Connor—would see a single
scrap of the data for at least a year, until the polio season had come and
gone and all the findings could be read and analyzed properly. If the trial
began early in the spring of 1954, that meant there'd be no information of
any kind forthcoming from his office until early in the spring of 1955. On
that point, more so than all the others, he would not be moved.

O'Connor agreed to every one of Francis's demands, and before his
quarry could get away again, approved a $1 million NFIP grant to set up
an office and staff for the work to begin. More funds would be made available if they were needed, which they probably would be during the course
of the long project. Within days, the Poliomyelitis Vaccine Evaluation
Center under the direction of Dr. Tommy Francis was opened in the Special Projects Research Building on the University of Michigan campus—
part of the very hospital where Jonas Salk's two older sons had been born.

No sooner did Francis take up residence in his new office than he began making it clear just how seriously he took his new role—particularly
the complete professional distance he'd now be keeping from his onetime
colleagues and peers. The foundation realized that during the course of the
field trial, it might have to call on the assistance of any number of grantee

labs to pitch in with a little impromptu work—isolating the odd virus or studying the odd side effect that might turn up among the subjects. Francis wanted to line up as many volunteer labs as he could in all of the states where the test would take place, so that they'd be ready to help if they were needed in the summer.

One morning, Salk received an envelope from Francis's office and opened it up to find a single-page letter inside. Salk's name and address and the salutation were hand-typed at the top. The rest of the letter was a mimeograph.

"Dear Dr. Salk," the only personalized passage of the letter read. "During the coming field trial of the poliomyelitis vaccine, certain concurrent investigations will be essential. Do you and your associates plan to carry out any serological studies related to the NFIP vaccination program in the coming season? Would you be willing to do so? Would you be willing to attend a meeting in the near future to plan the procedure? I would appreciate it if you would reply by special delivery as soon as is convenient. Sincerely yours, Thomas Francis, Jr."

Salk read the letter through and gave it to Lorraine Friedman to be filed. No special-delivery response would really be required, not from his lab at any rate. The full meaning of this communication had already been sent and received: There would be no appeals to friendship as the vaccine was being evaluated. Salk was now just another lab man to his onetime boss, and he would be treated as such. His work would succeed or fail on its merits alone.

Donna Salk had done a lot better than many people had thought she'd do living in the comparatively modest towns she'd called home since she and her doctor husband first left New York City. She'd thrived in both Ann Arbor and Pittsburgh, with barely a wistful thought of Manhattan. That was not to say that she didn't enjoy the occasional visit back.

More and more these days, Jonas had had to travel to New York for meetings, and now and then Donna and the boys would go along. Donna took the opportunity to visit friends, take in a show, and stay in one of the glamorous rooms at the Waldorf-Astoria or the St. Moritz where the foundation would put them up. The boys were thrilled, mostly by the four-propellor TWA Super Constellation that would fly them east from Pittsburgh to New York. During a visit in early 1954, however, Donna and Jonas had something on their minds.

Jonas had shared with Donna at least a few of the letters from parents who continued to write him at his lab, pleading for a bit of vaccine to protect their children before the polio season could arrive. He did not hide the anguish he felt at having to say no. The vaccine was still not an officially proven thing, and even if it were, there would not have been enough to satisfy the needs of even a fraction of the people who were seeking it. Jonas could not presume to choose who among the many reaching out to him most deserved one of the rare available vials. And that presented a problem.

On those occasions when the Salks socialized with friends and neighbors—infrequent occasions to be sure, given all the hours Jonas was spending in the lab—they were aware of an unexpressed tension. The Salk sons, unlike most other children in the world, had now been immunized against infantile paralysis. Jonas and Donna, by extension, enjoyed a freedom from fear that the other parents in their social circle did not know. They all also understood that Jonas had the power to remedy that problem.

Nobody ever mentioned all of this outright, but the matter hung in the air all the same. It was insupportable for Jonas to withhold protection he had the power to grant. And yet, as both he and Donna realized, it was equally insupportable—not to mention hypocritical—to offer it only to a handful of children in their charmed circle and not to those who happened to fall outside it.

This was the problem that was troubling Jonas and Donna during their trip to New York. In the days before they left, they took some time—out of range of the boys' hearing—and talked the matter out. Jonas spoke as the medical man he was, Donna spoke as the psychologist and social worker she was. They both spoke as two people caught in a moral bramble. It wasn't until after they arrived in New York, however, that they finally reached some kind of a solution. They would be governed, they decided, by simple arithmetic. Every child who received the vaccine would be one fewer who would ever become paralyzed. All young lives being essentially equal, Jonas and Donna would yield to the human impulse to protect the ones they cared for most.

Later that night, after they had checked into their rooms at the St. Moritz, on Central Park South, they waited until the boys were asleep, tore a sheet of paper from a hotel memo pad, and began to compose a list. Helen Press—now Helen Glickstein, the cousin who used to stay at Salk's home and made him hide his pickled pig fetus before she'd go to sleep at night—was the first name they entered. She would receive enough vials of vaccine to inoculate her son and two daughters. Belle Granick, a friend from Ann Arbor who had lost her husband in a car accident years ago and was raising her daughters, Jane and Judy, alone, would get enough for the two girls. Ruth Goodman, who had gone to college with Donna and had sat beside her at graduation when they heard themselves announced as the only two summa cum laudes in the school, would receive doses for her two children. All of Jonas's and Donna's nieces and nephews would be protected as well. In all, eight families, comprising twenty-three children, would make the list.

Not long after, when Salk had returned to Pittsburgh, he found yet another letter waiting for him, this one from Gale Walker, the superintendent at the Polk School, asking if Salk could see his way clear to providing a little vaccine for the two children of the school's long-serving dentist. Salk dictated his usual letter, apologizing for not being able to do more, but explaining, as he had explained so many times, that it was simply not possible.

Lorraine Friedman typed the letter as instructed and left it on his desk for his signature. Salk picked it up and gave it a long look; then, at the bottom of the unsigned letter, he scribbled an instruction to Lorraine: "Please send him whatever he needs."

Picking a date for a field trial and choosing a man to run it were among the easiest parts of actually getting the thing done. Mobilizing the medical war machine that would be necessary to pull it all off was another matter entirely. At the moment, one of the most rapid advances was being made by the drug companies.

As O'Connor had foreseen, the six firms that had shown the most interest in the vaccine during the November meeting—Eli Lilly, Wyeth, Sharp and Dohme, Pitman-Moore, Cutter, and Parke, Davis—indeed looked likely to sign on. Not all of the companies were learning to make the vaccine with equal skill and speed, but at Lilly and Parke, Davis the progress was impressive. Even now, virus grown in 2½-gallon culture bottles at Connaught Laboratories in Toronto was being pooled into larger, 10-gallon kegs, packed into refrigerated trucks, and shipped south in industrial bulk to the vaccine factories. There, scientists who had at last learned to follow Salk's recipe precisely were killing and clarifying the bug and processing it with increasing speed into pristine vaccine. When the work was done, they sealed samples of the preparation into one-ounce amber ampules and sent them to labs elsewhere in the factory as well as to Salk's lab and the National Institutes of Health for testing. An impressive percentage of the lots were coming up safe and clean and free of live virus.

That progress, however, did not mean that all the manufacturing problems were licked. For one thing, both the government and the drug companies continued to show a troubling inclination to fool with Salk's formula. The most meddlesome thing they were considering involved Merthiolate. During any drug-manufacturing process, it was always possible that stray bacteria or fungi could creep into the mix and contaminate it disastrously. The usual answer was to stir in a bit of Merthiolate toward the end of the process to kill any possible bugs. You wouldn't have to use a lot—perhaps no more than a 1-in-20,000 dilution. Such a stingy amount rarely did much harm and often did much good, and if it kept the product clean, what could be wrong with it?

Salk saw plenty. For one thing, the period of time between the points when the vaccine would be manufactured and when it would be used was so brief that even if a contaminant were present, it wouldn't have time to multiply sufficiently to do any harm. More important, Salk's vaccine had never been tested with Merthiolate—not in his lab anyway—and the idea of some other lab blithely tossing in a splash or two was both outrageous and dangerous. This wasn't a sauce recipe; this was a vaccine that had been invented in a very particular way under very rigid guidelines and would have to be produced that way if it was going to do any good.

Equally disturbing, even as Lilly and Parke, Davis were showing their increasing manufacturing prowess, other labs were having a terrible time getting the work done right. Cutter Laboratories in Berkeley, California, seemed to be struggling particularly hard. As the weeks went by, Salk became more than passingly familiar with the Cutter letterhead, as the company grew stuck and wrote to Pittsburgh with questions or concerns. If it wasn't a problem with growing the virus in the proper 5-liter flask, it was a question about formalin concentrations. If it wasn't that, it was confusion about techniques for examining monkey spines for polio symptoms. Salk would write back each time, offering extensive explanations and including detailed procedure sheets, and slowly Cutter seemed to be catching on. But slowly might not be good enough. All the progress reports from all the labs made their way to O'Connor, who, in turn, made a decision. The six companies would all be encouraged to continue their work so that they all might be ready if the time came to churn the vaccine out worldwide. Only Lilly and Parke, Davis, however, would be expected—or, for that matter, permitted—to produce the vaccine to be used in the trial itself.

In New York, the staffers in the NFIP headquarters were gearing up too. With the field trial now a dual trial, relying on both double-blind and observed controls, the number of children who would participate rose to 1.8 million. More than 400,000 of the boys and girls would receive real vaccine, more than 200,000 would receive the placebo, and nearly 1.2 million would receive nothing but would still have to be carefully tracked.

Overseeing and inoculating so huge a population scattered across forty-four states would require some 20,000 doctors, 40,000 nurses, and 1,000 supporting health workers and technicians. Since most of the injections would take place in schools, at least 14,000 principals and 50,000 teachers would have to be called on as well to coordinate injection schedules, keep parents informed, and maintain order as children queued up to get their shots. Most important—if least appreciated—would be the all-purpose

March of Dimes volunteers who would be needed to distribute forms, drive buses, collect funds, stuff envelopes, answer phones, man information tables, and otherwise tend to the more tedious tasks. The foundation conservatively estimated that it would need 200,000 of them.

If people were being recruited by the battalion, supplies were being ordered by the ton. Cotton, alcohol, bandages, scissors, drapes, masks, gloves, gowns, clipboards, pens, paper, lollipops, and other essentials would all have to be bought up in grosses of grosses, boxed up in shipping crates—which would themselves have to be purchased—and sent out to where they needed to go.

Syringes especially would be in keen demand. Under the original plans, the vaccine would be supplied to the field sites preloaded into single-dose shots, simplifying procedures at the inoculation tables. To eliminate the need for autoclaves and other sterilizers at each location, the NFIP had located a company that had recently invented a disposable syringe that could be filled up once and simply discarded after use. As it turned out, however, the syringes leaked and the manufacturer could not promise to cure the problem in time for the test. Instead, the NFIP opted for a half-measure, relying on traditional resuable shots but shipping each one with six replacement needles. Only the needles would have to be changed after every injection, with the syringe itself getting a full six uses before being cleaned. If any backwash of blood could be seen flowing into the shot, it would be tossed into the sterilizer immediately.

The foundation kept the printers and the post office busy too, running off and mailing millions of pieces of literature, including informational brochures, vaccination alerts, permission slips, legal waivers, public announcements, teachers' bulletins, inoculation cards, and blood-sample sheets. Multiply colored, multiply carboned, onionskin records would also be kept on every one of the 1.8 million children either injected or observed. Yellow forms would be used in the double-blind states, blue forms would be used in the observed-control states. Purple forms would be printed as well, to be used only if the virus in the vaccine went horribly awry. The heading at the top of the sheets—"Notification of Deaths and

Untoward Reactions"—left no doubt as to the seriousness of the business the documents were designed to address.

All of this earthmoving work took time, more time than Basil O'Connor had allowed when he held his boastful mid-November press conference announcing the February 9 target date. In early January, he called the press together again—this time with considerably less fanfare—to admit that that date was no longer realistic. The trial, he now said more vaguely, would begin sometime in March or perhaps early April. Of necessity, some Southern states might have to be dropped, since by then their polio seasons would surely have begun. They could be replaced by communities in the far north, perhaps even including a town or two in Canada.

To keep things simple for the press, O'Connor blamed the delay entirely on a lack of sufficient quantity of vaccine, which was true enough, though not the whole story. "We're shifting from production in a teacup to production in a barrel," he explained. "This is a complicated job."

Salk was generally pleased by the delay. He was having a hard enough time getting his little 10,000-person trial moving without having the juggernaut of the foundation's far larger one bearing down on him. For him, one of the biggest challenges was not a scientific one but a legal one. His letters to the parents of possible volunteers had gone out to twenty-four schools in and around Allegheny County and, as he'd hoped, had yielded thousands of positive responses. But a simple reply card indicating a willingness to participate in a trial was nothing compared with the more detailed legal waiver the parents would have to sign before a child could actually be injected.

Lawyers from both the University of Pittsburgh and the NFIP had been very specific about a handful of particular points the waiver would have to contain. The parents would have to acknowledge that they had been informed by Salk himself of the nature and purpose of the study; of the fact that the vaccine had been tried successfully in animals and that a subsequent inoculation similarly prepared—though not identically, since that was impossible to promise with absolute certainty—had been used successfully in humans too. The waiver would further have to disclose the rough ingredients of the injection and make it clear that a number of blood samples would have to be drawn from all the inoculated children to test its effectiveness. Finally, the parents would have to consent specifically to the participation of the child. For this form, there'd be no playing coy with words like "request." As long as all of these elements were included in the waiver, Salk could phrase the rest in as inviting a way as he pleased, though the lawyers would of course have to see his final draft before it was sent out.

One morning in early February 1954, Salk was taking his customary working lunch at the Bamboo Garden, staring sourly at yet another draft of the waiver and making revisions on a lined pad. His food sat next to him untouched. In recent weeks, John Troan had been devoting more and more time to the polio story, and had thus been taking more and more of his lunches at the Bamboo Garden too. He noticed that Salk seemed to welcome the brief lunchtime distraction more these days than he ever had before. Troan walked in, and when Salk spotted him, he smiled.

"Have a seat," he said. "Maybe you can help me with this."

Troan sat, ordered his now familiar egg foo young, and looked at the paper. He gave it a read and let out a breath. It was perfectly dreadful. Salk had kept it to a single page, which was good, but what that page was filled with was precisely what he'd have expected when a lawyer and a scientist got together to write something: unreadable.

"Well," he said judiciously, "it might need some revisions."

Troan spent the better part of the lunch hour working on the text—simplifying the medical gibberish, eliminating the legal windiness, un-knotting sentences that were hopelessly tangled up. When he was done, he sat back and read what he'd written, pleased with himself.

"Show this one to the lawyers," he said, "and don't let them go and mess it up again."

Salk read the text and thanked Troan happily, relieved that the dreary job was at last done. Unaccustomedly indebted to the reporter, he suggested a way he might pay him back. Assuming the waivers were sent out and returned promptly, Salk hoped to begin his mini-trial on February 23. At the request of the foundation, he'd be holding a press conference to announce this date within the next couple of days. Presumably all three local newspapers—the *Sun-Telegraph,* the *Post-Gazette,* and Troan's own *Pittsburgh Press*—would be in attendance, as would at least a couple of radio stations and all three of the new television stations now operating in the city. Salk would be happy to give Troan a jump on the story, provided the two men could come up with a way to do so without getting either of them into hot water with the rest of the local reporters.

"Tell you what," Troan said. "When you decide on the date for the press conference, give me twenty-four hours' notice. I'll write my story, file it the night before, and get it set in type. You meet the press at nine the next morning, I'll attend and ask one question just to cover myself, then I'll duck out, phone the *Press,* and give them the go-ahead to start printing."

The two men shook hands on the plan, and a few days later they executed it perfectly. Troan's page-one story ran a full 26 column inches and handily beat all the other coverage in town. Several days later, he ran into Bill Burns, Pittsburgh's most recognized television reporter and a man of the electronic media who wasn't accustomed to getting skunked by the plodding print media.

"John," Burns said with grudging admiration, "I never knew a man who could dictate a story as fast as you." Troan smiled in a way he hoped revealed nothing at all.

The poisonous letters continued to stream into the virus lab from Duon Miller and his Polio Prevention organization in Coral Gables, Florida. Lorraine Friedman opened them all and would have been just as happy to discard them. Salk, however, always insisted on seeing every piece of his mail, even the very worst of it. Most of the letters he received from Miller he ignored, but he still could not resist responding to one now and then, insisting that a reasoned answer to even the most irrational question could sometimes make an impression. Lorraine believed no such thing and would scold Salk when he handed her a response to be typed.

Salk seemed generally untroubled by Miller's ranting mail, and by Lorraine's admonition that he ignore it, but even he was stunned one day when the angry Florida man sent him the most venomous letter yet. "ISN'T IT A FACT," Miller wrote, "that a few years ago a 'fake' vaccine was tested on innocent little children? ISN'T IT A FACT . . . several of the children 'polluted' contracted POLIO? ISN'T IT A FACT . . . that the QUACK pseudo 'exspurt' responsible for this . . . committed suicide? MERELY A SUGGESTION . . . that's all."

This time Miller had crossed the line. It wasn't merely the whiff of a threat in his suggestion that Salk go the way of poor Maurice Brodie, it was the foul mention of the Brodie tragedy at all. A fool with a typewriter had no business invoking the name of a scientist who'd had a vision, no matter how imperfect or tragic that vision had proven to be. Salk was at last persuaded. Duon Miller would hear only silence from the virus lab from now forward, even weeks later when Miller wrote again, this time including the cover page of his soon-to-be published leaflet, which he called *Little White Coffins*. The leaflets, he threatened, would soon be distributed all over the country.

If Miller's bile was being widely disseminated, it wasn't making much of an impression on the press. The announcement of the coming trials had fired up the already overheated newspapermen, who continued to publish equally overheated reports on the progress of what they now universally referred to as the "Salk vaccine." The growing use of that label did not please either the NFIP or Salk.

From the beginning, Salk had done what he could to spread the credit for the virus lab's work as widely as possible. Papers published by his team never carried his name alone and often didn't even list it first. When he did receive top billing, the credit line always read, "by Jonas E. Salk with the collaboration of" whoever else had been involved in the work, no matter how many of them there were. On occasions when he was asked to approve the text of a press release or a magazine story, he always took care to insert the names of his associates there too, as well as a mention of the NFIP as a whole. And when the prestigous journal *Modern Medicine* planned to publish one of his papers and to commission a watercolor portrait of him to be featured on the cover—a rare honor much prized by scientists, particularly since they later got to keep the painting—Salk politely declined, asking that the paper still be published but that the portrait please be scrapped.

Even his entreaties, however, could not make the "Salk vaccine" label go away. Editors and reporters liked it because it was brief and punchy and, not incidentally, because Salk's four-letter name fit neatly into a headline. As an alternative, Salk requested that they try "Pitt vaccine," which required not a character more of space and far more accurately reflected how the work was getting done. Salk even made it a point to look up the rules of typesetting and learned that words with a lot of slender letters like *i* and *t* require less space on a page than words with fat ones, like *s* and *k*.

"Pitt only counts for three typographic units," Salk argued to John Troan. "Salk counts for four."

Troan laughed and agreed to try the name out in his column, but he knew it would be futile. The University of Pittsburgh was an institution and Salk was a man, and a person's name was always more compelling to readers. Even when Troan complied with Salk's request, an editor inevitably changed the phrasing back the other way.

No amount of finessing headlines or fiddling with bylines, however, could contain the burst of publicity that broke when the story Gil Cant had written at last ran in the March 9, 1954, issue of *Time* magazine. Salk had never considered that the story would be anything more than a science profile buried deep inside the latter pages of the magazine. It took him entirely by surprise, therefore, when he instead discovered his face on the cover.

The Salk family did not subscribe to *Time* magazine, and so Salk did not see the March 9 issue before he left the house on the Monday morning it was released. And since he drove to work rather than traveling by bus or train, he would not have seen it on a newsstand or in the hands of another commuter either. When he arrived at the hospital, however, there was no missing it. The little gift shop and candy stand next to the bank of first-floor elevators always carried a supply of magazines and newspapers, and Salk often gave them a glance as he passed by in the morning. When he saw his own face looking back at him, he was struck dumb.

254

The magazine, which preferred portraits to photographs for its covers, had produced quite a fine likeness of him. His painted face stared out with a pleasing earnestness that fell safely short of grimness. The rest of the cover, however, was a disaster. Drawings of frisky, healthy boys and girls frolicked at the top of the page, flying kites or tossing baseballs among the four letters in the magazine's familiar logo. Beneath, next to the picture of Salk, a pair of eerily empty braces accompanied by floating crutches lurched along as if operated by strings. A quiver of menacing-looking syringes pointed down at the crutches, and behind the whole tableau was a scattering of tiny pellets that resembled little sugar pills but were meant to represent an electron micrograph of the poliovirus.

"Polio Fighter Salk," the legend under the picture read. *"Is this the year?"*

Salk was horrified. As of this moment, his vaccine research had accomplished exactly nothing beyond burning through nearly $3 million of the NFIP's money and possibly protecting a flyspeck population of early volunteers. If there must be covers, save them for later, for the time the magazines could actually declare *This is the year,* tossing their cautionary question mark aside.

Salk bought a copy of the magazine, carried it to his office, and opened it with dread. The story, he found, was a different beast entirely.

No matter how objectionable some of Gil Cant's questions might have been, he had placed Salk's work in precisely the right perspective. The text was shot through with the names of the polio researchers who had gone before as well as the other men directing the research today. There were pictures of John Enders, Tommy Francis, Basil O'Connor, and even Albert Sabin. Enders's work particularly was featured, described as nothing short of virology's equivalent of the relativity equation—which was no exaggeration. If you saw nothing but the cover of *Time* magazine on the newsstand, you would have thought Jonas Salk a solitary visionary, doing battle with polio entirely on his own. If you took the time to read the story, you saw him for who he was—the point man, perhaps, in a larger war, but just one soldier nonetheless.

Salk said as little as he could about the story throughout the day, though it was hard to ignore the growing number of copies in hands and at lab stations. If only by his averted gaze, however, he made it clear he didn't care to talk about it. It was only when he got home that night that he spoke of it at all.

"I wouldn't have thought it," he conceded to Donna. "They got it right. Now if they could just tear off that cover."

Donna, who had already bought a stack of copies and planned to pick up more throughout the week, liked the cover just fine.

Two weeks before *Time* magazine appeared on the newsstands, Salk's little field trial actually got under way. *Time* hadn't made much of a fuss over that fact, devoting a single paragraph to it buried far down in the story. But for Salk, this was the real stuff of magazine covers.

The first 137 of the 10,000 boys and girls whose parents had volunteered them for the Allegheny County study received their shots at Pittsburgh's Arsenal Elementary School. It was an old building in an unlovely place, standing on a stretch of Fortieth Street just a couple blocks east of the Allegheny River. The raw February wind bringing grimy mist off the water did not do much to make the scene any more inviting, nor did the chilly gymnasium inside the school, where the injections would be administered.

Salk arrived at the school early in the morning accompanied by two of his lab researchers, four nurses, and Lorraine Friedman. They were all shown to the empty gym. As he had done so many times since his long-ago test of his flu vaccine on the young volunteers at the army's Camp Wellston, he set up his familiar folding table in the front of the room, spread out his familiar sterile cloth, and unpacked his kit bag of needles and vials. He had taken care to make sure that his nurses arrived in full uniform and that he and the two researchers were clad in lab coats. Only Lorraine Friedman was permitted business attire.

The setup work was conducted silently, and even the small knot of television, radio, and print reporters who had arrived and encamped in the back of the room kept their voices unaccustomedly low. Shortly after the morning bell rang, the first class of thirty children trooped into the room, steered by their teacher at the front of the line and the school's principal at the rear. Salk turned and saw them.

"Here they are!" he said brightly, as if he had been waiting for just this group of boys and girls for more or less his entire life—which, the fact of the matter was, he had.

There were no parents here today; nor, as Salk realized too late, were there any lollipops—a detail that he usually took care to remember whenever he was injecting children but that had somehow escaped him this morning. Instead, the boys and girls would have to be both assured and rewarded by his words alone.

He invited the class up to the front of the room, sat on the corner of the little folding table, and explained what would be in the shot they'd all be receiving that morning. When he was done, he asked if there were any questions, and there were indeed a few—the ones the children always asked: Would the injection give them polio? No, Salk assured them. Would it hurt? Yes, Salk conceded, a little, and then it would stop hurting.

When the questions were done, Salk called the children forward one after another, asked their names, asked if they were ready, and then administered the injection. When he was finished, he spent another moment with each of them, checking the injected spot, thanking them for being there—offering the only sweet reward he could. One girl out of the 137 thanked him in return, and then reached up for him to bend close. He did and she tightly hugged his neck. The reporters' flashbulbs, which had stayed mostly dark up until now, popped in unison at that, but the moment came and went so quickly that both the picture and the hug were largely lost to all but the man and the child who had so briefly shared it.

Monkey number 484 in the Eli Lilly laboratories in Indianapolis was never known by a more remarkable name—and never needed to be. It lived in its cage and ate its monkey mash and took its doses of the Salk vaccine just as all the other monkeys ahead of it had. Then, however, it did something more noticeable: It came down with a raging case of polio.

Number 484, like many of the monkeys in the Lilly lab, got its 2.5 ounces of polio vaccine from a freshly brewed lot—Lilly lot E-2178—made strictly according to Jonas Salk's recipe. Like the others too, 484 continued to frisk and play for another seventeen days. Then, on the eighteenth day after the inoculation, it seemed fatigued, feverish, and weak. By the morning of the twenty-first day, the weakness had progressed to paralysis. On the afternoon of the twenty-first day, number 484 was killed, and sections of its brain, brain stem, and spinal cord were removed and examined. They were shot through with polio lesions—damage that could only have been caused by Salk's vaccine.

That one Lilly animal, as it turned out, was not alone. Elsewhere in the same lab, other monkeys, newly shot up with Salk vaccine, were falling ill too, as were still others at the Parke, Davis lab in Detroit, and yet others at the National Institutes of Health in Bethesda. No one at any of the three labs knew of the contagion breaking out in the other two. For the moment, Salk himself did not know about any of them. As the monkeys were starting to fall ill, he was in New Orleans, addressing a gathering of the city's Graduate Medical Assembly, one of the rare public-speaking invitations the NFIP pressed him to consider and one of the rarer ones still he agreed to accept.

Salk took on the assignment partly because of the prestige of the New Orleans group, partly because the trip to the warm Crescent City during a chilly Pittsburgh March was a welcome break, and partly because, for once, he had a message he wanted to deliver. The closer the field trial grew, the more confident he became that it would succeed—and that the public needed to share that confidence. The speech he drafted for New Orleans was thus filled with an optimism—if not triumphalism—he didn't usually allow himself in public.

"One might question the justification for the conduct of a study such as the one under way," he said. "But what justification could there be for not proceeding with a test of a procedure that may well be capable of preventing paralysis? No experiment, well conceived, ever fails."

The audience members received the speech well, and since they were unfamiliar with the more circumspect tone Salk usually struck, saw nothing unexpected in it. His speech, however, wasn't the only one being delivered that day. Nine hundred miles away in Michigan, Albert Sabin was presenting an address of his own to another medical congress. The theme of his speech too was polio, and was in keeping with the approach he usually took to the topic. Just a few weeks before, *Life* magazine had devoted a full eleven pages to an exhaustive story on the history of infantile paralysis and the progress of the vaccine being developed against it. The article was a well-balanced one, offering at least a nod to all the usual polio figures. Like the *Time* story, however, it still focused principally on Salk, even opening with an oversized photograph of him in his lab, peering thoughtfully into a flask of virus.

"I felt certain that after you all read the *Life* magazine story on the conquest of polio, no one would be here," Sabin said to general laughter as he opened his remarks in Michigan. But that conquest, he spent the remainder of his speech arguing, was a long time away. It would not happen this year, it would not happen next year or maybe even the year after. When it did, it would not be a killed vaccine like Salk's that would be responsible, but a live vaccine like the one he was developing in his lab. Yes, the Salk vaccine had shown some early promise. But so had a lot of other scientific dead ends before they revealed themselves for what they were. "Let us not confuse optimisim with achievement," Sabin warned.

The newspapers, as always, carried both Salk's and Sabin's speeches, but Salk was untroubled by the Cincinnati scientist's crape-hanging. As the research proceeded and the sample group of inoculated children grew, it was becoming hard to deny both the safety and the potency of the killed vaccine. Voices like Sabin's might persist, but if they did, they'd simply find themselves consigned to the scientific margins, shouting out their despairing message to fewer and fewer listeners. That was what Salk believed when he returned to Pittsburgh from New Orleans, and received a letter from William Workman of the National Institutes of Health.

The details of the letter were stark. Lots 501, 502, 503, 504, and 506 of the Parke, Davis vaccine were causing animals to grow sick in the drug company's labs. Similar infections were being reported as a result of E-2178 at Lilly. Both companies, as required, had sent the potentially lethal vaccine to the NIH for testing even before they had completed their own studies. In both cases, the government analyses yielded the same troubling results.

"Needless to say," Workman wrote in flat understatement, "I am much disappointed in these results."

None of the flawed vaccine had been released to any of the boys and girls who had been vaccinated in the Allegheny County trial. But faith in the safety of the vaccine was decidedly shaken, and that would carry consequences. Workman instructed Salk to stop his Allegheny trial immediately. The larger field trial too would be postponed, and neither one would be allowed to resume until this latest problem was resolved. Salk and other representatives of the foundation were welcome to come to Bethesda to see if the mess couldn't be sorted out, but the brakes would be slammed on the whole project until they did.

The moment Salk read Workman's letter he phoned NFIP headquarters in New York. The foundation had received more or less the same letter and was already dispatching David Bodian, of Johns Hopkins, and Foard McGinnes—the public-health physician and former Red Cross executive O'Connor had recruited to help oversee vaccine procurement—to Bethesda to meet with the government. Salk booked a train south to meet them there, arriving in Bethesda late that night and presenting himself at NIH headquarters the next morning. McGinnes and Bodian were waiting for him. All three men would be powerful advocates for the safety of the vaccine, but all three also knew that it was Bodian who could be the most powerful of all.

In addition to all the polio work Bodian had conducted since 1940, he had recently turned his attention to the overall pathology of neurological diseases, making himself one of the world's most practiced diagnosticians of spinal illnesses in both humans and animals. If the sick monkeys indeed had polio, Bodian's sharp eye would confirm it.

Salk, McGinnes, and Bodian met with the worried Workman, who had had tissue samples and cell slides of the sickened monkeys prepared for their study. The four men examined the material together, but the other three retreated when Bodian leaned in for a closer look. He cast his practiced gaze on the slides and dishes, contemplated what he was seeing, and then announced his diagnosis: Four of the monkeys were sick all right, but it wasn't with polio. One of the others *might* have polio. The sixth one definitely did.

Things were bad, but better than they might have been. There was no telling how the four animals with nonpolio paralysis had fallen ill, but in the closed community of the lab, an unlucky wild infection of just one animal could easily have spread to others. It was the one suspected and one confirmed case of polio that were the real problems, and for the NIH, those cases were more than enough: The order halting the field trial would stand.

McGinnes, Bodian, and Salk pleaded for more time to call Basil O'Connor and Thomas Rivers, and Workman agreed. The foundation bosses listened silently to the news from Bethesda, then phoned Workman back, requesting seventy-two hours of grace so that they might look into the problem themselves. They would then come to the NIH and discuss whatever their internal investigation had revealed. A reluctant Workman agreed to that too.

O'Connor, Rivers, and a team of NFIP scientists spent the next three days grilling Lilly and Parke, Davis and quickly came up with some answers. Both companies acknowledged that they had been having manufacturing problems with some isolated lots—not much of a disclosure, given the dead monkeys. Each thought it knew where the difficulty lay. In Lilly's case, the problem had been poor filtration, which had allowed debris to remain in some of the culturing mix, protecting isolated virus particles from the toxic effects of the formalin. In Parke, Davis's case, the virus simply had not been exposed to the poison long enough, permitting some particles to survive. The bad lots, the labs reminded the NFIP, had been caught as they were supposed to be by the monkey tests, validating those measures and providing some reassurance that undiscovered bad lots hadn't slipped into the human subjects. If the labs could clean up their methods just a little bit more, the entire crisis might be resolved.

Rivers and O'Connor brought that message to Bethesda, but the NIH was not moved. Two institute epidemiologists were assigned to meet with the NFIP men. The government men stood by the suspension of the field trial, explaining that it could proceed only when there had been dramatic changes in the manufacturing and testing procedures for the vaccine. Most significant, the 54 monkeys that were now used to screen each lot were clearly not enough. At least 350 would have to be injected, sacrificed, and dissected for every lot any company produced. If that was done, and if all the monkeys tested clean, the government might let the trial go forward.

Rivers was furious. This wasn't a condition, this was a prohibition. The

NFIP couldn't breed monkeys fast enough for such testing. Even if it could, it couldn't afford them all. And even if it could afford them, it couldn't justify that kind of murderous excess. Sacrificing monkeys was one thing; slaughtering them to satisfy an arbitrary standard was something else entirely.

Rivers told the epidemiologists just what he thought of their numbers, reminding them that children would die this summer without the vaccine and that their blood would be on the NIH's hands. O'Connor, who knew a thing or two about negotiations, was cooler. He recognized the government's position as just an opening bid and suspected that they could be talked down from it if they were handled properly. The fuming Rivers was not the man to do that. During a break, O'Connor recommended—strongly—that Rivers return to New York and busy himself with other matters for a few days. Rivers reluctantly agreed, but he had one final thought for the NIH and its mathematicians:

"As far as I'm concerned," he said to the two men as the meeting reconvened, "you can take your pencil and paper and shove them up your ass."

Three days later, a more practical agreement was reached. With O'Connor patiently listening to the government men's arguments and with NFIP scientists coaching him by phone on how best to parry those points, the two sides met each other somewhere in the middle. The NIH's 350-monkey proposal would be scrapped, just as O'Connor had anticipated. Only 54 animals would be used per lot, precisely as before. From now on, however, all the labs would be required to produce no fewer than eleven straight lots of safe vaccine before any of them would be approved and released. There would be no selecting the clean lots out of the dirty ones. If the first ten in an eleven-lot run were good and the last one was bad, all of them would go into the trash.

The government imposed one more condition too. In the month since Salk's trip to Arsenal Elementary School, he had inoculated nearly 5,000 Allegheny County children, all of them with vaccine manufactured in his own lab. Since the purpose of the trial was simply to test the principle of the vaccine, no one had cared where it was made. So well had the vaccine performed so far that the NFIP had been set to pronounce itself satisfied with the 5,000 injections and not to require any more. Now, with confidence in the commercial labs shaken, the NIH ordered that 2,500 more children be recruited and that all of them be injected with existing Parke, Davis and Lilly product that had passed the new monkey tests. Only if all 7,500 children remained healthy could the larger field trial at last proceed, probably no sooner than April 19 or so. It was now March 28, a full week into the rapidly warming spring.

With all the journalists who were tracking the latest setback in the long march to the field trial, no one gave much thought to the likes of Walter Winchell, and with good reason. The broadcaster and reporter had a gossip columnist's attention span and a gossip columnist's taste for sensation. Medical stories did not typically provide the quick headline kick such a breed of journalist needed. That's what generally kept him off the beat, and made his broadcast on the night of Sunday, April 4, such a surprise.

"Good evening, Mr. and Mrs. America and all the ships at sea," he began the show, as he began all his shows. "Attention everyone. In a few moments I will report on a new polio vaccine—it may be a killer."

A commercial played and then Winchell was back. "Attention all doctors and families. The National Foundation for Infantile Paralysis plans to inoculate one million children this month. The U.S. Public Health Service tested ten batches of this new vaccine. They found, I am told, that seven of the ten contained live—not dead—virus. That it killed seven monkeys. The name of the vaccine is the Salk vaccine. The Michigan State Medical Society has refused approval. The polio foundation is trying to kill this story, but the U.S. Public Health Service will confirm it in about ten days. Why wait ten days?"

If Salk had been listening, he would have easily spotted the flecks of truth in Winchell's stew of lies. In the week since the monkeys had fallen sick, the Michigan State Medical Society had indeed withdrawn its approval for the trial, citing the bad lots of vaccine specifically. But the foundation believed the state officials might rethink their decision if they had a few more days to cool down. Winchell was similarly correct in reporting that several monkeys had died, but he said nothing about the fact that this only indicated that the safeguards had worked: the vaccine responsible had been found and the problem had been corrected. Already, both Lilly and Parke, Davis had resumed producing vaccine. Salk, similarly, was already vaccinating the 2,500 additional children with existing safe lots, and that appeared to be progressing uneventfully too. There were no naked lies in Winchell's broadcast, but virtually every word of it was a misuse of the truth—with the power to loose a panic.

Salk did not learn of what Winchell had said until the next morning in the virus lab, when his staff, many of whom had already bought newspapers carrying Winchell's column, filled him in. Immediately, the phones began ringing, mostly with reporters asking for quotes and local health officials demanding to know what the hell was going on. Dorothy Ducas of the NFIP press office and Hart van Riper phoned too. Despite how nonsensical Winchell's charges were, they said, a formal statement would have to be issued immediately—two statements actually: one from the foundation and one from Salk himself. Salk knew right away how to frame them.

"Don't answer Winchell directly," he said. "Certainly don't mention his name. Just use the science."

Within the hour, the statements were written and sent out wide. "Any product that contains live poliovirus is not the product developed by Dr. Jonas E. Salk," the foundation's release read. "A number of batches which failed to pass the required tests were eliminated by that testing. This demonstrates the validity of those tests and the safety they assure the public."

Salk's words were even more direct: "There is no possibility that live virus could have been contained in any inoculations given any children," his statement read. "All vaccine used has been tested and found to be completely safe."

The U.S. Public Health Service quickly weighed in with a statement of its own, one that was shot through with nervous hedges and careful conditionals but stood by the vaccine all the same. "There have been some difficulties in commercial processing," the agency admitted, "but we are confident no vaccine that was unsafe has been released for use. If any vaccine is found positive, it would not be released."

The formal statements were accurately quoted in the papers and dutifully read on the radio—and then were simply blown aside in precisely the storm of public anxiety Winchell had to have known he'd trigger. Within days, Minnesota announced that it was considering withdrawing from the trial; Virginia then followed suit. More than 150,000 children in the health districts still participating were pulled out by panicked parents. Reporters began turning up on the University of Pittsburgh campus and shadowing Salk in his off-hours. When O'Connor summoned him to New York for a quick meeting to discuss the crisis, the newspapermen followed him down to the train platform.

"What do you think of Walter Winchell's broadcast?" one of them shouted.

"Can't comment," Salk said. "I don't listen to him."

"Is the vaccine a killer?" another asked.

"No," Salk said emphatically. "There is absolutely nothing to be concerned about."

By the time Salk arrived in New York, the Associated Press had released the story, making little of what Salk had said but much of the hurried way he'd said it before boarding a train—as if he were a patent-medicine huckster leaving town just ahead of the tar bucket and feather bag.

Things only got worse when the reporters reached Albert Sabin. Winchell's charges were "intemperate," he agreed, but he couldn't say he was terribly surprised that this kind of problem had come up. "The field trial was always premature," he observed airily.

Salk, despite his best intention to let his pure-science statement speak for him, finally hit back, taking care to aim his blow not at any of the scientists or newspapermen whose good will he'd still need, but at Winchell alone.

"We will go on despite advice from sidewalk superintendents like Walter Winchell," he said to John Troan, when the *Pittsburgh Press* reporter phoned him for a quote. "He was wrong in his statistics and wrong about the danger. He was just interested in creating a sensation."

Winchell returned the punch the next week on the radio, repeating his earlier claims and adding the detail that thousands of white coffins were already being stockpiled around the country, ready to receive the withered remains of children killed by the Salk vaccine. Winchell was clearly echoing Duon Miller; the newsman did not directly cite the Florida pamphleteer, but he had obviously been influenced by his writings.

Winchell did mention one other name, however, one that was almost certainly lost on the majority of his listeners but that shocked Salk. Paul de Kruif, Winchell claimed, had been the source of his story, alerting him to the problem with the bad lots and campaigning personally for Michigan, his home state, to withdraw from the trial.

De Kruif was both the most likely and least likely person to have done such a thing. It was de Kruif whose subversive writings on the corrupted state of the medical community had gotten him sacked by Simon Flexner and the Rockefeller Institute in 1922; it was de Kruif whose spectacularly received *Microbe Hunters* had earned him far more recognition on the bestseller lists than he'd ever have achieved if he'd remained an academic. It was de Kruif who, as onetime head of Franklin Roosevelt's Birthday Ball commission, had campaigned so passionately for the new—and ultimately lethal—polio vaccine being developed by Drs. William Park and Maurice Brodie in 1935, seeing to it that the commission not only endorsed the field trial of the stuff but bankrolled it too.

De Kruif's name had been forever stained by his connection to the Park-Brodie-Kolmer disasters, and his presence on the Birthday Ball Commission as well as in the NFIP, afterward, had never again been welcome. Now, nineteen years after leaving the world of polio research, he was back, apparently hoping to upend that world with his mischief. It would be up to the foundation to set things right again.

Over the next several days, O'Connor, van Riper, and the other senior NFIP figures took to the road and worked the phones, calling or visiting the health officials and foundation chapters in all of the 211 communities in the forty-four states that had signed on for the field trial. Forced to choose between Walter Winchell, who trafficked in scandal, and the NFIP, which trafficked in science, surely they'd all know what decision to make. As it turned out, most of them did. Minnesota did pull out of the study, as did a scattering of counties in other states. But Michigan rejoined, and the defectors were quickly replaced. The field trial had been jolted but not derailed.

Several days after the crisis began to ebb, Bill Kirkpatrick sat down at his desk in his Pittsburgh home to write a letter. It had been nearly two years since the June day when Kirkpatrick had become the first of the paralyzed children at the D. T. Watson Home to receive Salk's vaccine. Though the inoculation could never do anything for his own illness, he'd been pleased to have played some role in the work. He was enraged at what Winchell had done, and he'd decided to write him personally at the *New York Daily Mirror,* his home newspaper. Kirkpatrick fired off his letter, telling Winchell who he was, how he had come to know Dr. Salk, and just what he thought of the radio man's attacks on the famous scientist.

Shortly afterward, he received an envelope from the *Mirror* offices on East Forty-fifth Street in New York City. Inside was a short note:

"Dear Mr. Kirkpatrick," it read. "Thank you for writing. I am glad you are walking without braces thanks to faith in God and Dr. Salk's vaccine. I never said I objected to it. I was requested by several medical groups to do so. I didn't report rumors. Everything I said was confirmed by the United States Department of Health. Good wishes, Walter Winchell."

Bill Kirkpatrick had to laugh. Winchell not only defamed Salk's vaccine, he had done so without even appearing to know what a vaccine was and what it could—and couldn't—do. Truly bad people needed to be challenged. Fools did not. Kirkpatrick would find it far easier to ignore the pitiably underinformed Walter Winchell now. He could only hope the country as a whole could do the same.

Ｂy the time the Walter Winchell episode was over, Basil O'Connor had had just about enough. He had had enough of the bad syringes and the sick monkeys and the arguments over the Merthiolate and the skittish health districts that were part of the field trial one day and not part of it the next. Most of all, he'd had it with the fact that the polio season had now arrived, at least in the Deep South, and still nothing was being done to prevent anyone from becoming paralyzed. Before April could melt away into May, he was determined that all the dallying would come to an end. The field trial would either begin straightaway or the plan would be scrapped until 1955 at the earliest. The children of 1954 would then simply have to survive the summer the best way they could. The matter, he decided, would be resolved within two weeks.

Settling things so certainly would require O'Connor to convene two meetings. The first would be held on Saturday, April 24, once again at the NIH offices in Bethesda. This gathering would be the more proletarian of the two, with Salk, Bodian, Workman, and a handful of other NFIP and NIH researchers gathering for one final review of all the vaccine data and one final memo summarizing that review. Their conclusions would be passed on to the Vaccine Advisory Committee, which would convene the next day at the Carlton Hotel in downtown Washington, D.C. If that committee approved the report, the field trial would begin the very next day.

None of the scientists attending the Saturday meeting at the NIH would be invited to the Sunday gathering. Salk would be permitted in the hotel—indeed, he'd be required to be there in case he was needed for something—but he would not be allowed into the meeting room proper.

In the days leading up to that weekend, Salk tried to keep his mind off the approaching meetings and on more-immediate matters concerning the field trial. As it turned out, he had little trouble doing that, since there were so many of those matters to address. For one thing, he learned, there was another problem with the syringes, this time the supposedly reliable reusable ones. The fit between the rubber plunger and the glass body was apparently imperfect, causing only 9.7 cubic centimeters of vaccine to be drawn up into the shot when a 10-cc load was needed. The 3 percent difference was far, far beyond what was acceptable in a study designed with such fine tolerances, and the syringes would either have to be fixed fast or completely replaced.

There was also the touchier matter of the Polio Pioneer buttons. The

foundation had decided that children who completed the full cycle of vaccine injections plus any necessary blood studies would receive campaign-
style buttons proclaiming them Polio Pioneers—an idea that was instantly
embraced by the local chapters, which were grateful for just about any inducement they could use to keep their volunteers happy and involved.
When word of the plan got back to Allegheny County, however, the parents of the 7,500 children whose inoculations were still being completed
seethed, figuring that if there were any pioneers in the study, those 7,500
were it. The *Pittsburgh Sun-Times* was being flooded with angry letters
from the parents, and Van Riper quickly contacted Salk, telling him that a
crate of buttons would be forwarded to his lab for distribution to the de-
serving children. Salk, who knew a thing or two about how a bit of political metal like a Support Our Allies button could stir up even a group of
full-grown medical interns, was not surprised that this kind of problem
had occurred.

When Friday finally arrived, Salk put these smaller troubles aside, packed
his bag, and made the familiar train trip from Pittsburgh to Bethesda. He
camped in a hotel overnight and showed up at the NIH early the next
morning. O'Connor, Workman, and Bodian were there already. So were
Tom Rivers and David Price, the assistant surgeon general of the United
States. So were small delegations of less prominent scientists from both the
NIH and the NFIP. Also in attendance was someone unexpected: Roderick Murray, one of Workman's senior colleagues at the NIH and a man
who typically didn't attend gatherings of this kind. The fact that he was
here today meant either that he wanted merely to observe the proceedings,
which was perfectly fine, or that he had some new and unexpected problem to discuss, which was less fine.

O'Connor called the men to their seats, and one final time they all reviewed what they already knew. They discussed the results of the long-ago
Watson Home work and the far more recent Allegheny trials. They discussed the latest reports from the drug companies; the progress being made
by NFIP headquarters, busy moving all the supplies and personnel into
place for the trial; the preparations being made by Tommy Francis to read

the results the field teams shipped back. O'Connor then asked if there were any final issues to address.

"Yes," Workman said. "We've got a problem with some mice."

In the last week, he explained, the NIH had been running routine toxicity tests on the vaccine, injecting it into mice to see how their systems tolerated it. The animals, he was pleased to report, showed no signs of being poisoned by the product. What they did show signs of, however, was polio.

Salk and the others fell silent. It was the sick monkeys all over again—this time barely two days before the trial was supposed to begin. But that simply oughtn't be possible, not with the safeguards now in place in the commercial labs, to say nothing of the ones that had always been in place in Salk's own.

Workman signaled to Murray, who in turn signaled for the lights to be dimmed; a projector that had until now stood unnoticed behind the men lit up and began to roll. The white wall at the front of the room came to life and the scientists watched as it filled with the images of horribly sickened mice. They limped as they walked, they dragged their rear legs, they sat stationary when they were too exhausted to move anymore. Ultimately, they fell on their sides, struggled for breath, and died. Every one of them had been injected with Jonas Salk's polio vaccine.

The lights came up to half, and most eyes, as if on cue, turned to David Bodian. There was a reason Bodian had been brought to Bethesda the month before to examine the slides of the monkey spines, and there was a reason he was here today.

"Well?" asked Workman.

Bodian took a thoughtful moment. "I don't know what it is," he answered. "But I know what it isn't: It isn't polio."

"What, then?" Workman asked.

"I'd call it Theiler's disease."

Most of the men had heard of Theiler's disease, but none of them had worked with it as closely as Bodian had. From what they knew, it was a rodent illness that could mimic polio but was in no way related to it.

Theiler's was a rare condition, and the fact that it would turn up at all was unusual. The fact that it would just happen to occur in a community of mice that had been freshly shot up with polio vaccine seemed unlikely in the extreme. Bodian acknowledged that that was true. But Theiler's disease *was* infectious, he reminded the other scientists, and if one of the mice contracted the virus, at least some of the others should have too.

He called for the film to be run again and walked the men through what he knew about the disease: the way the paralysis affected exclusively the hindquarters as opposed to all four limbs the way polio could; the complete flaccidity of the muscles, without the subtle degrees of paralysis that polio could cause. These animals fit the Theiler's arc precisely. The disease was a real one and some mice were bound to get it. Unluckily, several in this group had. Bodian was confident he was reading the fingerprint of the disease correctly. The other men here were free to believe him or not.

Salk looked at the faces around him anxiously. He had no concern that his vaccine had actually done the animals any harm. Even without Bodian's assurance, he knew that the principles behind his work were sound and that, by definition, the vaccine had to be safe. It was a scientific syllogism, nothing more. But Salk knew the men in the room did not share that certainty. They were the wild cards; the vaccine wasn't.

O'Connor turned to his committee with an inquiring expression. If the Theiler's diagnosis stood, the meeting would be adjourned and the Vaccine Advisory Committee would get a favorable report. If it didn't, the field trial would go down to defeat. O'Connor let the silence hold for several seconds waiting for an objection; then, without a whisper of protest from the group, he concluded the day's proceedings. Salk inwardly slumped in relief. The trial was halfway home.

Salk said his goodbyes the moment the meeting ended and left immediately for Washington, arriving that afternoon and checking into the Carlton, where he'd already booked a room. He'd used his own name in making the reservation, but beyond that would try to maintain the lowest profile possible. The foundation had not been shy about advertising the meetings taking place that weekend, partly because of the public relations value of the events, partly because the schools and chapters participating in the study would have to be ready to mobilize the moment the vote was taken, and the newspapers, television, and radio stations would be the most efficient way to get the word out. Reporters from all those outlets had already begun to mass.

To keep the Carlton quiet, the foundation had arranged for the press to be sequestered at the nearby Hotel Statler, where a media room had been established and regular updates would be delivered as the circumstances warranted. Already, the reporters had been told of the positive recommendation the first committee had passed onto the Vaccine Advisory Committee and they had dashed to the phones to file that news. Now, with the action moving to Washington itself, the journalists were getting harder to control, vanishing from the Statler whenever they could and slipping into the side doors of the off-limits Carlton. Two or three times a day, Dorothy Ducas, the foundation's public affairs director, would go corral them and herd them back to the Statler—usually delivering a scolding on the way.

Salk did a fair job of avoiding the press that Saturday night. The next morning, when the members of the Vaccine Advisory Committee—Tom Rivers, Joseph Smadel, Norman Topping, Thomas Turner, David Price, Ernest Stebbins, and Tom Murdock, along with Basil O'Connor—arrived, he didn't even need to try. Salk might be the man who'd invented the vaccine, but these were the ones who would determine what was to become of it. Snagging one of them for an unguarded quote about the prospects for the trial was a much bigger scoop than asking Salk how he was bearing up under the passive pressure of waiting for them to decide.

The committee members made their way as a group to a small banquet room down a dead-end corridor on the first floor. The hotel's own security guards kept this area clear of reporters, employees, and guests. Once the committee was sealed up inside, Salk too made his way to the little hallway and positioned himself on a divan just outside the door, ready to be summoned if he was needed.

Inside, O'Connor had no reason to call the men to order. He also had nothing at all of substance to say. The sick-mouse scare from yesterday had been a false alarm, and while today's committee had the report from yesterday's, there was really little in it that demanded a review. Nor was there anything to say about the two years' worth of human data that had been amassed since the very first vaccine injection, in 1952. The science spoke; O'Connor didn't need to. The next day, 1.8 million children would be asked either to step forward or stand down. O'Connor knew what he wanted them to do—and what he wanted his committee to do.

He asked the men if they were ready to vote. They murmured that they were. He asked who was in favor of proceeding with the trial. Seven hands went up. He asked—superfluously—who was opposed. No hands went up. The matter, at long last, was settled.

O'Connor solemnly produced a formal resolution he had drafted earlier in the week, complete with spaces for the committee members' signatures if the trial was approved. He had originally filled the document with a lot of phrases such as "whereas" and "be it resolved," but had later removed them, considering them fussy and decorative. The committee members read the resolution and requested that the excised language be restored. A typist was summoned and the changes were made. Then the revised document was passed around and ceremoniously signed. Finally, O'Connor opened the door and invited Jonas Salk inside. He was informed of the committee's decision and nodded his thanks.

The next night at 10:45, Salk and O'Connor returned to the same CBS radio studio from which they had addressed the nation thirteen months earlier. O'Connor once again introduced Salk, who spoke coast to coast for nearly fourteen minutes. He was decidedly more comfortable on the air than he had been the first time and decidedly more certain about what had just happened and what lay ahead.

"I do not share the view that polio has been with us a long time and therefore we can live with it another year," he said. "I do share the feeling that we must do all within our power to bring about the solution to the problem as soon as we can. Today, your children join mine in a program that will help us reach that goal."

In the hours before Salk and O'Connor even went on the air that night, the first few thousand of those new Polio Pioneers had gotten their shots, eaten their lollipops, and gone off to bed. Hundreds of thousands more would join them in the following days.

❧ 20 ❧

It was impossible to say who the first child was to receive the polio vaccine on the morning of Monday, April 26, 1954. That, however, did not stop people from trying to claim the title.

The reporters' favorite was Randy Kerr, the sweet-faced six-year-old boy in McLean, Virginia, whose school was located conveniently close to Washington. The NFIP had formally designated Kerr its first, and so the newspapermen obligingly trooped to his school, blinding the boy with a firestorm of flashbulbs at the same moment someone was jabbing a needle in his arm. It was a disagreeable way to get yourself in the papers, but on this day at least, a sure one.

Kerr was a pleasant enough child, and, predictably, a Caucasian one. If you were a Negro child, particularly a Negro child in the Midwest, you had a different Polio Pioneer. She was Precious Balentine, a second grader in the Douglas School in Kokomo, Indiana—one of the better Negro schools

in the state—where twelve children had enrolled in the field trial and dutifully queued up that morning to receive their shots. Dr. G. J. Smith, one
of the community's best Negro doctors, came to administer the injections.
Precious was the first in line, took the shot without a whimper, and received an orange lollipop for her trouble. She smiled gamely for the lone
newspaper photographer who had come to record the moment for the
local paper.

Much more conspicuous was the first official Pioneer in New York City,
seven-year-old Richard Dick, who early that morning trooped into a play-
room with the rest of his class at P.S. 61 on East Twelfth Street in Manhattan. Waiting for the children there was a midsized mob of doctors, nurses,
and reporters, along with twenty photographers and ten television cameramen, most of them paying no attention at all to the boys and girls. They
were instead focused on two men—a Dr. Van Riper and a Mr. O'Connor—
who did not appear to be here to administer the injections but who nonetheless seemed to be very important. When the time for the shots finally
came, Richard, as planned, was nudged forward first and received his dose
of vaccine from a tiny glass flask marked 08591QY, which, as his parents
had explained to him, might contain real medicine or might not. Then,
also as planned, he spoke to the reporters.

"My mother wanted me to have the injection because I had one type of
polio four years ago," he said, and he then made it clear his mother had explained other things to him too. "There are three types of polio. The inoculation may protect me from the other two." The newspapermen copied
down Richard's explanation.

All over the country that morning, tiny glass flasks like the ones in
Richard's school were being flown and trucked and trained to 211 health
districts in forty-four states in cardboard crates marked with bright red
lettering, "Polio Vaccine: Rush." Even before the vaccine arrived at the
14,000 schools that had signed on for the experiment, 14,000 field-trial
kits had already been shipped to them from the NFIP, containing all the
forms, instructions, and safety guidelines they would need to begin the injections immediately. With the idea of preloaded syringes having been
abandoned as largely unworkable, the health district officials were also told

precisely how to measure and administer the vaccine and even how to clean the needles afterward.

More than matériel flowed out from the foundation to the health districts in those first few days; personnel did too. The moment the field trial began, officials from New York were sent to tour the injection sites, making sure protocols were being followed and questions were being answered. Often, they weren't.

In Lexington, Kentucky, Elaine Whitelaw, the head of the NFIP Women's Activities Division, found an elementary school in disarray because one little girl had not shown up for the trial and the nurses did not want to begin the injections until all the children were accounted for. Whitelaw ordered the inoculations to begin, then dispatched the March of Dimes chapter director to the missing girl's home, which turned out to be a tumbledown house in a terrible neighborhood. The girl's mother, the chapter director discovered, didn't want her daughter to go to school that day because she simply didn't have a nice enough dress for the child to wear on such an important occasion. The chapter director helped the mother pretty the girl up as much as possible, then coaxed the child out of the house and drove her to school personally, where she joined the queue of her classmates and got her shot as planned.

In Quincy, Massachussetts, Whitelaw visited a parochial school where she noticed that while the boys and girls all appeared ready for their shots, there was no sign that they had filled out the necessary forms to allow their blood to be periodically drawn, an absolutely essential step if their antibody levels were going to be measured throughout the course of the trial.

"Sister," Whitelaw asked one of the nuns gently, "when do you plan on taking the samples?"

"Oh," the Sister answered brightly, "we're waiting for the little Lutheran school. The little Lutherans are going to give us the blood."

And indeed, as they watched, a school bus pulled up and a small group of Lutheran children climbed obligingly out. It was for Whitelaw to set things right, thanking the volunteers all the same but explaining to the Sister that it really was necessary that the blood for the studies come from the same veins that were about to receive the vaccine.

As much bustle as there was at the field-trial sites and the NFIP from the moment the test began, there was one place that stayed improbably quiet: the virus lab at the University of Pittsburgh. Tommy Francis had been very clear when he said that Jonas Salk and his staff would have no real role in the huge national experiment once it actually got under way, and now the Pittsburgh team could see that he meant it. Salk received no updates from the New York office on how the injections were progressing, few official reports from the NIH on how the vaccine manufacturing was going, no dispatches at all from the local chapters on polio outbreaks occurring in or near the field-trial sites. The man who had invented the vaccine had effectively been denied any official role in the test that would determine its worth. In place of that role, an unofficial one grew.

While the NIH and the NFIP had largely cut him out of things, the drug companies hadn't. Salk was still able to secure sample lots of vaccine when he wanted to so that he could continue to evaluate their quality. To his alarm, he was growing increasingly dissatisfied with what that spot-checking told him.

The argument about whether or not to include Merthiolate in the vaccine formula had raged for months before the field trial began. Salk had remained convinced that it was a dangerous mistake. It wasn't merely that the vaccine had not been designed with Merthiolate in mind, nor that a chemical intended to kill bacteria or fungi simply was not necessary given the brief amount of time the preparation was meant to remain on the shelf. The bigger problem, Salk had come to conclude, was that the very nature of his polio vaccine made it especially unsuited to such a toxic chemical.

The vaccine was a light, comparatively pristine preparation, without a lot of extraneous proteins in it that would absorb some of the Merthiolate. As a result, if the chemical didn't find any of the bacteria or fungi it had been added to the mix to kill, it might simply go to work on the inactivated viruses themselves, damaging their structure just enough that the immune system would fail to recognize them. This would not directly infect any children with polio, but it would fail to protect them from a wild infection that might later come along. Early blood studies in Salk's lab showed that not only might this be possible, it could happen when the

Merthiolate was used in concentrations as low as 1 in 10,000. If the vaccine absolutely had to have some protection against bacteria and fungi, other agents such as benzyl alcohol and phemerol would be preferable. Better still, the manufacturers could simply include an additional filtration step, clarifying the vaccine physically rather than chemically.

But Salk had lost the Merthiolate argument, and the chemical was included as part of the formula. Now the wrongheadedness of that decision seemed to be becoming apparent. Salk's studies of the sample lots suggested that even in concentrations as low as 1 in 20,000, the Merthiolate might cause the vaccine to lose 100 percent of its ability to trigger an immune response, at least against the Type I virus. A 1-in-80,000 concentration led to a 70 percent loss, and 1 in 100,000 cut the antigenicity by 50 percent. It was possible to get down to so low a Merthiolate level that the effectiveness of the vaccine wasn't harmed, but then the chemical lost its power to kill bacteria and fungi too, so there'd be no point in including it.

If the Merthiolate was in fact damaging the vaccine, it might already be having real consequences in the real world. Salk may not have been privy to any preliminary results from the field-trial sites, but he was free, like anyone else, to examine the government's monthly records of polio cases as they were compiled by the states and sent to Washington. In the health districts in which the field trial was taking place, there appeared to be a disproportionate number of Type I cases compared with the other two types, suggesting that the protection the vaccine might be offering against Types II and III was not present against Type I. It was entirely possible that this was purely coincidental—indeed, it wouldn't be known until the end of the summer if any formulations of the vaccine worked against any type of polio at all. But the bump in Type I cases was at least cause for worry.

Salk wrote Foard McGinnes with his analysis of five suspect lots of Parke, Davis vaccine. He asked McGinnes to request that the drug companies at least delay the addition of the Merthiolate until the last possible moment in the manufacturing process, since this would limit the amount of time in which it could do its damage. He also suggested that they store the vaccine at a lower temperature than they currently were, which might help slow the deterioration. Better than either of these measures, of course, they could simply leave the Merthiolate out. McGinnes forwarded Salk's ideas to the commercial labs, but without much of an endorsement.

"Recognizing that the vaccine you are producing is in accordance with the minimum requirements of the National Institutes of Health," he wrote, "I am not requesting you to carry out Dr. Salk's suggestion at the moment. However, I would appreciate your comments."

The companies were perfectly happy to offer the requested opinions. "Quite frankly," wrote a lab chief from Pitman-Moore, "we were very much surprised to learn that Dr. Salk was questioning the vaccine at this late date. It so happens that we do withhold the addition of Merthiolate until the product is ready for filling. There are limits, however, as to how long we can delay."

Salk, anticipating that this might be the companies' response, also sent off a telegram to O'Connor directly, summarizing his numbers and repeating his concerns. "Data from these experiments have not yet cooled off," he admitted. "But it is said that to await certainty is to await eternity." O'Connor, however, seemed content to wait, and like McGinnes, did nothing at all.

When June arrived, the Merthiolate matter was largely closed. By then, most of the children in the study had received their three required shots of vaccine, whether good or bad. All that was left now was to draw blood samples periodically and track the children's health as the year rolled out. It would not be until late February or early March that all the results would be in. For the virus lab, it looked like a quiet spring was going to turn into an even sleepier summer. The vaccine missile had been fired, and between the flame and noise of the launching and the landing would be nothing but the quiet arc of flight in the middle.

July played out precisely as uneventfully as it seemed it was going to, as did August. The only break in the comparative tedium came early in September, when the Third International Poliomyelitis Conference convened in Rome.

Like the first two conferences, this one would be a huge event, with more than 1,100 polio experts from forty-nine countries gathering at the Rome University Orthopedic Clinic for four days of seminars and presentations. Much of the debate would be about the usual mix of matters—epidemiology, rehabilitation, orthopedics, respiratory therapy. But just as much would be about the topic that was on all of the delegates' minds: the outlook for the new polio vaccine now undergoing its great test back in the United States.

Salk would have planned to attend the conference no matter what, but under the circumstances, he'd have no choice in the matter, if only to field the many questions that would surely be coming his way. As he had last time, he would be presenting a paper at the meeting, and he'd decided to make his address about the comparative virtues of the live and killed vaccines. It was always an explosive topic, but this was a curious time to address it. With a killed vaccine—his own killed vaccine—already at work in the bodies of so many children, the results that would soon be tabulated would either vindicate the principle or knock the legs out from under it. Delivering such a paper now could be taken as unnecessary crowing or premature hubris—neither of them good—depending on the actual results.

All the same, that was the topic that interested Salk and that was the one he wanted to discuss. He had been told he would deliver his paper during the morning session of the conference's third day. The schedule-makers, always hoping to keep things humming, had told Albert Sabin—who was also in attendance and had written a paper on the virtues of the live vaccine—that he would follow Salk.

Salk's address was a strong, if unsurprising, one. He touched on all the familiar points and made all the familiar arguments—nothing the attendees hadn't heard before. But the greater authority he now had gave him a freedom to speak his mind in ways he hadn't in the past. At the end of his speech, he seemed to decide to try out that new voice—and in so doing, to bury the live-virus question for good.

"In our early research," he said, "we addressed all of these issues and for a time proceeded to explore both vaccines at once. But further studies in our laboratory on the development of an attenuated virus have been postponed."

Postponed. It was a spectacularly understated word. Coming from the man who by himself seemed poised to silence the live-virus camp once and for all, it played as a splendid little slap that even if not aimed straight at Albert Sabin, landed there all the same. If Salk didn't mean the remark as a barb, he seemed curiously tone-deaf. If he did, he seemed gratuitously catty. He did not exhibit such inscrutable behavior often, but when he did, he rarely explained it. He concluded his remarks without revealing anything this time either.

Sabin took the dais, and given who he was and the tweak he'd just received, his response promised to be both arch and entertaining. But Sabin played his speech straight. His live-virus work was going well, he reported. He had discovered a number of weakened strains that seemed to work quite promisingly in a vaccine. He was already testing the preparation in chimpanzees and planning to progress to humans soon. He then ceded the microphone, with barely a nod in Salk's direction.

An open discussion followed, as with many of the conference presentations. Hilary Koprowski of Rockefeller University rose to speak first. If Sabin wasn't going to defend the principle behind the live virus, he was—and he was going to do so emphatically.

"We are living in the era of the live-virus vaccine," he said. It was science's job to follow well-established vaccine principles, "principles established by Jenner, by Pasteur, and by Theiler, and to apply them to poliomyelitis." Koprowski sat. It escaped no one's notice that the likes of Jonas Salk was conspicuously missing from the glittery list of names he'd mentioned.

Sven Gard, a Swedish researcher, then rose to echo Koprowski. He had worked with a killed-virus vaccine in his own lab and he had frankly not been impressed by what he saw. Certainly you could kill all the virus in a solution. Any chemist with a can of formaldehyde could do that. The hard part was getting those dead bugs to spark a reaction from the immune system—and his studies showed that simply could not be done. If Jonas Salk's vaccine was indeed immunizing subjects, it was only because undetected live virus remained stubbornly in the mix.

Gard made his case, and the chairman invited Salk to take a few moments to respond. Salk rose but declined the offer to hold the floor. "I can respond in less than a few moments," he said. "In our lab, live-virus research seems not to be a matter about which we need to have any concern."

A s fall turned to winter and 1954 drew to a close, so too did the observation period for the 1.8 million children in the field trial. Already, official tracking reports were beginning to trickle into Tommy Francis's Michigan office from the colder, more northerly regions of the country, where the polio season had started the latest and ended the earliest. Francis's statisticians promptly began stripping those anecdotal accounts to their arithmetical bones, and then crushing that information further into 144 million shards of data that would be transferred to IBM punch cards and fed into the huge, cabinet-sized computers the NFIP had leased for the work.

It would be a while, however, before the tabulators would have all the reports in hand so that Francis could read them and properly compose his report. Every state, it seemed, had a reason for a delay in submitting its results. In the Deep South it was a spell of unseasonable warmth that kept the poliovirus lingering and the case-counters' books open. In the West, it was the vast size of the participating states and the small number of field-trial children scattered within them, making the process of collection a long one. In New York, where all the children lived within easy reach of health officials in just three field-trial districts, in Manhattan, Brooklyn, and the Bronx, the sheer number of the subjects—14,233 in all—held things up.

Before the NFIP had Francis's analysis in hand, of course, the field-trial planners would have to decide how to release the news and manage the frenzy—good or bad—that would attend it. As early as January, Basil O'Connor, Dorothy Ducas, and Ed Stegen—an NFIP publicity man who specialized in communicating with the medical community—were already discussing their first concern: When the time was right, where should the critical announcement be made?

The NFIP offices at 120 Broadway were considered and quickly dismissed. The space was too small, the journey for reporters from the West and South was too long, and the feel of the place—a sparkly Wall Street office tower worlds away from the lunch-bucket states where the field trial was being conducted—was all wrong. The National Institutes of Health in Bethesda was ruled out for similar reasons. The University of Pittsburgh, where Salk and his team worked, was not even considered.

Finally, O'Connor decided on Rackham Lecture Hall at the University of Michigan. The sober, salmon-colored auditorium in the handsome deco-style building had just the right atmospherics, not to mention acres of peripheral classrooms and meeting rooms where dignitaries could be sheltered and reporters could be stored. The comparative heartland setting of the university made it a little inconvenient for almost everybody but not out of reach for anyone. Most important, Rackham Hall sent just the right message about the ownership of the event that would be held there. This might be Jonas Salk's vaccine and the NFIP's field trial, but it was Tommy Francis's study that would be presented. Francis ought to be allowed to play the day on his home field.

The question of when the event should be held was another matter. The urgency most people in the NFIP felt to get the results tabulated and the Francis report issued was a result of more than simply a desire to satisfy the curiosity of the press and the public. The sooner the efficacy of the vaccine was known, the sooner it could be mass-distributed. If that happened early enough in the spring, and if the pharmaceutical companies—which were still churning out vaccine—had manufactured enough, it might be possible to stop the 1955 polio season before it even broke from the gate.

O'Connor figured a Tuesday in early April was the most sensible date for any Rackham Hall event—April because that was the first realistic month the results could be known, a Tuesday because it was early enough in the week for the story to get maximum play, but not so early that the press staffers of the Universities of Pittsburgh and Michigan and of the NFIP itself wouldn't have at least a day to brace for the work. O'Connor thus narrowed his choice to either April 5 or April 12, then settled on the twelfth.

"Do any of you know the significance of that date?" O'Connor asked the headquarters staff when he chose it.

None did, but it was a date that had been weighing more and more heavily on O'Connor as it approached. Ten years earlier to the day, Franklin Roosevelt had been sitting for a portrait in his little home on the Warm Springs grounds, looking forward to a minstrel show and a Brunswick stew picnic, when a cerebral hemorrhage claimed his life. O'Connor had been hoping for a proper way to remember that loss, and this, surely, was it.

If an April 12 deadline was indeed going to be met, William Workman of the NIH had work to do too. Before Salk's preparation could be properly mass-distributed, it would have to be properly licensed. Before that could happen, the U.S. Public Health Service would have to approve of any favorable report Francis might issue. Then Oveta Culp Hobby, the secretary of health, education and welfare, would have to sign the licensing deals. Only then could the six drug companies begin to move the product they'd presumably been manufacturing. It was Workman's job, sometimes in collaboration with Salk, to see that all of these pieces were in place, which meant consulting with the drug companies, briefing the Public Health Service, and poking the department of HEW—a notoriously slow beast—so that the licenses would be drawn up on time and could simply await Hobby's signature.

Throughout January and February 1955, all this work at NIH and the NFIP pressed steadily ahead. So too did matters in Francis's office, where the field-trial results finally began pouring in so steadily and quickly that by March 9, the last of them had arrived, allowing Francis to start composing his report. It was around that time too that the seal of secrecy Francis had so carefully built around the work started to turn to cheesecloth.

No one in the Michigan office discussed any of the field-trial developments with anyone outside the office—least of all the press. But no one could control the thousands of people out in the health districts who collated the data before it was sent in and who were free to talk to anyone at all. As this chatter inevitably grew, the press inevitably began circling. Before long, even scientific sources, who ought to have known better, began talking out of turn.

John Troan had continued to report the polio story both aggressively and thoroughly. But for weeks now, he had found it increasingly difficult to get ahold of Salk. It may have been simply that Salk didn't have much information for him; it may have been that he did, but that for the first time in years he was choosing not to share it. Whatever the reason, Troan felt the loss acutely, both for sentimental reasons and because the absence of inside access was beginning to pinch his reporting. Periodically, he'd call Ed Stegen in the NFIP office in New York and press him for any information he might have.

"John," Stegen would answer helplessly, "it's all out in Michigan."

Toward the end of March, however, Troan got a lead of his own. As he was completing a nonpolio story he was writing for the Sunday edition, his phone rang in the *Press* newsroom.

"John?" said a voice. "It's Jim Lewis."

Lewis, the animal man in the Pittsburgh lab, had been the one who'd originally tipped Troan off about Salk's habitual visits to the Bamboo Garden. Over the years, Lewis and Troan had developed a quiet professional friendship of their own, and now and again Lewis would fill the newsman in on details and developments when Salk himself either couldn't or wouldn't.

"Thought you'd like to know that William Workman is here," Lewis now said.

"Workman . . . ," Troan repeated, briefly failing to put the name to the person.

"From the National Institutes of Health. He's locked up with Jonas drawing up the final protocols for the vaccine. It looks like a done deal."

Troan, surprised, thanked Lewis, and hung up the phone. Neither Salk nor Workman could know the results of Tommy Francis's study, but they were clearly proceeding as if they did. Troan began calling around to his sources at the drug companies to get their read on the situation. They didn't know whether or not it was true that Workman was in Pittsburgh, nor why he'd be there even if he was, but their collective gut told them something good was up. Troan's gut told him the same.

"The Salk polio vaccine will be released for general use," he wrote in his column the next day, a column that was picked up by United Press International and distributed far beyond Pittsburgh. "The word in drug circles is that the vaccine is 'terrific.' The fact that the National Foundation for Infantile Paralysis has organized a special scientific meeting for the occasion is indicative of the vaccine's success. 'If the vaccine hadn't worked,' one scientist pointed out, 'they'd have given it a decent burial. They wouldn't schedule a feast.'"

Troan's instincts and sources may or may not have steered him right. One thing for sure was that if even he had begun handicapping the matter, it was time for Francis to come forward and settle things. And so the invitations at last began to go out:

> The National Foundation for Infantile Paralysis
> and the
> University of Michigan
> have the honor to invite you to a scientific meeting
> at the University of Michigan
> Rackham Lecture Hall, Ann Arbor, Michigan
> Tuesday morning, April twelfth
> from 10 a.m. to 1 p.m.
> *To hear a report of the evaluation of the efficacy of the*
> *poliomyelitis vaccine used in a field study sponsored by the*
> *National Foundation for Infantile Paralysis in the spring of 1954*

The engraved announcement—along with an offer of hotel accommodations and all incidental courtesies—was sent mostly to dignitaries in the scientific and political communities, people who had backed the work of the NFIP up to that point and whose good will would continue to be needed no matter what the results of the trial were. A less formal notice went out to the press, informing them of the event, inviting them to cover it, and providing them with a list of hotels near the campus where they were welcome to make themselves a reservation. Fifty-four thousand physicians around the country would also be invited to look in on the proceedings, thanks to a $250,000 closed-circuit television hookup paid for by the Eli Lilly company, which was only too happy to have the doctors watching. They were the ones who would eventually be ordering and buying any vaccine that was cleared and licensed.

Salk was free to invite whomever he wanted, within practical limits. Having his entire lab staff of fifty attend was not possible. He instead selected eleven senior staffers—including Lewis, Byron Bennett, Julius Youngner, Elsie Ward, and Lorraine Friedman. Salk also wanted Donna and the boys to come to Michigan, and Donna agreed, though whether Jonathan, not yet four, could sit through such a long event was open to serious doubt. Salk's brothers, Lee and Herman, along with their wives, were also invited, as were his parents, still living in New York. Salk also reserved Daniel and Dora a spot at one of New York's closed-circuit gatherings, at the Waldorf-Astoria Hotel, suspecting that they might not want to make the long trip to the Midwest. That, as it turned out, was what they preferred.

Rackham Hall would have to be modified for the announcement, equipped with an eight-foot-long platform at the back of the auditorium to give the television and newsreel cameras a clear shot at the stage. The temporary addition would eliminate the last two rows of seats, reducing the number of people who could witness the announcement in person, but it would exponentially increase the number who could see it from a distance. The newspaper reporters would not be treated as hospitably as the camera crews, kept in a holding room three floors above the main venue, where they would have access to desks and telephones so that they could write and call in their stories. They'd be expected to remain there except for the three hours or so when the presentation and speeches were being made, during which they could stand in the back of the hall and observe.

Such brusque treatment notwithstanding, Francis and the NFIP were willing to extend the newspapermen a courtesy that even the leaders of the foundation wouldn't enjoy. The secrecy surrounding the field-trial findings was a more than minor inconvenience to Hart van Riper, Thomas Rivers, Basil O'Connor, William Workman, and Salk himself. All of them and a few others would be expected to present speeches after Francis's pivotal one April 12. But since none of them had any idea whether their talks would be celebrations or lamentations, they had to draft two different versions and deliver one of them only after they heard what Francis had to say.

The men of the press would not be able to compose alternative stories in advance and would instead need to write their stories on the fly. This meant they would require a single, central place where they could all get the news they needed in a digestible way, and get it at least at the same time as—or even shortly before—Francis made his presentation. The only way that information could be provided to them, however, was if somebody knew everything Francis knew and could write up the necessary press releases. Francis understood that. Not long before the Tuesday meeting, he summoned Lou Graff, the University of Michigan's public affairs officer for medical matters, to a closed-door meeting in his office and opened up his notebooks to him.

Graff and Francis remained sequestered for hours. When the meeting broke up, Graff was to go straight back to his office, write his press release, and personally make hundreds of mimeographed copies. He was then to place the copies under lock and key and destroy the stencil that was used to make them. The releases would not be unlocked until Tuesday morning as the press conference was beginning.

On April 10 and 11, the newspapermen decamped from their home cities for the journey to Michigan. Trains departing from New York were especially stuffed with reporters, since so many of the routes for men covering the story for smaller, East Coast papers ran first through Manhattan before heading west. Along the way from New York to Michigan even more newspapermen came aboard. Eyeballing one another in the crowded coaches, they saw for the first time just how keenly they'd all be competing for pay phones and live quotes within the next couple of days. Many wondered just what the point of covering so overcovered an event would even be.

"You ready for the story?" Troan asked William Laurence, the esteemed science writer from the *New York Times* as he settled into his seat next to him on the train.

"What story?" Laurence grumbled.

"You mean there ain't no meat left on the bone?" Troan said.

"There ain't even a bone left."

On the way, Troan also ran into Al Bloom, the medical writer from the rival *Pittsburgh Post-Gazette.* Bloom, who had not made the polio story the mission Troan had, had been unable to book himself a hotel room. Ordinarily, this might have given Troan no little pleasure, but the collegial feel aboard the train that morning softened his competitive edge somewhat. What's more, today Bloom might be a man on whose good side it would pay to be. Early reservations might secure a hotel room in Ann Arbor, but no amount of advance planning could ensure any of the newspapermen seats in the university town's handful of restaurants. Already the reporters were beginning to fret about how they would manage to eat over the next 48 hours. Bloom had no such concerns. He was an observant Jew and was traveling during the Passover week, so he had brought his own breakfasts with him. The hard-boiled eggs and matzoh muffins with which he planned to fortify himself were not what Troan was used to eating on the road, but tomorrow morning they'd look pretty good. If Bloom would be willing to share his food, Troan proposed, Troan would be willing to share his room. Later that day, the men arrived in Ann Arbor and checked into their quarters.

The Salk family and Basil O'Connor arrived that Monday morning too. They and other key guests had been spared the nuisance of staying in a hotel and were instead put up at Inglis House, a spacious campus residence that had once been the home of the university president. Unattached women like Lorraine Friedman and Elsie Ward who were part of the NFIP party would stay at one of the campus coeds' residences, since single women weren't permitted in Inglis House. Also bunking close by would be Tom Coleman, a public affairs official the University of Pittsburgh had assigned to shadow the Salk family and manage the maelstrom that would surround them. Salk himself doubted Coleman would be needed. The university did not agree.

Monday afternoon and evening passed quietly in Inglis House. The Salk boys played with a kite they had brought with them from Pittsburgh, which they tried to fly in a small yard behind the house. Donna busied herself unpacking and hanging up the sport jackets, trousers, and ties she had brought for the boys to wear the next day. Jonas passed the hours refining and rehearsing his two speeches—knowing he'd be delivering only one.

On the morning of April 12, Rackham Hall opened to the University of Michigan custodial crew well before it opened to anyone else. The carpenters had already built the platform for the cameras in the back of the hall, but on the stage, there were still things to do. A heavy lectern with a large blue-and-gold University of Michigan banner draped over the front had to be rolled into place. Behind it, the workmen had to arrange a panel of desks on a low riser and another panel on a slightly more elevated riser behind that.

Place cards positioned at each of the spots in the twin rows of desks identified who would be sitting where. In the first row, just behind and to the right of the rostrum as seen from the audience, would be a Dr. Salk from the University of Pittsburgh. Farther off to the right would be a Dr. Rivers, a Mr. O'Connor, and a Dr. Workman. Just behind and to the left of the podium would be a Dr. Francis, along with Dr. Bodian, Dr. van Riper, and Dr. Harlan Hatcher, the president of the University of Michigan. Behind them on the second riser would be eight other men, including Drs. Stebbins, Topping, Turner, and Smadel.

The work on the stage was completed and the doors of the building were opened an hour or so before the event. The reporters, as expected, were the first to arrive. Streaming inside, they headed straight for the auditorium proper, but were steered away and sent up to their holding room on the third floor, where the desks had been set up and the phones were working. They'd be called out of the room shortly before the meeting to receive the press release Lou Graff had composed and an abstract of Francis's findings. Only then would they be permitted back downstairs and into the hall itself.

The dignitaries and other guests arrived at the building shortly after the reporters did. Polio researchers who were not themselves assigned a spot onstage took seats in the audience. The eleven-person team from the Pittsburgh Virus Lab arrived as a group and sat together. William McEllroy, dean of the University of Pittsburgh School of Medicine; Rufus Fitzgerald, chancellor of the University of Pittsburgh as a whole; and Dr. Jessie Wright, superintendent of the D. T. Watson Home for Crippled Children, showed up as well. Hundreds of other researchers from dozens of other institutions filed in too, taking every available seat in the hall. Among the last to appear, in the careful custody of Tom Coleman, were Donna, Peter, Darrell, and Jonathan Salk, accompanied by the younger of Jonas's two brothers, Lee. Coleman pointed them to a row of seats that had been saved for them.

With the audience in place, most eyes turned toward the stage. There was still nobody up there at all, but the rostrum and daises were promisingly lit by a bright bath of theater lights. After a moment, there was a shifting in the wings, and two lines of business-suited scientists, Salk among them, walked awkwardly onto the stage and took their seats with a scraping of chairs. A large bank of brighter, hotter lights flared to life in the back of the hall as the sixteen television and newsreel cameras began to roll. For all the preparation that had gone into this day, Salk was struck by the drama of the moment. He had been wholly immersed in his work until now, with this morning's meeting in Rackham Hall merely a prospective event scheduled for some future time. Now that time was upon him, and he tensed with uncharacteristic anticipation.

At precisely five minutes after ten, Hart van Riper rose from his seat on the far left side of the front panel and stepped to the rostrum. He was greeted by respectful applause.

"In a letter to Mary Gladstone," he began, "Lord Acton wrote: 'The great object in trying to understand history is to get behind men and grasp ideas.' More and more, history has been shaped and charted in the colleges and universities of the world. In having us here today, the University of Michigan demonstrates not only that it is a gracious host, but that it fulfills the responsibilities imposed on it by its own greatness."

In her seat in the middle of the auditorium, Donna Salk noticed her sons already beginning to squirm. Jonathan, the youngest, was the worst.

"Lee," she whispered, leaning over the boys to her brother-in-law. "Would you . . . ?" She gestured to Jonathan.

Lee nodded, lifted Jonathan from his seat, and carried him quietly up the aisle and out of the room.

Van Riper went on. "While you and I have gathered in this auditorium today to hear history reported, or at least we hope"—he held for expected laughter and got a bit—"we must remember that the bone and sinew of that history was made in many places. It was made in a former maternity hospital on this campus where Dr. Francis and his associates undertook the massive task of vaccine evaluation. It was made in universities and laboratories across the nation; in classrooms of thousands of schools. On behalf of all of these, and in the name of the National Foundation for Infantile Paralysis, I welcome you."

Van Riper stepped away from the podium and returned to his seat, and all eyes turned expectantly to Tommy Francis. He made no sign of moving. Instead, Hatcher, the university president, rose and took the microphone.

"Before we proceed," he said, "I'd just like to ask the platform party"—he gestured broadly at Salk, O'Connor, and all the other men behind him—"to move off the stage and occupy the first two rows of the lecture hall. This is to spare you the lights and make it possible to see the charts in the talks to come."

The men on the twin panels looked at one another and did as they were told, standing and moving to either side of the stage, where they lined up to descend the two short staircases leading down to the audience. Only Tommy Francis remained where he was.

"Now," said Hatcher, just as it had been scripted, "I have the pleasure of presenting Dr. Thomas Francis, Jr., director of the Poliomyelitis Vaccine Evaluation Center of the University of Michigan."

Hatcher left the stage and Francis rose. He wore a black suit, his mustache was neatly trimmed, his glasses glinted. He approached the podium and positioned himself behind it. For Salk, low in his front-row seat, Francis was not easy to see. Francis shuffled the thick sheaf of papers he carried and settled himself. At precisely 10:20, he began to speak.

"During the spring of 1954," he read, "an extensive field trial of the effectiveness of a formalin-inactivated poliomyelitis vaccine, as developed by Dr. Jonas Salk and his associates, was initiated by the National Foundation for Infantile Paralysis. The Poliomyelitis Vaccine Evaluation Center was established at the University of Michigan for the purposes of collating and analyzing data collected during the trial."

Francis spoke with little inflection, reading the text cold from the page. This, of course, was the way protocol demanded it be done at a scientific conference. And for all the lights and press and sensation here today, that's what this was. Francis would thus frame his address by those rules, spending long minutes reviewing things everyone here already knew—the field trial's sampling methods, the size of its subject groups, the history of the vaccine the study was testing. Within the auditorium, the audience listened silently. Beyond the walls of the big room, the press waited invisibly. In cities around the country, 54,000 doctors stared fixedly at their closed-circuit television screens. Francis talked on, his dense, slow prose leading seemingly nowhere at all. Finally, well into the patient presentation, were three exquisite bits of information, held fast in the thick amber of what Francis had come here to say.

"In placebo-controlled areas," he read, "the poliomyelitis vaccination was 68 percent effective against polio Type I, 100 percent effective against Type II, and 92 percent effective against Type III."

Then, for those who didn't understand the enormous meaning of those numbers, he said it another way. "The vaccine works. It is safe, effective, and potent."

An absolute silence continued to fill the hall, still required by the rules of the day. But there is silence and there is silence, and this one was filled with a noisy uncoiling. It was the uncoiling of a spring that had been wound tight since 1916, when 9,300 boys and girls in New York City were claimed by the twin furnaces of the summer and the virus. It was a spring that had been wound since 1935, when 19,000 children had consumed a bad vaccine and waited to see if it would save them or kill them. It was a spring that had been wound since 1952, when 57,879 children were inked into the virus-counter's casebook. And it was a spring that had been wound since the summer of 1921, when a tall man with presidential ambitions contracted a children's disease, losing even the ability to rise back up to his full height, never mind—or so it seemed—become the global leader he wanted to be.

It was a spring that it had seemed would never uncoil, and now it did with a sudden whipcrack that was nearly deafening—save for the fact that it made no sound at all. Jonas Salk, in his front-row seat in Rackham Hall, showed no reaction. People who discreetly craned their necks to look at him—and many did—may have expected smiles, may have expected tears. But they saw neither. For Salk, Francis's dramatic announcement held no drama at all. He had already consulted the final authorities on his work: his data, his cultures, nature itself. Today's announcement might confirm all those facts to the public, but in Salk's mind they had been confirmed long ago.

Donna Salk's own face ran with tears. Without looking away from the stage, she reached out and clutched the hands of her sons Peter and Darrell. Tears streamed too on the faces of the eleven people from the Pittsburgh Virus Lab, on the face of Jessie Wright of the Watson School, and on the faces of other men and women around the hall. Outside in the small, barbaric world inhabited by the journalists in the building, things were different.

"It works! It works!" the reporters upstairs shouted, charging back to their phones and typewriters as they clutched the announcements that had been kept locked up and then distributed to them only moments before Francis had begun to speak. A pair of clerks from the Michigan press office had brought the reports in a hand truck up to the third floor, planning to roll them over to the reporters' room and hand them out there. The reporters, however, had been waiting for them by the elevator and set upon them the moment the doors opened, stampeding over one another to tear the stapled packets from the metal carts. Lou Graff, who had come up in the adjacent passenger elevator, stared in alarm at the mob in front of him, leapt on a table, and began tossing packets to reporters, knowing that the only way to disperse them was to give them precisely what they were grappling for.

"Lou! Throw me one, throw me one!" the newsmen cried to Graff. Most of them had never met him before but seemed to hope that the familiar use of his first name might catch his attention faster. When they snagged their copy and read the opening line Graff had written, they whooped and hooted.

"The vaccine works," were the first three words of Graff's release. Everything else was for the rewrite men to figure out.

John Troan was in the tangle of men battling for a pair of reports. Back in the press room, he had dialed his news desk and enlisted Al Bloom to stay on the phone and keep the line open while he ran out to get them both copies. When he got back, he dictated a summary of the report back to the *Press,* then ran down to the auditorium to catch the presentation live. Bloom kept hold of the phone, called his own story in, then charged downstairs to join Troan.

There was, it turned out, a lot more of the presentation to go. Francis spoke for a full hour and thirty-eight minutes. He explained all the nuances of the numbers, comparing the placebo group with the vaccine group with the observed group; comparing the entire 1.8 million field-trial population with the nation at large. But it was the three numbers he kept coming back to—68 percent, 92 percent, and 100 percent—that held the listeners fast. This was far better than even some of the optimists had expected—far, far better than the 15 percent the drug companies would have considered adequate for marketing. And the 68 percent, the least impressive of the three findings, was almost certainly a result of the Merthiolate that had so weakened the Type I formula. Francis did not say so explicitly, but he did say that Type I infection was particularly evident in children who had been inoculated with so-called "poor lots" of vaccine. No one who had been following the field trial had to ask what ingredient had made those lots so poor; none doubted that that ingredient would promptly be eliminated.

Francis concluded his talk and left the stage to strong but still-controlled applause. Other speakers from the front row then climbed to the rostrum to make their own remarks, tucking away the forlorn speech they would have delivered if Francis's news had been bad. David Bodian described the work that had been done in the years leading up to the field trial, tipping his hat to everyone who had contributed in any way to the new vaccine. Thomas Rivers spoke about the grave responsibility science now bore to use the solution both wisely and swiftly. Basil O'Connor spoke about Franklin Roosevelt and his NFIP and the millions of givers whose donated dimes had paid for the foundation's research for the past seventeen years and who, in a very real sense, held title to the vaccine that was being celebrated today.

Finally, at 12:05, O'Connor looked down at the front row of the auditorium and introduced Jonas Salk of the University of Pittsburgh Virus Lab. Now, at long last, decorum broke down.

At the mention of Salk's name, a roar of applause filled the hall, and the audience members—laypeople and scientists alike—rose to their feet. The noise of the ovation was almost a physical thing, sealed in as it was by the walls of the auditorium. Cheers and whistles joined the applause. Salk stood awkwardly in the front row, blinking a little in the camera lights. He mounted the few steps to the stage and the noise only grew. Finally, as he took his spot behind the rostrum, the audience began to exhaust itself, became quieter, and sat.

"While many like to listen to music," Salk began, "those who know how a musical score is put together can appreciate the creation of a theme from notes that to others of us are merely disconnected sounds. The gigantic task which Dr. Thomas Francis and his staff completed today could only have been accomplished by one of the great masters."

The crowd applauded, more politely now, resuming the restraint it had so raucously abandoned. Salk went on with his talk, sharing out the credit for the success of the vaccine that had been announced here today and that, he argued, wrongly bore his name alone. He thanked Harry Weaver, who had so inspired his work, and Thomas Rivers, who had so focused it. He thanked Foard McGinnes and Hart van Riper, who had shaped the field trial. He thanked the children of the Polk School and the D. T. Watson Home—not to mention all the others in the field trial proper—who had been brave foot soldiers when they were asked to be. He thanked too Dean McEllroy and Chancellor Fitzgerald, who had provided a place for his work to proceed, and Connaught Laboratories in Toronto, which had provided something as unglamorous as his Medium 199.

Finally, of course, he thanked Basil O'Connor, who, if the vaccine was truly going to be named after a man, deserved the honor most. As Ralph Waldo Emerson—the great-grand-uncle of Haven Emerson, the New York City health commissioner during the polio plague of 1916—had said, " 'The reward of a thing well done is to have done it.' Mr. O'Connor," Salk concluded, "can indeed enjoy that reward."

It was a perfectly fine talk—if not a terribly surprising one—but Salk could have recited multiplication tables today and he still would have thrilled this crowd. When he concluded his remarks and surrendered the podium, the applause exploded again—in all but one row of the hall.

Somewhere in the middle of the auditorium, the small delegation from the Pittsburgh Virus Lab sat shocked and silent. There had been not a word, not a nod of acknowledgment from the man with whom they'd worked so hard for so many years. Each time in his speech that Salk seemed ready to recognize his team—"There is a group," he'd say, "that gave so much more than they received, that I cannot find analogies to say what I mean"—they'd sit forward expectantly, only to slump back when he directed his thanks toward someone else. He'd found room in his remarks to acknowledge strangers; he'd found room to acknowledge a corporation; he'd found room for 1.8 million boys and girls whose names he didn't know. But he hadn't found room for eleven other people with whom he'd worked and lived as if in a crucible for nearly eight years.

In the back of the hall, John Troan narrowed his eyes in confusion and made himself a note to ask Salk what he was thinking. Salk hadn't thanked John Enders, Fred Robbins, and Thomas Weller either, but that was a minor oversight. Their work had been widely recognized—and widely celebrated—in the polio community for years, and their contribution to the success of the day went without saying. The names of the people in the virus lab were nowhere near such a given. Perhaps, Troan thought, it was merely a terrible oversight. Salk didn't often address such large groups at such dramatic moments, and he could be forgiven an amateur's mistake.

Perhaps—this was most likely—it was simply the naïve scientist's belief that the world understood that research like this is almost never done alone. If the flood of virus lab papers published under the names of multiple authors hadn't made that point over the years, Salk himself had surely made it again and again, each time he'd pointedly added the names of his staffers to every press release or magazine story that had ever crossed his desk for approval. A scientist thanking his team today was a bit like a runner thanking his lungs and muscles for helping to carry him the distance: You might do it, but it really was understood that the organism functioned as a whole. But Salk was not merely a lab man now. As of this morning, he'd become something far, far larger. With a bank of television and newsreel cameras facing him and reporters scrambling for a piece of him, he'd fumbled one of his first and biggest jobs in his new role.

The Rackham Hall event finally adjourned at one P.M., but so great was the crush of people and press that it took at least another hour for Salk to move beyond the front of the room, grab hold of Donna's and the boys' hands, and fight the family's way out of the building. Before he could, Edward R. Murrow, the admired CBS journalist and former war correspondent, caught his ear for a quiet aside.

"Young man," he told him, "a great tragedy has befallen you. You've lost your anonymity."

The men and women from the Pittsburgh Virus Lab suffered no such tragedy. They easily exited the building and scattered back to the local airport or train station for the trip home to Pittsburgh. Byron Bennett, whom Salk had always taken respectful care to address as Major Bennett and whom he had worked so hard to keep focused and sober, cried freely on the train ride home.

It had been folly for the Salk family to believe they'd be able to leave Ann Arbor just a day or two after Tommy Francis's announcement. That had been their plan, and they even had plane tickets in hand for a trip back to Pittsburgh on Thursday, April 14. Salk had gone so far as to send Tom Coleman on ahead, telling the University of Pittsburgh media man that he'd be of much greater help back home, managing the flood of questions that would surely be pouring in from the public and press.

"Are you sure you can handle this?" Coleman asked.

"I'm sure," Salk said. "Go."

Coleman did as he was told, caught the next flight out, and a few hours later landed back in Pittsburgh. Before he left the airport he heard himself paged.

"It's Jonas," the voice on the other end of the line said to him when he picked up the message phone. "Please come back."

Salk had reason to call for help. Tommy Francis's announcement had been only part of the news that was made that first day in Michigan. Before HEW secretary Oveta Culp Hobby could sign the licensing deals permitting the vaccine to be manufactured, government rules required that William Workman of the NIH recommend the action to her officially. And before he could do that, the rules further required him to convene a panel of experts to make that same recommendation to him. As it happened, of course, all the experts he could possibly need for such an impromptu committee were already in Ann Arbor for the Rackham Hall announcement. Almost immediately, he collared a handful of handy researchers, including William Hammon and—in the interests of balance—Albert Sabin, and pulled them into a closed-door meeting. It took the men the better part of the afternoon to reach an agreement, but just after five P.M., Workman emerged and announced that he was ready to phone Washington, where Hobby was standing by with the licenses on her desk. He placed the call and, with a flourish, she signed the papers.

"It's a great day," Hobby said to the press assembled at HEW headquarters. "It's a wonderful day for the people of America and the whole world."

Six drug companies—Lilly, Pitman-Moore, Wyeth, Sharp and Dohme, Cutter, and Parke, Davis—would be cleared to manufacture and distribute the vaccine immediately, Hobby said. The NFIP already had its own stockpile on hand, and that would be shipped straightaway to states in the Deep South where the polio season was under way. Within a week, nearly 5.8 million cc's of commercial vaccine should follow, with much more to come after that. The poliovirus would soon be feeling the wrath of organized science.

"POLIO IS CONQUERED," John Troan's *Pittsburgh Press* shouted in a thick black banner headline. "U.S. APPROVING VACCINE SALES."

"POLIO ROUTED!" crowed the *New York Post*.

The *New York Times* was marginally more reserved. "SALK POLIO VACCINE PROVES SUCCESSFUL," it reported. "MILLIONS WILL BE IMMUNIZED SOON." On the front page of that edition was a picture of Jonas Salk on the Rackham Hall stage, sharing a private word with Thomas Francis while pointing sagely to something out of frame.

The world reacted to such sensational news just as would be expected. The United Nations formally hailed what Salk had done, announcing that it had already set up regional centers at Yale University in Connecticut and Hadassah Medical School in Jerusalem to help speed the new vaccine to the people who needed it. Similar facilities would soon open up in Europe, Africa, the western Pacific, and Southeast Asia.

Governments in Europe and elsewhere were not waiting for the UN to act. Sweden immediately announced plans to buy enough American-made vaccine to inoculate 100,000 people, and that was only a start. The Netherlands cabled Tommy Francis directly to inquire into purchasing supplies of its own. Switzerland, Denmark, and Germany all announced that they'd be shopping for vaccine in the American market too. President Eisenhower quickly issued an executive order requiring that all information necessary for manufacturing the Salk vaccine be passed on, free of any charge, to seventy-five countries around the globe, including the Soviet Union. The move was both humane and tactical, a way to spread the life-saving vaccine as widely as possible, while protecting American shores from being stormed by foreign health officials. The only major exception to Eisenhower's largesse was Red China, whose 607 million people did not make the president's list. But few in Washington doubted—or objected to—the likelihood that the USSR would simply pass the information on to its Socialist brother.

In the United States, local governments sprang to act too. Massachusetts declared its intention to begin large-scale inoculations of at least 250,000 schoolchildren the first week in May. New Jersey, with only a small supply of vaccine in hand, nonetheless announced that it would soon begin injections of 300,000 children. Pennsylvania planned on a full half-million, with 64,519 in Salk's Allegheny County alone.

Though the sensation caused by the vaccine moved quickly beyond the little greensward of the University of Michigan, the reporters staking out the campus showed no inclination to leave, as long as the Salk family was in residence. Salk, in turn, was expected to stay and respond to all the demands for interviews and profiles that the NFIP wanted him to satisfy. Reporters and television cameras swirled thick as yellow jackets around the

Salks whenever they emerged from Inglis House. Photographers blinded the family with flashbulbs, demanding all manner of awkwardly posed pictures—the five Salks waving, grinning, sitting, chatting, or most preposterously of all, clustered in the Inglis House yard while Jonas held the damnable kite, appearing to explain to the three attentive boys, all of whom were wearing jackets and ties, how to fly it. Donna stood smiling behind them all. And always, when the photos were done, the reporters would ask Jonas what he planned to work on next.

"I just want to continue perfecting the vaccine," he'd say.

"What about other diseases?" they'd persist. "Any plans to tackle cancer?"

"I just want to continue perfecting the vaccine," he'd repeat.

It was four days before the press decamped from the university, allowing Salk and his family—with Tom Coleman now by their sides—to catch their much delayed flight back to what they hoped would be a far more sedate Pittsburgh. But Pittsburgh, as it turned out, was not nearly as calm as they expected. A crowd of 500 people was waiting for the family when they landed at the airport. Before they could even climb down the gangway, Mrs. A. W. Conover, head of the Pittsburgh Chamber of Commerce, climbed up and presented Donna with three dozen roses and a card that read, "From the grateful people of Pittsburgh."

When they all descended the steps to the tarmac, the crowd was so thick that airport police were needed to lead the Salks to a waiting city car; a knot of police motorcycles then escorted the car back to the Salk home. Peter, Darrell, and Jonathan were thrilled by the noise and lights. Donna was mortified. When they reached their block, the escorts—trained in getting the people in their charge to where they were going by the shortest route possible—purposely headed the wrong way down the Salk's one-way street. Donna told the driver of the car not to dare, ordering him to double back and go around the proper way. When the family finally reached their driveway, the confused motorcycle escorts were waiting for them there.

The scene at the Salks' front door—as well as back at the virus lab—was overwhelming: In both places, a mountain of telegrams, letters, and gifts had accumulated.

"How does it feel to have changed the world?" cabled actress Helen Hayes, who had lost a daughter to polio years before.

"Along with millions of Americans, I send you my congratulations and blessings," wrote Eddie Cantor, whose "March of Dimes" brainstorm sixteen years earlier had made him a favorite son of the NFIP ever since.

"Please accept this message as a small gesture of indebtedness for your diligence and humanity," telegrammed Marlon Brando.

Parents wrote too—from the United States, from the Americas, from Europe and Asia—applauding what Salk had done and thanking him for having done it. Letters from children followed.

"Dear Dr. Salk," wrote a seven-year-old from Chicago, "I am glad you discovered the shot. If it was not for you we would all get polio."

"Dear Dr. Salk," echoed an eight-year-old from Indiana, "Thank you very, very much for finding the Salk vaccine."

A kindergartner from San Diego wrote simply, "My sister and brother had polio. We love you."

After the letters came the gifts. Most of what was sent was money: a dollar or two at a time pouring in from individuals and families; checks of $50 or $100 from schools and civic clubs. A man in Sioux Falls began a nationwide chain letter, asking that every person in the chain forward Salk $1, promising that this would soon make the deserving scientist a very, very rich scientist. An Amarillo, Texas, radio station held a thank-Dr.-Salk drive with the aim of collecting $3,000. Instead, the station raised $6,500, which it used to buy a new Oldsmobile Holiday coupe, outfit it with air conditioning, and ship it north to Salk personally. Other, smaller gifts arrived: framed poems, handmade plaques; songs with titles like "A Man Named Salk" or "Hi-Ho, Hi-Ho, We'll Lick the Polio." Someone else sent a wooden cigarette box. Still another sent marmalade and nuts.

Business proposals were mixed in with the gifts. Publishers from most of the big New York houses wrote to offer book deals. Movie producers came calling too, sometimes through intermediaries. Hollywood giant Samuel Goldwyn let on to Edward R. Murrow that he'd be interested in a Salk biography, and Murrow passed that news on to Salk in a two-line note. Another offer arrived from an apparel manufacturer, hoping to market a collection of shirts, sweaters, and hats branded with the NFIP's emblem and the legend "Thank you, Dr. Salk." This, the man assured Salk, would "bring the name and work of the Foundation to the attention of every parent in America"—a job he evidently felt a line of clothing could do better than the polio vaccine itself.

Salk's policy toward all of this mail was firm: Cash or checks would be sent straight to the NFIP for the purchase of vaccine. Costly gifts would be either declined, with thanks, or sold, with the proceeds also going to the foundation. Gifts with no real monetary value would be kept. All business offers of any kind would be rejected. Anyone who had taken the time to write anything at all would be acknowledged and thanked by mail.

On April 21, the protocol liaison from the White House phoned with his own congratulations as well as a request from President Eisenhower that Salk and his family visit him the next day. Salk said that he'd be honored. A few moments later, HEW secretary Hobby called personally to ensure that Salk was indeed responding to the presidential summons.

The next morning, a black government car was waiting on the curb to collect Tom Coleman and the Salks. When heavy rain and heavy traffic slowed their route to the airport, the driver pulled over in front of a police station and Coleman jumped out.

"I've got Jonas Salk in the car," he announced to the desk sergeant. "He's late for a meeting with the president."

The sergeant came outside, peered through the partly fogged windows of the car, and spotted the familiar face in the back seat. Then he raised his hand and signaled for his motorcyclists to mount up. A few moments later, an embarrassed Donna Salk was riding in her second motorcade that week. A few hours after that, she and her family were standing on a dais in the Rose Garden, with the press corps and the president in front of them.

Eisenhower spoke about Salk's dedication to service, thanked him and his family for all the sacrifices they'd made, and offered the applause of a grateful nation. Salk then read a few remarks of his own, deflecting credit from himself and out to the hundreds of thousands whose contributions—

financial and otherwise—had made the vaccine possible. After the addresses, the president invited the family into the Oval Office for a brief private visit—a visit that almost came to grief.

"So what do you do besides play golf?" young Darrell asked Eisenhower, apropos of nothing at all. He was echoing his mother, a zealous Adlai Stevenson supporter who often claimed that practicing putting on the South Lawn was all the dull pretender in the Oval Office did with his time. Donna winced; Eisenhower smiled.

"Well," he said with a small laugh, "I like to paint."

Darrell surveyed the portraits that decorated the Oval Office walls, all on loan from the Smithsonian Institution. "Did you paint those?"

"No," the president answered. "They were done by much better painters than me."

Donna rested a restraining hand on Darrell's shoulder to prevent him from going any further and reminded him that the president was a very busy man. Eisenhower agreed, thanked the entire family for coming, and presented the boys with pens and pen knives stamped with the presidential seal. Donna thanked him on the boys' behalf. She let them keep the pens. The knives, she would later confiscate.

The next day, the Salks headed back to Pittsburgh, this time to stay. With the sensation of the Ann Arbor announcement at last beginning to fade and with the drug companies and the March of Dimes busying themselves with the less glamorous work of getting the newly licensed vaccine made and distributed, Salk had reason to hope things might at last begin to settle a bit. That's exactly what they started to do too—until word began to go around about a small group of healthy children in California who had been freshly injected with Salk vaccine and who had promptly begun to develop polio.

For all the global giddiness that followed Ann Arbor, nobody pretended that there wouldn't still be significant problems associated with the vaccine—the biggest concerning the supply. The drug houses' target production of 5.8 million cc's was a good start, but it was a modest one, and the fact of the matter was that barely a drop of it had been manufactured yet. The NFIP's stockpile amounted to about 9 million doses, enough for a three-dose cycle for 3 million children. That might help create a small viral firebreak in the Deep South, but it was far short of the vaccine needed for the 46 million boys and girls whose parents would be clamoring for it. Even with the manufacturers working around the clock, the most optimistic projections called only for a big enough supply for about a quarter of the vulnerable population by the beginning of July and not enough for the remainder until the beginning of November, when the polio season would be over. And all that assumed that the drug companies could avoid the numerous production problems that had plagued them since they first got hold of Salk's vaccine recipe.

Even the limited stockpile of vaccine that was already on the shelves was less than it appeared to be. Pharmaceutical companies typically loaded 10 cc's of any preparation into vials for every 9 cc's needed, in order to compensate for the few drops that are unavoidably lost when physicians change needles. This baker's-dozen packaging was no problem when there was a reliable supply of a product already available, but when every cc is being measured and rationed, the practice could lead to significant shortfalls in inventory. Compounding this, some of the vaccine that had already been counted as part of the national reserves had to be pulled when random testing showed that vials were cracked or damaged, or the vaccine had somehow leaked or spoiled. Since the companies had already logged the bad vaccine in, the states and cities to which it had been promised had to alter their vaccination plans when their shipments came up short.

All these problems caused Eisenhower to take another step to protect the domestic supply, slapping an immediate export embargo on all foreign sales of the Salk vaccine until American demand was satisfied. Governments overseas, which had received the formula free of charge and were now gearing up to churn the vaccine out, could not do much more than grumble at this choking off of supplies that they had hoped would carry them until they produced their own supply. In the United States, where the stockpile was in reach but tightly controlled, people could do more than merely complain: Quickly—and predictably—a quasi-legal gray market began to emerge. Almost nobody, of course, tried bootlegging vaccine, since no one beyond the experts knew how to handle such potentially lethal stuff. But plenty of people were willing to try filching it. All over the country, caches of vaccine that had been stashed in pharmaceutical depots or entrusted to druggists for distribution to physicians somehow began leaking away, with contraband vials winding up in completely unauthorized places.

"Never mind where I got them," one New Orleans mother instructed her family physician as she appeared in his office with her daughter at her side and produced a pair of one-cc vaccine vials from her purse. "Just use them." The doctor did as he was told.

As frustrations with the shortage mounted, it was Washington that came in for the most blistering criticism. Almost daily, Democratic congressmen accused the Republican White House of muddleheadedness and ineptitude in planning the manufacturing and distribution process. HEW Secretary Hobby only made things worse when she tried to explain the problem away.

"No one," she said, in a statement that drew incredulous hoots, "could have foreseen the public demand for the vaccine."

It was in the midst of all these distractions that case-counters first took note of the five polio infections that popped up in California sometime around April 26—two in San Diego and one apiece in Ventura, Oakland, and Napa. The reports raised few eyebrows since the polio season was well under way in the Far West and some cases among the unvaccinated were inevitable. Even when health officials learned that the children had indeed received their polio shots just days before falling ill, there was still no cause for panic.

Most such cases of postinjection infection could be traced easily back to an infected family member or classmate with whom the child had come into contact before being inoculated, and not to the vaccine. Even when the source could not be pinpointed, a more generalized local outbreak was usually to blame. In California, however, the results were different. The five children did not appear to have been exposed to polio anywhere in their schools or homes. Worse, when health officials checked the records of the particular vials of vaccine from which the children had been inoculated, they found that they had all come from the same few lots, produced by Cutter Laboratories in Berkeley, California.

Immediately after the California cases, a similar postvaccine infection popped up in Chicago—then three in Idaho, two in Washington, and one in Colorado. Then, alarmingly, seven more flared in California. All those children in all those places had been injected with vaccine cooked up in Cutter's Berkeley plant. So far, the company had shipped vaccine to at least eighteen states. In Los Angeles alone, 30,000 children had been injected with the Cutter product.

The states acted fast. Utah, which lay deep in the Cutter market, immediately suspended all use of the company's vaccine. California did the same, as did Idaho, Colorado, Massachussetts, and the city of Philadelphia. The Public Health Service in Washington made the ban uniform, suspending the use or distribution of Cutter vaccine anywhere in the country. Parents whose children had received Cutter shots ran panicked to their doctors. Parents whose children had gotten vaccine from another company nonetheless began pulling the boys and girls from the vaccination programs after they'd received only one or two of the three injections they'd need. The National Institutes of Health tried to prevent the hemorrhaging, declaring that it continued to have "great confidence" in the Salk vaccine, even as it dispatched two investigators from Bethesda to Berkeley to sweep the Cutter plant, sit down with the corporate scientists, and see what in the world was going on out there.

Salk himself learned of the nightmare news in a phone call from the NIH, and was summoned to Bethesda for a meeting on the morning of April 29. He spent the evening of the twenty-eighth huddled with Coleman in the Salk family's dining room, studying health reports from around the country and trying to make at least preliminary sense of what the numbers were telling him. So far, there were twenty-nine cases of apparently Cutter-related polio. A handful of the children had landed in iron lungs, struck by the often-lethal bulbar type. Others had milder cases. It was exceedingly likely—though not certain—that live virus in the vaccine lots was responsible. Just where the breakdown in the manufacturing cycle had occurred, however, and whether other companies were fumbling the same way, was impossible to say.

The meeting in Bethesda included Salk, Workman, O'Connor, various NFIP grantees, and representatives from all six drug companies. The first step in determining how the Cutter problem had occurred, they knew, would be to conduct exhaustive tests of the company's lots to determine whether live virus was in fact present. If it was, the factory's production methods would have to be stripped apart and studied one step at a time. It went without saying that Cutter vaccine would continue to be barred from distribution, but the product from the other five companies would remain in circulation, at least as long as they all continued to test clean. Of course, until faith in the vaccine as a whole could be restored, far fewer people would be coming forward for any of the shots at all.

Workman got the testing under way immediately, enlisting numerous corporate and NFIP labs, including Salk's own, to conduct the studies. The work began early in May, and it looked likely that it would continue deep into the summer.

Political critics of the vaccination program feasted on the new problem. Congressmen demanded the resignation of Surgeon General Leonard Scheele and then, almost as an afterthought, tossed Hobby's name onto the pyre too. One representative spread the word, *sotto voce,* that Cutter Laboratories would never have been licensed for vaccine production in the first place if it hadn't been for a "prominent California politician" who leaned on Hobby to sign six licenses instead of five. Nobody said out loud that the prominent politician was Vice President Richard Nixon, but nobody doubted that that was the implication. Nixon and Hobby vehemently denied the charge.

Scientific critics weighed in too. Albert Sabin, to no one's surprise, was very clear on the matter. "Both vaccine production and inoculation must be stopped," he declared, "until the vaccine can be made consistently safe."

Basil O'Connor, who had spent years appeasing the prickly Sabin, had no patience for him this time. "This is old stuff," he said. "He's been using it for years. He's been using it on every possible occasion to stop the use of the Salk vaccine." O'Connor then took pains to remind the Cincinnati scientist just who was paying for the research he was conducting. "The National Foundation has supported Sabin's work to the tune of $853,314.71," he said. "We'll continue to support him, but let's not have the Salk vaccine talked to death."

Other scientists and officials—ones O'Connor couldn't silence—took pokes at Salk too. The state of Idaho was being hit hard by the bad vaccine and made it clear where it affixed the responsibility for the crisis. "The department does not blame Cutter Laboratories," the state's health director declared, "because they were only carrying out the procedures outlined by Dr. Salk."

Salk responded in as politic a way as he could. "The people of Idaho have had a tragic experience," he said. "Our deep concern has not been a secret. But only when all of the evidence is available will the state be in a position to draw a sound conclusion."

No such conclusion was available throughout May or June, but in early July, the NIH and the private labs were at last able to reveal what they knew: Live virus, as anticipated, had indeed been found in the Cutter vaccine and, so far as it was possible to tell, only Cutter vaccine. The problem was not with Salk's methods but with the lab's execution of those methods, compounded by a bit of vagueness in the NIH's written protocols for vaccine manufacturing. Since not every badly manufactured vial actually contained live vaccine, the dangerous lots were able to slip through the animal-testing nets, with lucky monkeys receiving good vials and some unlucky children receiving bad ones. The protocols would be rewritten and clarified and additional testing steps would be imposed, including better filtration, larger sampling of lots, and more accurate tissue testing. The Mahoney strain of the Type I virus would also be replaced with a less virulent strain.

In the end, 79 children inoculated with the Cutter vaccine were struck by polio and 105 of their playmates and family members contracted it from them. Eleven people died. Cutter would be largely responsible for cleaning up the mess of the inevitable lawsuits that would follow.

After the NIH findings were known, the House of Representatives called hearings to determine officially if the vaccination program should be allowed to proceed. The Health and Science Subcommittee convened a panel of fifteen experts on viral diseases, including John Enders, William Hammon, John Paul, and Jonas Salk. The scientists and congressmen worked through all the relevant facts and all the relevant arguments for and against the vaccine. Then the science panel voted: Eight were in favor of proceeding, three were opposed, four abstained. Salk, who could hardly cast an objective vote, was among the abstentions. The congressmen then cast their own votes and agreed to proceed too. The vaccine that had been a source of such global joy in April—and such sorrow in May and June— would be offered to the world again.

EPILOGUE

efore the celebrated year of 1955 came to a close, 28,985 children and adults in the United States contracted polio; 13,850 of them were left permanently paralyzed. Although virtually all of the cases were among people who had not received timely doses of Salk's vaccine, the numbers were still a disappointment. They were better than the previous two years to be sure—and far better than the 57,879 claimed in the plague season of 1952. But in a year in which 10 million children—more than 20 percent of all the boys and girls in the nation—had received at least one or two of the Salk shots, surely the outcome should be more encouraging than this.

There were a lot of reasons it wasn't. The vaccination program started late, for one thing, and was not available in many areas at all. When it finally did reach some communities, it didn't do so until autumn or winter, when the year's viral hammer had already fallen. Any benefit from the shots could thus not be determined until the following summer.

Already, however, there were some promising signs that lay a little deeper in the epidemiological numbers. In communities in which children had been vaccinated early and uniformly, the polio count dropped much more precipitously. In the Deep South, where vaccine was rushed first, the caseload was slashed by more than half compared with the previous year. In regions in the East or Midwest, where less vaccine had been available, it ticked down only slightly.

Often, getting any amount of vaccine at all into a community helped protect not only children who received the inoculations but uninoculated ones as well. Any person vaccinated with Salk's killed virus would be knocked permanently out of the infection chain. Remove enough of these carriers, and there simply won't be enough active virus going around to get any kind of contagion going in the unvaccinated population. Epidemiologists called this the herd effect, and for all the inelegance of its bovine name, it helped save a lot of lives.

Salk and the NFIP were counting on a much more organized and vigorous vaccination program to bring the case count down in the summers that would follow—and that was precisely what they got. In 1956, the polio total in the United States was cut nearly in half, to 15,150. In 1957, it was cut by another two-thirds, to just 5,467. The number stabilized in 1957 and actually rallied a bit to 8,425 in 1958—mostly because of the failure of some families to ensure that children completed the entire three-shot cycle. That threw a scare into a lot of complacent parents, who came swarming back to doctors' offices and vaccination centers. In 1961, only 1,312 American children contracted infantile paralysis, a 98 percent improvement over the epidemic of just nine years earlier. The poliovirus, it was clear, had been largely flushed from the human population.

But not everyone saw things in so rosy a way. Salk may have been adored by the parents of children whose lives and legs had been saved by his vaccine, but the scientists in whose circles he worked were far less charmed. None of them had cared for his appearances on radio and, ultimately, television, before and after the grand announcement at the University of Michigan. Such behavior, they felt, was showmanship at its shabbiest, not at all the way serious science was done. His artless, if inadvertent, snub of his staff during his Rackham Hall remarks only convinced some people further that he was a self-promoter, and a rather clumsy one at that.

In the decades that followed, Salk never talked much about the Rackham Hall gaffe, even to his family. While his sons came to see him the way all children see their parents—as complex and inevitably flawed, capable both of greatness and of moments of behaving badly or selfishly—they continued to believe there was no malice in the hurt he had inflicted on his staff. Most people on the staff accepted that the seeming slight was a mere oversight and forgave him, including Jim Lewis and Lorraine Friedman. A few never did.

In 1954, John Enders, Thomas Weller, and Frederick Robbins were awarded the Nobel Prize for their breakthrough in polio tissue culturing. After the field-trial triumph of 1955, the press and public assumed that such an award would surely be coming Salk's way too. But people within the scientific community suspected otherwise: The Nobel committee, they believed, was unlikely ever to recognize Salk, or even seriously consider him. What he'd done was merely "kitchen science," his critics sniffed—a lot of mixing and warming of ingredients other people had provided him, but surely nothing original or inspirational. Awards weren't granted for that, particularly when the potential recipient himself was, well, a little controversial.

What's more, even as the polio numbers fell lower and lower, some people remained unpersuaded by the principle of the killed vaccine. Live-virus partisans continued to argue that immunity achieved with a living pathogen was simply longer-lasting and more powerful than anything that came from a dead bug. Moreover, since killed virus couldn't grow in the gut and then make its way to the bloodstream, where immunity was established, it would never be possible to deliver the Salk vaccine orally, meaning that the messiness of an injection would always be part of the process. Live vaccine could be administered in something as benign as a dropper or a sugar cube. While this was not a critical advantage in the developed world, it made a real difference in other, more rugged places, where it would be necessary to conduct massive numbers of injections in the field and where strangers descending with vials and needles were not necessarily welcome.

Finally, advocates argued, there was one more advantage to the live vaccine. When a living but weakened virus was introduced into the body, at least some of it would later be sneezed, coughed, or excreted out. At large in the world, it would then be free to infect other people, once again causing an asymptomatic case of polio that would immunize but never sicken. The vaccinated could thus become vaccinators, spreading health and protection to the community as a whole.

The problem was that the tendency of viruses to mutate could also present the risk that a harmless bug might revert to virulence, becoming dangerous and even deadly once again. In some cases it was possible that a single passage through a body would be enough for the transformation to take place.

Without any real experience in large-scale use of a live polio vaccine, however, there was no way to be sure if reversion to virulence on any meaningful scale was real or just a ghost story. Given that, and the undeniable ease of an orally administered vaccine, the live-virus idea persisted, kept burning by the inexhaustible Albert Sabin. Pressing on with his studies, he developed a preliminary vaccine that he was given permission to test on volunteers in an Ohio penitentiary in 1955. The results were good. Broader studies of larger populations followed, and again the outcome was encouraging. After that, however, testing stalled. With the United States having just finished one massive field trial of the killed vaccine, it was not about to mount another with the live version.

This was not the case in the Soviet Union. Moscow had experimented with Salk vaccine in 1957 and found it hard to make and inconvenient to administer. In 1958, Sabin was thus invited to the USSR and Czechoslovakia to see if he could do better. He leapt at the offer. By 1959, he had inoculated nearly 13 million Communist-bloc children and adults with his live vaccine. There too polio was now in retreat.

This gave Sabin all he needed to return home in scientific triumph and renew his call to push aside the Salk product and replace it with his, making all the familiar arguments, with his wealth of new data from the East now available to back him up. To Salk's surprise, the government agreed. Sabin's product could go promptly into large-scale production, Washington ruled, and would soon be given to every schoolchild in the country, even those who had already taken the Salk shots.

Sugar-cube inoculations with Sabin vaccine began in 1962. By 1969, there were only twenty cases of polio anywhere in the United States. By 1974, there were seven. From 1984 through 1998, the numbers almost never rose out of the single digits. In 1999 and 2000, there were none at all. Salk brought the polio caseload down from 50,000 to 1,000. It took Sabin to carry the baton the rest of the way.

Or so it seemed. But things were much more complicated than that. The Salk vaccine had been in use for only seven years before Sabin's was introduced, and had been on a glide path that, the numbers suggested, would have achieved the same polio eradication given a few years' more time. The Sabin vaccine got decades. What's more, the biggest misgiving about the live formulation appeared to be well founded.

The last wild case of polio in the United States occurred in 1979. All of the tiny number of cases since then have been directly traceable to the virus in the live vaccine. Often the infection appeared not in the vaccinated child but in a vulnerable adult living in the household. The more infirm the victim already was, the higher the risk of infection became. People who were taking immunosuppressive drugs to prevent transplant rejection or who were infected with HIV—a virus the likes of which Basil O'Connor's polio foundation had never even imagined—were especially vulnerable. In the developing world, where live vaccine was all there was, it was impossible to determine how many cases of the disease were blowback infections like this and how many were simply a result of the lack of uniform inoculation programs. Both causes were almost certainly involved.

For the rest of Salk's life, he would never see the argument between the live and killed factions fully settled. As he got older, he liked to say that when you're arguing for an unpopular idea, there are three stages of truth. First, your opponents say it can't be true. Next they say if it's true, it can't be very important. Finally they say well, we've known it all along. Salk did not always make that point without anger, but in fact he came to long for stage three, if only because it would mean that his ideas had been universally accepted.

Salk spent the decades that followed his polio triumph doing far more than waging this ideological war. In 1962, he and his family moved to La Jolla, California, where he established the Salk Institute for Biological Studies, a sweeping facility overlooking the Pacific Ocean. Many of the still-loyal members of his Pittsburgh staff joined him there. Today, the institute employs a full-time faculty of 56 and a scientific staff of 850 and serves as a learning and research center for more than 500 undergraduate, graduate, and postdoctoral students. Over the years the institute has trained five scientists who went on to win Nobel Prizes. Seven other Nobel laureates are currently either on the faculty or working as nonresident fellows. For decades, Salk, who had so often felt shut out of the world's circle of scientists, thrived in the circle he'd created on his own. He continued conducting research in a range of areas, improving his polio vaccine, studying multiple sclerosis, and, in the 1980s, working to develop a vaccine against AIDS.

The National Foundation for Infantile Paralysis lives on but is now known exclusively as the March of Dimes, battling premature births, birth defects, and genetic disorders.

Jonas and Donna's marriage did not survive. They divorced in 1967, and Jonas married artist Françoise Gilot in 1970. Peter, Darrell, and Jonathan all became physicians, and are now living and working in La Jolla, Seattle, and Los Angeles.

Albert Sabin was the first of the two polio giants to go, dying in 1993 at the age of eighty-six. He is buried at Arlington National Cemetery. Salk did not live much longer, succumbing to congestive heart failure on June 23, 1995, at the age of eighty.

Several months before he died, he was still deeply involved with his AIDS research, juggling monkey studies and government clearances and other associated problems. Speaking to Peter on the phone one evening, a weary Salk asked his oldest son, "Where do you think I should be pushing this now? What should I be doing next?"

"Nothing," Peter said quietly. "There's nothing you have to do."

The year after Salk died, the Centers for Disease Control ruled that in order to eliminate the final lingering cases of polio in the United States, the live vaccine invented by Albert Sabin would be phased out and replaced by the killed formulation invented by Jonas Salk. On January 1, 2000, that transition was complete and the Salk vaccine returned, at least in the United States.

Around the world, there were fewer than 700 polio cases in 2003, three-quarters of them in Nigeria, Pakistan, and India. The World Health Organization has set itself the goal of eradicating the very last case of the disease, driving the poliovirus over the cliff of extinction and into medical history.

ACKNOWLEDGMENTS

Trying to do narrative justice to a figure who was such a tectonic force in scientific history is a presumptuous undertaking. To the extent that I was successful, I owe a lot of thanks to a lot of people, most of whom are mentioned here and all of whom are described in greater detail in the Source Notes that follow.

Most valuable in my research—and most deeply appreciated—were Jonas Salk's three sons, Peter, Jonathan, and especially Darrell, who all agreed to sit down for conversations and interviews, read portions of the manuscript, and provided wise guidance and insight. If I have been able to incorporate into this work even a portion of what they offered, I have done my job. If I haven't, the fault is entirely mine. Thanks too to Helen Glickstein (née Helen Press) and Sylvia Salk, who knew Jonas Salk as only family members could and offered a glimpse into that exclusive world.

Other members of the small group of people who were involved in the remarkable events of half a century ago and generously agreed to be interviewed include Sylvia Clark, Hilary Koprowski, Frederick Robbins, William Kirkpatrick, James Sarkett, and Don Wegemer. I am in their debt. Special thanks go to John Troan—one of those extraordinary journalists who set the professional bar so damnably high for the rest of us—for his time, his patience, and his willingness to share the extraordinary things he knows.

I could not have written this book without the remarkable resources of Jonas Salk's collection of private papers in the Mandeville Special Collections at the University of California at San Diego, or the equally rich library at the March of Dimes headquarters in White Plains, New York. And I would not have been able to find my way through the thicket of all that material without the able assistance of archivists Lynda Corey Claasen and Steven Coy at UCSD and David Rose at the March of Dimes. Many thanks for all the time they spent pointing me along the paper trail.

Numerous fine books, all cited in the Source Notes, provided special research insight. Principal among them were *Breakthrough,* by Richard Carter; *Patenting the Sun,* by Jane S. Smith; *A Summer Plague,* by Tony Gould; and *Passport to Adventure,* by John Troan. Thanks to all these authors for providing such an extraordinary historical framework and such a high reportorial standard.

I would not, of course, have had a book to write in the first place if not for the patience and gentle care of the wonderful folks at the Joy Harris Literary Agency, particularly Joy Harris, Alexia Paul, Stephanie Abou, and Leslie Daniels. I first walked in Joy's door thirteen years ago; it's a number that has always served us well and I hope for thirteen more at the very least. I am also happily indebted to Jennifer Hershey at Putnam, who recognized that the Salk story was one richly worth telling, and whose brilliant editorial guidance restrained the worst of my excesses and brought forth the best of the rest. For editing two different books by two different members of the same mad family alone, she wins my admiration.

I want to add a word of acknowledgment and my deep respect to the folks at the Christopher Reeve Paralysis Foundation and the Miami Project to Cure Paralysis. I have closely followed and occasionally been privileged to cover both groups over the years, and if there are any organizations today that are the true spiritual descendants of the National Foundation for Infantile Paralysis, it is they. Spinal cord injury is the poliomyelitis of our time. The Chris Reeve Foundation and the Miami Project deserve our profound appreciation—and our support.

More personal acknowledgments are due to a handful of precious others. Appreciation and admiration go to the indomitable Hilde Gerst, for her elegance, grace, and courage. Thanks and love to Richard and Phyllis Kluger, for always good counsel and always great fun. Much love to Splash Kluger, who never saw a single thing wrong with her four sons pursuing what they loved in life, and is one of the reasons that they went ahead and did just that. Love too to my sibs and sisters-in-law: Steve, Garry, Bruce, Adam, and Allison Kluger, Alene Hokenstad, and Lori Oliwenstein. *Besos y besos* to my sweet *sobrinos,* Bridgette, Mateo, Emily, Audrey, Julian, and Noah.

Finally, my deepest love to Alejandra, Elisa, and Paloma—my home and heart, all day, every day, forever and ever.

SOURCE NOTES

Most of the research references that follow are self-explanatory, but some abbreviations and initials may require clarification. Five members of the Salk family kindly agreed to be interviewed and offer their thoughts as I was researching and writing the manuscript. They are: Peter Salk, Darrell Salk, and Jonathan Salk (Jonas Salk's three sons); Helen Glickstein, née Helen Press (Salk's cousin); and Sylvia Salk (Salk's sister-in-law). For simplicity's sake, they are cited throughout the source notes by their initials: P.S., D.S., J.S., H.G., and S.S. Some of the information from these sources was drawn from formal interviews I conducted with them; some came from more casual conversations or discussions of portions of the manuscript. I indicate this with such citations as "interview with D.S." or "conversations with sons."

The list of surviving scientists, polio patients, and others who were involved in some way in the Salk vaccine story is a necessarily short one, that story having played out half a century ago. The few who were available and were able to share their time with me were Sylvia Clark, a former patient at the D. T. Watson Home; William Kirkpatrick, a polio survivor and the first person to receive the experimental vaccine; Hilary Koprowski, who developed an early version of the live vaccine in 1951; Frederick Robbins, cowinner of the 1954 Nobel Prize for Medicine and codeveloper of the method for cultivating poliovirus in non-nervous-system tissue; James Sarkett, the polio survivor who lent his slightly misspelled name to the Type III strain of the poliovirus Salk used in his work; John Troan, the inexhaustible journalist from the *Pittsburgh Press* who better than anyone of his day chronicled the polio story; and Don Wegemer, a leading researcher in Salk's lab. All of these sources, when cited, are cited by their names rather than by initials.

The documentary resource that was most valuable to me in my research was the massive collection of Jonas Salk's personal papers, archived in the Mandeville Special Collections at the Theodore S. Geisel library at the University of California, San Diego (UCSD). The Salk records, which currently fill 683 file boxes, include lab notes, memos, correspondence, telegrams, scientific papers, contracts, research proposals, writings, lectures, interviews, photographs, awards, newspaper clippings, and more. The collection covers the period from 1916 (two years after Salk's birth) to 1995 (the year of his death). The large majority of documents cited below were drawn from this collection. In most cases, the date of the document is included. Where the date was not visible or was obscured, I have tried to include the number of the file box and folder in which the document was found, though on occasion this information was not available either.

Also essential to my research was the extensive documentary collection at the March of Dimes headquarters in White Plains, New York. The material there was indispensable in helping me piece together the history of the Georgia Warm Springs Foundation, the National Foundation for Infantile Paralysis, and the March of Dimes. I identify records drawn from the March of Dimes collection with a parenthetical M.O.D.

A number of books were helpful as well in providing me background to the Salk story, the Warm Springs story, and the Franklin Roosevelt story. Those books are:

Kathryn Black, *In the Shadow of Polio: A Personal and Social History*
Richard Bruno, *The Polio Paradox*
Richard Carter, *Breakthrough: The Saga of Jonas Salk*
Frank Freidel, *Franklin D. Roosevelt: The Ordeal*
Tony Gould, *A Summer Plague: Polio and Its Survivors*
Stephanie Sammartino McPherson, *Jonas Salk: Conquering Polio*
Ted Morgan, *FDR: A Biography*
Nina Gilden Seavy, Jane S. Smith, and Paul Wagner, *A Paralyzing Fear: Conquering Polio in America*
Jane S. Smith, *Patenting the Sun*
John Troan, *Passport to Adventure*
Turnley Walker, *Roosevelt and the Warm Springs Story*
Geoffrey C. Ward, *A First-Class Temperament*

All books mentioned in the Source Notes are cited by the author's last name, followed by the applicable page numbers.

Newspaper and magazine clippings came from a variety of sources, including the New York Public Library, the libraries at the Time-Life Building in Rockefeller Center in New York, the Salk collection at UCSD, and John Troan's personal files. Whenever possible, the date and name of the newspaper or magazine and the headline of the story are included.

PROLOGUE

1 **All the talk about the little white coffins:** Various sources including Smith, p. 257.

2 **after inoculating all of them had he similarly treated:** NFIP minutes, Vaccine Advisory Committee, 11/13/53 (M.O.D.).

2 **In the summer of 1952 alone:** International Polio Network, "Incidence Rates of Poliomyelitis in USA."

2 **The following summer, over 35,000:** Ibid.

3 **"Good evening, Mr. and Mrs. America":** Various sources, including *New York Daily Mirror* typescript, 4/5/54.

4 **But the pitch would continue:** Various sources, including author conversations with sons, and Smith, p. 257.

4 **Salk himself was unaware:** Author conversations with sons.

4 **"You heard?" a technician asked:** Ibid.

5 **What he didn't know:** Carter, pp. 233–37.

CHAPTER ONE

7 **There was a time when a black car:** *Brooklyn Eagle,* "Mothers Will Do Anything to Keep Sick Babies at Home," date missing but between 8/25/16 and 8/29/16. (All *Brooklyn Eagle* clips from Box 131, Folder 8, of UCSD collection.)

7 **from Madison Avenue:** Address from Carter, p. 29.

7 **116,000 of them were now registered:** *New York Times,* "A Million in Motor Fees," 8/24/16.

8 **a mandatory trip to Swineburne Island:** *New York Times,* "Defense League of 21,000 Citizens Fights Paralysis; Swineburne Island Ready for Patients," 7/9/16; *Brooklyn Eagle,* "Mothers Will Do Anything to Keep Sick Babies at Home."

8 **It had happened that way back in 1907:** Various sources, including *New York Times,* "Day Shows 12 Dead by Infant Paralysis," 7/1/16; *Brooklyn Eagle,* "46 More Infant Paralysis Cases; Girl of 14 Dies," date missing but after 6/28/16 and before 7/1/16.

8 **"INFANTILE PARALYSIS," the signs would announce:** *Brooklyn Eagle,* "Quarantine Notice From the Board of Health," date missing but shortly after 7/1/16; photo, placard on wall of Brooklyn house under quarantine in 1916 (Range, Bettmann Archive/UPI).

9 **After the placards appeared:** *Brooklyn Eagle,* "21 Deaths; 68 New Cases of Paralysis; 200 in Hospital," date missing but shortly after 7/1/16; *New York Times,* "Paralysis Cripples Glad to Aid Others," 8/9/16.

9 **tickets for free ice:** *New York Times,* "Paralysis Crest Believed Passed," 8/22/16.

10 **Dora Salk made it a point:** Author interview with S.S., 8/20/02.

10 **Mothers did not surrender:** *Brooklyn Eagle,* "Mothers Will Do Anything to Keep Sick Babies at Home"; *Brooklyn Eagle,* ". . . Still Fail to Enforce Paralysis Quarantines," headline incomplete and date missing; *New York*

Times, "Defense League of 21,000 Citizens Fights Paralysis; Swineburne Island Ready for Patients," 7/9/16.

11 **The first thing the doctor would do:** Ibid.

11 **the windows would be closed:** *Brooklyn Eagle,* "Flies May Carry Germs Says Dr. Simon Flexner," 7/1/16.

12 **Dora Salk—or Dora Press:** Author interviews with S.S., 8/20/02 and 9/25/02; author interview with H.G., 8/20/02.

13 **"Can you help me read that?":** Author interview with S.S., 8/20/02.

13 **regularly rinsed with a solution:** *Brooklyn Eagle,* "How Best to Ward Off Infantile Paralysis," 7/1/16.

14 **By the first of July, 350 children:** *Brooklyn Eagle,* "20 P.C. Mortality in Epidemic; Cases Total Reaches 350," date missing, but shortly after 7/1/16; *New York Times,* "Day Shows 12 Dead by Infant Paralysis," 7/1/16.

14 **New York was not alone:** *New York Times,* "Paralysis Kills 22 More Babies in New York City; Disease in Other Cities," 7/8/16; *New York Times,* "Paralysis in 33 States," 8/18/16.

14 **The Fourth of July:** *New York Times,* "Lights to Spell Out High Ideals on 4th," 7/2/16.

14 **France and Great Britain had just mounted:** *New York Times,* "French Thrust Nears Perrone, Capturing Five Towns on the Way," 7/2/16.

15 **On the afternoon of July 2:** *New York Times,* Weather, 7/2/16; *New York Times,* "Bar All Children from the Movies in Paralysis War; Plans for 15 Celebrations Cancelled at Request of Dr. Emerson," 7/4/16.

15 **At the Polo Grounds:** *New York Times,* "Schauer and Schupp, Doing Relief Duty, Wilt and Champions Make Score 9 to 2," 7/2/16; *New York Times,* "Weather Bothers Wavering Giants," 7/4/16.

15 **Of the sixty biggest celebrations:** *New York Times,* "Bar All Children from the Movies in Paralysis War: Plans for 15 Celebrations Cancelled at Request of Dr. Emerson," 7/4/16.

15 **113 new cases checked into hospitals:** *New York Times,* "City to Provide $80,000 to Fight Paralysis Peril," 7/6/16.

16 **and 87 followed:** *New York Times,* "Paralysis Kills 22 More Babies in New York City," 7/8/16.

16 **For every five cases, at least one:** *Brooklyn Eagle,* "20 P.C. Mortality in Epidemic; Cases Total Reaches 350"; *New York Times,* "Paralysis Gains Following Lull," 8/16/16.

16 **When the weekend arrived:** *Brooklyn Eagle*, "Cool Weather Gives Hope in Epidemic," 8/10/16; *Brooklyn Eagle*, "'Tuesday Increase' in Paralysis Cases Now Shows Decline," 8/22/16.

16 **Cats, many people concluded:** *Brooklyn Eagle*, "Infantile Paralysis Kills 42 Children in a Week," date missing but before 7/1/16; *New York Times*, "Paralysis Kills 22 More Babies in New York City; Disease in Other Cities," 7/8/16; *New York Times*, "72,000 Cats Killed in Paralysis Fear" (per Gould, p. 8).

16 **If it wasn't mosquitoes:** *New York Times*, "Paralysis Fighters Expect a Rest Soon," 8/28/16.

16 **In train terminals in all the boroughs:** Various clips, including *New York Times*, "25 More Deaths from Paralysis; Exodus of 50,000 Children," 7/5/16; *Brooklyn Eagle*, "Mothers Hurrying out of City with Children," date missing but early July 1916.

17 **In the first full week of July:** *Brooklyn Eagle*, "Week's Paralysis Cases," 7/15/16.

17 **the ancient carving of an Egyptian boy:** Various sources, including photo, Egyptian stele showing polio victim, 1580–1350 B.C.; photo part of March of Dimes Birth Defects Foundation collection.

17 **They knew the great names:** Various sources, including Bruno, chap. 4; Smith, pp. 34–37; Carter, pp. 8–11.

18 **An informational meeting would be held:** *New York Times*, "Day Shows 12 Dead by Infantile Paralysis," 7/1/16.

18 **Emerson rapped the table:** *Brooklyn Eagle*, "Flies May Carry Germs, Says Dr. Flexner" and "How Best to Ward Off Infantile Paralysis," 7/1/16; "20 P.C. Mortality in Epidemic; Cases Total Reaches 350"; *New York Times*, "Day Shows 12 Dead by Infantile Paralysis," 7/1/16.

20 **By August, polio brushfires:** *New York Times*, "New Cases and Deaths," 8/1/16, 8/2/16, 8/18/16.

20 **The black cars came:** Ibid.

20 **Camphor, it had been said:** *Brooklyn Eagle*, "Camphor Not Cure but Demand Is Big," date missing but shortly before 7/20/16.

20 **"Leave your shoes outside":** Author interviews and conversations with H.G., S.S., P.S., D.S., J.S.

21 **As the middle of August approached:** *Brooklyn Eagle*, "Big Paralysis Drop; 31 New Cases Here," 8/15/16.

21 **Money or other resources collected:** Various sources, including *New York Times,* "Paralysis Gains Following Lull," 8/16/16.

21 **the wealthy summer residents of the Rockaway Peninsula:** *New York Times,* "Threaten to Wreck Paralysis Hospital," 8/27/16; *New York Times,* "Oyster Bay Still Seething," 8/30/16.

24 **In the end, the doctors counted:** New York City Department of Health Poliomyelitis Records, Background Note.

CHAPTER TWO

25 **Helen Press and her parents:** Author interview with H.G.

25 **But while Salk could be a serviceable enough athlete:** Author interview with H.G., S.S., and sons.

26 **But that kind of compliance came only:** Author interviews with D.S.

26 **While only a middling asset:** Ibid.

26 **Once every few years, he'd give:** Author interview with S.S.

27 **Sharing this decision with his mother:** Author interview with D.S.

29 **The tall man left a trail:** Walker, pp. 6–9; Ward, pp. 650–52; Freidel, pp. 119–20; author visit to 120 Broadway.

29 **Roosevelt arrived that morning:** Walker, pp. 6–9; Ward, pp. 650–52; Freidel, 119–20.

29 **where he had worked as a branch chief:** Various sources, including Ward, pp. 560–63; Morgan, pp. 246, 263–64.

30 **That problem began in the summer of 1921:** Various sources, including Ward, pp. 581–90; Morgan, pp. 246–49.

31 **"It's perfectly clear," the doctor said:** Ward, p. 590.

31 **The long, shiny car came to a stop:** Walker, pp. 6–9; Ward, pp. 650–52; Freidel, pp. 119–20.

32 **Jonas Salk entered New York University Medical School:** Author conversations with Salk sons.

32 **"Would you mind taking that thing with you?":** Author interview with H.G.

33 **his social skills began to look a lot like:** Author interviews with D.S., P.S., J.S., S.S., and H.G; Salk, Academy of Achievement interview, conducted 5/16/91, File 1, p. 6.

33 **It showed itself mostly with the handful of fast friends:** Ibid.

34 **most memorably during his first-year study:** Salk, Academy of Achievement interview, File 1, p. 1.

35 **While unpredictable things like vaccines troubled Salk:** Author interview with D.S.

36 **During Salk's first year in medical school:** Salk, Academy of Achievement interview, File 2, p. 1.

36 **"I want you to think about leaving school":** Salk, Academy of Achievement interview, File 2, p. 1; author interviews with sons.

36 **Cannan was studying the streptococcus bacterium:** "Method for Separation of Micro-organisms from Large Quantities of Broth Culture," by Jonas E. Salk (introduction by R. Keith Cannan), *Procedures of the Society of Experimental Biology and Medicine* 38: 228–30, 1938; author interviews with D.S.; Salk, Academy of Achievement interview, File 2, p. 1; Carter, pp. 32, 35.

37 **By himself, Franklin Roosevelt could never climb:** "Notes on Georgia Warm Springs Foundation," compiled by Adam W. Lunow, pp. 1–6 (M.O.D.).

38 **People both inside and outside Meriwether County:** Ibid., pp. 2–4.

38 **story got around about the young civil engineer:** Ibid., pp. 7–8.

38 **Roosevelt . . . was not always entirely rational:** Morgan, pp. 274–76; Ward, pp. 660–69, 709.

39 **A crowd of Georgians:** Walker, pp. 18–24.

39 **Franklin Roosevelt had gotten such wild business notions:** Ward, pp. 658–60.

39 **In the two years since he took his fall:** Walker, pp. 118–22; Morgan, pp. 266, 276–77; Ward, pp. 657, 715; Freidel, p. 143; Carter, pp. 11–12; Smith, pp. 52–57.

40 **Basil O'Connor was a different breed:** Basil O'Connor, curriculum vitae (M.O.D.); Smith, pp. 52–54.

40 **He was admitted to the New York bar:** Basil O'Connor, curriculum vitae (M.O.D.).

41 **the New York Democratic Party found itself:** Morgan, pp. 289–96, Ward, pp. 788–99.

42 **"Take over Warm Springs, old fella":** Gould, p. 45; Carter, p. 12.

42 **As Roosevelt had predicted:** Notes on Georgia Warm Springs Foundation," p. 9 (M.O.D.).

43 **the $47 per week that was the per-patient fee:** Georgia Warm Springs Foundation admissions brochure (M.O.D.).

43 **Wouldn't they like to celebrate:** Carter, pp. 13–24; Smith, p. 70; Walker, pp. 223–27.

44 **"As the representative of hundreds of thousands":** Carter, p. 14.

44 **On September 23, 1937, he signed:** "Milestones in History of National Foundation for Infantile Paralysis," p. 7 (M.O.D.); Gould, p. 73.

44 **Jonas Salk's class at New York University:** Author conversations with sons.

46 **Dr. Salk began his internship:** Ibid.

47 **If Jonas's studies denied him free time:** Ibid.

49 **Salk knew that by any responsible measure:** Author conversations with sons; Carter, pp. 42–44; Smith, pp. 103–6.

49 **soon found himself running virus samples:** Author conversations with sons; *New York Sun,* "Radiation Might Help Fight Flu," 1/3/41; *New York Herald Tribune,* "New Treatment for Influenza Vaccine Found," 1/4/41.

50 **Salk wrote Francis a letter:** Author conversations with sons; Smith, pp. 103–6.

50 **In the United States, more than 550,000 people died:** *Time* Almanac 2004, p. 601.

CHAPTER THREE

51 **Brodie was a physician at Montreal's McGill:** Numerous sources, including *Tom Rivers: Reflections on a Life in Science and Medicine,* pp. 182–83.

52 **The state of polio science had advanced:** "Report on the Brodie Vaccine," March of Dimes Historical Division, 5/21/54 (M.O.D.).

52 **De Kruif was once a researcher:** "The Life and Legacy of Paul DeKruif," by Robin Marantz Henig.

54 **He asked the old man directly:** Carter, p. 21.

54 **the Birthday Ball Commission . . . agreed to allocate:** "Report on the Brodie Vaccine," March of Dimes Historical Division (M.O.D.).

54 **At Temple University, physician John Kolmer:** Ibid., p. 2.

54 **"ANTI-PARALYSIS SERUM REPORTED A SUCCESS":** *New York Times,* 2/3/35.

54 **But that dazzling figure:** "Report on the Brodie Vaccine," March of Dimes Historical Division (M.O.D.); *New York Times,* "Paralysis Vaccine Discontinued Here," 12/27/35; Carter, pp. 22–23; Gould, pp. 66–69.

55 **"FLEXNER REJECTS PARALYSIS VACCINE":** *New York Times,* 11/1/35.

55 **But it didn't compare with:** *Tom Rivers: Reflections on a Life in Science and Medicine,* pp. 182–83.

55 **There would be two presentations:** Ibid.

55 **Dr. Kolmer . . . might as well be guilty:** Ibid.

56 **"It looks as though according to Dr. Rivers":** Ibid.

56 **Even as the promise of the vaccines:** *New York Times* (editorial page), "The Fight Against 'Polio,'" 12/28/35.

CHAPTER FOUR

57 **It was probably inevitable:** Salk, handwritten notes from preliminary visits to Wellston, 7/29/43 and 7/31/43.

58 **So the Wellston men had spent:** Self-profiles of Wellston volunteers, Box 189, Folder 13, in UCSD collection.

58 **In September 1943, word got around:** Salk, typed and handwritten notes for 9/15/43 and 9/16/43 visit to Wellston.

58 **Donna and Jonas came to Ann Arbor:** Author interviews with D.S.

58 **far too tony for the $2,100 per year:** Carter, p. 44.

59 **The Salks moved into their new home:** Author interviews with D.S.

60 **So this is what this is like:** Ibid.

60 **It had been only nine years:** Salk notes from slide presentation, Box 287, Folder 15, in UCSD collection.

61 **The alternative was blood cells:** Francis and Salk, "A Simplified Procedure for the Concentration and Purification of Influenza Virus," *Science,* 11/27/42.

62 **Not long after, Francis and Salk completed:** Author interview with D.S.

63 **Over the next year, Salk startled Francis:** Ibid.

64 **The procedure Salk envisioned:** Salk, typed notes, "Rules and Regulations Governing the Influenza Experiment Beginning Sept. 15 or 16," Box 189, Folder 12, in UCSD collection.

64 **On September 15, 1943, Salk arrived:** Ibid.

65 **The boy's name was on the card:** Handwritten self-profile of R.D. Boynton, 7/20/43.

65 **"All right if we begin, then?":** Author conversations with sons.

65 **he began to compose a story:** Salk, fable composed at Camp Wellston, Box 189, Folder 13 in UCSD collection.

66 **Three days later, Salk called his volunteers:** Francis and Salk, "A Clinical Evaluation of Vaccine Against Influenza," *Journal of the American Medical Association*, 4/1/44.

66 **"To All Guinea Pigs":** Salk, fable composed at Camp Wellston.

66 **In all the time Franklin Roosevelt:** Numerous sources, including Morgan, p. 710.

67 **Since the very first of the Birthday Balls:** Various materials, including, "Notes on Georgia Warm Springs Foundation," compiled by Adam W. Lunow; birthday-card lists, state by state, 4/22/41; "The Story," Georgia Warm Springs Foundation, no visible page number (all from M.O.D. collection).

67 **Each year, the NFIP sponsored:** Author interview with D.S.

68 **Cities took to launching their own:** Text of radio spots (M.O.D. collection).

68 **"How many dimes in a mile?":** Ibid.

68 **As the funds streamed into foundation accounts:** Grants-in-Aid and Appropriations, 1939, pp. 16–40 in NFIP annual report (M.O.D.).

69 **No matter how the NFIP chose to spend:** International Polio Network, "Incidence Rates of Poliomyelitis in USA."

69 **The cabin was decorated modestly:** "The Little White House, Warm Springs, Georgia" (M.O.D.).

69 **At about one-thirty, shortly before his lunch:** Various sources, including Morgan, p. 763.

69 **"Here's where I make a law":** Ibid.

70 **At the moment Franklin Roosevelt lay dying:** Entire story drawn from "Notes on Georgia Warm Springs Foundation," pp. 30–31, recollections of Mrs. Mabel Irwin (M.O.D.).

72 **"Flu Preventive Developed Here by Francis and Salk":** *Ann Arbor News*, 3/31/44.

72 **"Influenza Vaccine Developed at U-M":** *Detroit Free Press*, 4/1/44.

72 **the report that appeared in the esteemed pages of the *Journal*:** Francis and Salk, "A Clinical Evaluation of Vaccine Against Influenza," *Journal of the American Medical Association*, 4/1/44.

72 **"Just wondering if you saw this":** Author interview with D.S.

73 **He visited Buckley and Lowry fields:** Various sources, including Minutes

of the Meeting of Commission on Influenza, Rockefeller Institute, 6/21/45; Francis, Report of Commission on Influenza, May 1945–April 1946; memo, Salk to Brigadier General S. Bayne-Jones, 6/45; memo, Salk to Bayne-Jones, 1/21/46; Francis, Report of Commission on Influenza.

73 **"Every case of disease poses several questions":** Salk, handwritten class notes, 7/1/46, Box 287, Folder 9, in UCSD collection.

74 **the modest farmhouse in the Michigan wild:** Author conversations with sons.

74 **"That's a closet?":** Author interviews with S.S. and H.G.

74 **Two weeks before the baby was due:** Author interview with D.S.

74 **making him plate after plate:** Author interview with P.S.

75 **In May 1947, just such an opportunity:** Letters, Salk to Malcolm Merrill of the California Department of Public Health, 5/23/47; Walter Schlesinger to Salk, 6/12/47.

75 **For several years, the University of Pittsburgh:** Exchange of eleven letters between Salk and Lauffer, from 5/27/47 to 7/21/47.

76 **"Dear Dr. Salk," wrote Max Lauffer:** Lauffer to Salk, 5/27/47.

76 **Salk could see why he'd loathed:** Author interview with D.S.

77 **the job would come with a salary of $7,500:** Letter, Salk to Lauffer, 6/27/47.

77 **"I think I fell in love with the place":** Various sources, including author interviews wirh D.S.; Carter, p. 53.

77 **On a hot morning at the beginning of August:** Letter, Salk to W. C. Price, 8/7/47.

CHAPTER FIVE

78 **Cutting hay on a murderously hot day:** Author interview with James Sarkett.

79 **At some point within the last two weeks:** Bruno, pp. 20–37.

80 **That was what was happening in the body:** Author interview with Sarkett.

81 **The epidemiological lottery of 1947:** International Polio Network, "Incidence Rates of Poliomyelitis in USA."

81 **In 1946, a staggering 25,698 Americans:** Ibid.

82 **The new woman's name was Elaine Whitelaw:** Oral history, interview with Elaine Whitelaw conducted 6/8/84 (M.O.D.).

85 **With the help of Whitelaw and public affairs director:** Ibid.

85 **In 1947, foundation revenues soared:** NFIP, Tenth Annual Report, Period Ending 12/31/47 (M.O.D.).

85 **"The public can't see you only":** Oral history, interview with Dorothy Ducas, conducted 3/26/84 (M.O.D.).

CHAPTER SIX

86 **Deep in the autumn of 1947:** Letter from Salk to Stella Barlow, 11/10/47.

86 **"I am not too surprised to learn":** Barlow to Salk, 11/20/47.

87 **The couple compromised:** Letter from Salk to Walter M. Mack, 8/26/47; author interviews with sons.

87 **things were far less pleasant on the morning of October 1:** Letter from Salk to Dionys Blaskovic, 10/17/47.

88 **"Subject or subjects of investigation":** Salk, principal investigator's memo.

88 **The officers in the army's medical division:** Memo, Salk to McEllroy, 12/9/47; Salk letter to Lauffer, 8/28/47.

89 **There were a lot of ways:** Memo, Salk to McEllroy, 12/9/47.

89 **But polio turned at least some:** Various sources including Bruno, p. 41; Gould, pp. 26–27; Smith, pp. 35–36.

89 **David Bodian of Johns Hopkins University:** Various sources, including Bruno, p. 72.

90 **Salk . . . had selected several possible roads:** Memo, Salk to McEllroy, 12/9/47.

91 **he turned his attention to the business of hiring:** Salk, principal investigator's memo.

91 **"Dear Dr. Lauffer," he wrote:** Salk to Lauffer, 11/5/47.

92 **"I've become a bureaucrat":** Author conversations with sons: letter, Salk to Joseph Baird, 11/22/47.

92 **Finally, not long before the holidays:** Salk, Academy of Achievement interview, conducted 5/16/91.

92 **Weaver had been chosen:** Various sources, including Carter, p. 56; Smith, pp. 11–14.

94 **The foundation, he explained, was looking:** Salk, Academy of Achievement interview, conducted 5/16/91, File 2, p. 3.

94 **It was the kind of slow, repetitive:** Memo, undated, "The Objectives of the Program for the Differentiation of the Immunological Types of the Virus Poliomyelitis . . ."

95 **Salk learned that his opportunity:** Letter, Weaver to Salk, 12/15/47; Salk response, 12/18/47.

96 **The Washington meeting had been planned:** Letter, Weaver to Francis, 11/7/47.

97 **Seated a few places away:** NFIP revised list of conference participants, January 7–8, 1948 (M.O.D.).

97 **Barely eight years Salk's senior:** Various sources: Throughout Carter, McPherson, Gould, Smith. Author interviews with sons.

99 **"Gentlemen," Weaver said:** NFIP Transcript of conference, p. 2 (M.O.D.).

99 **The three types of poliovirus were very different:** Various sources, including Bruno, pp. 279–81; and author interviews with D.S.

100 **Before a virus sample's type was known:** "Immunologic Classification of Poliomyelitis Viruses," *American Journal of Hygiene,* 6/4/51; Salk memo, undated, "The Objectives of the Program for the Differentiation of the Imunological Types of the Virus Poliomyelitis . . ."; author interview with D.S.

101 **At its most basic, typing a virus :** Memo, undated, "The Objectives of the Program for the Differentiation of the Immunological Types of the Virus Poliomyelitis . . ."; author interview with D.S.

101 **Shortly after the discussions got under way:** NFIP transcript of conference, pp. 91–97 (M.O.D.).

103 **"Your premise is that you'll infect the animal":** NFIP transcript of conference, pp. 134–39 (M.O.D.).

103 **But what Dr. Turner meant:** Author interview with D.S.; memo, Salk to Weaver, 12/1/48.

105 **Salk received his minutes in the mail:** Letter, Salk to T. E. Boyd, 1/31/48.

CHAPTER SEVEN

106 **There was no real reason for John Enders:** Author interview with Frederick Robbins.

107 **set about pursuing a Ph.D. in philology:** *The Harvard University Gazette,* "John Enders' Breakthrough Led to Polio Vaccine," by Alvin Powell, 10/8/98.

107 **"I mouth the strange syllables":** *Boston Globe,* "Nobel Recipient John Enders, 88, Virus Work Led to Polio Vaccine," by Edgar J. Driscoll, 9/10/85.

107 **The research Enders was doing:** Author interview with Robbins.

108 **Even coming from a greenhorn researcher:** Ibid.

109 **Enders, who had no reason:** Ibid.

110 **Sabin and Olitsky had been wrong:** Ibid.

CHAPTER EIGHT

111 **The monkeys easily outnumbered:** Author interview with Don Wegemer; memo, Salk to Weaver, 8/24/48.

112 **The coveted morgue was now wholly Salk's:** Author interview with Wegemer.

112 **"Dear Dr. McEllroy," he wrote:** Letter, Salk to McEllroy, 8/23/48.

112 **"What are you doing?":** Donna Salk interview, Seavey, Smith, Wagner, p. 200; conversations with sons.

113 **The most important if least scientific:** Author interview with D.S.

114 **One of Salk's earliest . . . recruits was Byron Bennett:** Author interview with Wegemer.

114 **Also joining Salk's inner circle:** Author interview with Wegemer; Youngner recruitment letter, Salk to Harry Eagle, 7/2/48.

115 **Most of the monkeys that would live:** Letter, Salk to Lauffer, 12/11/47; memo, Weaver to all NFIP grantees, 3/31/48.

116 **That work would be unpleasant:** Undated Salk memo, "Standard Technique for Virus Preparation and Titration: Intracerebral Inoculation"; additional lab memo, 3/30/49.

116 **Salk had developed his own system:** Salk lab memo, 9/13/49.

116 **There was, Salk knew:** Author interview with Wegemer.

117 **The mix came in 25-pound bags:** Letter, Weaver to Salk, 4/29/49.

117 **in Salk's lab the extra calories would not be provided:** Letter, secretary of Paul Bodian to Salk, 9/1/48; lab memo, 3/15/52.

117 **Troan was an inexhaustible science reporter:** Troan, pp. 12, 61, 146; author interview with Troan.

119 **He made himself an indefatigable presence:** Author interviews with Troan.

119 **Troan was pointed to a fair number:** Troan, p. 178.

120 **The answer . . . was something known as an adjuvant:** Troan, p. 180; author interviews with Troan; author interviews with D.S.

121 **Salk, as luck would have it, was traveling:** Troan, p. 178; author interviews with Troan.

121 **Most nights, the lights of the lab:** Author conversations with sons.

123 **With extraneous administrative matters off his mind:** Letter, Weaver to Salk, 3/11/49.

123 **"I am attaching hereto a list":** Letter, Weaver to Salk, 9/2/49.

123 **In Salk's lab, more than 1,800 animals:** Letter, Salk to Weaver, 8/16/49; Carter, p. 73.

123 **Isabel Morgan, whom Salk had met at the typing meeting:** Various sources, including Carter, p. 85; Smith, p. 129.

125 **"If you could arrange for us to get":** Letter, Salk to Weaver, 9/7/49.

125 **"This is in response to your kind letter of September 7":** Weaver to Salk, 9/12/49.

125 **"Dear Dr. Enders," he wrote:** Salk to Enders, 9/17/49.

126 **Hamlin wrote back promptly:** Hamlin Insurance to Salk, 9/28/49.

CHAPTER NINE

127 **It took more than 250 miles:** Author interview with William Kirkpatrick.

CHAPTER TEN

130 **addressing a group of fretful parents:** *Pittsburgh Post-Gazette,* "War on Polio Is Gaining," 6/7/50.

130 **In 1948 . . . 27,726 American children:** International Polio Network: "Incidence Rates of Poliomyelitis in the USA."

130 **In 1949, that already alarming toll:** Ibid.

130 **filling every seat in Chicago's Wrigley Field:** *World Almanac and Book of Facts,* 1999 edition, p. 951.

131 **the clumsy hunks of rotating hardware:** Author interview with D.S.; photos of lab.

131 **expected they'd cost at least $7,500:** Letters, Weaver to Salk and Salk to Weaver, 4/7/50; Carter, p. 95; Smith, pp. 127–28.

132 **Rivers was born in Jonesboro, Georgia:** Thomas M. Rivers papers, American Philosophical Society, Philadelphia.

133 **he remembered him both for his brains and his religion:** Carter, p. 42.

134 **"Dear Dr. Weaver," he typed:** Letter, Salk to Weaver, 6/16/50.

135 **Weaver answered Salk's eight-page manifesto:** Letter, Weaver to Salk, 6/22/50.

136 **It was with that easy combination:** *Pittsburgh Post-Gazette,* "War on Polio Is Gaining," 6/7/50.

137 **33,300 American children were struck:** International Polio Network, "Incidence Rates of Poliomyelitis in the USA."

137 **nearly four times the battlefield deaths:** *World Almanac and Book of Facts,* 1999 edition, p. 166.

137 **A disturbing and disproportionate 134:** Cases of Poliomyelitis Hospitalized in Pittsburgh by County of Residence, 9/16/50.

137 **When John Troan first started:** Author interview with John Troan.

140 **Most researchers studying the trio of polioviruses:** Various sources, including Bruno, pp. 279–80; and Gould, pp. 160–61.

141 **John Kolmer's discredited vaccine relied:** Various sources, including *New York Times,* "Flexner Rejects Paralysis Vaccine," 11/1/35.

141 **Deep in a memo to Byron Bennett and Jim Lewis:** Undated memo to Bennett and Lewis.

142 **when the NFIP's Committee on Immunization met at the Hotel Commodore:** Proceedings of the Committee on Immunization transcript, 5/17/51.

142 **There were twenty other members of the panel:** Ibid., list of attendees

142 **with the far less permanent tactic of passive immunity:** Various sources, including author interviews with D.S.; Gould, pp. 22, 130–31.

143 **during the . . . epidemic of 1916, panicky New Yorkers:** *New York Times,* "Find Hope for Cure in Paralysis Serum," 8/1/16.

143 **"I think we are all agreed that gamma globulin contains":** Proceedings of the Committee on Immunization transcript, 5/17/51, pp. 19–48.

145 **The people of Utah County:** Subsequent meeting, Proceedings of the Committee on Immunization transcript, 12/4/51, pp. 5–13 principally.

CHAPTER ELEVEN

148 **In the same hot week . . . William Hammon was traveling:** Second International Poliomyelitis Conference, formal agenda, September 1951.

148 **The cabin-for-one would set the NFIP back:** Letters, Thos. Cook & Sons to Salk, 4/12, 4/16, and 4/17, 1951.

148 **Salk's trip home:** Ibid.

149 **he'd been chosen to present the findings:** Immunological Classification of Poliomyelitis Viruses, text, Second International Poliomyelitis Conference, formal agenda, September 1951.

149 **Of all the samples tested:** Ibid., p. 11.

150 **"I note your continued enthusiasm":** Letter, Salk to Sabin, 3/1/51.

151 **fired back a four-line response:** Letter, Sabin to Salk, 3/3/51.

151 **"Dear Albert," he wrote in response:** Letter, Salk to Sabin, 3/7/51.

151 **"It is a pleasure to read":** Letter, Sabin to Salk, 6/20/51.

151 **"Your suggestion with regard to the wording":** Letter, Salk to Sabin, 6/27/51.

151 **Salk's presentation took place early:** Second International Poliomyelitis Conference, formal agenda, pp. 12–13.

152 **Bettyann had been struck by her own case of polio:** Various sources, including Seavey, Smith, and Wagner, p. 168.

152 **In 1950, the plague had hit especially hard:** Lincolnshire Post-Polio Library, online.

152 **"Daddy," she said in a telephone call:** Various sources, including Seavey, Smith, and Wagner, p. 168.

153 **During mealtimes, he found that one of the best:** Various sources, including Carter, pp. 113–14; Smith, pp. 170, 172, 372; author interviews with D.S.

153 **Salk told her that that was evident:** Author interviews with D.S.

154 **Bill Kirkpatrick was getting to know a . . . redheaded girl:** Author interview with Bill Kirkpatrick; author interview with John Troan; Troan, p. 194.

157 **This Commodore Hotel meeting would be attended:** Proceedings on the Committee on Immunization, 12/4/51, attendees page.

157 **"With your permission," he said:** Ibid., p. 1.

158 **"I think we will all have to admit":** Ibid., p. 3.

158 **"The situation of formalinized vaccine":** Ibid., p. 33.

159 **Under the new rules, scientists would be required:** Wikipedia, Nuremberg Code, online.

159 **"I think," said Norman Topping:** Proceedings on the Committee on Immunization, 12/4/51, p. 41.

CHAPTER TWELVE

160 **At least fifty technicians and scientists:** Author interview with Don Wegemer.

160 **In addition to the Salks, the Dize family:** Author conversations with sons.

161 **The NFIP's 1952 grant to the Pittsburgh Virus Lab:** Letter, Salk to university news service director, 1/7/52.

162 **Developing a killed vaccine would not be a linear process:** Author interview with D.S.

162 **After a monkey was sedated and killed:** Troan, pp. 185–89.

162 **a rich goo of nutrients known as Medium 199:** Author interview with D.S.; numerous letters, including Salk to Connaught, 1/10/52.

163 **Viruses in solution tend to clump:** Various published papers, particularly, D. and S. Salk, "Vaccinology of Poliomyelitis," *Vaccine,* 3/84; J. Salk, "Studies in Human Subjects on Active Immunization Against Poliomyelitis," *Journal of the American Medical Association,* 3/28/53; and J. and D. Salk, "Control of Influenza and Poliomyelitis with Killed Virus Vaccines," *Science,* 3/4/77.

164 **it was still necessary to test:** Ibid.

164 **But performing the actual injection took some practice.:** Author interview with D.S.

165 **"How's that culture look to you?":** Author interview with Wegemer.

166 **"Assignments for the Week":** Undated memo, Salk to staff.

166 **cigarette smoke—courtesy of a new habit:** Author interview with Wegemer.

167 **"What Dr. Salk and his associates are primarily":** NFIP press release, 1/2/52.

167 **pointedly scratched out the word "primarily":** Ibid.

167 **To the unacquainted eye, the Polk State School:** Services and New Admissions Procedures at Polk School, 4/25/52.

167 **the state of Pennsylvania loosely called mental defectives:** Written opinion of H. J. Woodward, Deputy Attorney General of Pa., 8/10/44.

169 **"We regard what we are doing":** January draft of letter, Salk to Polk.

169 **there had been a frightening flurry of cases:** Letter, Gale Walker, Polk superintendent, to Pa. secretary of welfare, 1/29/52.

169 **send out a feeler to the state's attorney general:** Ibid.

169　**The Watson Home had been in operation:** Times/Beaver Newspapers, "A Legacy of Caring," by Patti Conley, 8/24/98; author interview with Betty Gundelfinger, former Watson nurse.

170　**What Salk envisioned doing:** Various sources, including Troan, p. 196.

171　**Salk thus began another round:** Letter, Salk to Jessie Wright, superintendent of Watson Home, 3/14/52.

171　**Wright was celebrated in the field:** Various sources, including Gould, p. 197.

171　**even going so far as to send back a list of fifty-two:** Letter, Wright to Salk, 3/6/52.

171　**The insurers wrote back promptly:** Letter, Medical Protective Company to Salk, 6/4/52.

172　**that was before the sheriffs from upstate New York:** Author interview with Wegemer.

172　**There was the housewife from Toronto, Ohio:** Letter, M. Robinette to Salk, January 1951.

172　**There was the far more poignant plea:** Letter, T. Shimrock to Salk, 4/30/51.

173　**It was early in the morning when the lawman:** Author interview with Wegemer.

174　**They found the proper thermometer setting:** Various sources and papers, particularly D. and S. Salk, "Vaccinology of Poliomyelitis," *Vaccine,* vol. 2, 3/84; J. and D. Salk, "Control of Influenza and Poliomyelitis with Killed Virus Vaccines," *Science,* vol. 195, pp. 834–37, 3/4/77.

174　**Salk developed a logarithm:** Ibid.

174　**As it happened, the state's attorney general:** Letter, Pa. commissioner of public health to Walker, 3/18/52.

175　**Ultimately the parents of 47 Polk . . . and 40 Watson patients:** Letter, Salk to Walker, 10/14/52; letter, Wright to Salk, 3/6/52.

176　**Salk set out for the eighty-mile drive:** Various sources, including Smith, p. 139.

176　**the uncounted parties that were routinely held:** *News-Letter,* Polk State School, September 1952.

176　**the so-called no-productive patients:** Ibid.

176　**She fell quiet at the sight of the near-adults:** Various sources, including conversations with sons; Carter, p. 137.

177 **Salk pressed gently ahead:** Ibid.

177 **"If this were all there was to the job":** Ibid.

178 **Salk and the nurses arrived:** Various sources, including author interview with Bill Kirkpatrick.

180 **On July 2, he would return:** Smith, p. 141.

CHAPTER THIRTEEN

181 **Troan published . . . "Where Do We Stand on Polio?":** Troan, *Pittsburgh Press,* 6/8/52.

182 **Bill Jacobs, the paper's assistant city editor:** Interview with Troan.

CHAPTER FOURTEEN

184 **Half past seven in the morning was the time:** Author interviews with Don Wegemer and D.S.

185 **In the summer of 1952, Ward's station:** Ibid.

185 **viral researchers had to make their determination:** Ibid.

185 **Healthy cells . . . would have a characteristic plumpness:** Ibid.

185 **The color of the tubes would be an even more direct signal:** Ibid.

186 **Just recently, Salk had gotten around:** Ibid.

186 **One morning in mid-September, Elsie Ward:** Ibid.

187 **Salk didn't begin his workday:** Ibid.

189 **The paralysis season began in early June:** NFIP booklet, *1952: The Worst Polio Year of All Time.*

189 **The summer of 1951 had been the third-worst:** International Polio Network, "Incidence Rates of Poliomyelitis in USA."

189 **The 1952 season more than doubled:** Ibid.

190 **Attendance at Forbes dropped:** Various sources, including Marc Selvaggio, "The Making of Jonas Salk," *Pittsburgh Magazine,* June 1984; *The Baseball Encyclopedia,* ninth edition, 1993.

190 **pulling in a staggering $28 million:** NFIP booklet *1952: The Worst Polio Year of All Time.*

190 **Inevitably, he'd have one or two small scraps:** Author interview with D.S.

191 **Salk's sample group . . . had grown to 161:** Numerous sources, including memo, "Sera to be tested from patients in Watson Home Experiments," 9/18/52; letter, Salk to Walker, 10/14/52; letter, Salk to University of Pittsburgh bursar for expenses reimbursement, 11/18/52; Troan, p. 197.

191   **The hotel was a palatial building:** Author visit to Hotel Hershey.

192   **with an endowment of $255,472:** Letter, Salk to Campbell Moses, 3/7/53.

192   **"How are things going?":** Author interview with Troan.

192   **Sabin had been on the road:** Carter, p. 142.

192   **on the eleven A.M. train from Pittsburgh to Harrisburg:** Correspondence between Lorraine Friedman and Hotel Hershey, Jan. 2 and 5, 1953; correspondence between Salk and Sabin, 1/8/53 and 1/12/53.

192   **But he also had questions:** J.S. oral history interview, p. 12, conducted 9/8/84 (M.O.D.).

194   **Tommy Turner of Johns Hopkins rose:** Carter, p. 145.

194   **"When are you going to do your Provo test?":** Ibid.

194   **He responded by declaring the card:** Ibid.

195   **In 1953, the board was made up of thirty-eight:** NFIP Annual Report, 1953, pp. 86–87 (M.O.D.).

195   **to convene the trustees' meeting as early as January 26:** Text of Weaver's address to trustees, p. 1.

196   **"I am very conscious that it is impossible":** Ibid.

197   **The Lilly Pharmaceutical company wrote:** Letter, Eli Lilly company to Salk, 2/9/53.

197   **"My feeling," said Thomas Rivers:** All quotations here from transcript of 2/26/53 meeting.

198   **"Studies in Human Subjects on Active Immunization Against Poliomyelitis":** Salk, *Journal of the American Medical Association,* 3/28/53, pp. 1081–98.

198   **under the starry-eyed title:** *Cincinnati Post,* "What It Means to Be an Ohioan," by David Wecker, 1/2/03.

199   **"No," Howe said, "that's not me":** Academy of Achievement interview with Salk, 5/16/91, File 3, p. 3.

199   **"NEW POLIO VACCINE!":** Various sources, including Smith, p. 186.

199   **"This is a huge embarrassment":** Author interview with D.S.

200   **"The Scientist Speaks for Himself!":** Transcript, "The Scientist Speaks for Himself," 3/26/53.

202   **John Troan . . . phoned Salk's home:** Author interview with Troan.

202   **"John," Donna said with a laugh:** Ibid.

CHAPTER FIFTEEN

203 **No matter what Darrell Salk said:** Author interview with sons.

CHAPTER SIXTEEN

207 **But 1953 . . . started out even worse than 1952:** NFIP, state-by-state incidence rates, 5/30/53 to 9/13/53.

208 **The NFIP . . . now found itself ginning up:** Elaine Whitelaw oral history, conducted 6/8/84, p. 34 (M.O.D.).

209 **Miller was a wealthy marketer:** *New Republic,* "Vitamins and Racism," 9/12/55, pp. 4–5.

209 **"When a child's bloodstream is polluted":** Ibid.

210 **"The article in the Miami Daily News":** Letter, Duon Miller to Salk, 3/27/53.

210 **a group that included Morris Bealle:** *New Republic,* "Vitamins and Racism."

210 **"I'm going to answer this man":** Author conversations with sons.

210 **"I am sure that your objective":** Letter, Salk to Miller, 4/4/53.

211 **"I am the mother of 13 children":** Letter, M. L. Novelli to Salk, 5/4/53.

211 **"It is extremely difficult to have to say":** Letter, Salk to Novelli, 5/18/53.

211 **circulating a twelve-page fact sheet:** Memo, O'Connor to chapter chairmen, 5/14/53.

212 **Of all the firms, it was Parke, Davis:** Carter, p. 164.

212 **"Parke, Davis has been working jointly":** Press release, Thoburn Wiant and Thorn Kuhl, Bureau of Industrial Services, Inc.

212 **"Dr. Salk works for Parke, Davis":** Unnamed Detroit newspaper, 3/27/53; transcribed clipping in Box 130, Folder 4, of UCSD collection.

212 **"Parke, Davis announced that there is":** Wire service story picked up by *Sun-Telegraph,* Box 130, Folder 4.

212 **Salk fired off a telegram to the company president:** Salk to H. J. Lloyd, 3/27/53.

212 **apologizing for what he called a "gross misunderstanding.":** Lloyd response to Salk, date not legible.

213 **Peter, Darrell, and Jonathan Salk could not be certain:** Author conversation with sons.

215 **Both Gale Walker and Jessie Wright of the Polk and Watson homes:** Letter, Gale Walker to Polk parents, 4/25/53.

215 **volunteers at the Industrial Home for Crippled Children:** Letters, Salk to Edouard de May, superintendent of Industrial Home, 6/25/53 and 6/30/53; de May to Salk, 6/22/53.

215 **Sewickley enrolled children from kindergarten through twelfth grade:** Salk to Clifford Nichols, Sewickley headmaster, 10/28/53; Nichols to Salk, 11/3/53; Sewickley website, www.sewickley.org.

215 **Percival Bazeley took the lead:** Author interview with Don Wegemer.

216 **the difference between the aqueous formulation:** J. Salk, "Use of Adjuvants in Studies on Influenza Immunization," *Journal of the American Medical Association,* 4/4/53, pp. 1169–75.

216 **developed a sort of immunological memory:** Author interview with D.S.

216 **The paraffin adjuvants used at the beginning of the century:** J. Salk and D. Salk, "Control of Influenza and Poliomyelitis with Killed Virus Vaccines," *Science,* pp. 834–47, 3/4/77; *JAMA,* 4/4/53.

217 **mineral oils supplied . . . by the Standard Oil Company:** *JAMA,* 4/4/53.

217 **Sabin wrote him a letter decorously damning it:** Letter, Sabin to Salk, 3/24/53.

218 **Sabin wasn't through, however:** Author interview with Troan.

218 **John Troan attended the meeting:** Ibid.

220 **Weaver nonetheless set about drafting a memo:** Weaver memo, undated, Box 125, Folder 1, of UCSD collection.

221 **announced the formation of a new executive panel:** Various sources, including Gould, p. 139; Carter, pp. 175–76.

221 **he'd once again have to call on Basil O'Connor:** Author interview with D.S.; Carter, pp. 170–74.

222 **"Mass Field Test Slated for Polio Vaccine":** *Pittsburgh Press,* 7/14/53.

223 **He fired Harry Weaver:** Various sources, including Gould, p. 139; Carter, pp. 181–82.

223 **"Either he goes or I go":** Ibid.

223 **"It is with considerable regret":** Letter, Weaver to Salk, 9/1/53.

CHAPTER SEVENTEEN

226 **The committee thus decided that hearings:** Excerpts from Congressional hearing transcript, sent by committee clerk to Salk, 11/20/53.

226 **The congressmen would instead:** Ibid.

226 **The culturing and inactivating experiments:** Author interview with Wegemer.

227 **One of Jim Lewis's cynomolgus monkeys:** Ibid.

227 **a lovely, almost grand house:** Author interview with P.S.

227 **the seven-minute commute from the new home:** Letter, Salk to Sabin, 12/3/53.

228 **"I have noticed that Dr. Salk has been modest":** Hearing transcript excerpts, pp. 775–79, 849–50.

229 **"I had a call from Bill Jacobs today":** Author interview with Troan.

231 **"I am instructing every member of the staff":** NFIP memo to division heads and field staff, 11/18/53.

231 **an arranged marriage between Parke, Davis and the virus lab:** Carter, pp. 184–85.

232 **arranged for a visit by Parke, Davis representatives:** Letter, NFIP to Parke, Davis, 9/23/53.

232 **The Detroit operation was . . . huge and unwieldy:** Letter, Thomas Weller to Foard McGinnes, 1/18/54.

233 **the first 30-liter batch . . . was not even remotely ready:** Various sources including letters, Joseph A. Bell to Parke, Davis, 9/23/53; Salk to Van Riper, 10/16/53; Salk to O'Connor, 12/1/53; H. J. Lloyd to O'Connor, 12/17/53.

233 **It was a question of scientific ideology:** Author conversations with D.S. and J.S.

235 **O'Connor scheduled a meeting for November 11:** Various sources, including memo, NFIP to drug companies, 11/4/53; letter, NFIP to Salk, 11/4/53.

236 **According to Salk's data, it would take 10 days:** NFIP, minutes of 11/11/53 meeting.

236 **O'Connor . . . posed a question:** Carter, p. 198.

237 **scheduling one more meeting for . . . November 13:** NFIP minutes, Vaccine Advisory Committee, 11/13/53 (M.O.D.).

237 **The debate over the aqueous and oily formulations:** Partial NFIP transcript of 11/13/53 meeting, p. 17 (M.O.D.).

237 **the committee also settled the double-blind matter:** 1955 March of Dimes fact sheet on polio field trial (M.O.D.).

238 **A small pilot trial would be scheduled:** Minutes of 11/13/53 meeting (M.O.D.).

238 **"Basil just wants to make sure":** Author interview with Troan.

CHAPTER EIGHTEEN

239 **The 35,592 cases of infantile paralysis:** International Polio Network, "Incidence Rates of Poliomyelitis in USA."

240 **From April 17 through November 24, 1953, fully 391:** Letter, T. S. Danowski, acting medical director, to Salk, 12/5/53.

240 **Salk took pains to avoid . . . the word "volunteer":** *Time* magazine, "Polio Pioneers," 4/26/54, p. 53.

240 **"We're providing a good thing":** Author conversations with sons.

241 **What was needed was Tommy Francis:** Various sources, including Gould, pp. 139–40; Smith, pp. 225–29; Carter, pp. 202–6.

244 **Salk received an envelope:** Letter, Francis to Salk, 2/5/54.

244 **Jonas had had to travel:** Author conversations with sons.

245 **On those occasions when the Salks socialized:** Ibid.

246 **tore a sheet of paper from a hotel memo pad:** Page from St. Moritz memo pad and accompanying page of notes, Box 95, Folder 6, in UCSD collection.

246 **Helen Press—now Helen Glickstein:** Author interview with D.S.

246 **he found yet another letter . . . from Gale Walker:** Letter, Walker to Salk, 6/7/54.

246 **"Please send him whatever he needs":** Memo, Salk to Lorraine Friedman, 6/11/54.

247 **virus grown in 2½-gallon culture bottles:** *National Foundation News,* April 1954 edition; *Time* magazine, "Closing in on Polio," 3/29/54, p. 56.

247 **perhaps no more than a 1-in-20,000 dilution:** Salk, "Specifications and Minimum Requirements for an Experimental Poliomyelitis Vaccine (Aqueous)," 11/25/53, p. 8.

248 **Cutter Laboratories . . . seemed to be struggling:** Letters, Cutter to Salk, 11/23/53, 12/4/53, 12/11/53, 3/12/54, 4/20/54; Salk to Cutter, 12/4/53.

248 **the staffers in the NFIP headquarters:** NFIP fact sheet for 1955, "The Polio Vaccine Field Trials" (M.O.D.).

250 **In early January, he called the press:** NFIP draft of press release, 1/15/54.

250 "We're shifting from production in a teacup": Ibid.

250 Lawyers from both the University of Pittsburgh: Draft copy of waiver letter, Salk to NFIP, 1/22/54; author interviews with Troan.

251 One morning in early February 1954: Author interview with Troan.

252 The poisonous letters continued to stream: Letters, Miller to Salk, 12/8/53, 3/23/54.

253 what they now universally referred to: Author interview with Troan; Troan, p. 213.

253 And when the prestigous journal *Modern Medicine:* Letters, Mark Parker, executive editor of *Modern Medicine* magazine, to Salk, 11/27/53 and 12/1/53.

254 gift shop and candy stand: Author interview with Wegemer.

255 The magazine, which preferred portraits: *Time* magazine, 3/29/54.

255 Salk said as little as he could: Author interview with Wegemer.

256 received their shots at Pittsburgh's Arsenal Elementary School: Associated Press article, "Pittsburgh Children Given First Polio Vaccine Shots," Box 94, Folder 2, in UCSD collection.

256 Salk arrived at the school early: Author interview with Troan.

256 the first class of thirty children: Ibid.

CHAPTER NINETEEN

258 Monkey number 484 in the Eli Lilly: Letter from Lilly Research Laboratories to Salk, 2/24/54

259 as were still others at the Parke, Davis lab: Carter, p. 221.

259 he was in New Orleans, addressing: Ibid., p. 219.

259 Just a few weeks before, *Life: Life* magazine, "Tracking the Killer," by Robert Coughlan, 2/22/54.

260 "I felt certain": Carter, p. 219.

260 The details of the letter: Gould, p. 140; Carter, p. 221.

261 In addition to all the polio work: Gould, p. 140.

261 Salk, McGinnes, and Bodian met with: Gould, p. 140; Carter, p. 220; Smith, p. 253.

262 At least 350 would have to be injected: Ibid.

263 "As far as I'm concerned,": Carter, p. 224.

263 Three days later, a more practical agreement: Gould, p. 140; Carter, p. 220; Smith, p. 253.

264 **"Good evening, Mr. and Mrs. America":** Various sources, including *New York Daily Mirror* typescript, 4/5/54.

265 **"Any product that contains live poliovirus":** Carter, p. 232.

265 **"There is no possibility that live virus":** Ibid.

266 **"There have been some difficulties":** Associated Press typescript, 4/5/54.

266 **Minnesota announced that it was considering:** Carter, pp. 232–33.

266 **"There is absolutely nothing":** Typescript, Associated Press story, 4/4/54.

266 **"The field trial was always premature":** Wire service typescript, 4/5/54; Troan, p. 218.

266 **"We will go on despite advice":** Various sources, including Troan, p. 217.

267 **adding the detail that thousands of white coffins:** Smith, pp. 257–58.

268 **Bill Kirkpatrick sat down:** Author interview with Kirkpatrick.

269 **Their conclusions would be passed on:** Draft press release of Vaccine Advisory Committee meeting, 4/22/54.

269 **there was another problem with the syringes:** Letter, Fred Stimpert to Foard McGinnes, 4/7/54.

269 **There was also the touchier matter:** Letter, Hart Van Riper to Salk, 4/23/54.

270 **O'Connor called the men to their seats:** Various sources, including Carter, pp. 233–37; Gould, pp. 146–47; Smith, pp. 258–60; McPherson, p. 75.

274 **O'Connor solemnly produced:** Recommendations of Vaccine Advisory Committee and Statement of U.S. Public Health Service, 4/25/54.

274 **The next night at 10:45:** Typescript, WCBS Radio, 4/26/54.

CHAPTER TWENTY

275 **The reporters' favorite was Randy Kerr:** Various sources, including Black, p. 222; Troan, p. 218.

275 **She was Precious Balentine:** Clip from unidentified Kokomo, Indiana, newspaper, 4/29/54, Box, 95, Folder 1, in UCSD collection.

276 **the first official Pioneer:** *New York Times*, "14,233 Injected Here in Polio Test," by Robert K. Plumb, 4/28/54.

276 **14,000 field-trial kits had already been shipped:** Oral history, Elaine Whitelaw, interview conducted 6/8/85, p. 19 (M.O.D.).

277 **In Lexington, Kentucky, Elaine Whitelaw:** Ibid., p. 20.

277 **"Sister," Whitelaw asked:** Ibid., p. 22.

278 **he was growing increasingly dissatisfied:** Details on Merthiolate contamination available in numerous documents including: Exchanges between Foard McGinnes and Pitman-Moore, 10/5/54, 10/27/54, and 10/29/54; Salk to Workman, 10/9/54; Roderick Murray, Public Health Service, to Salk, 10/13/54; NFIP memo, 11/1/54; O'Connor to Foard McGinnes, talking points for NFIP meeting, 11/17/54.

278 **if the chemical didn't find any of the bacteria:** Ibid.

279 **even in concentrations as low as 1 in 20,000:** Ibid.

279 **Salk wrote Foard McGinnes:** Letter, Salk to McGinnes, 9/30/54.

280 **"Recognizing that the vaccine you are producing":** Form letter, McGinnes to six drug companies, 9/13/54.

280 **"Quite frankly," wrote a lab chief:** Letter, Pitman-Moore to McGinnes, 10/5/54.

280 **"Data from these experiments":** Telegram, Salk to O'Connor, 11/8/54.

280 **Like the first two conferences:** Third International Poliomyelitis Conference program, Sept. 6–10, 1954.

281 **address about the comparative virtues:** Third International Poliomyelitis Conference press release, 9/8/54.

281 **"In our early research":** Carter, pp. 247–49.

283 **144 million shards of data:** Basil O'Connor address to National Conference of Organizations, 9/12/55, p. 5 (M.O.D. collection).

283 **It would be a while, however:** Ibid.

284 **Finally, O'Connor decided on Rackham Lecture Hall:** Ibid., p. 8.

285 **"Do any of you know the significance":** Carter, p. 266.

286 **"John," Stegen would answer helplessly:** Author interview with Troan.

287 **"The Salk polio vaccine will be released":** *Pittsburgh Press,* "Salk's Polio Vaccine Ready for Public Use," 4/3/55 by John Troan; also, various Associated Press pickups, 4/2/55.

287 **"The National Foundation for Infantile Paralysis":** Formal invitation to Ann Arbor conference (M.O.D.).

287 **Fifty-four thousand physicians around the country:** Various sources, including "54,000 Physicians See Digest on TV," *New York Times,* 4/13/55; "Polio Vaccine Gets Go-Ahead," clip from unidentified magazine, Box 135, Folder 5, in UCSD collection.

288 **He instead selected eleven senior staffers:** Letter from Salk to NFIP, 3/21/55.

288 **Salk also wanted Donna and the boys:** Author conversations with sons.

288 **an eight-foot-long platform:** *New York Times,* "Salk Polio Vaccine Proves Success," 4/13/55.

288 **kept in a holding room three floors above:** Author interview with Troan.

289 **Lou Graff, the University of Michigan's public affairs officer:** Smith, pp. 311–12.

289 **"You ready for the story?":** Author interview with Troan; Troan, pp. 221–22.

290 **The Salk family and Basil O'Connor:** O'Connor schedule for April 11 and 12, 1955 (M.O.D.); author conversations with sons.

291 **lectern with . . . University of Michigan banner:** *New York Times,* "Fanfare Ushers Verdict on Tests," 4/13/55.

291 **Place cards positioned:** Hand-drawn diagram, Platform Party Seating Arrangement (M.O.D.).

292 **For all the preparation that had gone:** J.S. oral history, 9/8/84, p. 19 (M.O.D.).

292 **At precisely five minutes after ten:** Annotated Agenda, April 12 Meeting of the National Foundation for Infantile Paralysis, p. 1 (M.O.D.).

292 **Donna Salk noticed her sons:** Author conversations with sons.

293 **"Before we proceed":** Annotated Agenda, April 12 Meeting of the NFIP, p. 2 (M.O.D.).

293 **He wore a black suit:** *New York Times,* "Fanfare Ushers Verdict on Tests," 4/13/55.

294 **"During the spring of 1954":** Abstract, "Evaluation of 1954 Field Trial of Poliomyelitis Vaccine" (M.O.D.).

295 **"It works! It works!":** Troan, p. 223.

296 **"The vaccine works":** Ibid., and text of press release (M.O.D.).

296 **There was . . . a lot more:** Annotated Agenda, April 12 Meeting of the NFIP (M.O.D.).

296 **Other speakers . . . then climbed:** Collection of speeches, 4/12/55 (M.O.D.).

297 **decorum broke down:** Author interviews with Troan; Carter, p. 278; *New York Times,* "Fanfare Ushers Verdict on Tests," 4/13/55.

297 **"While many like to listen to music":** Transcript of Salk remarks, 4/12/55 (M.O.D.).

298 **In the back of the hall, John Troan:** Author interview with Troan.

299 **The Rackham Hall event finally adjourned:** Annotated Agenda, April 12 Meeting of the NFIP (M.O.D.).

299 **"Young man," he told him:** Salk, Academy of Achievement interview, conducted 5/16/91, File 3, p. 4.

299 **Major Bennett . . . cried freely:** Author interview with Troan; Carter, p. 279.

CHAPTER TWENTY-ONE

300 **"Are you sure you can handle this?":** Author interview with sons.

301 **Almost immediately, he collared:** Carter, pp. 281–82.

301 **"It's a great day":** Handwritten statement of Jack Russell, press relations officer, H.E.W. (M.O.D.).

301 **Six drug companies . . . would be cleared:** *New York Times*, "Six Vaccine Makers Get U.S. Licenses," 4/13/55.

301 **"POLIO IS CONQUERED":** *Pittsburgh Press*, 4/13/55.

301 **"POLIO ROUTED!":** *New York Post*, 4/13/55.

301 **"SALK POLIO VACCINE PROVES SUCCESSFUL":** *New York Times*, 4/13/55.

302 **The United Nations formally hailed:** *New York Times*, "U.N. Health Agency Welcomes Vaccine," 4/13/55.

302 **Sweden immediately announced:** *New York Times*, "Vaccinations Planned in Europe," 4/13/55.

302 **The Netherlands cabled Tommy Francis:** Ibid.

302 **Switzerland, Denmark, and Germany all announced:** Ibid.

302 **President Eisenhower quickly issued:** *Chicago Tribune*, "Ike Orders Salk Data Be Given to Reds, 74 Others," by Joseph Hearst, 4/13/55.

302 **In the United States, local governments:** Various wire service items, *New York Times*, 4/13/54.

302 **Pennsylvania planned on:** Ibid.

302 **Reporters and television cameras swirled thick:** Author interviews with sons.

303 **A crowd of 500 people:** *Louisville Courier-Journal*, "Dr. Salk Returns to Pittsburgh, Vows to Try to Perfect Vaccine," 4/16/55.

303 **Peter, Darrell, and Jonathan were thrilled:** Author conversations with sons.

304 **"How does it feel to have changed":** Copy of telegram from Helen Hayes, 4/11/55.

304 **"Along with millions of Americans":** Copy of telegram from Eddie Cantor, 4/13/55.

304 **"Please accept this message as a small gesture":** Copy of telegram from Marlon Brando, 4/18/55.

304 **"Dear Dr. Salk," wrote a seven-year-old:** Handwritten letter from Lynn Weston.

304 **"Dear Dr. Salk," echoed an eight-year-old:** Handwritten letter from Sara Kathryn Wright.

304 **"My sister and brother had polio":** Handwritten letter from Pat Higgins.

304 **A man in Sioux Falls began:** *Minneapolis Star,* "In This Corner, with Cedric Adams."

304 **An Amarillo, Texas, radio station:** Telegram from KGNC-TV to Salk, 4/18/55.

304 **Other, smaller gifts arrived:** List of gifts, possibly in Lorraine Friedman's handwriting, Box 110, Folder 3, in UCSD collection.

304 **Samuel Goldwyn let on to Edward R. Murrow:** Letter from Murrow to Salk, 4/27/55.

305 **Another offer arrived from an apparel manufacturer:** Letter from commercial attorney to Salk, 6/13/55.

305 **Salk's policy toward all of this mail:** Various sources, including author conversations with sons.

306 **The drug houses' target production:** *Newsweek,* "The Polio Scramble: It's Not as Bad as the Headlines," 5/2/55.

307 **The NFIP's stockpile amounted:** *New York Times,* 4/13/55.

307 **Pharmaceutical companies typically loaded:** *Time* magazine, "Vaccine Snafu (Cont'd.)," 5/30/55.

307 **All these problems caused Eisenhower:** Wire service story, 4/13/55.

307 **a quasi-legal gray market:** Various sources, including United Press, "Gray Market in Polio Vaccine Said Uncovered," 4/28/55.

308 **"Never mind where I got them":** *Newsweek,* 5/2/55.

308 **"No one . . . could have foreseen":** Various sources, including *Time* magazine, 5/30/55.

308 **five polio infections that popped up in California:** "Polio Vaccine Ban Sensation," wire service story (clip service), 4/27/55.

309 **Immediately after the California cases:** Ibid., and various other sources, including United Press story, 4/28/55; wire service story (clip service), 4/30/55.

309 **Utah, which lay deep:** Wire service story (clip service), 4/28/55.

309 **California did the same:** Various sources, including wire service stories (clip service), 5/5/55.

309 **continued to have "great confidence":** Associated Press clip (clip service), 5/8/55.

309 **He spent the evening of the twenty-eighth:** Author interview with sons.

310 **The meeting in Bethesda included:** Various sources, including Carter, p. 317.

310 **Workman got the testing under way:** Letter, Workman to Salk, 5/2/55.

310 **Political critics of the vaccination program:** Various sources, including *Newsweek*, "Polio: A Political Storm," 6/6/55; wire service story (clip service), 5/9/55.

310 **Albert Sabin . . . was very clear:** Various sources, including *Time* magazine, 7/4/55.

310 **"This is old stuff":** Various sources, including *Time* magazine, "Vaccine Safety," 7/4/55; and Carter, p. 337.

311 **"The department does not blame Cutter":** Statements to Associated Press, 6/28/55.

311 **Live virus, as anticipated:** Numerous sources, including Report of the Technical Committee on Poliomyelitis Vaccine, 10/27/55.

311 **The protocols would be rewritten:** Ibid.

311 **In the end, 79 children":** Numerous sources, including Smith, p 366

311 **the House of Representatives called hearings:** *Time* magazine, 7/4/55.

EPILOGUE

313 **28,985 children and adults in the United States:** International Polio Network, "Incidence Rates of Poliomyelitis in USA."

314 **In the Deep South, where vaccine was rushed:** Poliomyelitis 1955, Annual Statistical Review; NFIP Case Reports, weeks 21 to 38 of 1955.

314 **Epidemiologists called this the herd effect:** Numerous sources, including author conversations with D.S.

314 **the polio total in the United States was cut:** International Polio Network, "Incidence Rates of Poliomyelitis in USA."

315 **A few never did:** Author conversations with sons.

315 **In 1954, John Enders, Thomas Weller, and Frederick Robbins:** Numerous sources, including *Time* Almanac 2004, p. 51.

315 **What he'd done was merely "kitchen science":** Various sources, including author interviews with D.S.

316 **the tendency of viruses to mutate:** Ibid.

316 **volunteers in an Ohio penitentiary:** Carter, pp. 357–84; Gould, pp. 173–209; Smith, pp. 383–92.

317 **Sugar-cube inoculations:** Ibid.

317 **The last wild case of polio in the United States:** Numerous sources, including Anita Manning, "Oral Polio Vaccine Out; Shots to Be Standard," *USA Today,* 1999.

317 **All of the tiny number of cases:** Ibid.

318 **there are three stages of truth:** Salk, Academy of Achievement interview, conducted 5/16/91, File 2, p. 5.

318 **In 1962, he and his family moved:** Author interviews with sons.

318 **Albert Sabin was the first of the two polio giants:** Many public sources, including Albert B. Sabin Archives, University of Cincinnati Medical Heritage Center.

318 **Salk did not live much longer:** Author conversations with sons.

319 **"Where do you think I should be pushing this now?":** Author interview with P.S.

319 **the Centers for Disease Control ruled:** CDC, *Parents' Guide to Childhood Immunization.*

319 **there were fewer than 700 polio cases:** World Health Organization epidemiological report.

PHOTO CAPTIONS

page 1.   Jonas Salk and his lab staff study the action of poliovirus and polio vaccine in vitro. If the pinkish dye changed color to red or yellow, the vaccine was working.

page 7:   A New York mother airs her sickened baby during the polio epidemic of 1916. The house and the entire block were under quarantine.

page 25:   Franklin Roosevelt blows out his candles during the first of the anti-polio Birthday Balls, January 30, 1934.

page 51:   A polio nurse holds a stricken boy. His right arm, clinging to her shoulder, is the only one of his limbs apparently not affected.

page 57:   Roosevelt, his dog Fala, and an unidentified girl at the Warm Springs rehabilitation facility in Georgia.

page 78:   The March of Dimes coordinated its fund-raising drives with major cultural events, and the Miss America Pageant was one of the biggest.

page 86:   Salk enters Municipal Hospital in Pittsburgh on a blustery day.

page 106:   Children in rehab learned balance with the aid of parallel bars. Their braced legs would support them, but never effectively transport them.

page 111:   Cat-sized cynomolgus monkeys were used by the thousands in virus-typing studies and vaccine tests.

page 127:   During epidemics, communities that had not yet been affected posted signs denying entry to children from communities that had.

page 130:   A family of newly injected girls leaves one of the Utah community centers where gamma globulin injections were administered in 1951.

page 148:   A child confined to an iron lung is loaded into an ambulance, to be transferred from one hospital to another.

page 160:   Salk injects a subject with what he by then felt confident was a safe and effective vaccine.

page 181:   Admiring cheerleaders pay tribute to Salk, part of the national adulation that grew as he closed in on the vaccine.

page 184:   Basil O'Connor with Salk at the CBS radio studios on the evening of March 26, 1953. Salk was appearing on the program *The Scientist Speaks for Himself* to explain a major paper that was about to report success in the early trials of his vaccine.

page 203:   Salk inoculates his youngest son, Jonathan, with polio vaccine. Salk's wife, Donna, and a nurse assist.

page 207:   Albert Sabin with Salk at a professional conference. Basil O'Connor is visible behind them.

page 225:   Salk and a member of his team work with one of the oversized flasks used for culturing virus.

PHOTO CAPTIONS

page 239: In one of the laboratory photo sessions Salk found so tedious, he posed with a rack of test tubes similar to the ones in which he first mixed live virus with his experimental vaccine. The vaccine stopped the virus in its tracks.

page 258: Polio vaccine is packed and readied for shipment in anticipation of the go-ahead to begin the field trial.

page 275: Newspapers around the world hailed the success of the field trial. The sensational news set off a global stampede for the vaccine; in most cases, the demand could not remotely be met.

page 300: President Eisenhower honors Salk and welcomes him and his family to the White House. Standing next to Salk is Basil O'Connor.

page 313: Children line up to receive the vaccine after it is declared safe, effective, and potent.

page 325: Four of the first girls to receive the vaccine. The title "Polio Pioneer" was much coveted.

INDEX

ABOUT THE AUTHOR

Jeffrey Kluger is a senior writer at *Time*. He is the coauthor, with Jim Lovell, of *Lost Moon: The Perilous Voyage of Apollo 13*, which was the basis for the movie *Apollo 13*. He has written for numerous other publications, including *The New York Times Magazine, Newsday, New York* magazine, *Family Circle, Cosmopolitan, McCall's, GQ,* and *Discover.* He lives in New York City with his wife, Alejandra, and their daughters, Elisa and Paloma.